volume **5**

Wered

by ADAM WARREN

cover colors by **RYAN KINNAIRD** empowered logo by **EUGENE WANG**

ninjutsu linguistic assistance by **TOMOKO SAITO**

DARK HORSE BOOKS®

publisher
Mike Richardson

editor
Chris Warner

designer
Josh Elliott

art director
Lia Ribacchi

EMPOWERED VOLUME 5

© 2009 by Adam Warren. Empowered, Ninjette, Thugboy, and all prominent characters and their distinctive likenesses are trademarks of Adam Warren. All rights reserved. Dark Horse Books® and the Dark Horse logo are registered trademarks of Dark Horse Comics, Inc. All rights reserved. No portion of this publication may be reproduced or transmitted, in any form or by any means, without the express written permission of the copyright holders. Names, characters, places, and incidents featured in this publication are either the product of the author's imagination or are used fictitiously. Any resemblance to actual persons (living or dead), events, institutions, or locales, without satiric intent, is coincidental.

Dark Horse Books
A division of Dark Horse Comics, Inc.
10956 SE Main Street
Milwaukie, OR 97222

darkhorse.com

To find a comics shop in your area, call the Comic Shop
Locator Service toll-free at 1-888-266-4226

First edition: June 2009
ISBN 978-1-59582-212-3

1 3 5 7 9 10 8 6 4 2

Printed in the United States of America

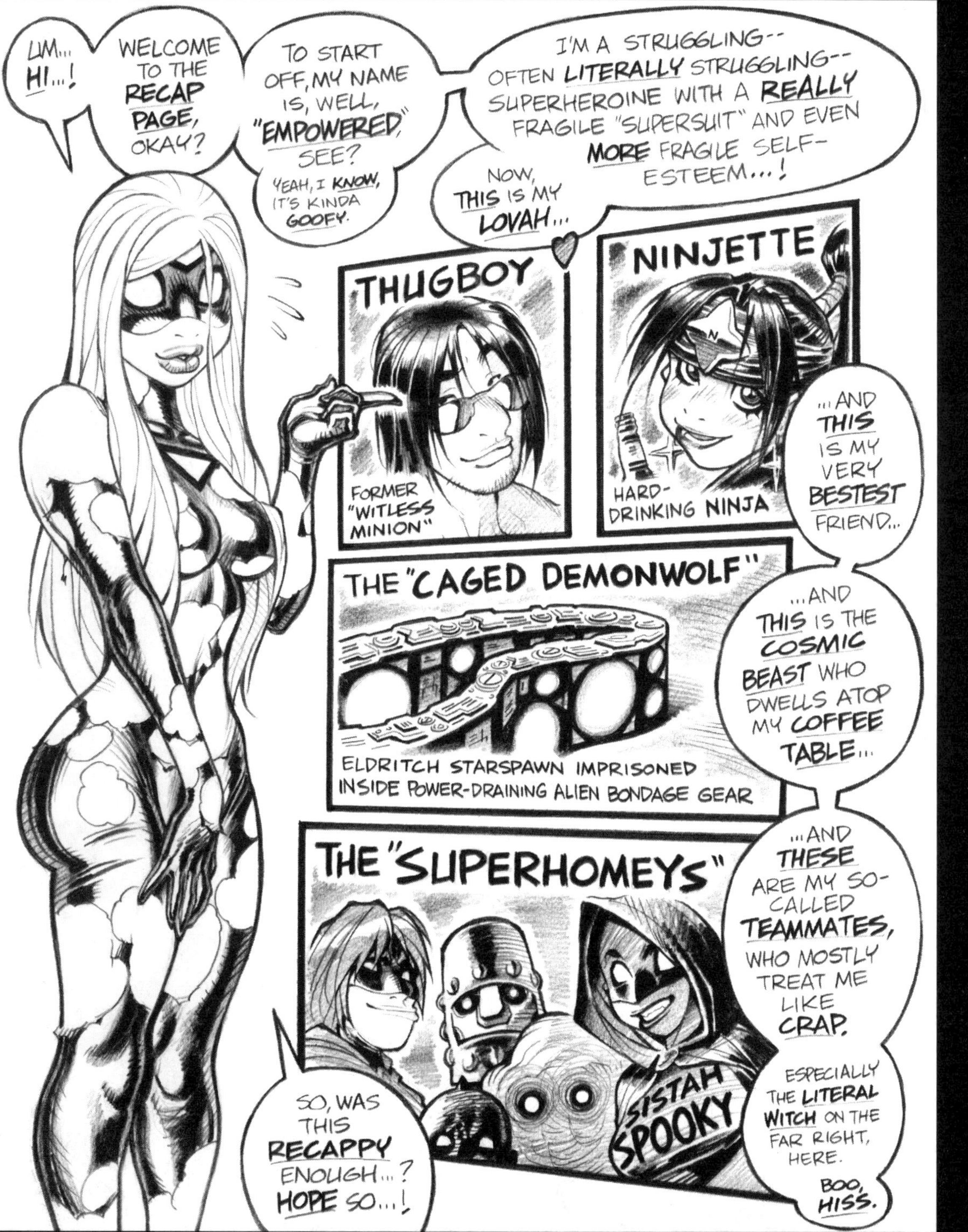

UM... HI...!
WELCOME TO THE RECAP PAGE, OKAY?
TO START OFF, MY NAME IS, WELL, "EMPOWERED," SEE?
YEAH, I KNOW, IT'S KINDA GOOFY.
I'M A STRUGGLING--OFTEN LITERALLY STRUGGLING--SUPERHEROINE WITH A REALLY FRAGILE "SUPERSUIT" AND EVEN MORE FRAGILE SELF-ESTEEM...!
NOW, THIS IS MY LOVAH...
THUGBOY
FORMER "WITLESS MINION"
NINJETTE
HARD-DRINKING NINJA
...AND THIS IS MY VERY BESTEST FRIEND...
THE "CAGED DEMONWOLF"
ELDRITCH STARSPAWN IMPRISONED INSIDE POWER-DRAINING ALIEN BONDAGE GEAR
...AND THIS IS THE COSMIC BEAST WHO DWELLS ATOP MY COFFEE TABLE...
THE "SUPERHOMEYS"
...AND THESE ARE MY SO-CALLED TEAMMATES, WHO MOSTLY TREAT ME LIKE CRAP.
SISTAH SPOOKY
ESPECIALLY THE LITERAL WITCH ON THE FAR RIGHT, HERE.
BOO, HISS.
SO, WAS THIS RECAPPY ENOUGH...? HOPE SO...!

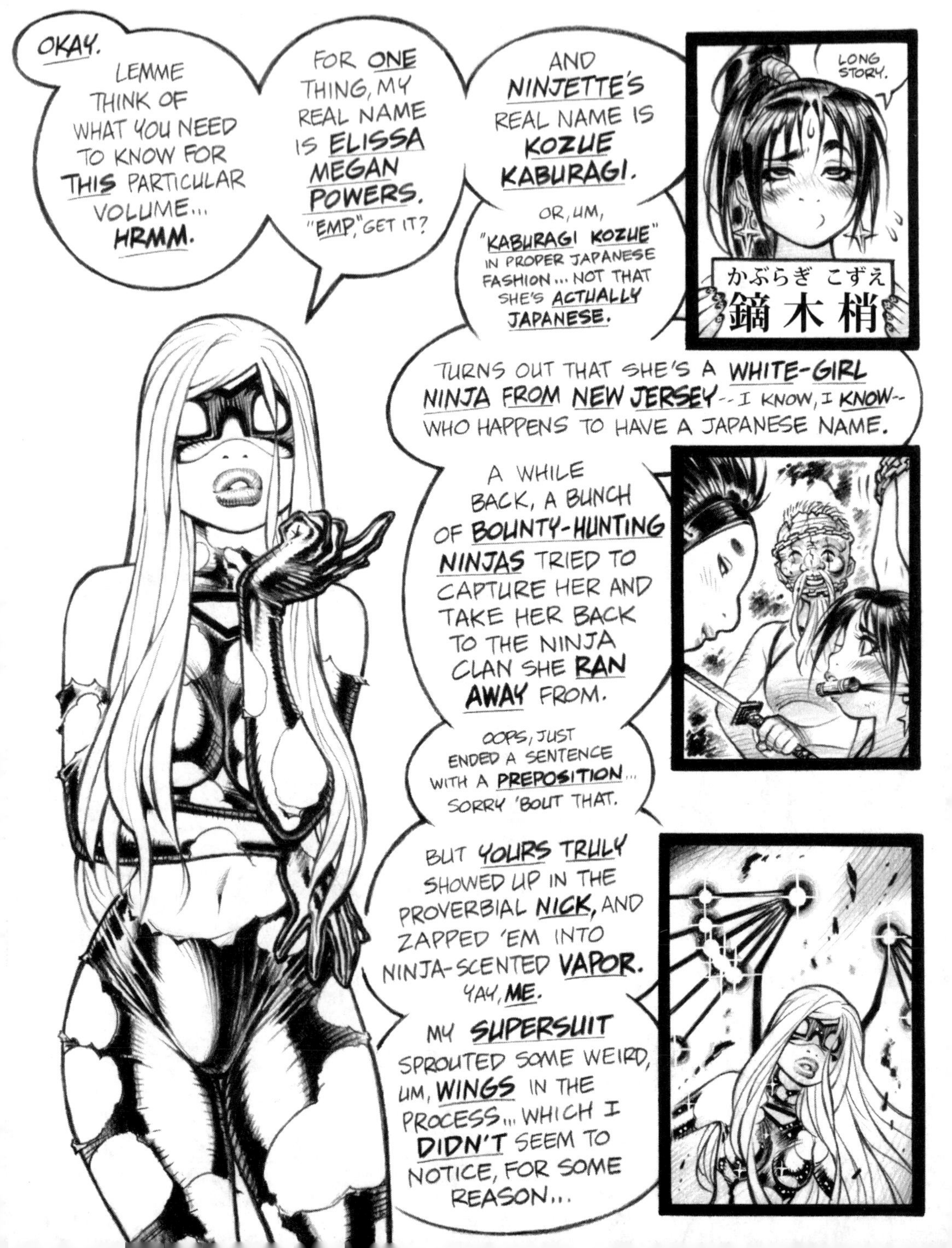

OKAY.
LEMME THINK OF WHAT YOU NEED TO KNOW FOR THIS PARTICULAR VOLUME... HRMM.
FOR ONE THING, MY REAL NAME IS ELISSA MEGAN POWERS. "EMP," GET IT?
AND NINJETTE'S REAL NAME IS KOZUE KABURAGI.
OR, UM, "KABURAGI KOZUE" IN PROPER JAPANESE FASHION... NOT THAT SHE'S ACTUALLY JAPANESE.
LONG STORY.
かぶらぎ こずえ
鏑木梢
TURNS OUT THAT SHE'S A WHITE-GIRL NINJA FROM NEW JERSEY-- I KNOW, I KNOW-- WHO HAPPENS TO HAVE A JAPANESE NAME.
A WHILE BACK, A BUNCH OF BOUNTY-HUNTING NINJAS TRIED TO CAPTURE HER AND TAKE HER BACK TO THE NINJA CLAN SHE RAN AWAY FROM.
OOPS, JUST ENDED A SENTENCE WITH A PREPOSITION... SORRY 'BOUT THAT.
BUT YOURS TRULY SHOWED UP IN THE PROVERBIAL NICK, AND ZAPPED 'EM INTO NINJA-SCENTED VAPOR. YAY, ME.
MY SUPERSUIT SPROUTED SOME WEIRD, UM, WINGS IN THE PROCESS... WHICH I DIDN'T SEEM TO NOTICE, FOR SOME REASON...

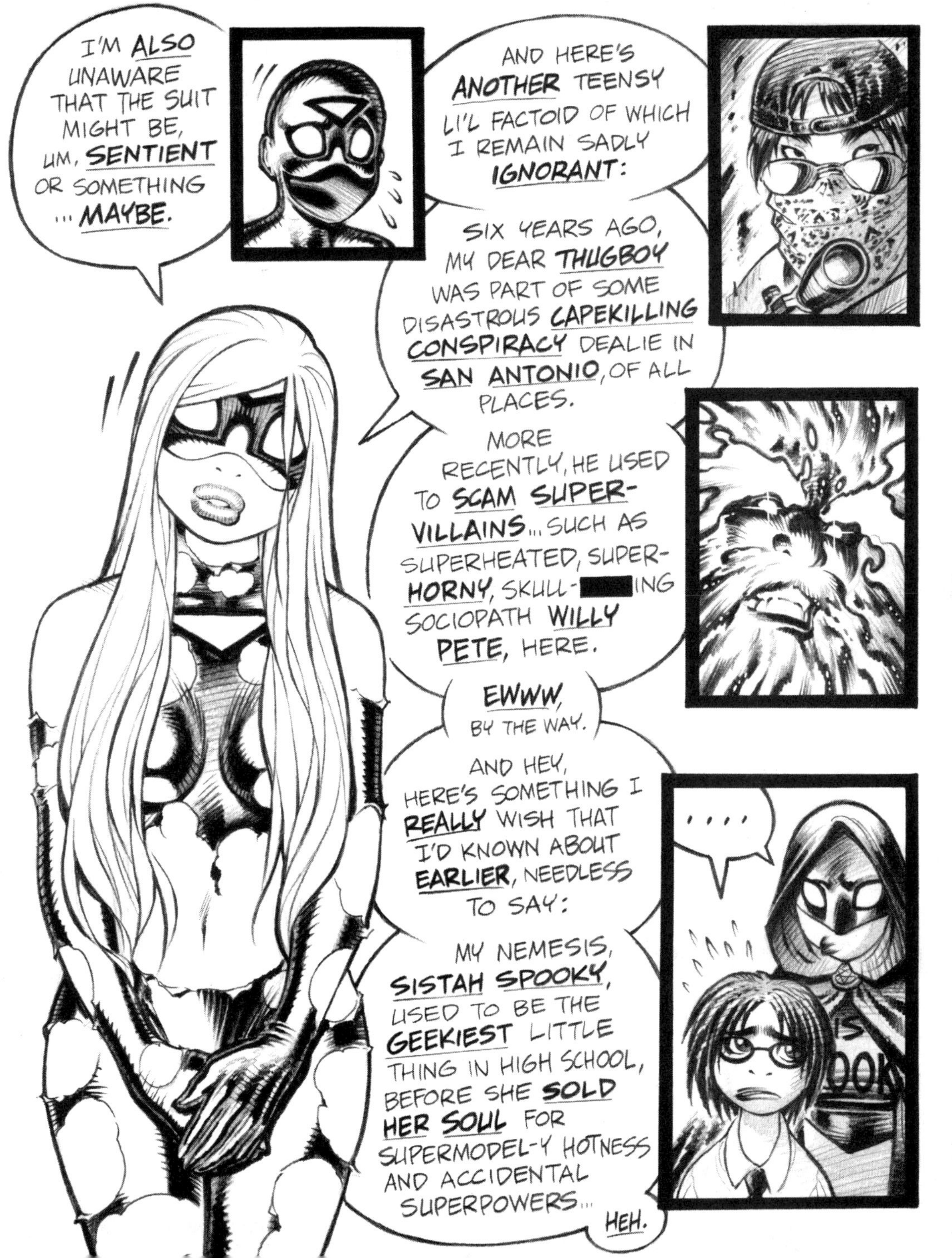

I'M ALSO UNAWARE THAT THE SUIT MIGHT BE, UM, SENTIENT OR SOMETHING ...MAYBE.
AND HERE'S ANOTHER TEENSY LI'L FACTOID OF WHICH I REMAIN SADLY IGNORANT:
SIX YEARS AGO, MY DEAR THUGBOY WAS PART OF SOME DISASTROUS CAPEKILLING CONSPIRACY DEALIE IN SAN ANTONIO, OF ALL PLACES.
MORE RECENTLY, HE USED TO SCAM SUPER-VILLAINS... SUCH AS SUPERHEATED, SUPER-HORNY, SKULL-[redacted]ING SOCIOPATH WILLY PETE, HERE.
EWWW, BY THE WAY.
AND HEY, HERE'S SOMETHING I REALLY WISH THAT I'D KNOWN ABOUT EARLIER, NEEDLESS TO SAY:
MY NEMESIS, SISTAH SPOOKY, USED TO BE THE GEEKIEST LITTLE THING IN HIGH SCHOOL, BEFORE SHE SOLD HER SOUL FOR SUPERMODEL-Y HOTNESS AND ACCIDENTAL SUPERPOWERS...
HEH.
....

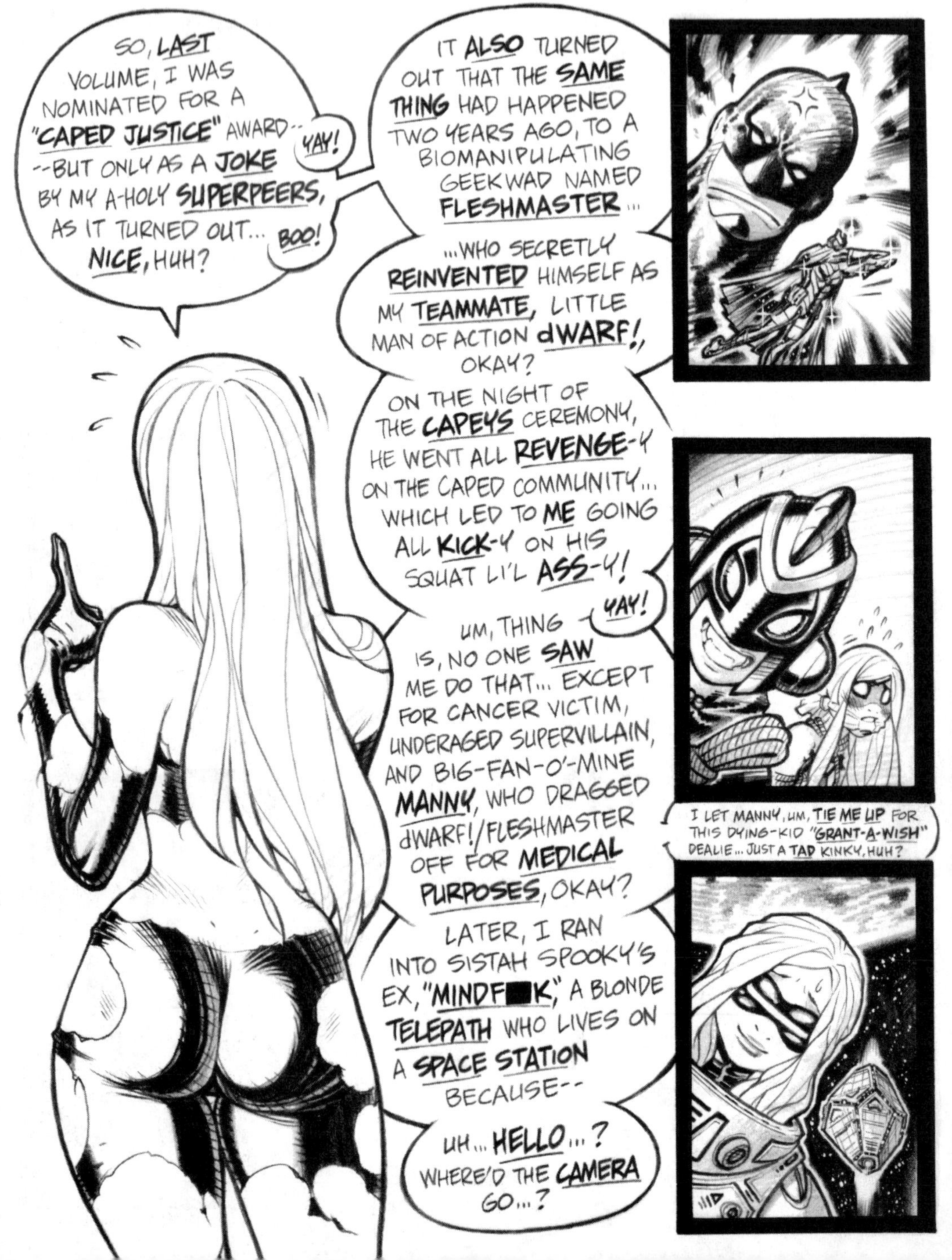

SO, LAST VOLUME, I WAS NOMINATED FOR A "CAPED JUSTICE" AWARD--
YAY!
--BUT ONLY AS A JOKE BY MY A-HOLY SUPERPEERS, AS IT TURNED OUT...
BOO!
NICE, HUH?
IT ALSO TURNED OUT THAT THE SAME THING HAD HAPPENED TWO YEARS AGO, TO A BIOMANIPULATING GEEKWAD NAMED FLESHMASTER...
...WHO SECRETLY REINVENTED HIMSELF AS MY TEAMMATE, LITTLE MAN OF ACTION dWARF!, OKAY?
ON THE NIGHT OF THE CAPEYS CEREMONY, HE WENT ALL REVENGE-Y ON THE CAPED COMMUNITY... WHICH LED TO ME GOING ALL KICK-Y ON HIS SQUAT LI'L ASS-Y!
YAY!
UM, THING IS, NO ONE SAW ME DO THAT... EXCEPT FOR CANCER VICTIM, UNDERAGED SUPERVILLAIN, AND BIG-FAN-O'-MINE MANNY, WHO DRAGGED dWARF!/FLESHMASTER OFF FOR MEDICAL PURPOSES, OKAY?
I LET MANNY, UM, TIE ME UP FOR THIS DYING-KID "GRANT-A-WISH" DEALIE... JUST A TAD KINKY, HUH?
LATER, I RAN INTO SISTAH SPOOKY'S EX, "MINDF[redacted]K," A BLONDE TELEPATH WHO LIVES ON A SPACE STATION BECAUSE--
UH... HELLO...? WHERE'D THE CAMERA GO...?

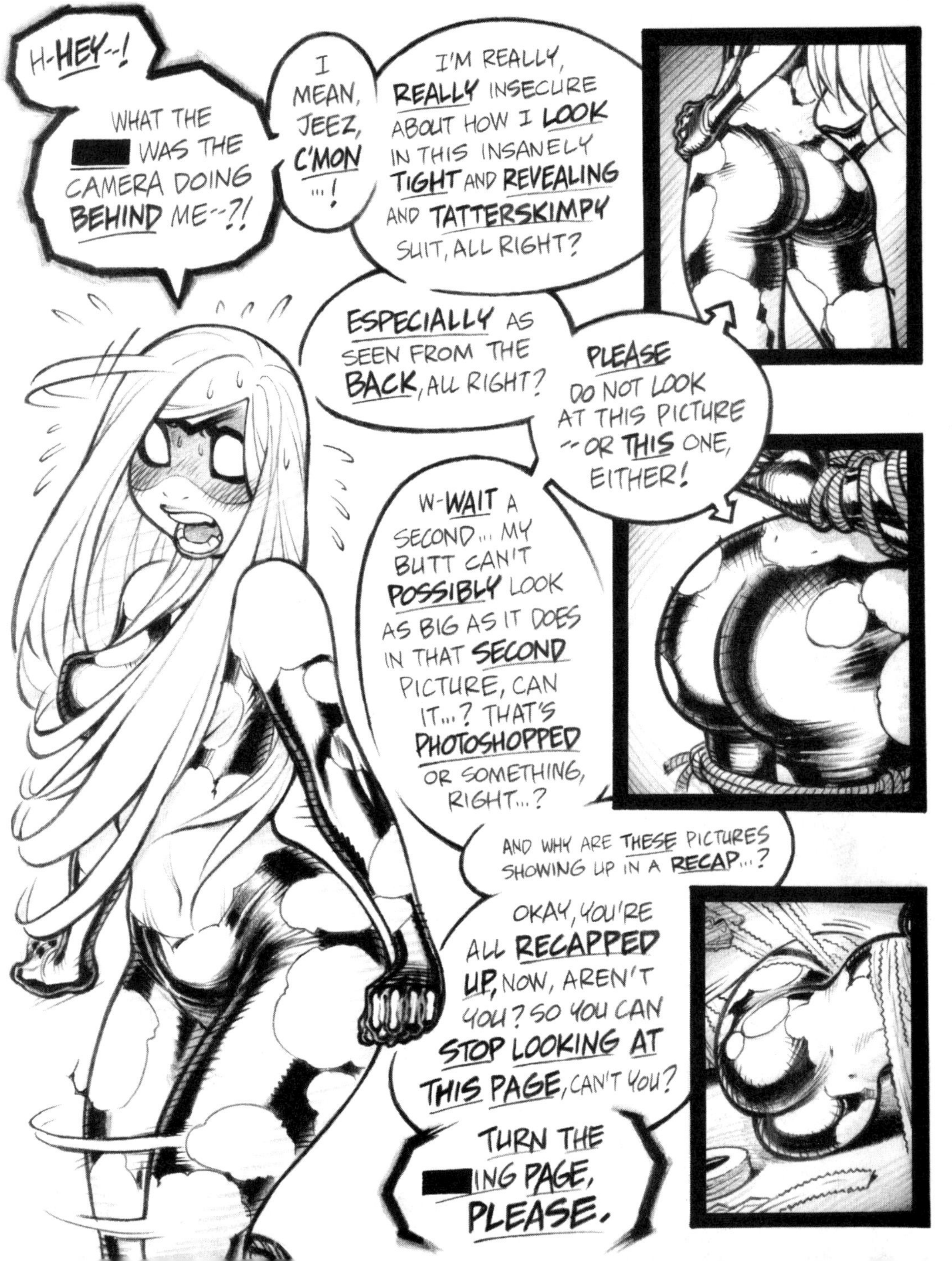
H-HEY--!
WHAT THE [redacted] WAS THE CAMERA DOING BEHIND ME--?!
I MEAN, JEEZ, C'MON ...!
I'M REALLY, REALLY INSECURE ABOUT HOW I LOOK IN THIS INSANELY TIGHT AND REVEALING AND TATTERSKIMPY SUIT, ALL RIGHT?
ESPECIALLY AS SEEN FROM THE BACK, ALL RIGHT?
PLEASE DO NOT LOOK AT THIS PICTURE --OR THIS ONE, EITHER!
W-WAIT A SECOND... MY BUTT CAN'T POSSIBLY LOOK AS BIG AS IT DOES IN THAT SECOND PICTURE, CAN IT...? THAT'S PHOTOSHOPPED OR SOMETHING, RIGHT...?
AND WHY ARE THESE PICTURES SHOWING UP IN A RECAP...?
OKAY, YOU'RE ALL RECAPPED UP, NOW, AREN'T YOU? SO YOU CAN STOP LOOKING AT THIS PAGE, CAN'T YOU?
TURN THE [redacted]ING PAGE, PLEASE.

Empowered™

Reducing the Uppity

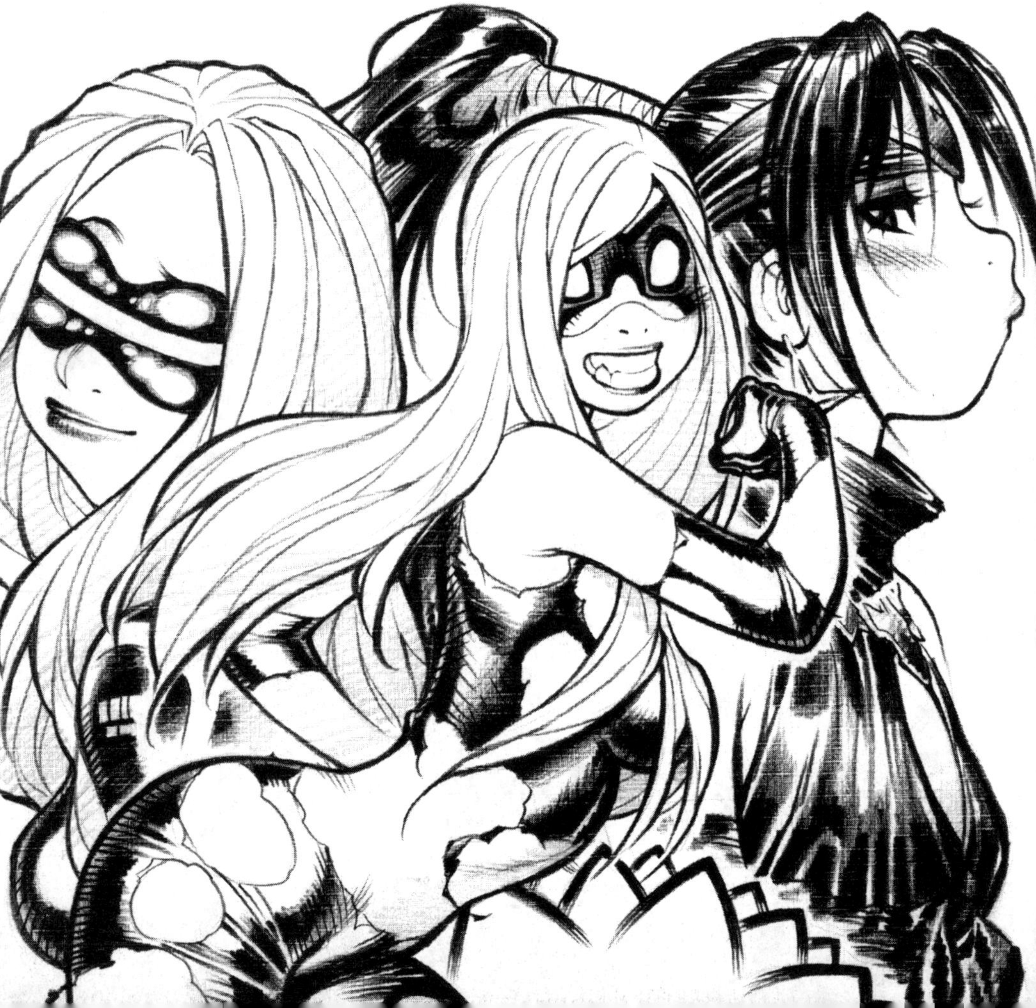

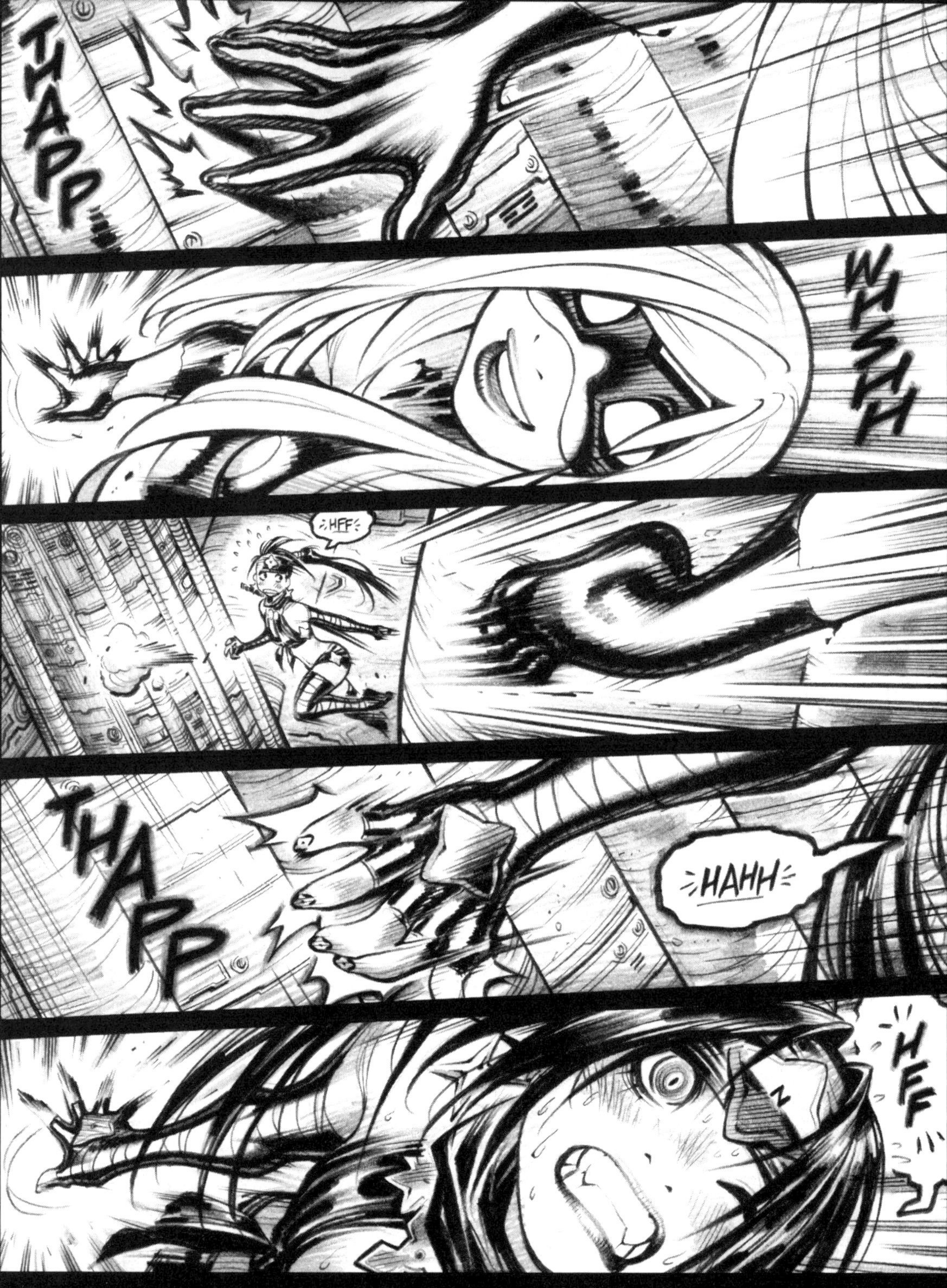
THAPP
WHSHH
HFF
THAPP
HAHH
HFF

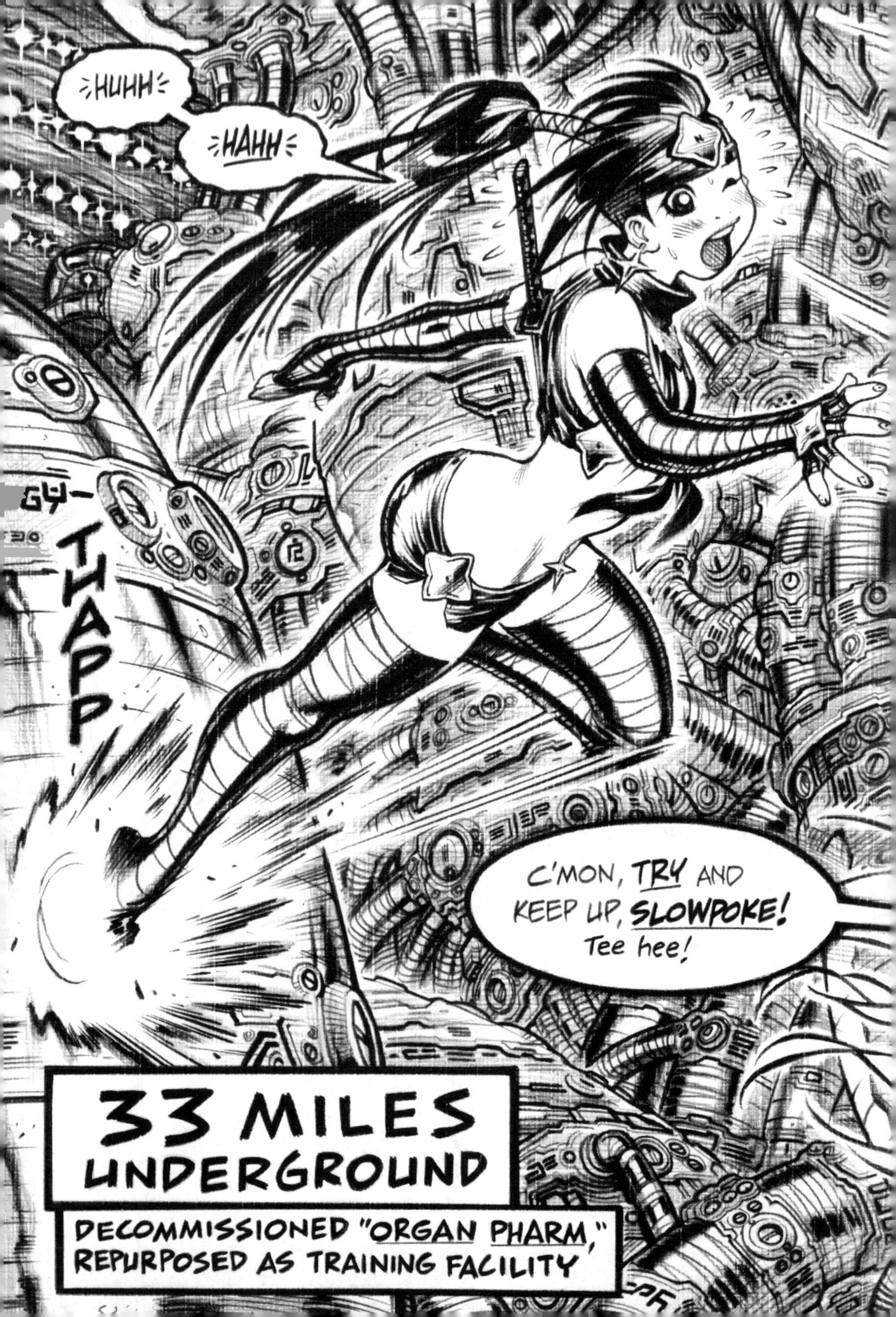
HUHH
HAHH
GY-THAPP
C'MON, TRY AND KEEP UP, SLOWPOKE! Tee hee!
33 MILES UNDERGROUND
DECOMMISSIONED "ORGAN PHARM," REPURPOSED AS TRAINING FACILITY

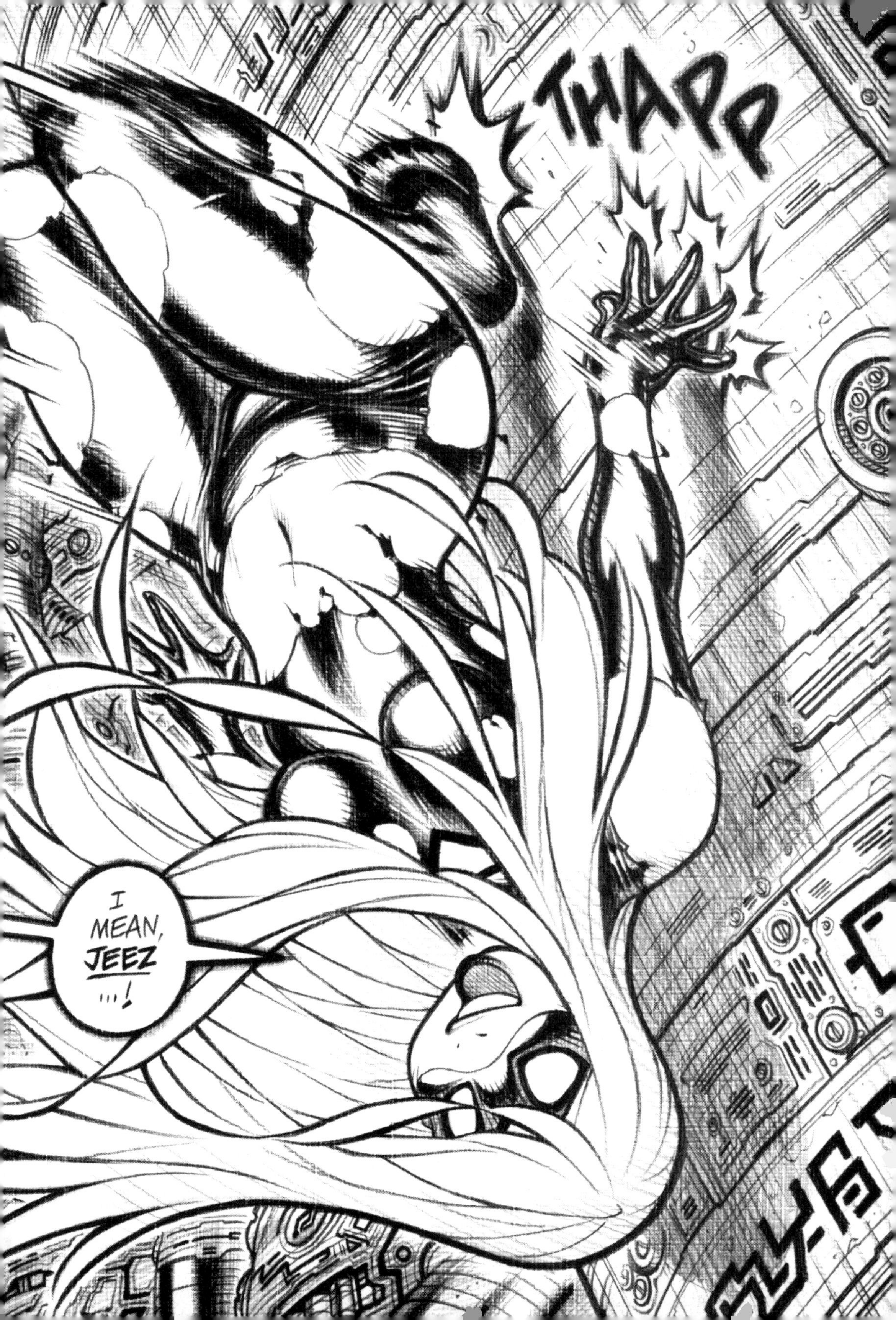
THAPP
I MEAN, JEEZ ...!

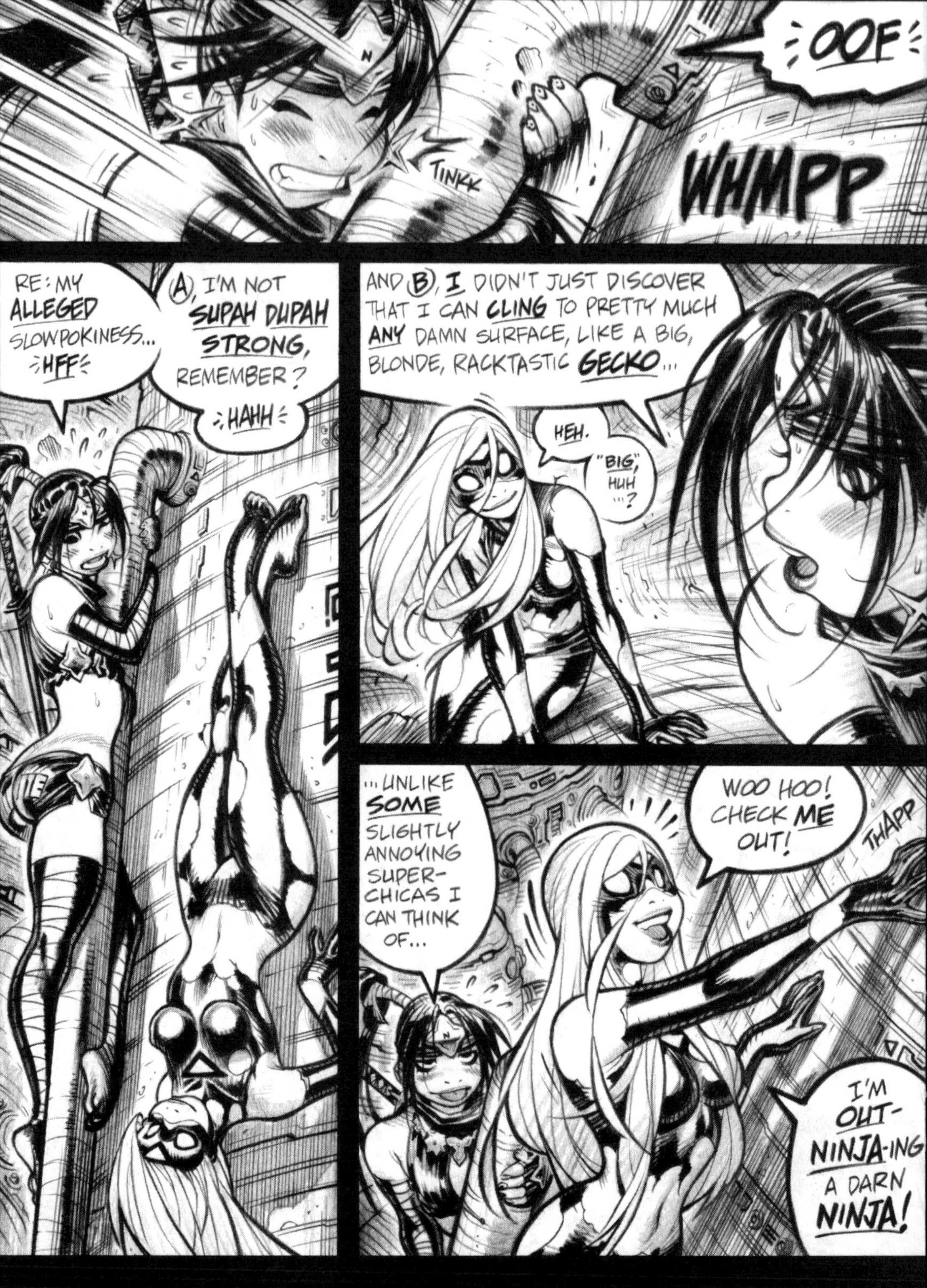
OOF
TINKK
WHMPP
RE: MY ALLEGED SLOWPOKINESS... HFF
A), I'M NOT SUPAH DUPAH STRONG, REMEMBER? HAHH
AND B), I DIDN'T JUST DISCOVER THAT I CAN CLING TO PRETTY MUCH ANY DAMN SURFACE, LIKE A BIG, BLONDE, RACKTASTIC GECKO...
HEH.
"BIG," HUH...?
...UNLIKE SOME SLIGHTLY ANNOYING SUPER-CHICAS I CAN THINK OF...
WOO HOO! CHECK ME OUT!
THAPP
I'M OUT-NINJA-ING A DARN NINJA!

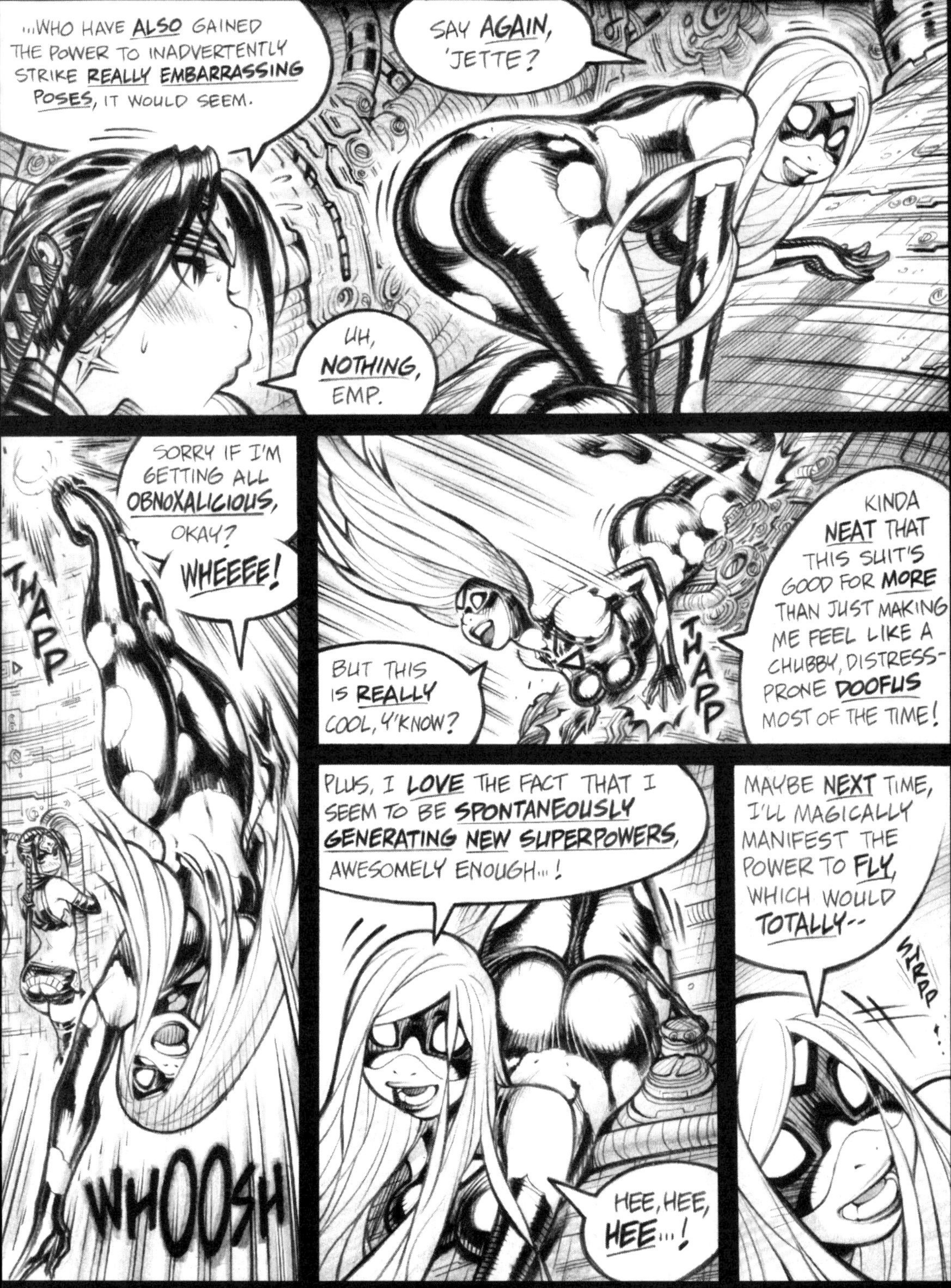

...WHO HAVE ALSO GAINED THE POWER TO INADVERTENTLY STRIKE REALLY EMBARRASSING POSES, IT WOULD SEEM.
SAY AGAIN, 'JETTE?
UH, NOTHING, EMP.
SORRY IF I'M GETTING ALL OBNOXALICIOUS, OKAY?
WHEEEE!
THAPP
WHOOSH
KINDA NEAT THAT THIS SUIT'S GOOD FOR MORE THAN JUST MAKING ME FEEL LIKE A CHUBBY, DISTRESS-PRONE DOOFUS MOST OF THE TIME!
BUT THIS IS REALLY COOL, Y'KNOW?
THAPP
PLUS, I LOVE THE FACT THAT I SEEM TO BE SPONTANEOUSLY GENERATING NEW SUPERPOWERS, AWESOMELY ENOUGH...!
HEE, HEE, HEE...!
MAYBE NEXT TIME, I'LL MAGICALLY MANIFEST THE POWER TO FLY, WHICH WOULD TOTALLY--

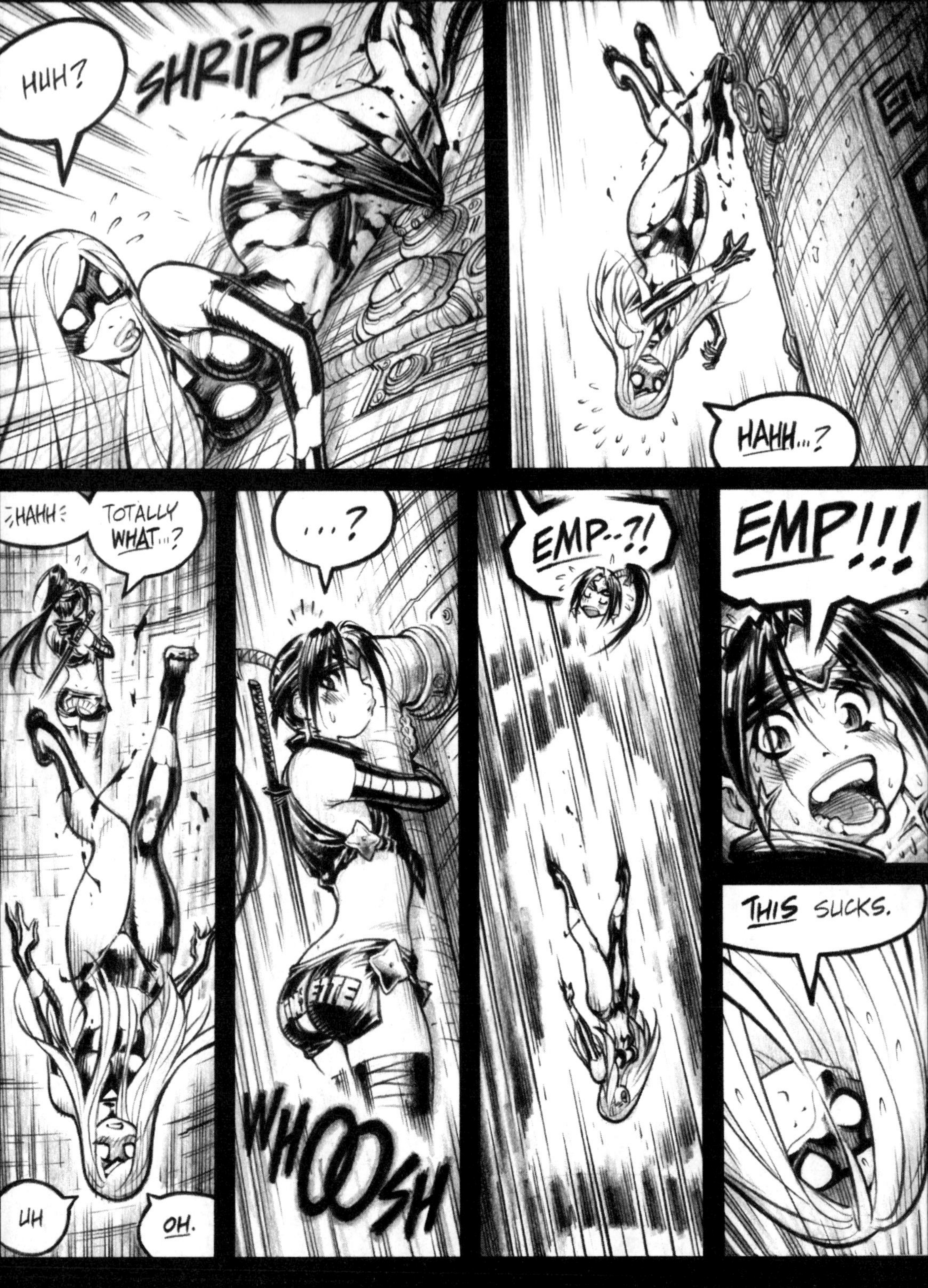
HUH?
SHRIPP
HAHH...?
HAHH
TOTALLY WHAT...?
UH
OH.
...?
WHOOSH
EMP--?!
EMP!!!
THIS SUCKS.

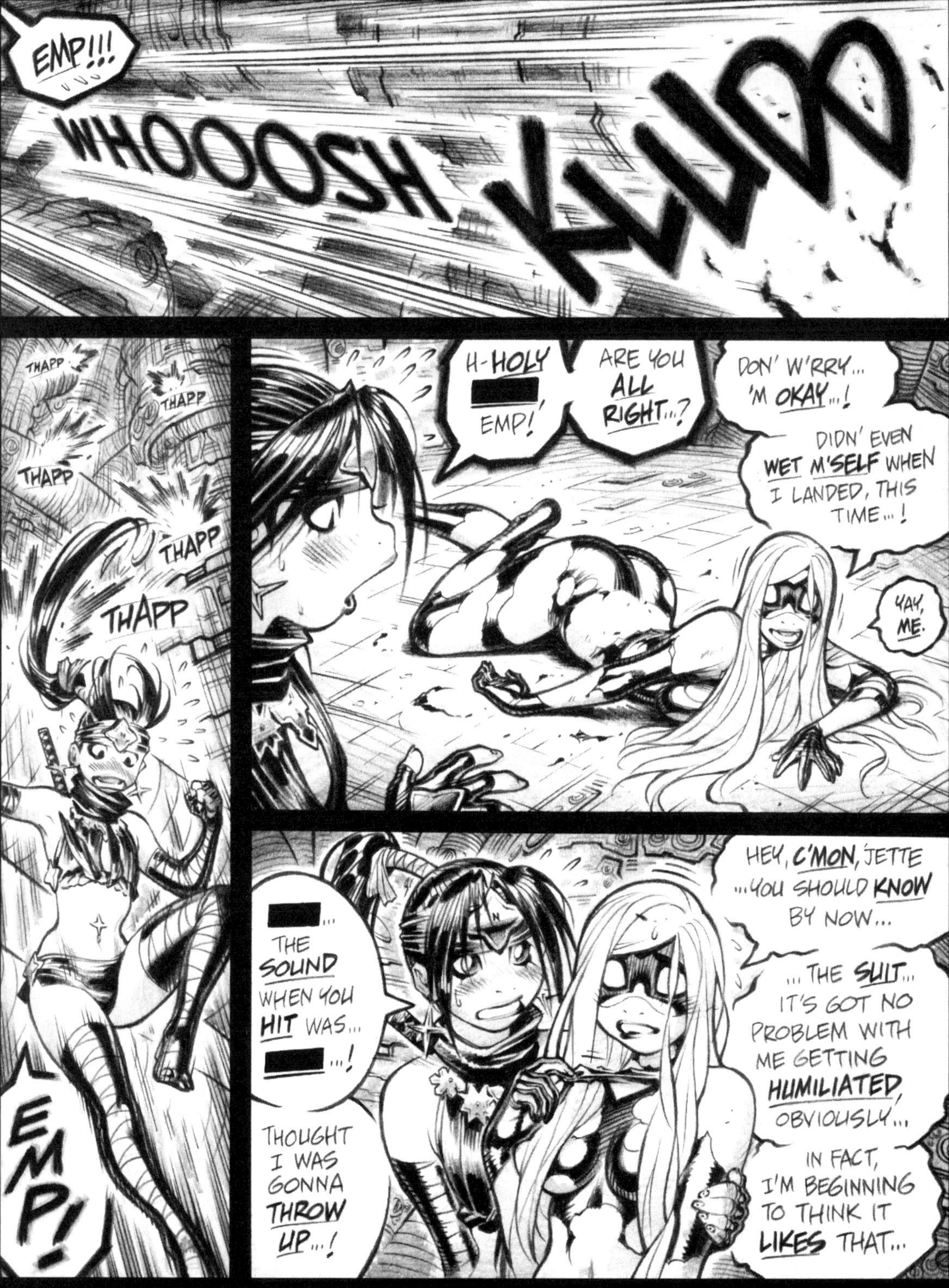

EMP!!!
WHOOOSH
KLUDD
THAPP
THAPP
THAPP
THAPP
THAPP
EMP!
H-HOLY [redacted], EMP!
ARE YOU ALL RIGHT...?
DON' W'RRY... 'M OKAY...!
DIDN' EVEN WET M'SELF WHEN I LANDED, THIS TIME...!
YAY, ME.
[redacted]... THE SOUND WHEN YOU HIT WAS... [redacted]...!
THOUGHT I WAS GONNA THROW UP...!
HEY, C'MON, JETTE ...YOU SHOULD KNOW BY NOW...
...THE SUIT... IT'S GOT NO PROBLEM WITH ME GETTING HUMILIATED, OBVIOUSLY...
IN FACT, I'M BEGINNING TO THINK IT LIKES THAT...

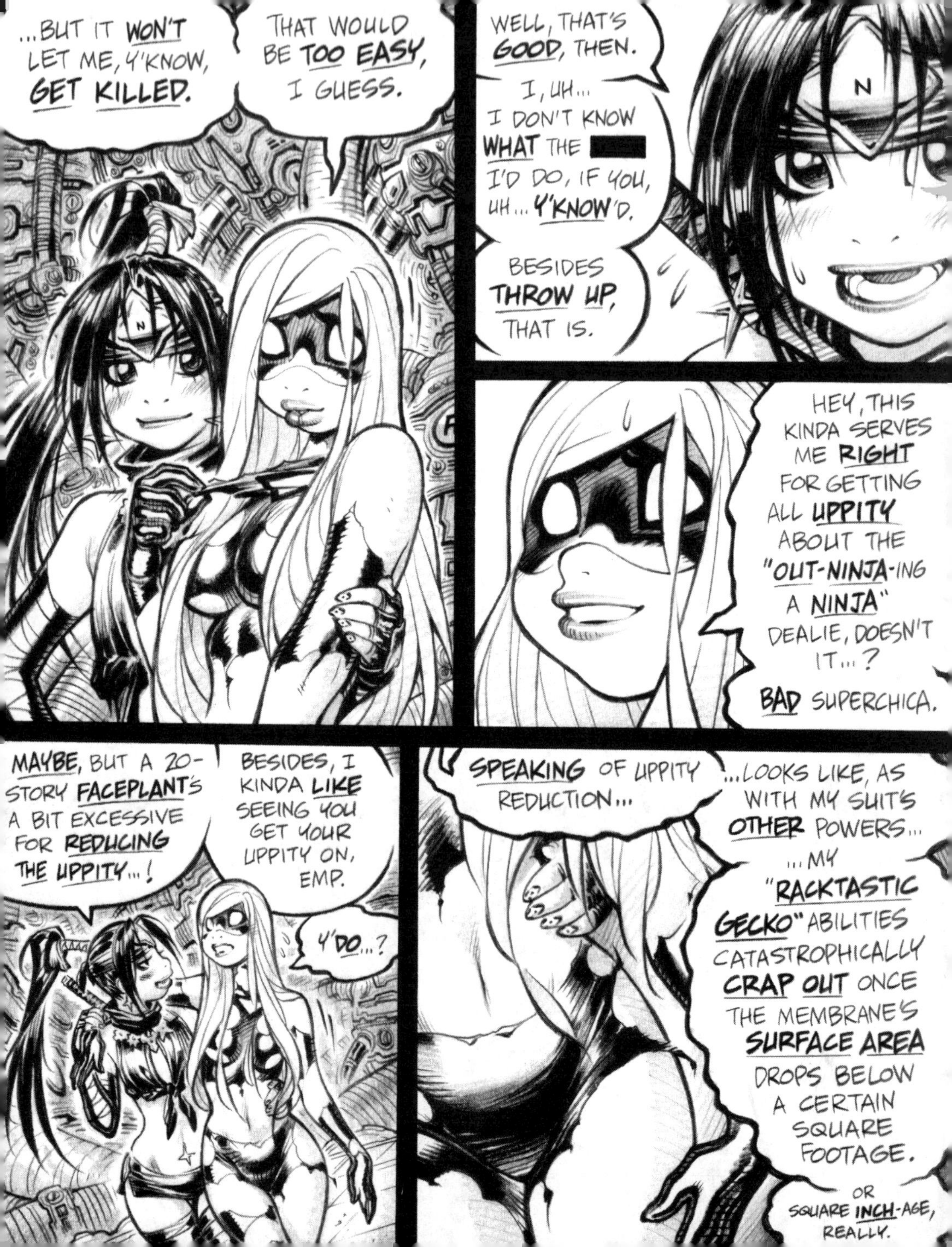
...BUT IT WON'T LET ME, Y'KNOW, GET KILLED.
THAT WOULD BE TOO EASY, I GUESS.
WELL, THAT'S GOOD, THEN.
I, UH... I DON'T KNOW WHAT THE [redacted] I'D DO, IF YOU, UH... Y'KNOW'D.
BESIDES THROW UP, THAT IS.
HEY, THIS KINDA SERVES ME RIGHT FOR GETTING ALL UPPITY ABOUT THE "OUT-NINJA-ING A NINJA" DEALIE, DOESN'T IT...?
BAD SUPERCHICA.
MAYBE, BUT A 20-STORY FACEPLANT'S A BIT EXCESSIVE FOR REDUCING THE UPPITY...!
BESIDES, I KINDA LIKE SEEING YOU GET YOUR UPPITY ON, EMP.
Y'DO...?
SPEAKING OF UPPITY REDUCTION...
...LOOKS LIKE, AS WITH MY SUIT'S OTHER POWERS...
...MY "RACKTASTIC GECKO" ABILITIES CATASTROPHICALLY CRAP OUT ONCE THE MEMBRANE'S SURFACE AREA DROPS BELOW A CERTAIN SQUARE FOOTAGE.
OR SQUARE INCH-AGE, REALLY.

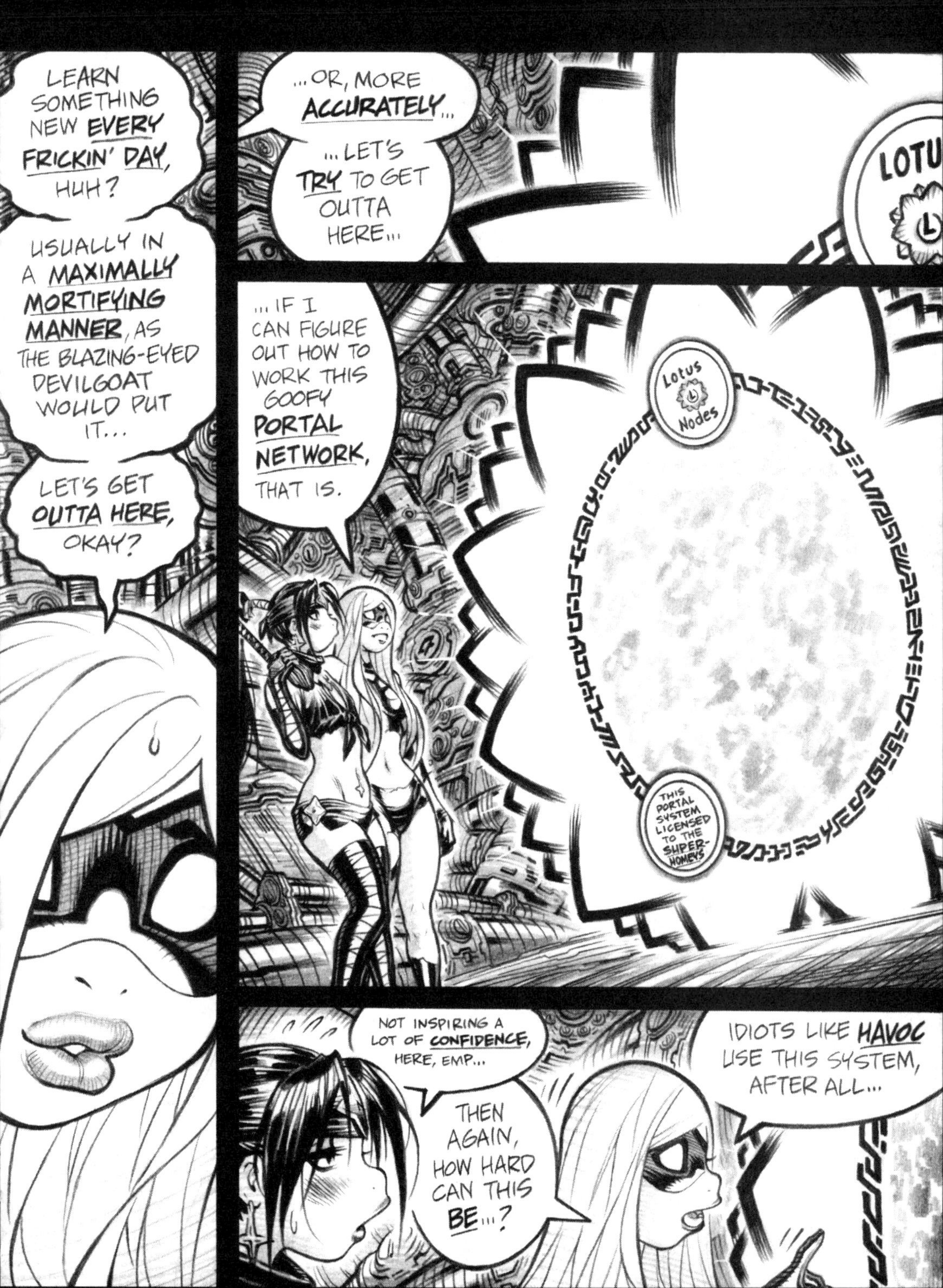
LEARN SOMETHING NEW EVERY FRICKIN' DAY, HUH?
USUALLY IN A MAXIMALLY MORTIFYING MANNER, AS THE BLAZING-EYED DEVILGOAT WOULD PUT IT...
LET'S GET OUTTA HERE, OKAY?
...OR, MORE ACCURATELY...
...LET'S TRY TO GET OUTTA HERE...
...IF I CAN FIGURE OUT HOW TO WORK THIS GOOFY PORTAL NETWORK, THAT IS.
Lotus Nodes
THIS PORTAL SYSTEM LICENSED TO THE SUPER-HOMEYS
NOT INSPIRING A LOT OF CONFIDENCE, HERE, EMP...
IDIOTS LIKE HAVOC USE THIS SYSTEM, AFTER ALL...
THEN AGAIN, HOW HARD CAN THIS BE...?

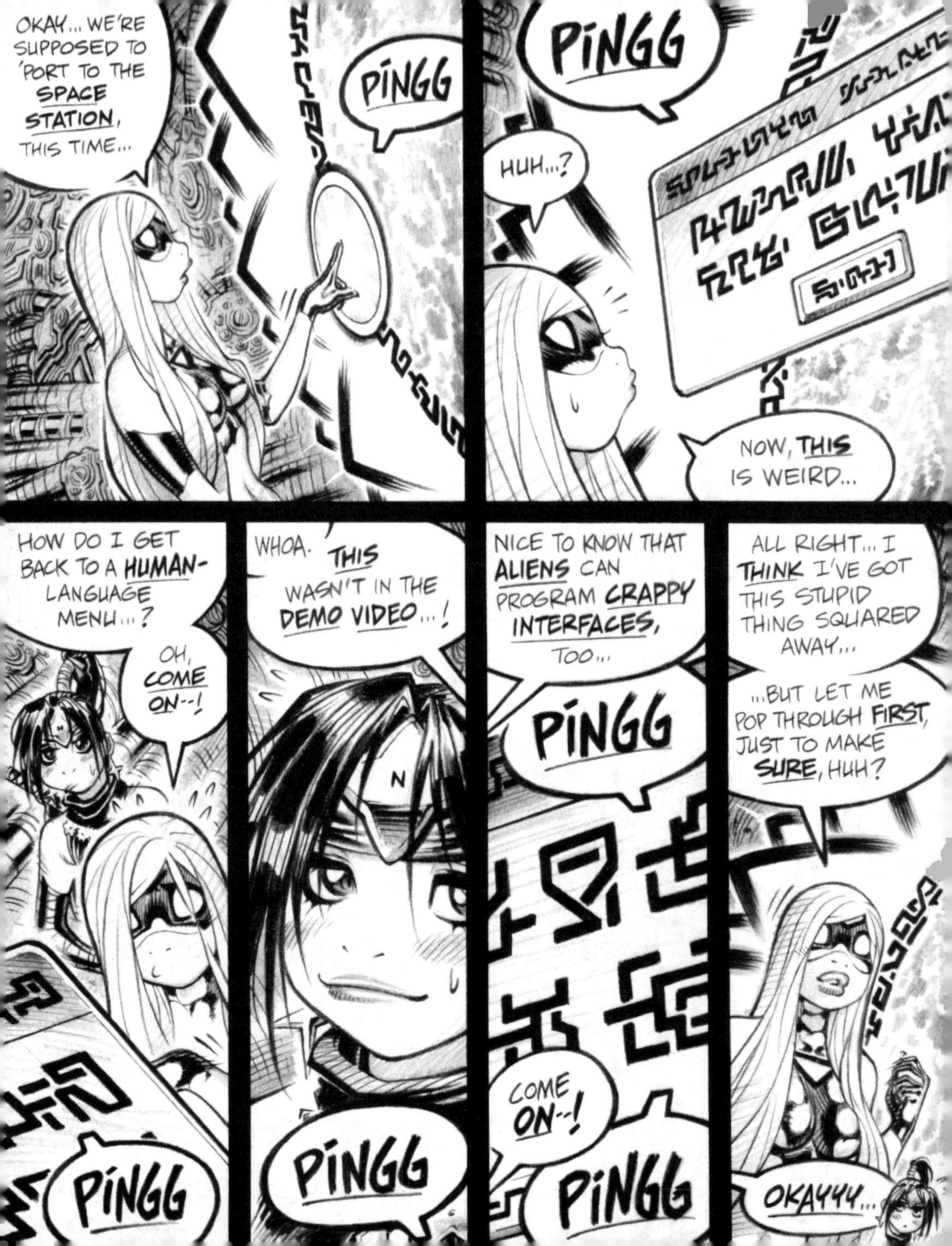
OKAY... WE'RE SUPPOSED TO 'PORT TO THE SPACE STATION, THIS TIME...
PINGG
PINGG
HUH...?
NOW, THIS IS WEIRD...
HOW DO I GET BACK TO A HUMAN-LANGUAGE MENU...?
OH, COME ON--!
PINGG
WHOA. THIS WASN'T IN THE DEMO VIDEO...!
PINGG
NICE TO KNOW THAT ALIENS CAN PROGRAM CRAPPY INTERFACES, TOO...
PINGG
COME ON--!
PINGG
ALL RIGHT... I THINK I'VE GOT THIS STUPID THING SQUARED AWAY...
...BUT LET ME POP THROUGH FIRST, JUST TO MAKE SURE, HUH?
OKAYYY...

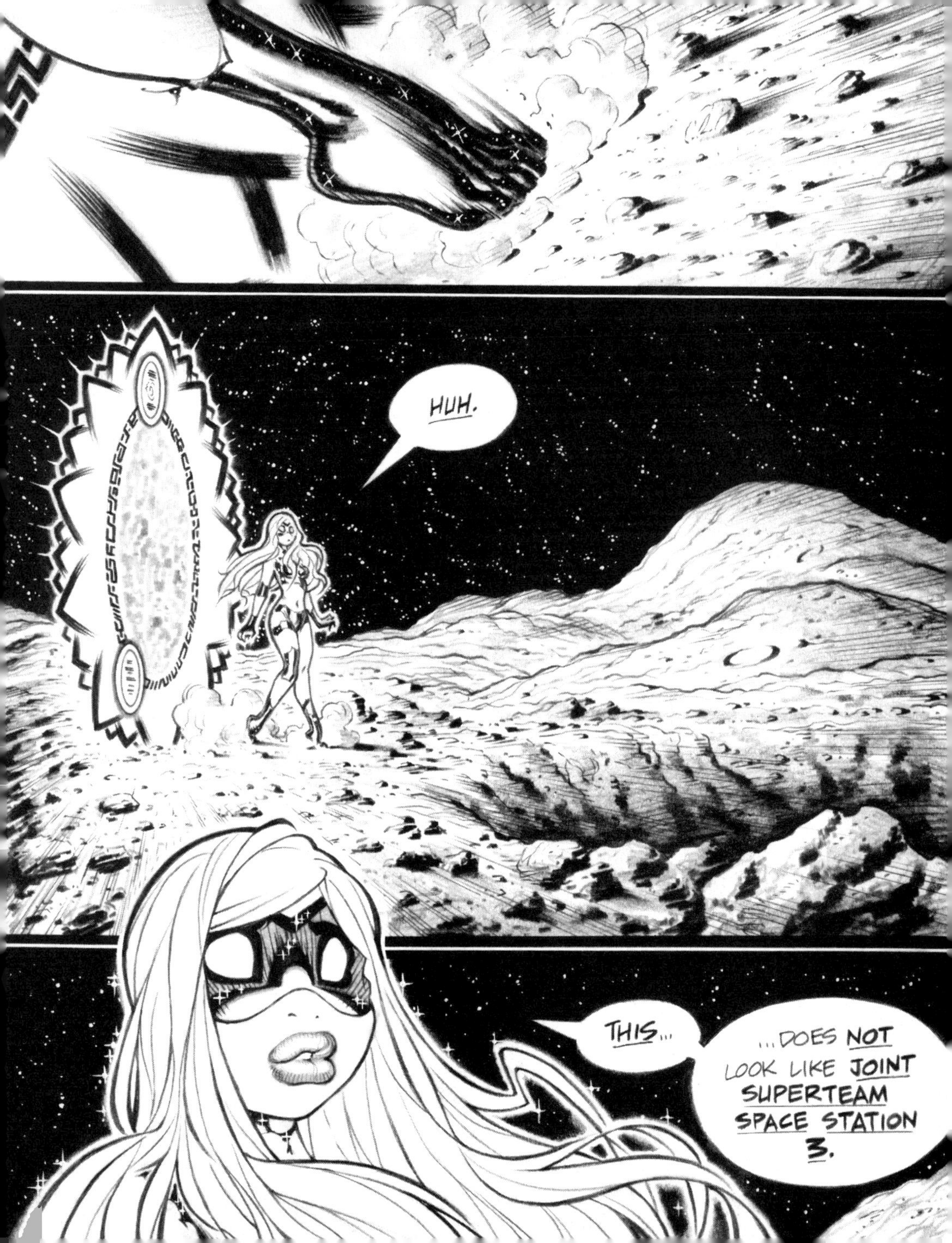
HUH.
THIS...
...DOES NOT LOOK LIKE JOINT SUPERTEAM SPACE STATION 3.

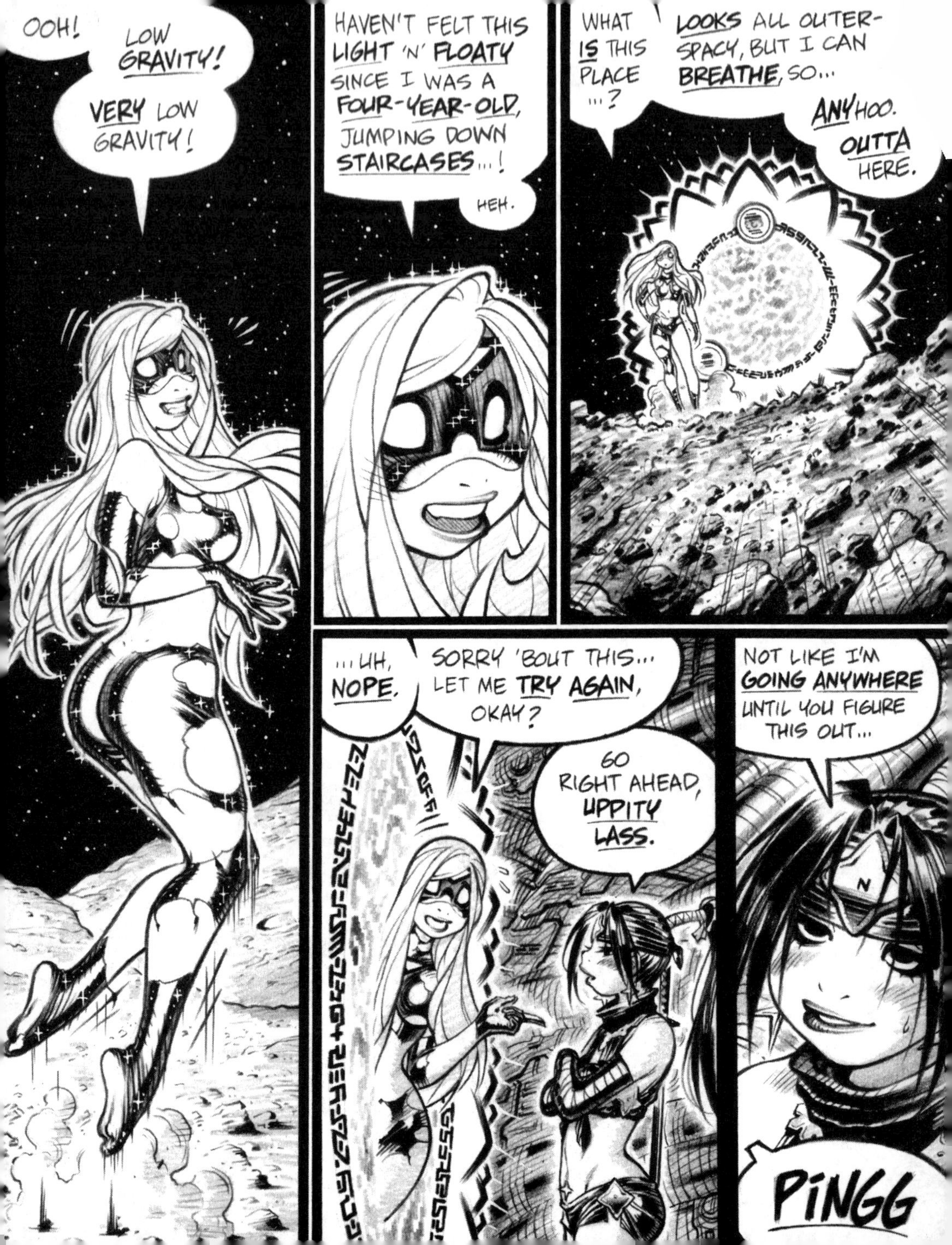
OOH!
LOW GRAVITY!
VERY LOW GRAVITY!
HAVEN'T FELT THIS LIGHT 'N' FLOATY SINCE I WAS A FOUR-YEAR-OLD, JUMPING DOWN STAIRCASES...!
HEH.
WHAT IS THIS PLACE ...?
LOOKS ALL OUTER-SPACY, BUT I CAN BREATHE, SO...
ANYHOO. OUTTA HERE.
...UH, NOPE.
SORRY 'BOUT THIS... LET ME TRY AGAIN, OKAY?
GO RIGHT AHEAD, UPPITY LASS.
NOT LIKE I'M GOING ANYWHERE UNTIL YOU FIGURE THIS OUT...
PINGG

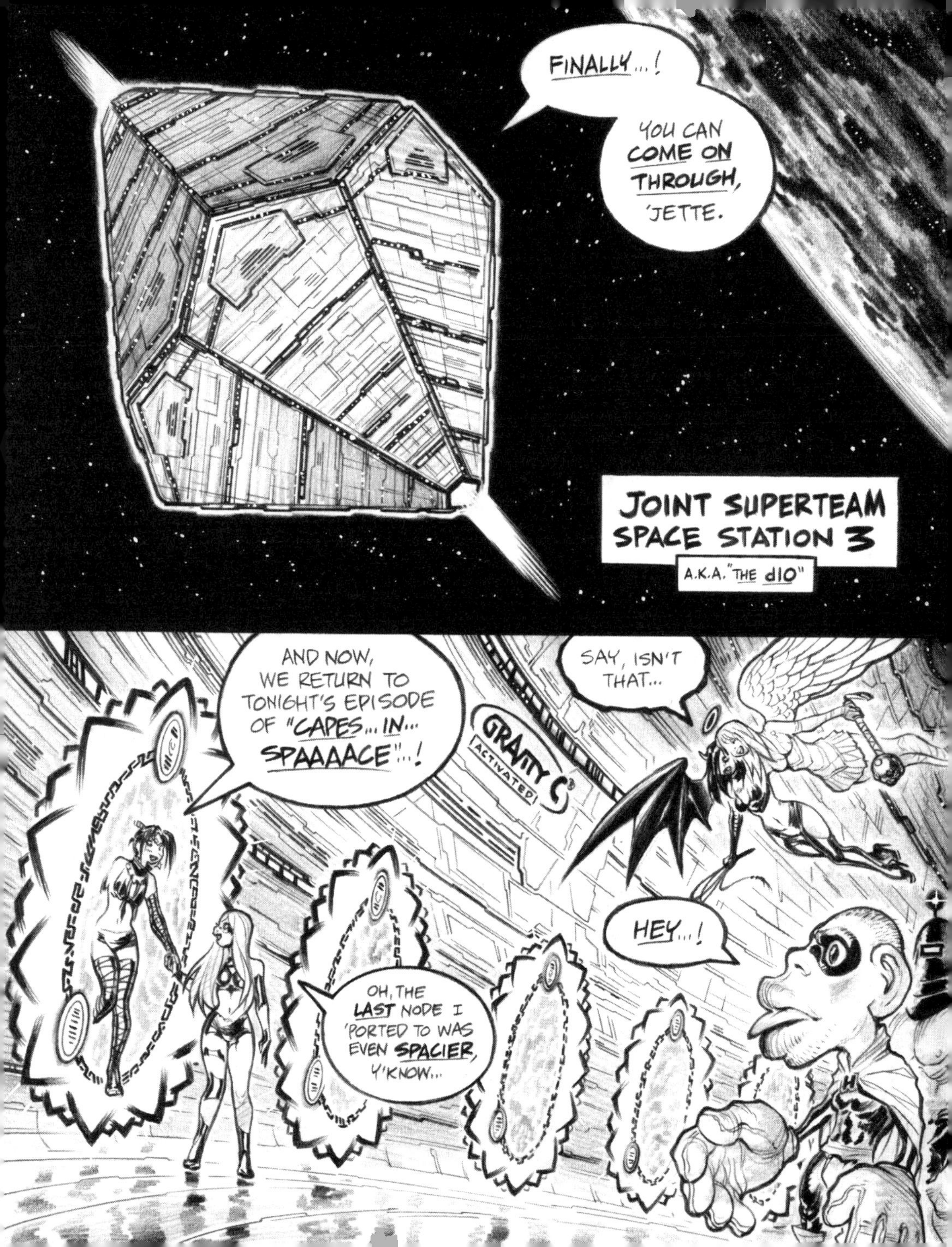
FINALLY...!
YOU CAN COME ON THROUGH, 'JETTE.
JOINT SUPERTEAM SPACE STATION 3
A.K.A. "THE d10"
AND NOW, WE RETURN TO TONIGHT'S EPISODE OF "CAPES... IN... SPAAAACE"...!
GRAVITY ACTIVATED
SAY, ISN'T THAT...
HEY...!
OH, THE LAST NODE I 'PORTED TO WAS EVEN SPACIER, Y'KNOW...

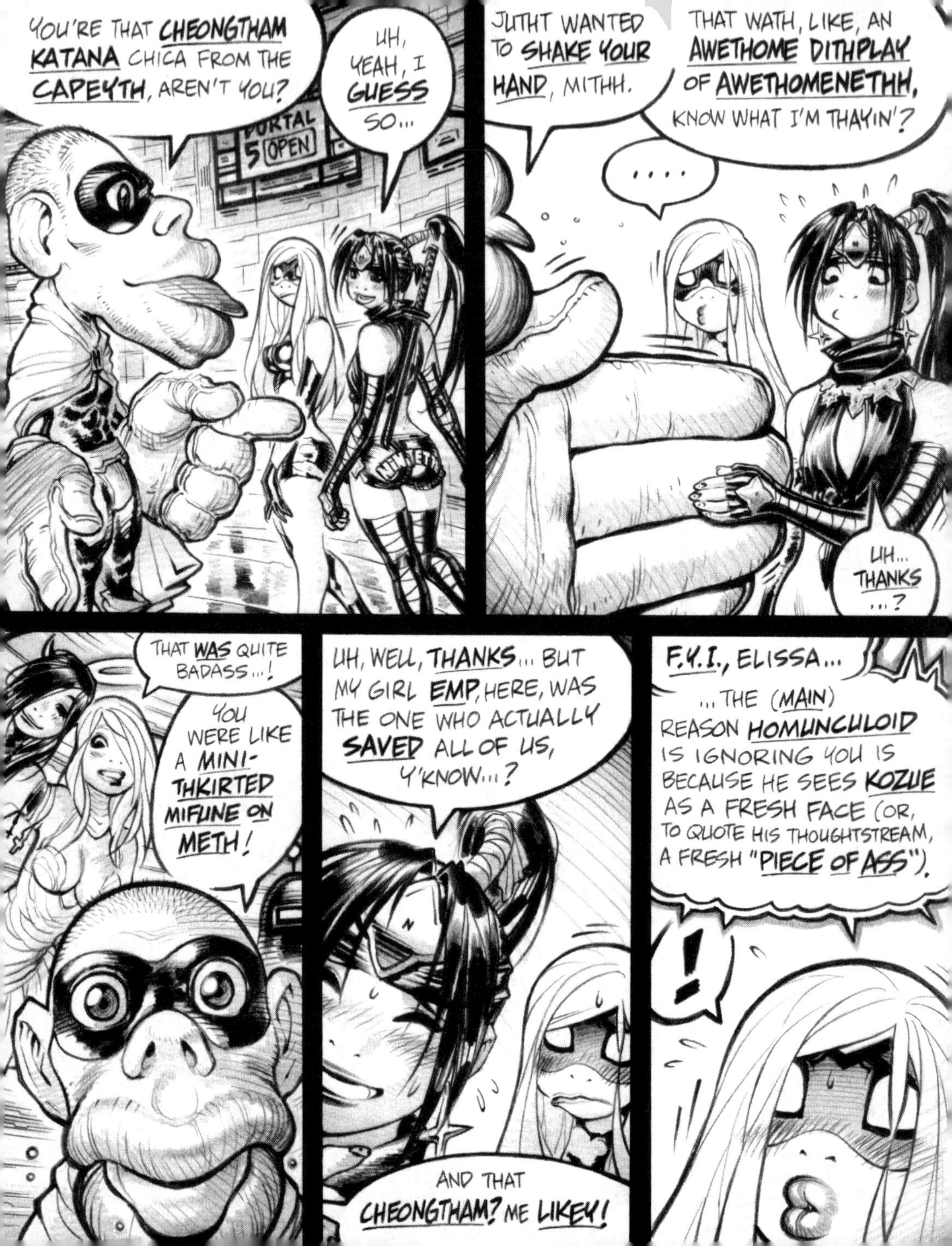
YOU'RE THAT CHEONGTHAM KATANA CHICA FROM THE CAPEYTH, AREN'T YOU?
UH, YEAH, I GUESS SO...
PORTAL 5 OPEN
JUTHT WANTED TO SHAKE YOUR HAND, MITHH.
THAT WATH, LIKE, AN AWETHOME DITHPLAY OF AWETHOMENETHH, KNOW WHAT I'M THAYIN'?
....
UH... THANKS ...?
THAT WAS QUITE BADASS...!
YOU WERE LIKE A MINI-THKIRTED MIFUNE ON METH!
UH, WELL, THANKS... BUT MY GIRL EMP, HERE, WAS THE ONE WHO ACTUALLY SAVED ALL OF US, Y'KNOW...?
AND THAT CHEONGTHAM? ME LIKEY!
F.Y.I., ELISSA...
...THE (MAIN) REASON HOMUNCULOID IS IGNORING YOU IS BECAUSE HE SEES KOZUE AS A FRESH FACE (OR, TO QUOTE HIS THOUGHTSTREAM, A FRESH "PIECE OF ASS").
!

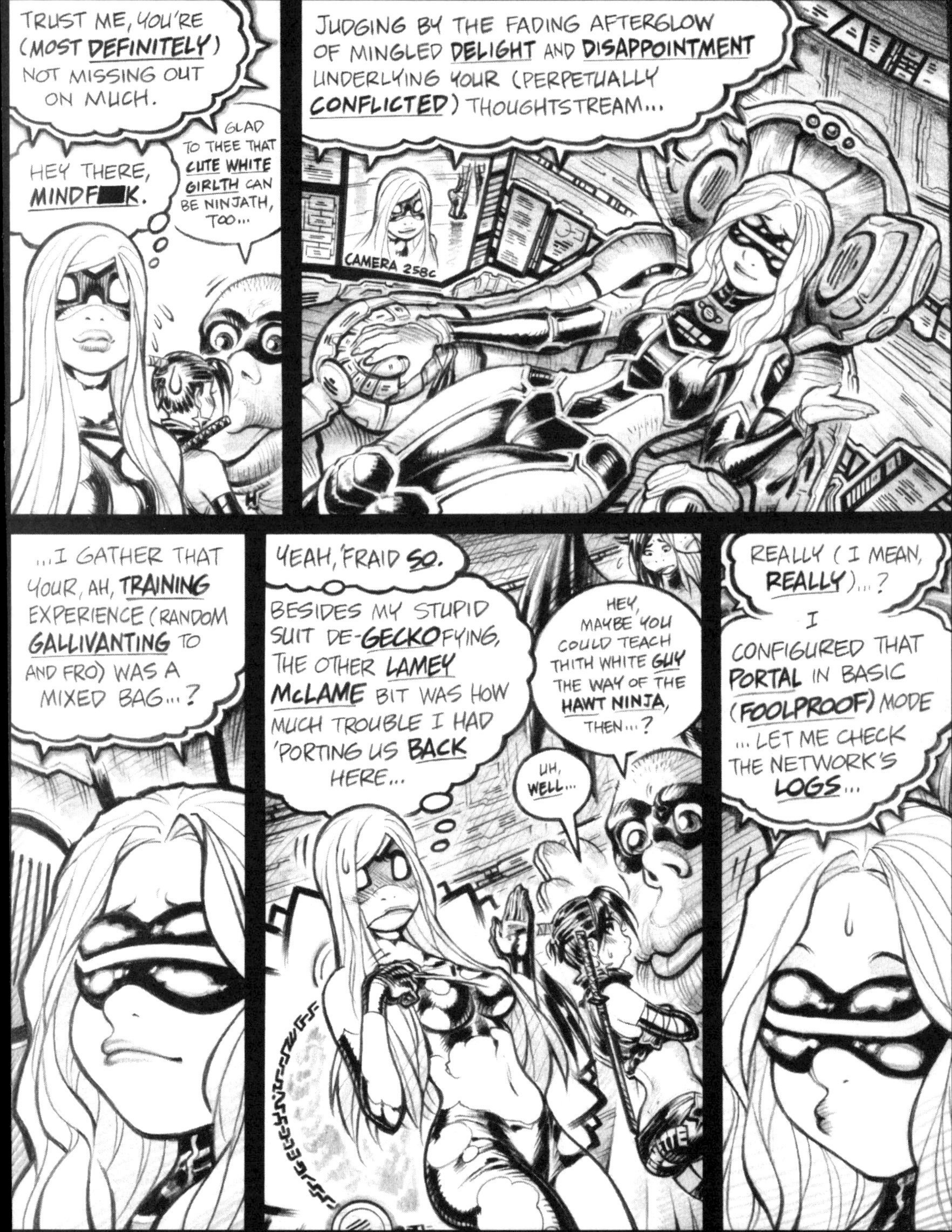
TRUST ME, YOU'RE (MOST DEFINITELY) NOT MISSING OUT ON MUCH.
HEY THERE, MINDF[redacted]K.
GLAD TO THEE THAT CUTE WHITE GIRLTH CAN BE NINJATH, TOO...
JUDGING BY THE FADING AFTERGLOW OF MINGLED DELIGHT AND DISAPPOINTMENT UNDERLYING YOUR (PERPETUALLY CONFLICTED) THOUGHTSTREAM...
CAMERA 258c
...I GATHER THAT YOUR, AH, TRAINING EXPERIENCE (RANDOM GALLIVANTING TO AND FRO) WAS A MIXED BAG...?
YEAH, 'FRAID SO.
BESIDES MY STUPID SUIT DE-GECKOFYING, THE OTHER LAMEY McLAME BIT WAS HOW MUCH TROUBLE I HAD 'PORTING US BACK HERE...
HEY, MAYBE YOU COULD TEACH THITH WHITE GUY THE WAY OF THE HAWT NINJA, THEN...?
UH, WELL...
REALLY (I MEAN, REALLY)...?
I CONFIGURED THAT PORTAL IN BASIC (FOOLPROOF) MODE ...LET ME CHECK THE NETWORK'S LOGS...

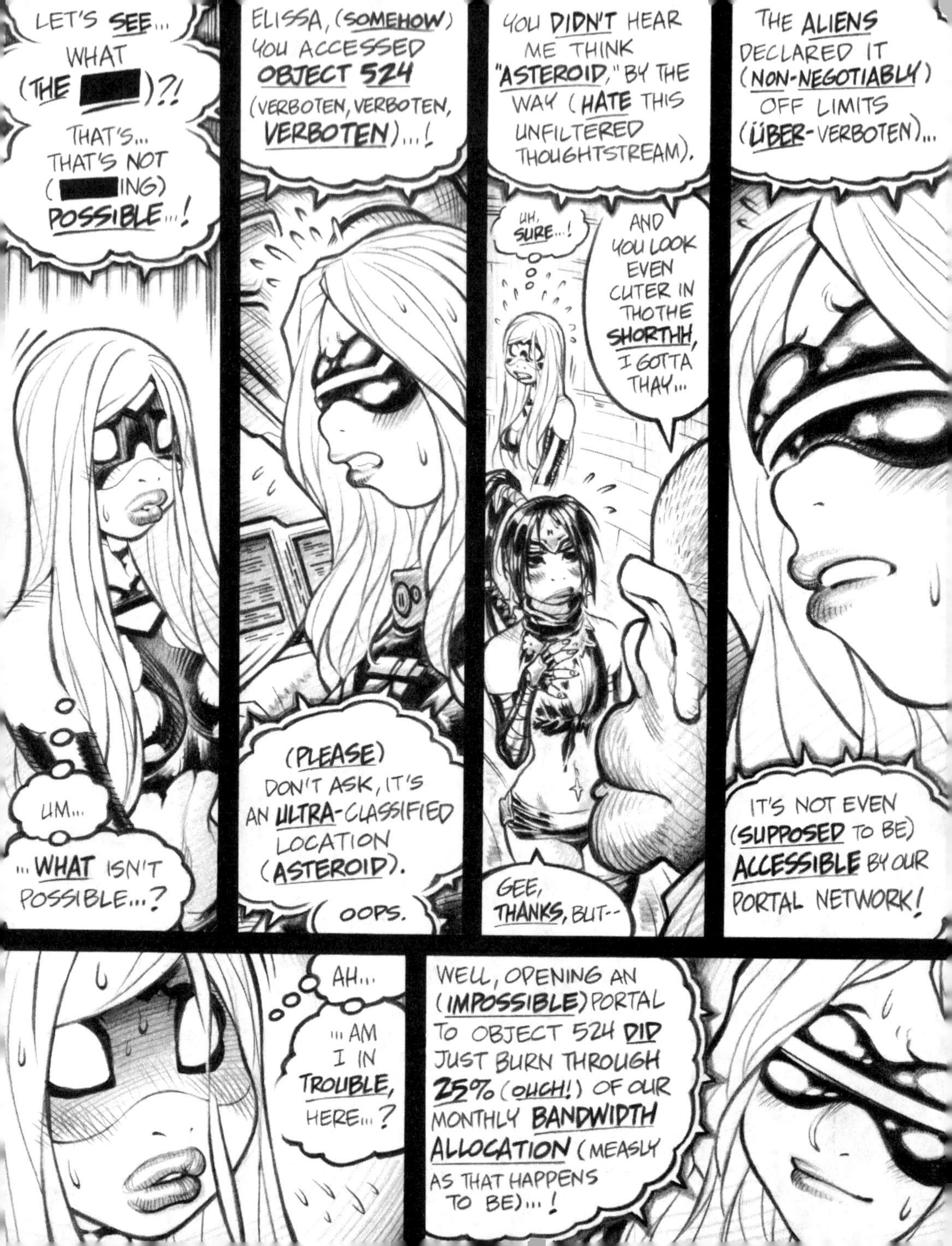

LET'S SEE... WHAT (THE [redacted])?!
THAT'S... THAT'S NOT ([redacted]ING) POSSIBLE...!
UM...
...WHAT ISN'T POSSIBLE...?
ELISSA, (SOMEHOW) YOU ACCESSED OBJECT 524 (VERBOTEN, VERBOTEN, VERBOTEN)...!
(PLEASE) DON'T ASK, IT'S AN ULTRA-CLASSIFIED LOCATION (ASTEROID).
OOPS.
YOU DIDN'T HEAR ME THINK "ASTEROID," BY THE WAY (HATE THIS UNFILTERED THOUGHTSTREAM).
UH, SURE...!
AND YOU LOOK EVEN CUTER IN THOTHE SHORTHH, I GOTTA THAY...
GEE, THANKS, BUT--
THE ALIENS DECLARED IT (NON-NEGOTIABLY) OFF LIMITS (ÜBER-VERBOTEN)...
IT'S NOT EVEN (SUPPOSED TO BE) ACCESSIBLE BY OUR PORTAL NETWORK!
AH...
...AM I IN TROUBLE, HERE...?
WELL, OPENING AN (IMPOSSIBLE) PORTAL TO OBJECT 524 DID JUST BURN THROUGH 25% (OUCH!) OF OUR MONTHLY BANDWIDTH ALLOCATION (MEASLY AS THAT HAPPENS TO BE)...!

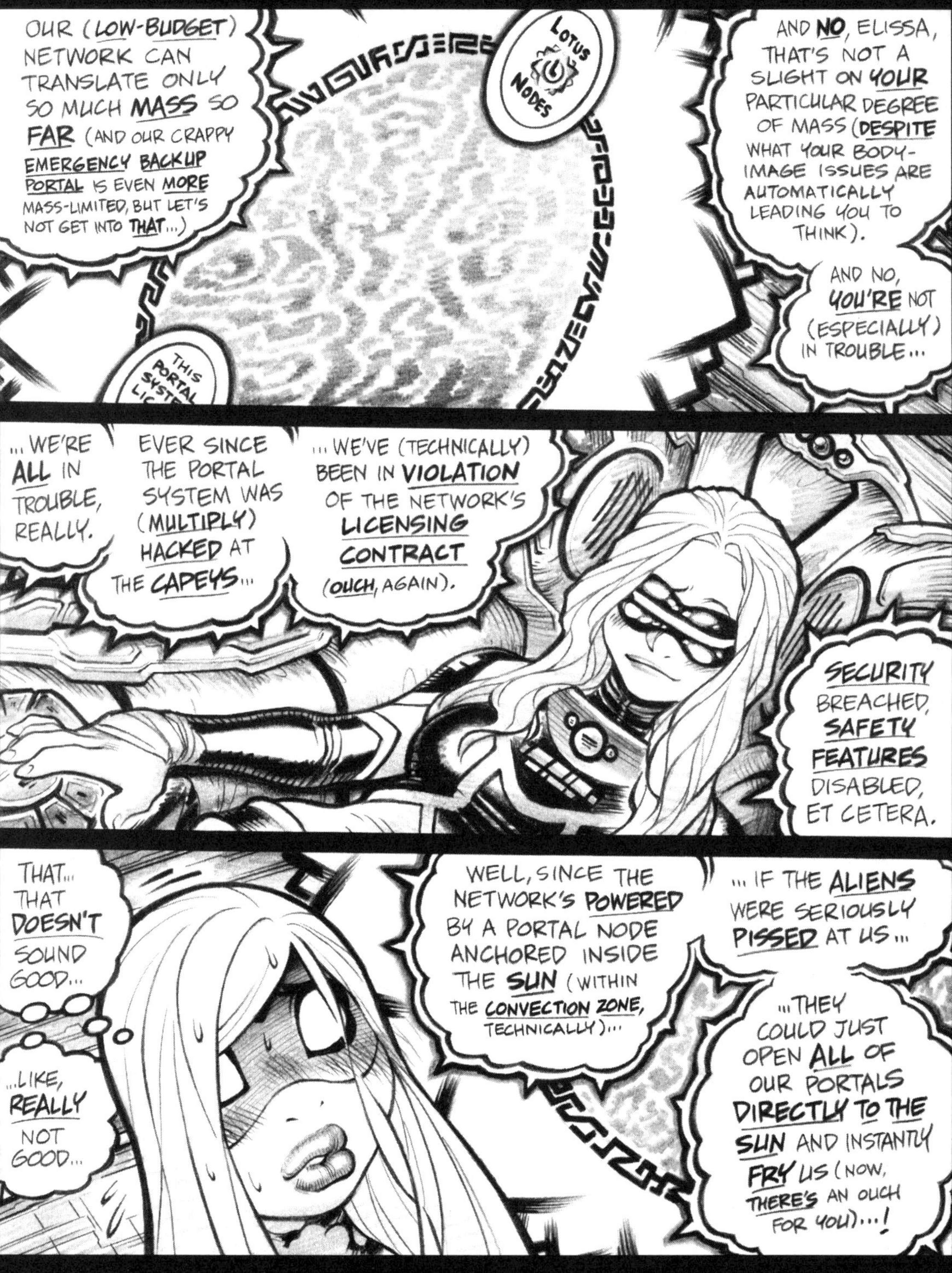
OUR (LOW-BUDGET) NETWORK CAN TRANSLATE ONLY SO MUCH MASS SO FAR (AND OUR CRAPPY EMERGENCY BACKUP PORTAL IS EVEN MORE MASS-LIMITED, BUT LET'S NOT GET INTO THAT...)
LOTUS NODES
AND NO, ELISSA, THAT'S NOT A SLIGHT ON YOUR PARTICULAR DEGREE OF MASS (DESPITE WHAT YOUR BODY-IMAGE ISSUES ARE AUTOMATICALLY LEADING YOU TO THINK).
AND NO, YOU'RE NOT (ESPECIALLY) IN TROUBLE...
...WE'RE ALL IN TROUBLE, REALLY.
EVER SINCE THE PORTAL SYSTEM WAS (MULTIPLY) HACKED AT THE CAPEYS...
...WE'VE (TECHNICALLY) BEEN IN VIOLATION OF THE NETWORK'S LICENSING CONTRACT (OUCH, AGAIN).
SECURITY BREACHED, SAFETY FEATURES DISABLED, ET CETERA.
THAT... THAT DOESN'T SOUND GOOD...
...LIKE, REALLY NOT GOOD...
WELL, SINCE THE NETWORK'S POWERED BY A PORTAL NODE ANCHORED INSIDE THE SUN (WITHIN THE CONVECTION ZONE, TECHNICALLY)...
...IF THE ALIENS WERE SERIOUSLY PISSED AT US...
...THEY COULD JUST OPEN ALL OF OUR PORTALS DIRECTLY TO THE SUN AND INSTANTLY FRY US (NOW, THERE'S AN OUCH FOR YOU)...!

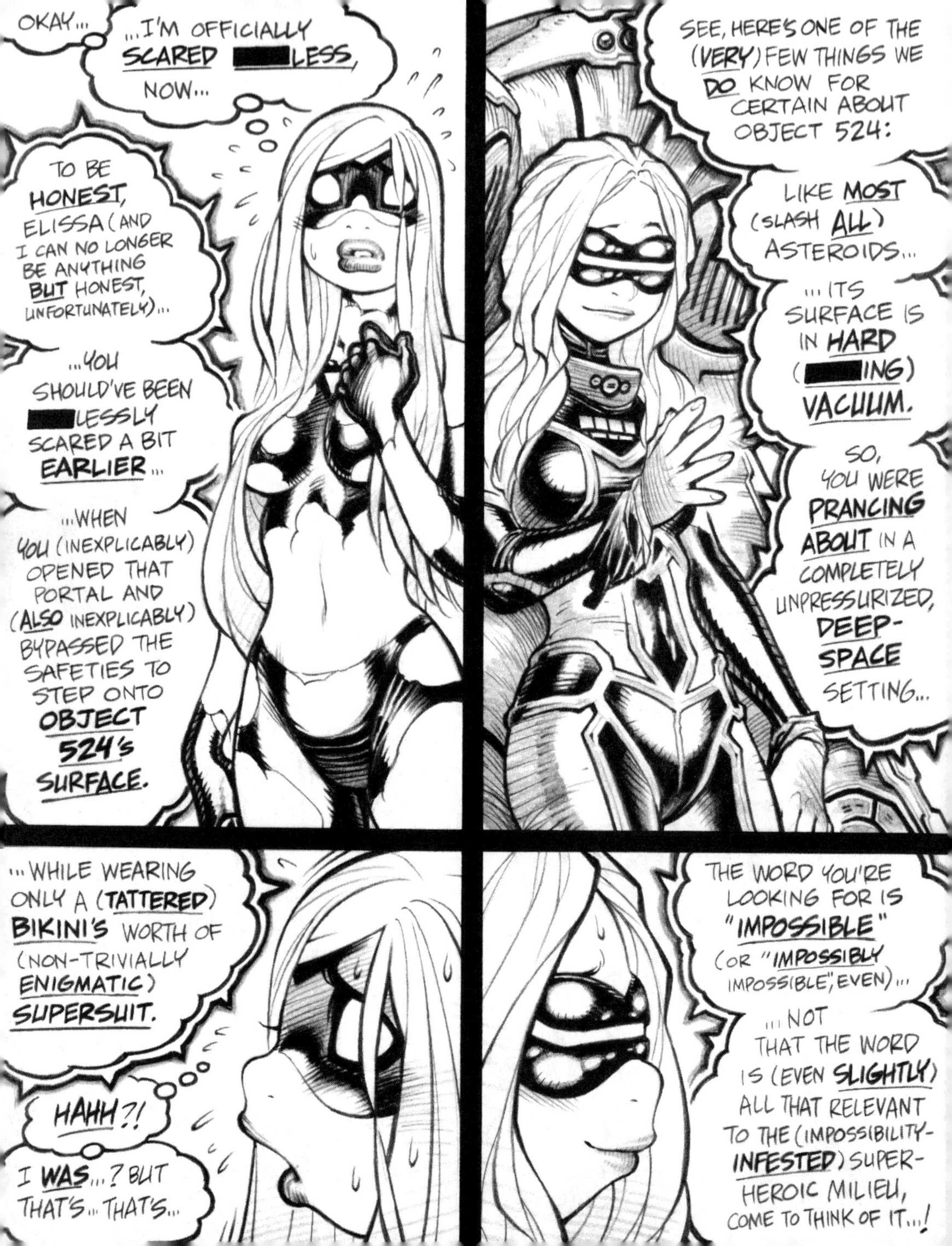
OKAY...
...I'M OFFICIALLY SCARED [redacted] LESS, NOW...
TO BE HONEST, ELISSA (AND I CAN NO LONGER BE ANYTHING BUT HONEST, UNFORTUNATELY)...
...YOU SHOULD'VE BEEN [redacted] LESSLY SCARED A BIT EARLIER...
...WHEN YOU (INEXPLICABLY) OPENED THAT PORTAL AND (ALSO INEXPLICABLY) BYPASSED THE SAFETIES TO STEP ONTO OBJECT 524's SURFACE.
SEE, HERE'S ONE OF THE (VERY) FEW THINGS WE DO KNOW FOR CERTAIN ABOUT OBJECT 524:
LIKE MOST (SLASH ALL) ASTEROIDS...
...ITS SURFACE IS IN HARD ([redacted] ING) VACUUM.
SO, YOU WERE PRANCING ABOUT IN A COMPLETELY UNPRESSURIZED, DEEP-SPACE SETTING...
...WHILE WEARING ONLY A (TATTERED) BIKINI'S WORTH OF (NON-TRIVIALLY ENIGMATIC) SUPERSUIT.
HAHH?!
I WAS...? BUT THAT'S... THAT'S...
THE WORD YOU'RE LOOKING FOR IS "IMPOSSIBLE" (OR "IMPOSSIBLY IMPOSSIBLE", EVEN)...
...NOT THAT THE WORD IS (EVEN SLIGHTLY) ALL THAT RELEVANT TO THE (IMPOSSIBILITY-INFESTED) SUPER-HEROIC MILIEU, COME TO THINK OF IT...!

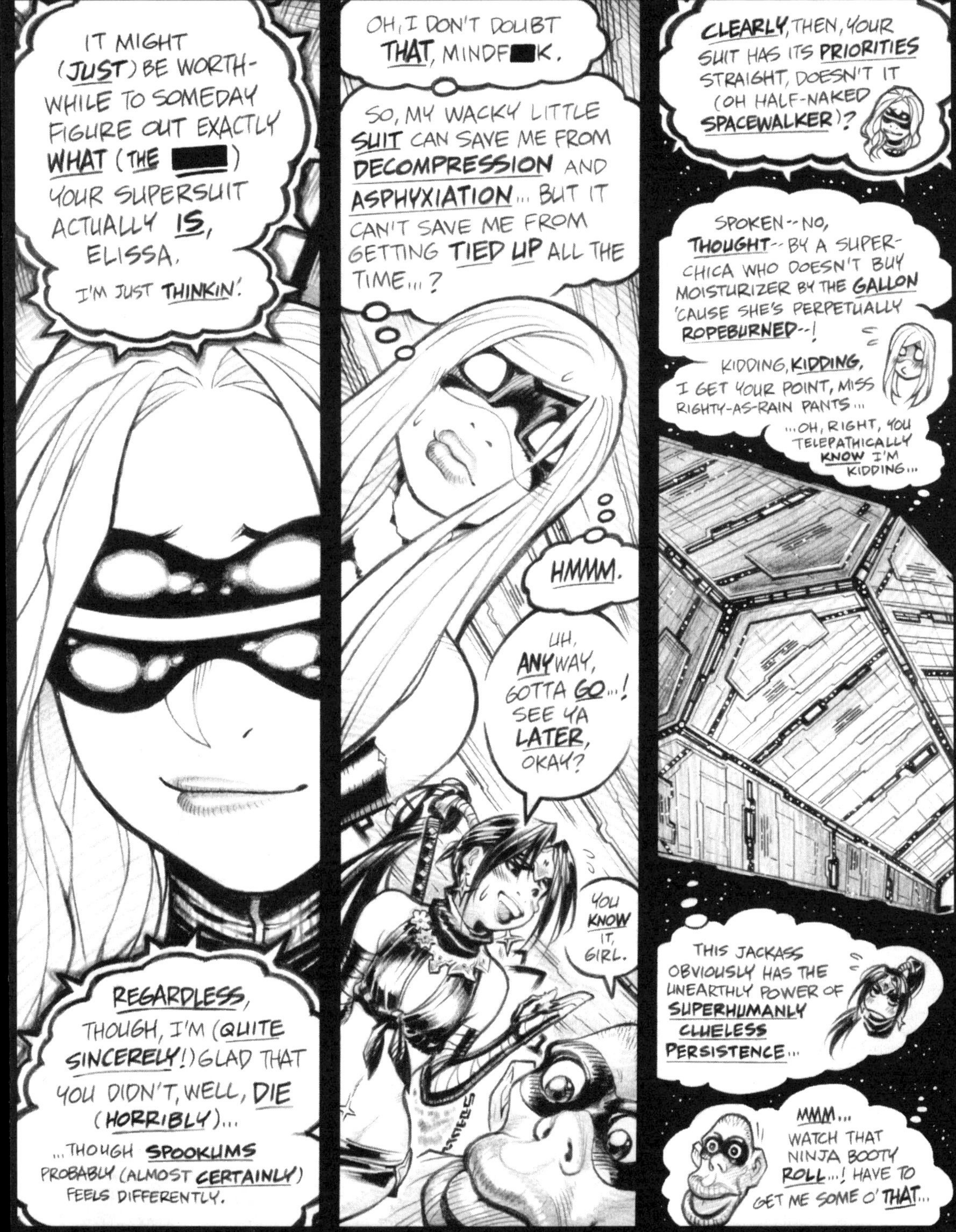
IT MIGHT (JUST) BE WORTH-WHILE TO SOMEDAY FIGURE OUT EXACTLY WHAT (THE [redacted]) YOUR SUPERSUIT ACTUALLY IS, ELISSA.
I'M JUST THINKIN'.
REGARDLESS, THOUGH, I'M (QUITE SINCERELY!) GLAD THAT YOU DIDN'T, WELL, DIE (HORRIBLY)...
...THOUGH SPOOKUMS PROBABLY (ALMOST CERTAINLY) FEELS DIFFERENTLY.
OH, I DON'T DOUBT THAT, MINDF[redacted]K.
SO, MY WACKY LITTLE SUIT CAN SAVE ME FROM DECOMPRESSION AND ASPHYXIATION... BUT IT CAN'T SAVE ME FROM GETTING TIED UP ALL THE TIME...?
HMMM.
UH, ANYWAY, GOTTA GO...! SEE YA LATER, OKAY?
YOU KNOW IT, GIRL.
CLEARLY, THEN, YOUR SUIT HAS ITS PRIORITIES STRAIGHT, DOESN'T IT (OH HALF-NAKED SPACEWALKER)?
SPOKEN--NO, THOUGHT--BY A SUPER-CHICA WHO DOESN'T BUY MOISTURIZER BY THE GALLON 'CAUSE SHE'S PERPETUALLY ROPEBURNED--!
KIDDING, KIDDING, I GET YOUR POINT, MISS RIGHTY-AS-RAIN PANTS...
...OH, RIGHT, YOU TELEPATHICALLY KNOW I'M KIDDING...
THIS JACKASS OBVIOUSLY HAS THE UNEARTHLY POWER OF SUPERHUMANLY CLUELESS PERSISTENCE...
MMM... WATCH THAT NINJA BOOTY ROLL...! HAVE TO GET ME SOME O' THAT...

empowered™

Denial at Flood Stage

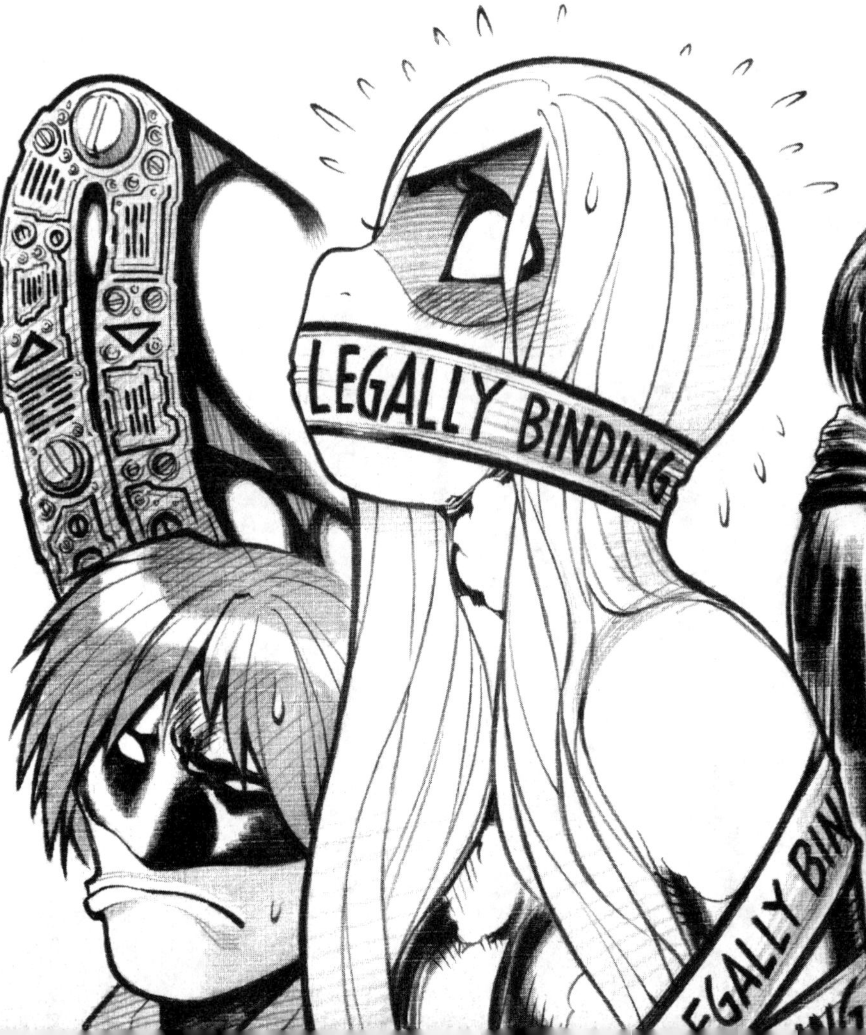
LEGALLY BINDING

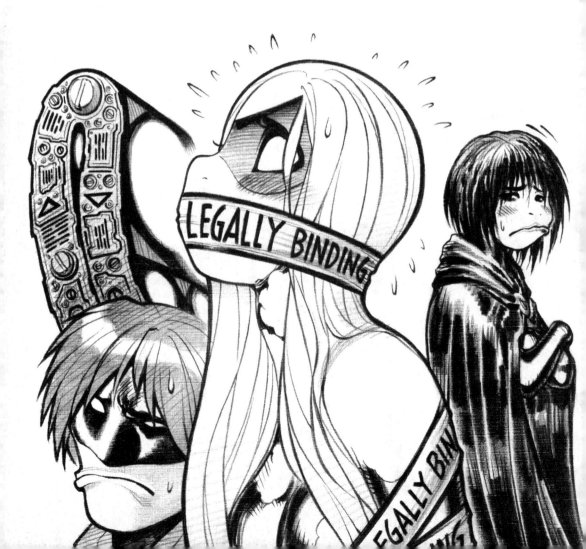

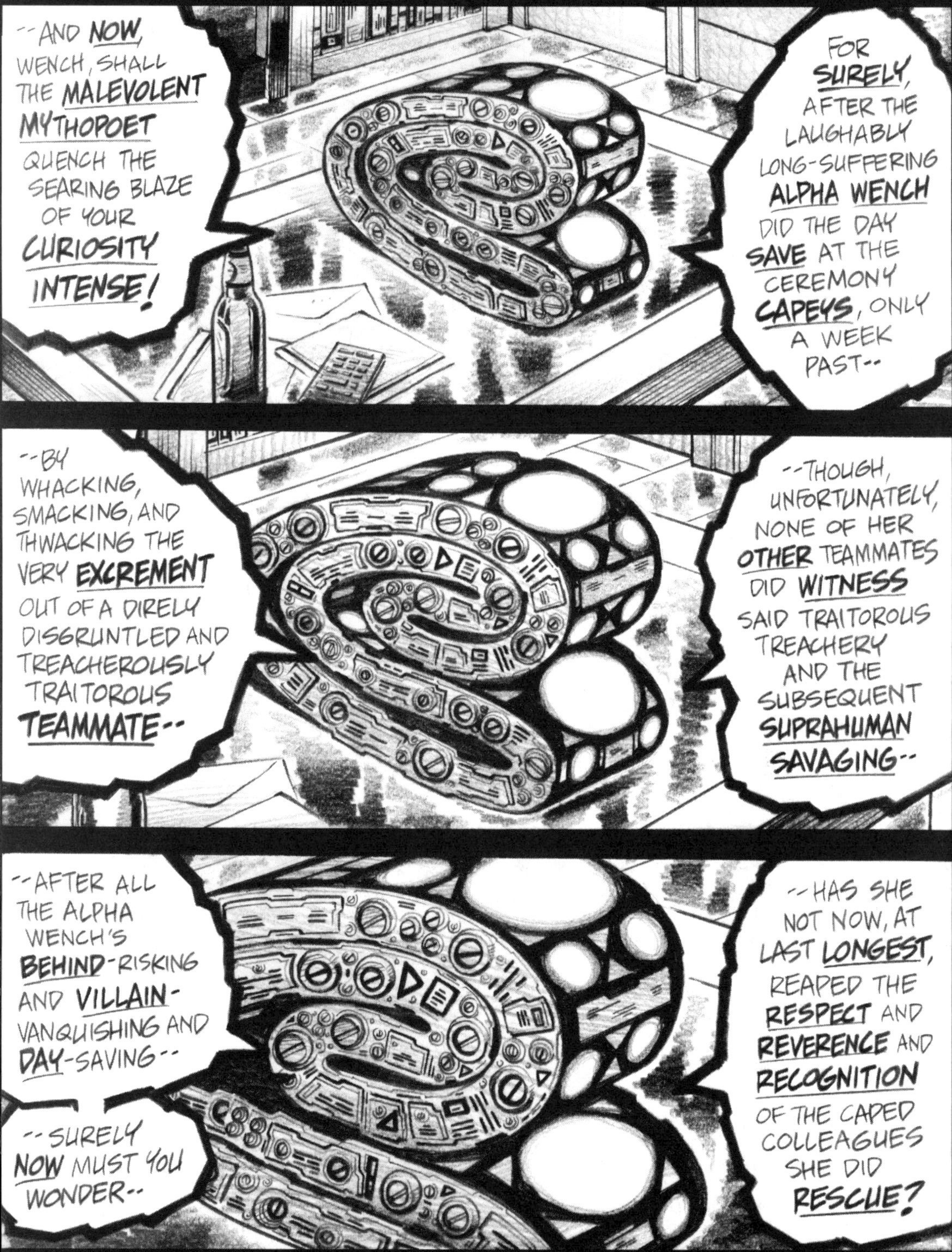
--AND NOW, WENCH, SHALL THE MALEVOLENT MYTHOPOET QUENCH THE SEARING BLAZE OF YOUR CURIOSITY INTENSE!
FOR SURELY, AFTER THE LAUGHABLY LONG-SUFFERING ALPHA WENCH DID THE DAY SAVE AT THE CEREMONY CAPEYS, ONLY A WEEK PAST--
--BY WHACKING, SMACKING, AND THWACKING THE VERY EXCREMENT OUT OF A DIRELY DISGRUNTLED AND TREACHEROUSLY TRAITOROUS TEAMMATE--
--THOUGH, UNFORTUNATELY, NONE OF HER OTHER TEAMMATES DID WITNESS SAID TRAITOROUS TREACHERY AND THE SUBSEQUENT SUPRAHUMAN SAVAGING--
--AFTER ALL THE ALPHA WENCH'S BEHIND-RISKING AND VILLAIN-VANQUISHING AND DAY-SAVING--
--SURELY NOW MUST YOU WONDER--
--HAS SHE NOT NOW, AT LAST LONGEST, REAPED THE RESPECT AND REVERENCE AND RECOGNITION OF THE CAPED COLLEAGUES SHE DID RESCUE?

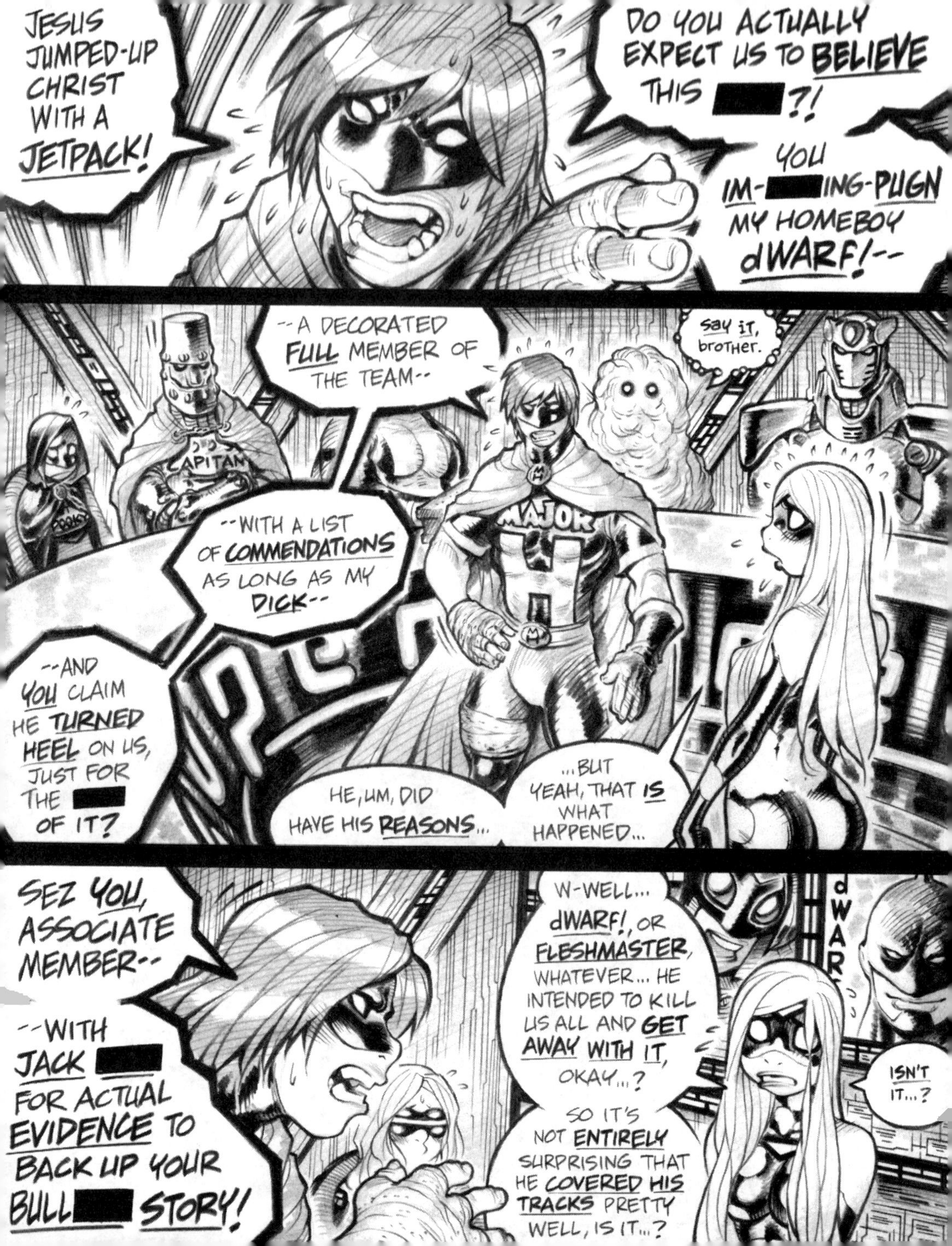

JESUS JUMPED-UP CHRIST WITH A JETPACK!
DO YOU ACTUALLY EXPECT US TO BELIEVE THIS [redacted]?!
YOU IM-[redacted]ING-PUGN MY HOMEBOY dWARF!--
--A DECORATED FULL MEMBER OF THE TEAM--
Say it, brother.
CAPITAN
MAJOR
--WITH A LIST OF COMMENDATIONS AS LONG AS MY DICK--
--AND YOU CLAIM HE TURNED HEEL ON US, JUST FOR THE [redacted] OF IT?
HE, UM, DID HAVE HIS REASONS...
...BUT YEAH, THAT IS WHAT HAPPENED...
SEZ YOU, ASSOCIATE MEMBER--
--WITH JACK [redacted] FOR ACTUAL EVIDENCE TO BACK UP YOUR BULL[redacted] STORY!
W-WELL... dWARF!, OR FLESHMASTER, WHATEVER... HE INTENDED TO KILL US ALL AND GET AWAY WITH IT, OKAY...?
SO IT'S NOT ENTIRELY SURPRISING THAT HE COVERED HIS TRACKS PRETTY WELL, IS IT...?
ISN'T IT...?

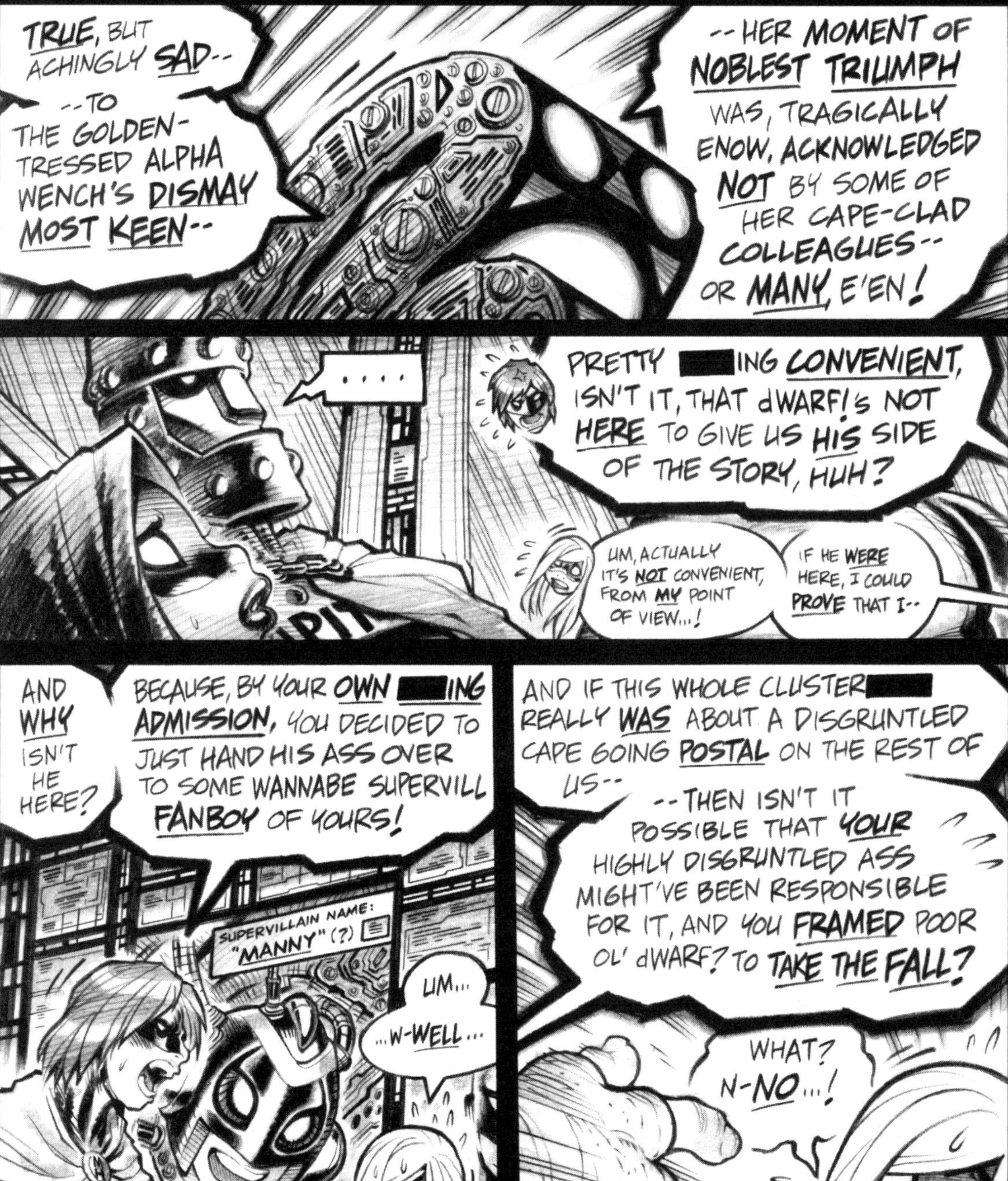
TRUE, BUT ACHINGLY SAD-- --TO THE GOLDEN-TRESSED ALPHA WENCH'S DISMAY MOST KEEN--
--HER MOMENT OF NOBLEST TRIUMPH WAS, TRAGICALLY ENOW, ACKNOWLEDGED NOT BY SOME OF HER CAPE-CLAD COLLEAGUES-- OR MANY, E'EN!
....
PRETTY [redacted]ING CONVENIENT, ISN'T IT, THAT dWARF!'s NOT HERE TO GIVE US HIS SIDE OF THE STORY, HUH?
UM, ACTUALLY IT'S NOT CONVENIENT, FROM MY POINT OF VIEW...!
IF HE WERE HERE, I COULD PROVE THAT I--
AND WHY ISN'T HE HERE?
BECAUSE, BY YOUR OWN [redacted]ING ADMISSION, YOU DECIDED TO JUST HAND HIS ASS OVER TO SOME WANNABE SUPERVILL FANBOY OF YOURS!
SUPERVILLAIN NAME: "MANNY" (?)
UM... ...W-WELL...
AND IF THIS WHOLE CLUSTER[redacted] REALLY WAS ABOUT A DISGRUNTLED CAPE GOING POSTAL ON THE REST OF US--
--THEN ISN'T IT POSSIBLE THAT YOUR HIGHLY DISGRUNTLED ASS MIGHT'VE BEEN RESPONSIBLE FOR IT, AND YOU FRAMED POOR OL' dWARF? TO TAKE THE FALL?
WHAT? N-NO...!

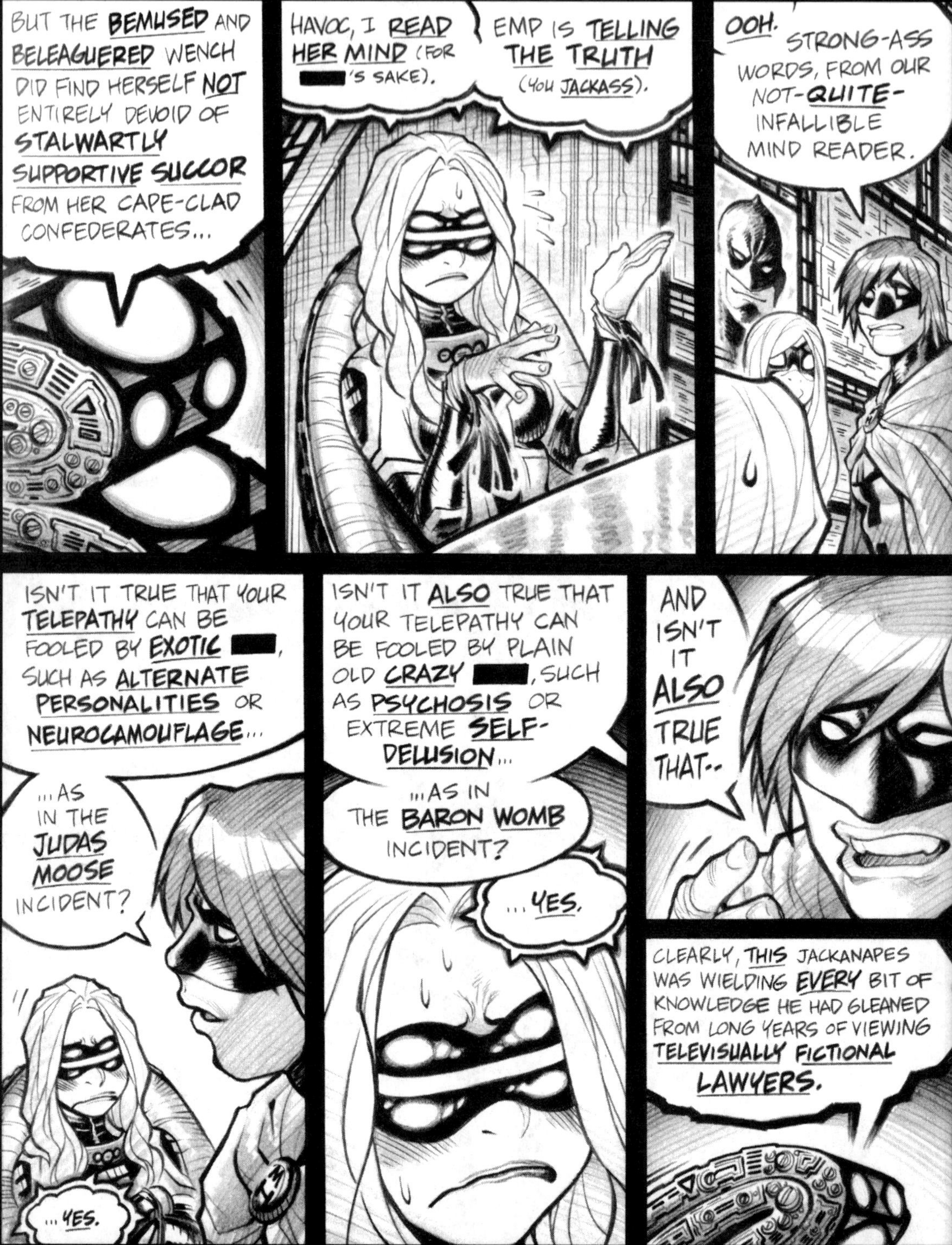
BUT THE BEMUSED AND BELEAGUERED WENCH DID FIND HERSELF NOT ENTIRELY DEVOID OF STALWARTLY SUPPORTIVE SUCCOR FROM HER CAPE-CLAD CONFEDERATES...
HAVOC, I READ HER MIND (FOR [redacted]'S SAKE).
EMP IS TELLING THE TRUTH (YOU JACKASS).
OOH. STRONG-ASS WORDS, FROM OUR NOT-QUITE-INFALLIBLE MIND READER.
ISN'T IT TRUE THAT YOUR TELEPATHY CAN BE FOOLED BY EXOTIC [redacted], SUCH AS ALTERNATE PERSONALITIES OR NEUROCAMOUFLAGE...
...AS IN THE JUDAS MOOSE INCIDENT?
...YES.
ISN'T IT ALSO TRUE THAT YOUR TELEPATHY CAN BE FOOLED BY PLAIN OLD CRAZY [redacted], SUCH AS PSYCHOSIS OR EXTREME SELF-DELUSION...
...AS IN THE BARON WOMB INCIDENT?
...YES.
AND ISN'T IT ALSO TRUE THAT--
CLEARLY, THIS JACKANAPES WAS WIELDING EVERY BIT OF KNOWLEDGE HE HAD GLEANED FROM LONG YEARS OF VIEWING TELEVISUALLY FICTIONAL LAWYERS.

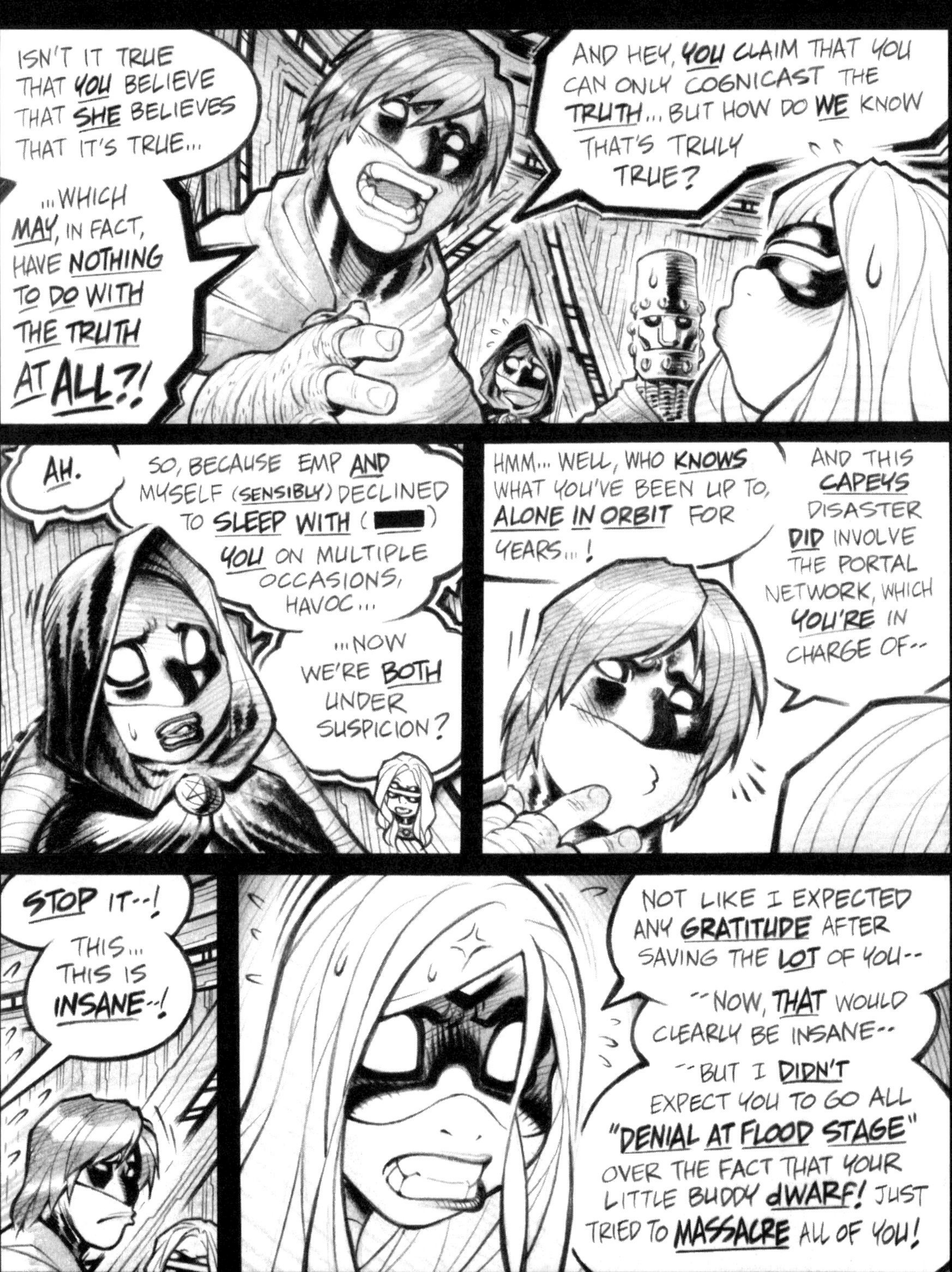
ISN'T IT TRUE THAT YOU BELIEVE THAT SHE BELIEVES THAT IT'S TRUE...
...WHICH MAY, IN FACT, HAVE NOTHING TO DO WITH THE TRUTH AT ALL?!
AND HEY, YOU CLAIM THAT YOU CAN ONLY COGNICAST THE TRUTH... BUT HOW DO WE KNOW THAT'S TRULY TRUE?
AH.
SO, BECAUSE EMP AND MYSELF (SENSIBLY) DECLINED TO SLEEP WITH ([redacted]) YOU ON MULTIPLE OCCASIONS, HAVOC...
...NOW WE'RE BOTH UNDER SUSPICION?
HMM... WELL, WHO KNOWS WHAT YOU'VE BEEN UP TO, ALONE IN ORBIT FOR YEARS...!
AND THIS CAPEYS DISASTER DID INVOLVE THE PORTAL NETWORK, WHICH YOU'RE IN CHARGE OF--
STOP IT--!
THIS... THIS IS INSANE--!
NOT LIKE I EXPECTED ANY GRATITUDE AFTER SAVING THE LOT OF YOU--
--NOW, THAT WOULD CLEARLY BE INSANE--
--BUT I DIDN'T EXPECT YOU TO GO ALL "DENIAL AT FLOOD STAGE" OVER THE FACT THAT YOUR LITTLE BUDDY dWARF! JUST TRIED TO MASSACRE ALL OF YOU!

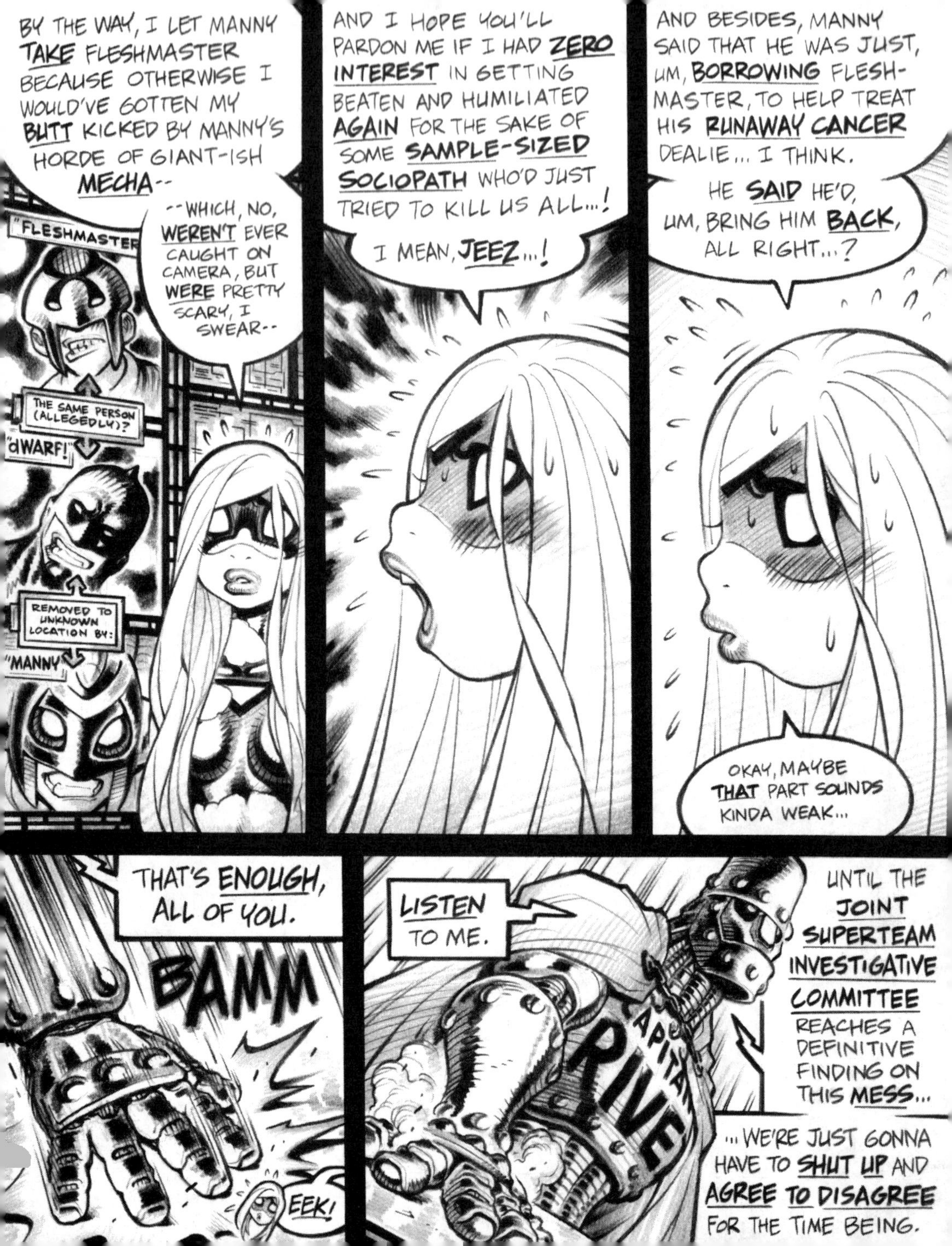

BY THE WAY, I LET MANNY TAKE FLESHMASTER BECAUSE OTHERWISE I WOULD'VE GOTTEN MY BUTT KICKED BY MANNY'S HORDE OF GIANT-ISH MECHA--
"FLESHMASTER"
THE SAME PERSON (ALLEGEDLY)?
"dWARF!"
REMOVED TO UNKNOWN LOCATION BY:
"MANNY"
--WHICH, NO, WEREN'T EVER CAUGHT ON CAMERA, BUT WERE PRETTY SCARY, I SWEAR--
AND I HOPE YOU'LL PARDON ME IF I HAD ZERO INTEREST IN GETTING BEATEN AND HUMILIATED AGAIN FOR THE SAKE OF SOME SAMPLE-SIZED SOCIOPATH WHO'D JUST TRIED TO KILL US ALL...!
I MEAN, JEEZ...!
AND BESIDES, MANNY SAID THAT HE WAS JUST, UM, BORROWING FLESH-MASTER, TO HELP TREAT HIS RUNAWAY CANCER DEALIE... I THINK.
HE SAID HE'D, UM, BRING HIM BACK, ALL RIGHT...?
OKAY, MAYBE THAT PART SOUNDS KINDA WEAK...
THAT'S ENOUGH, ALL OF YOU.
BAMM
EEK!
LISTEN TO ME.
UNTIL THE JOINT SUPERTEAM INVESTIGATIVE COMMITTEE REACHES A DEFINITIVE FINDING ON THIS MESS...
...WE'RE JUST GONNA HAVE TO SHUT UP AND AGREE TO DISAGREE FOR THE TIME BEING.

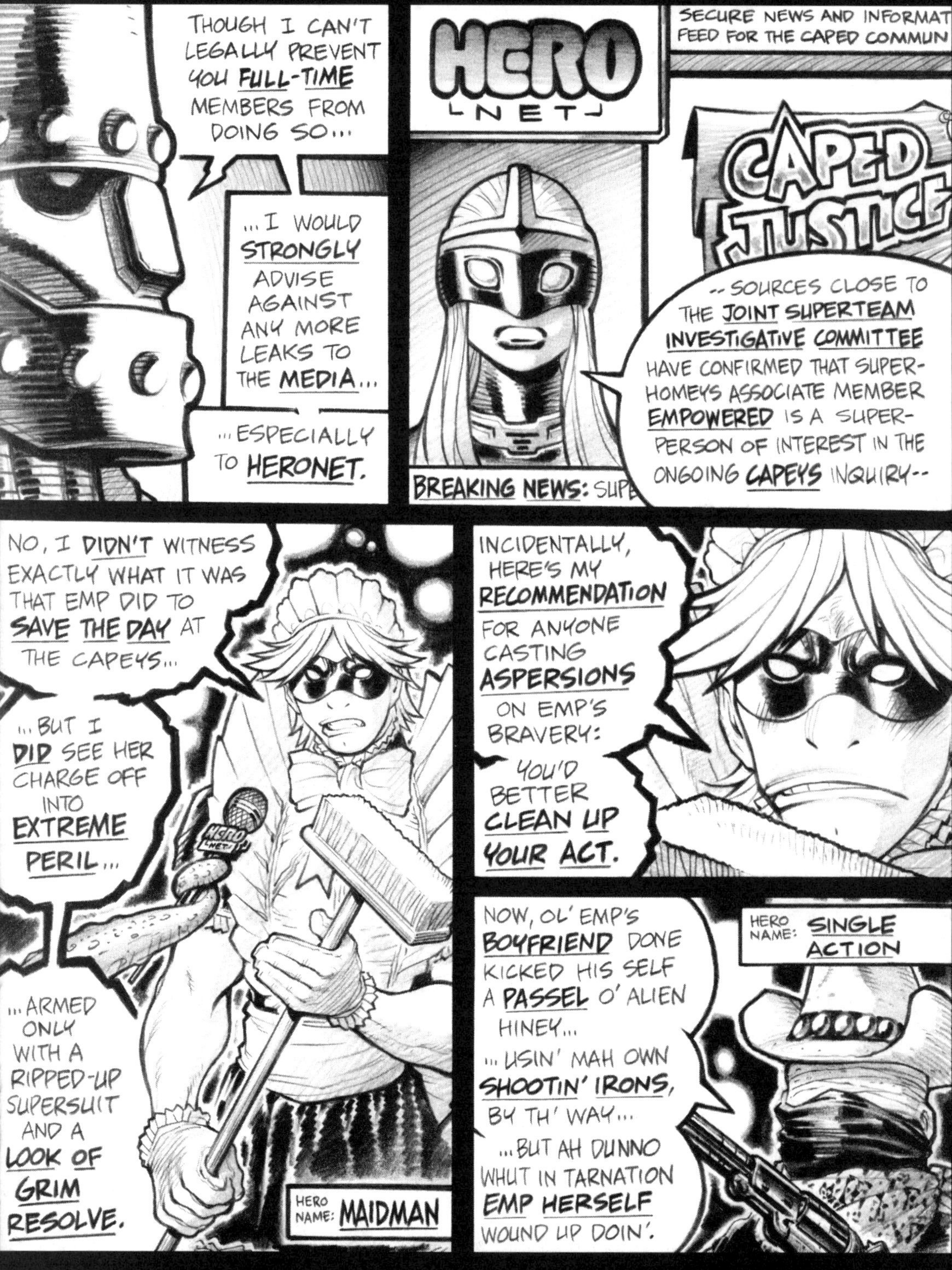
THOUGH I CAN'T LEGALLY PREVENT YOU FULL-TIME MEMBERS FROM DOING SO...
...I WOULD STRONGLY ADVISE AGAINST ANY MORE LEAKS TO THE MEDIA...
...ESPECIALLY TO HERONET.
HERO NET
SECURE NEWS AND INFORMAT
FEED FOR THE CAPED COMMUN
CAPED JUSTICE
BREAKING NEWS: SUPE
--SOURCES CLOSE TO THE JOINT SUPERTEAM INVESTIGATIVE COMMITTEE HAVE CONFIRMED THAT SUPER-HOMEYS ASSOCIATE MEMBER EMPOWERED IS A SUPER-PERSON OF INTEREST IN THE ONGOING CAPEYS INQUIRY--
NO, I DIDN'T WITNESS EXACTLY WHAT IT WAS THAT EMP DID TO SAVE THE DAY AT THE CAPEYS...
...BUT I DID SEE HER CHARGE OFF INTO EXTREME PERIL...
HERO NET
...ARMED ONLY WITH A RIPPED-UP SUPERSUIT AND A LOOK OF GRIM RESOLVE.
HERO NAME: MAIDMAN
INCIDENTALLY, HERE'S MY RECOMMENDATION FOR ANYONE CASTING ASPERSIONS ON EMP'S BRAVERY:
YOU'D BETTER CLEAN UP YOUR ACT.
NOW, OL' EMP'S BOYFRIEND DONE KICKED HIS SELF A PASSEL O' ALIEN HINEY...
...USIN' MAH OWN SHOOTIN' IRONS, BY TH' WAY...
...BUT AH DUNNO WHUT IN TARNATION EMP HERSELF WOUND UP DOIN'.
HERO NAME: SINGLE ACTION

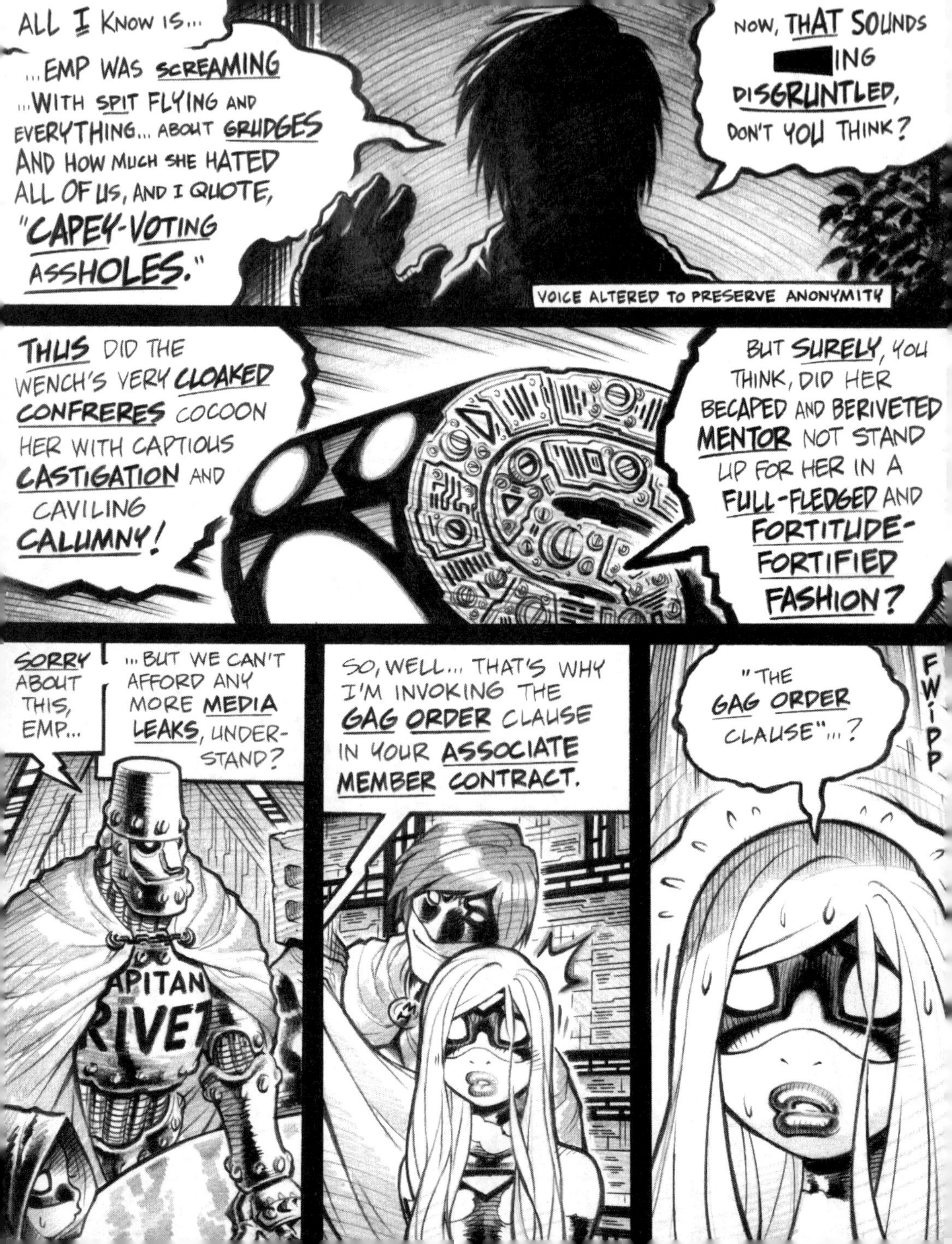
ALL I KNOW IS...
...EMP WAS SCREAMING ...WITH SPIT FLYING AND EVERYTHING... ABOUT GRUDGES AND HOW MUCH SHE HATED ALL OF US, AND I QUOTE, "CAPEY-VOTING ASSHOLES."
NOW, THAT SOUNDS [redacted]ING DISGRUNTLED, DON'T YOU THINK?
VOICE ALTERED TO PRESERVE ANONYMITY
THUS DID THE WENCH'S VERY CLOAKED CONFRERES COCOON HER WITH CAPTIOUS CASTIGATION AND CAVILING CALUMNY!
BUT SURELY, YOU THINK, DID HER BECAPED AND BERIVETED MENTOR NOT STAND UP FOR HER IN A FULL-FLEDGED AND FORTITUDE-FORTIFIED FASHION?
SORRY ABOUT THIS, EMP...
...BUT WE CAN'T AFFORD ANY MORE MEDIA LEAKS, UNDER-STAND?
APITAN
RIVET
SO, WELL... THAT'S WHY I'M INVOKING THE GAG ORDER CLAUSE IN YOUR ASSOCIATE MEMBER CONTRACT.
"THE GAG ORDER CLAUSE"...?
FWIPP

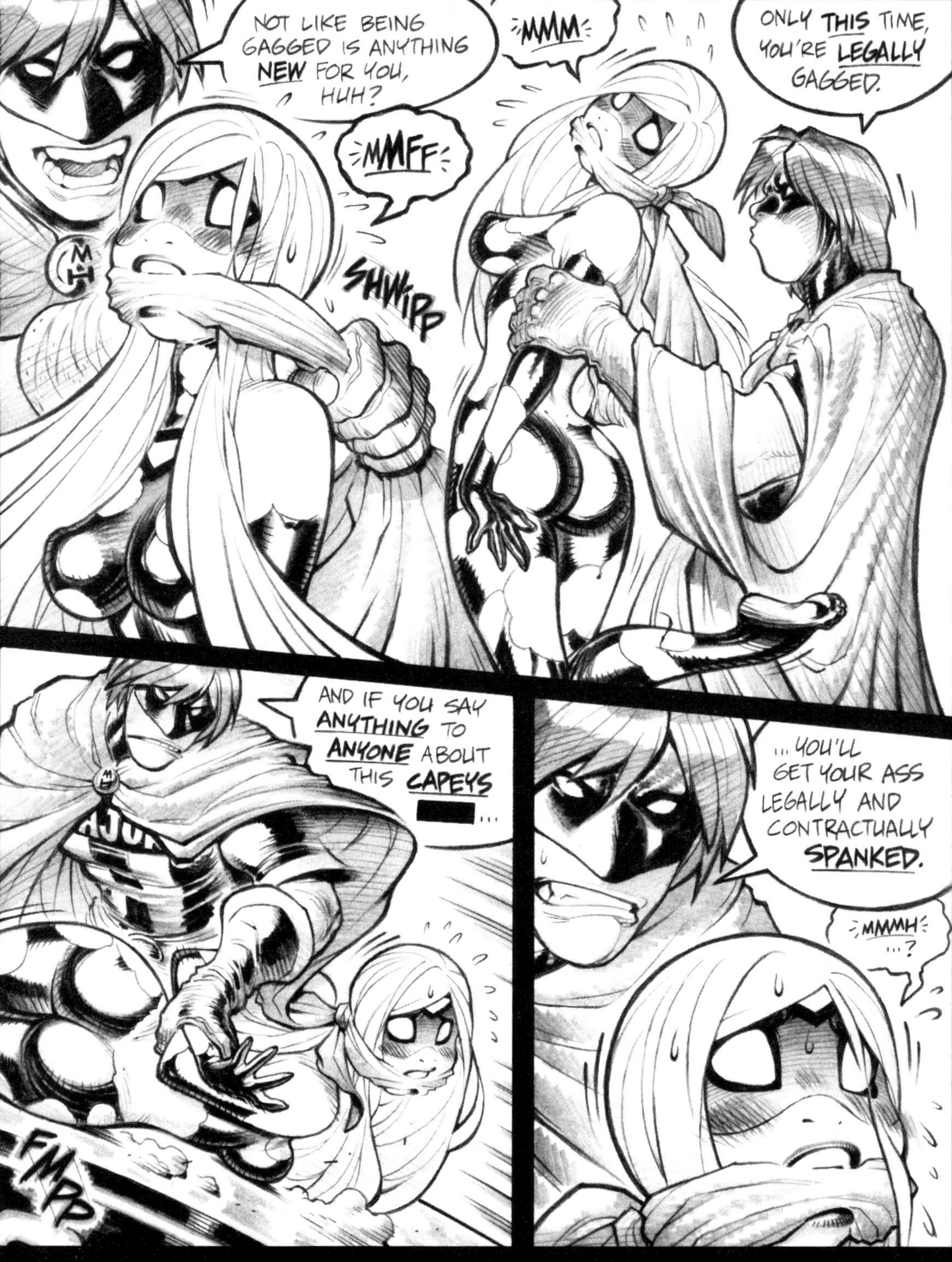
NOT LIKE BEING GAGGED IS ANYTHING NEW FOR YOU, HUH?
MMFF
SHWIPP
MMM
ONLY THIS TIME, YOU'RE LEGALLY GAGGED.
AND IF YOU SAY ANYTHING TO ANYONE ABOUT THIS CAPEYS [redacted]...
FMPP
...YOU'LL GET YOUR ASS LEGALLY AND CONTRACTUALLY SPANKED.
MMMH ...?

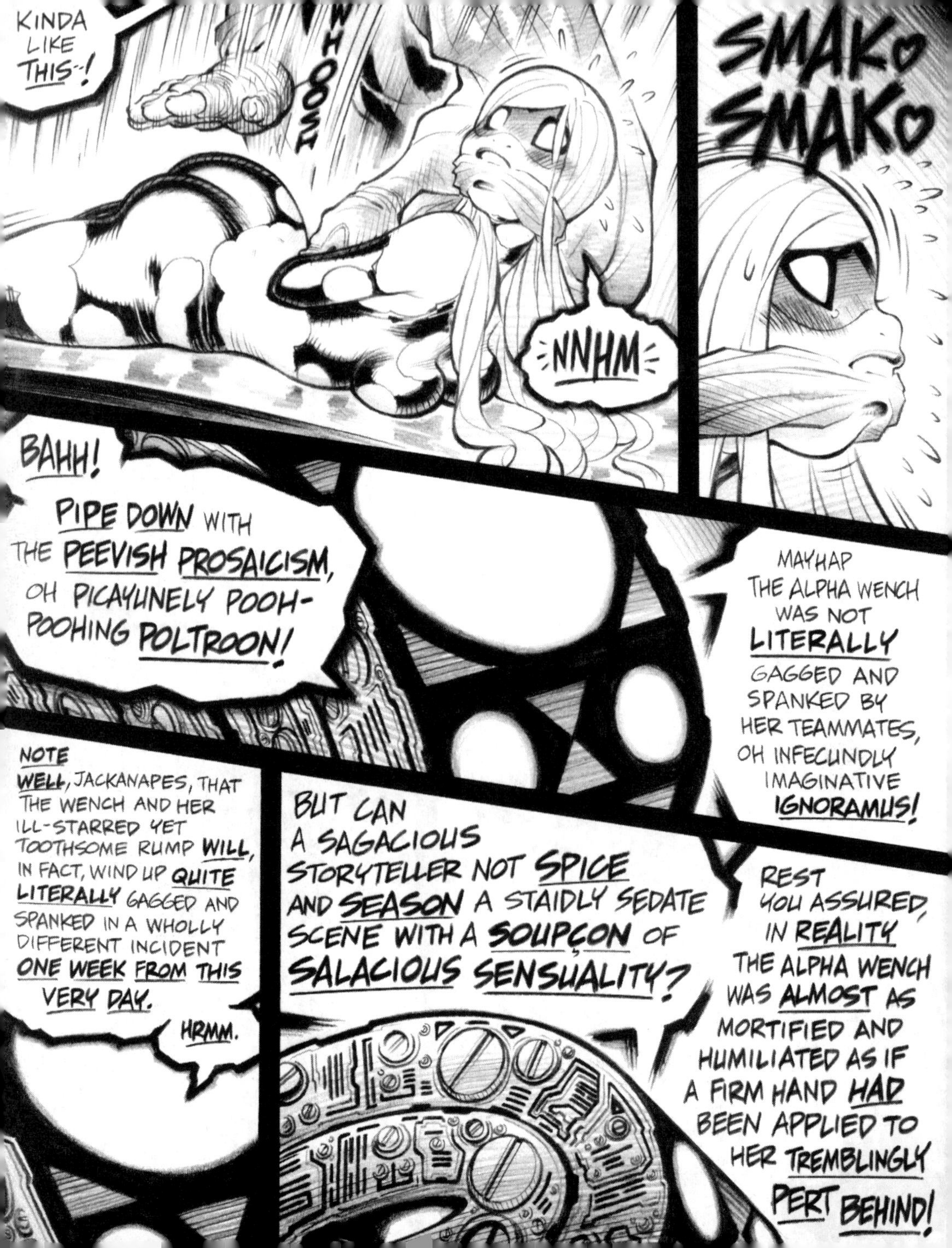

KINDA LIKE THIS--!
WHOOSH
NNHM
SMAK♡ SMAK♡
BAHH!
PIPE DOWN WITH THE PEEVISH PROSAICISM, OH PICAYUNELY POOH-POOHING POLTROON!
MAYHAP THE ALPHA WENCH WAS NOT LITERALLY GAGGED AND SPANKED BY HER TEAMMATES, OH INFECUNDLY IMAGINATIVE IGNORAMUS!
NOTE WELL, JACKANAPES, THAT THE WENCH AND HER ILL-STARRED YET TOOTHSOME RUMP WILL, IN FACT, WIND UP QUITE LITERALLY GAGGED AND SPANKED IN A WHOLLY DIFFERENT INCIDENT ONE WEEK FROM THIS VERY DAY.
HRMM.
BUT CAN A SAGACIOUS STORYTELLER NOT SPICE AND SEASON A STAIDLY SEDATE SCENE WITH A SOUPÇON OF SALACIOUS SENSUALITY?
REST YOU ASSURED, IN REALITY THE ALPHA WENCH WAS ALMOST AS MORTIFIED AND HUMILIATED AS IF A FIRM HAND HAD BEEN APPLIED TO HER TREMBLINGLY PERT BEHIND!

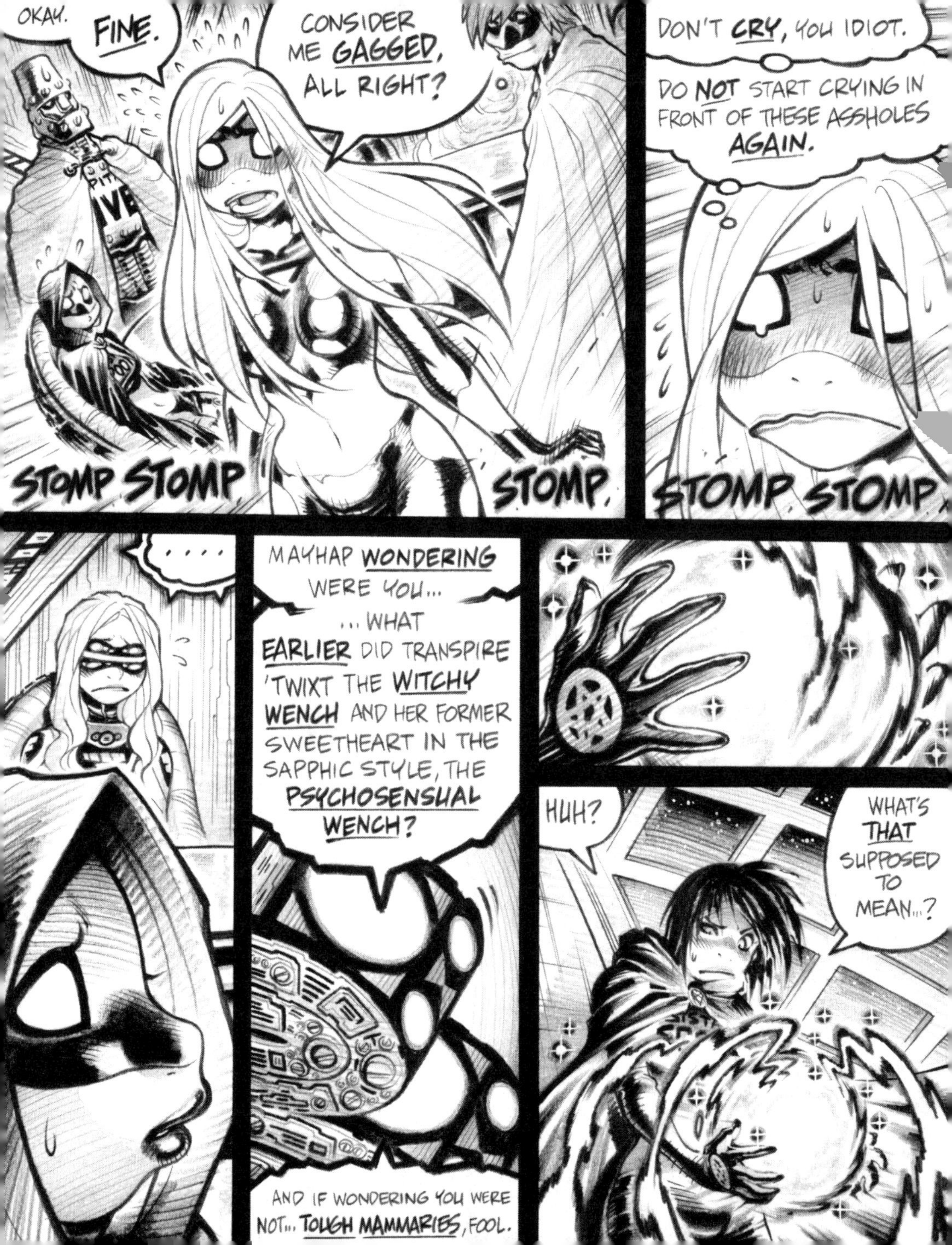
OKAY.
FINE.
CONSIDER ME GAGGED, ALL RIGHT?
STOMP STOMP
STOMP.
DON'T CRY, YOU IDIOT.
DO NOT START CRYING IN FRONT OF THESE ASSHOLES AGAIN.
STOMP STOMP
.....
MAYHAP WONDERING WERE YOU...
...WHAT EARLIER DID TRANSPIRE 'TWIXT THE WITCHY WENCH AND HER FORMER SWEETHEART IN THE SAPPHIC STYLE, THE PSYCHOSENSUAL WENCH?
AND IF WONDERING YOU WERE NOT... TOUGH MAMMARIES, FOOL.
HUH?
WHAT'S THAT SUPPOSED TO MEAN...?

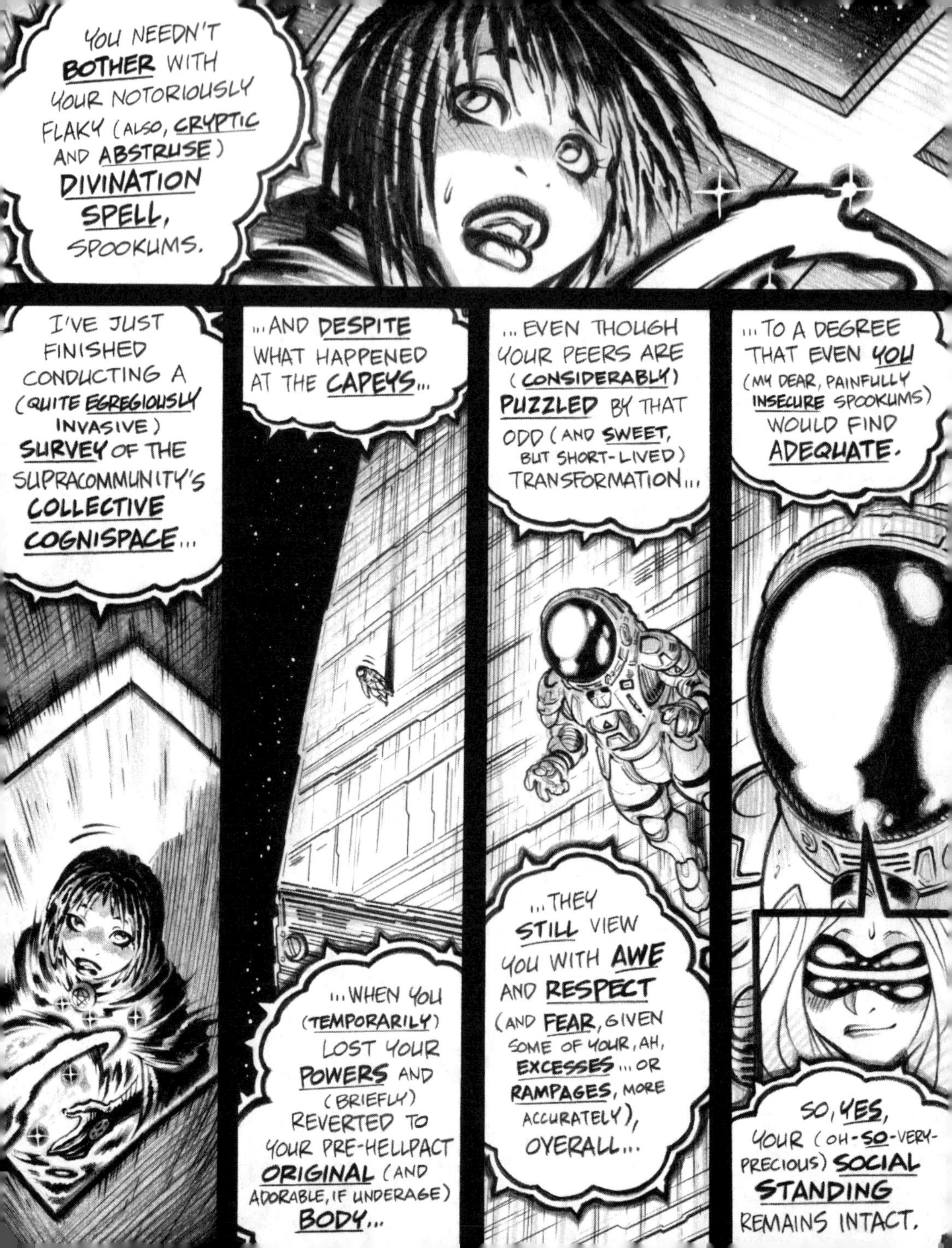

YOU NEEDN'T BOTHER WITH YOUR NOTORIOUSLY FLAKY (ALSO, CRYPTIC AND ABSTRUSE) DIVINATION SPELL, SPOOKUMS.
I'VE JUST FINISHED CONDUCTING A (QUITE EGREGIOUSLY INVASIVE) SURVEY OF THE SUPRACOMMUNITY'S COLLECTIVE COGNISPACE...
...AND DESPITE WHAT HAPPENED AT THE CAPEYS...
...WHEN YOU (TEMPORARILY) LOST YOUR POWERS AND (BRIEFLY) REVERTED TO YOUR PRE-HELLPACT ORIGINAL (AND ADORABLE, IF UNDERAGE) BODY...
...EVEN THOUGH YOUR PEERS ARE (CONSIDERABLY) PUZZLED BY THAT ODD (AND SWEET, BUT SHORT-LIVED) TRANSFORMATION...
...THEY STILL VIEW YOU WITH AWE AND RESPECT (AND FEAR, GIVEN SOME OF YOUR, AH, EXCESSES... OR RAMPAGES, MORE ACCURATELY), OVERALL...
...TO A DEGREE THAT EVEN YOU (MY DEAR, PAINFULLY INSECURE SPOOKUMS) WOULD FIND ADEQUATE.
SO, YES, YOUR (OH-SO-VERY-PRECIOUS) SOCIAL STANDING REMAINS INTACT.

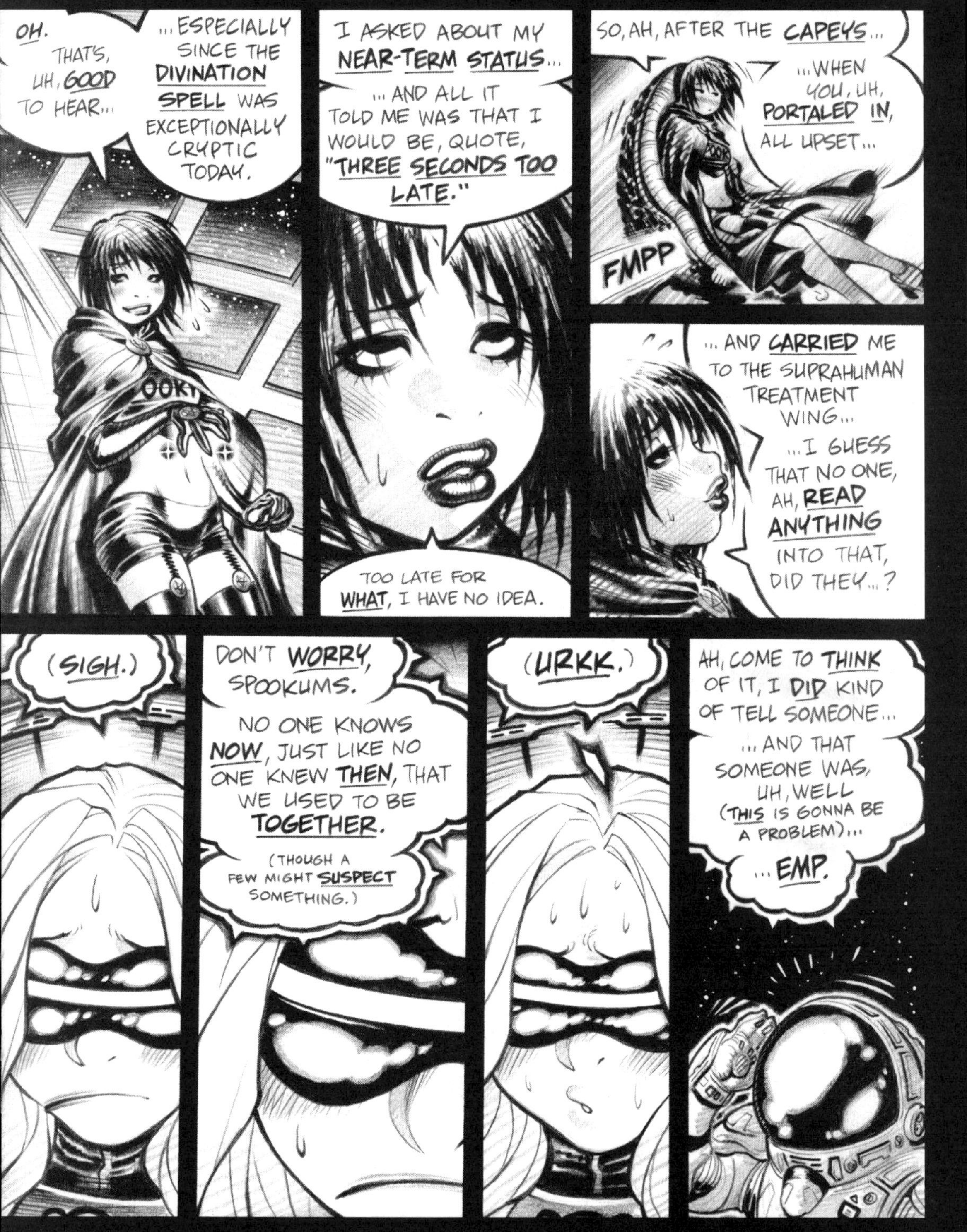
OH. THAT'S, UH, GOOD TO HEAR...
...ESPECIALLY SINCE THE DIVINATION SPELL WAS EXCEPTIONALLY CRYPTIC TODAY.
OOKY
I ASKED ABOUT MY NEAR-TERM STATUS...
...AND ALL IT TOLD ME WAS THAT I WOULD BE, QUOTE, "THREE SECONDS TOO LATE."
TOO LATE FOR WHAT, I HAVE NO IDEA.
SO, AH, AFTER THE CAPEYS...
...WHEN YOU, UH, PORTALED IN, ALL UPSET...
FMPP
...AND CARRIED ME TO THE SUPRAHUMAN TREATMENT WING...
...I GUESS THAT NO ONE, AH, READ ANYTHING INTO THAT, DID THEY...?
(SIGH.)
DON'T WORRY, SPOOKUMS.
NO ONE KNOWS NOW, JUST LIKE NO ONE KNEW THEN, THAT WE USED TO BE TOGETHER.
(THOUGH A FEW MIGHT SUSPECT SOMETHING.)
(URKK.)
AH, COME TO THINK OF IT, I DID KIND OF TELL SOMEONE...
...AND THAT SOMEONE WAS, UH, WELL (THIS IS GONNA BE A PROBLEM)...
...EMP.

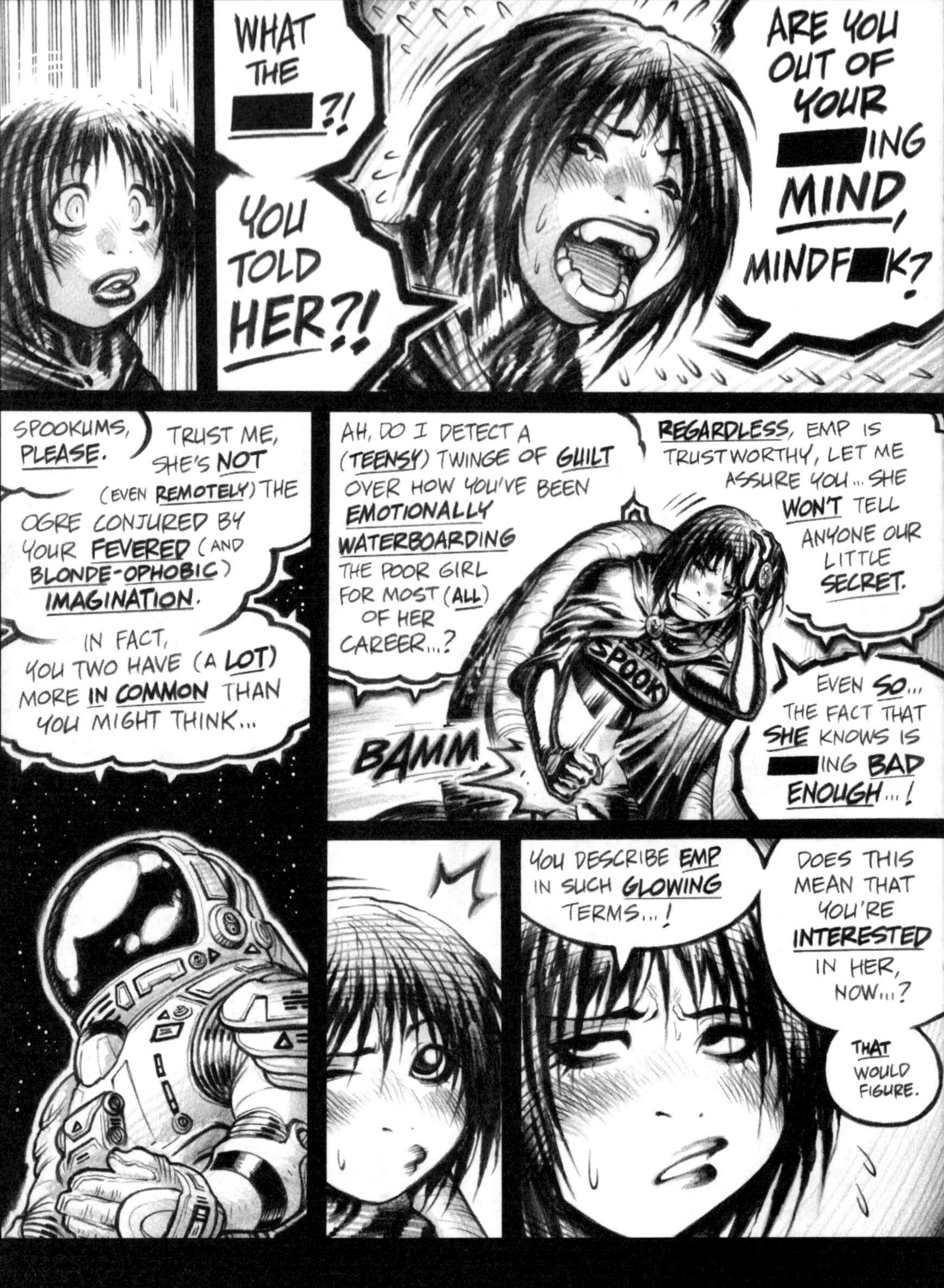
WHAT THE [redacted]?!
YOU TOLD HER?!
ARE YOU OUT OF YOUR [redacted]ING MIND, MINDF[redacted]K?
SPOOKUMS, PLEASE.
TRUST ME, SHE'S NOT (EVEN REMOTELY) THE OGRE CONJURED BY YOUR FEVERED (AND BLONDE-OPHOBIC) IMAGINATION.
IN FACT, YOU TWO HAVE (A LOT) MORE IN COMMON THAN YOU MIGHT THINK...
AH, DO I DETECT A (TEENSY) TWINGE OF GUILT OVER HOW YOU'VE BEEN EMOTIONALLY WATERBOARDING THE POOR GIRL FOR MOST (ALL) OF HER CAREER...?
REGARDLESS, EMP IS TRUSTWORTHY, LET ME ASSURE YOU... SHE WON'T TELL ANYONE OUR LITTLE SECRET.
SPOOK
BAMM
EVEN SO... THE FACT THAT SHE KNOWS IS [redacted]ING BAD ENOUGH...!
YOU DESCRIBE EMP IN SUCH GLOWING TERMS...!
DOES THIS MEAN THAT YOU'RE INTERESTED IN HER, NOW...?
THAT WOULD FIGURE.

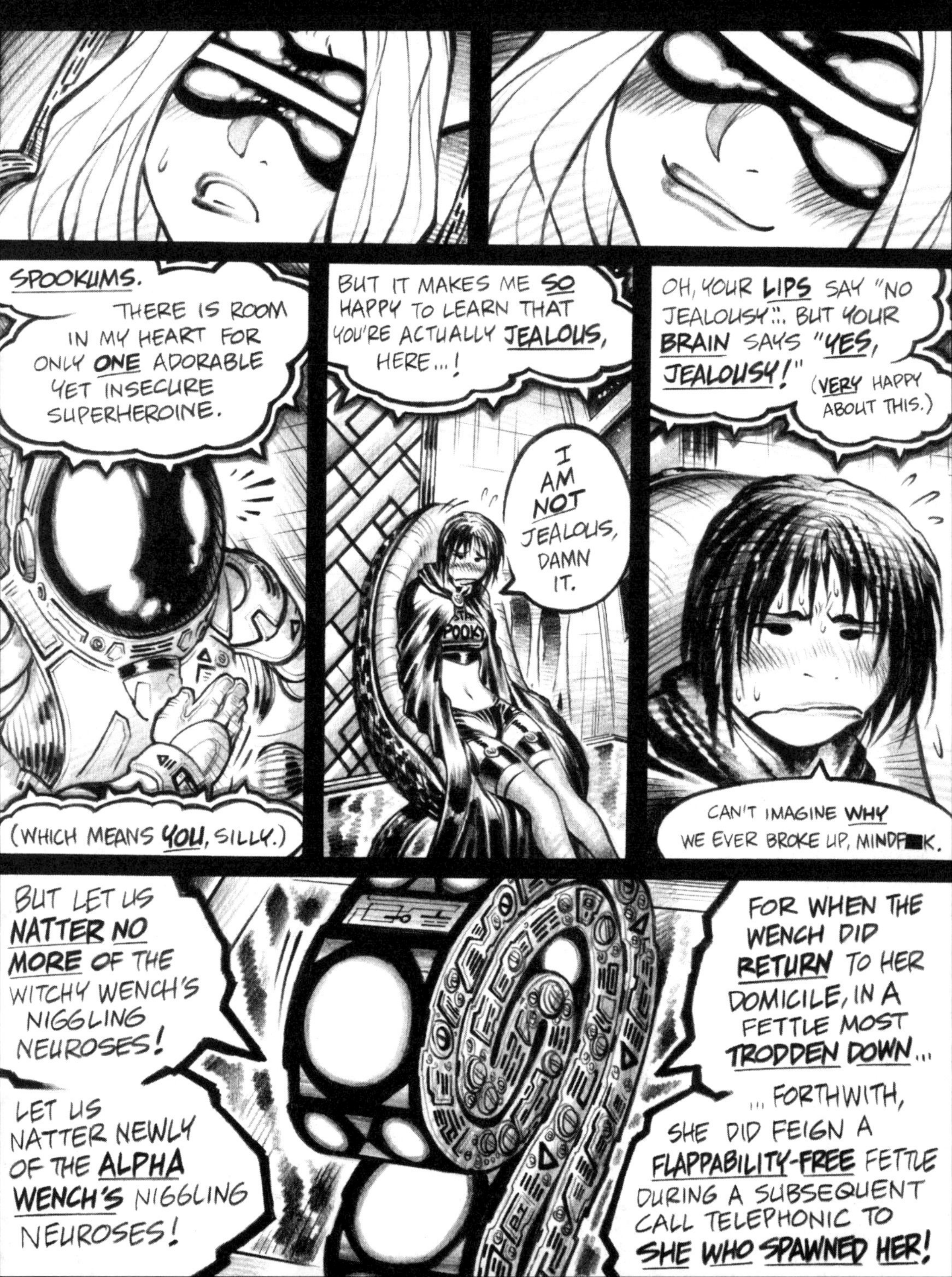
SPOOKUMS. THERE IS ROOM IN MY HEART FOR ONLY ONE ADORABLE YET INSECURE SUPERHEROINE.
(WHICH MEANS YOU, SILLY.)
BUT IT MAKES ME SO HAPPY TO LEARN THAT YOU'RE ACTUALLY JEALOUS, HERE...!
I AM NOT JEALOUS, DAMN IT.
OH, YOUR LIPS SAY "NO JEALOUSY"... BUT YOUR BRAIN SAYS "YES, JEALOUSY!"
(VERY HAPPY ABOUT THIS.)
CAN'T IMAGINE WHY WE EVER BROKE UP, MINDF[redacted]K.
BUT LET US NATTER NO MORE OF THE WITCHY WENCH'S NIGGLING NEUROSES!
LET US NATTER NEWLY OF THE ALPHA WENCH'S NIGGLING NEUROSES!
FOR WHEN THE WENCH DID RETURN TO HER DOMICILE, IN A FETTLE MOST TRODDEN DOWN...
... FORTHWITH, SHE DID FEIGN A FLAPPABILITY-FREE FETTLE DURING A SUBSEQUENT CALL TELEPHONIC TO SHE WHO SPAWNED HER!

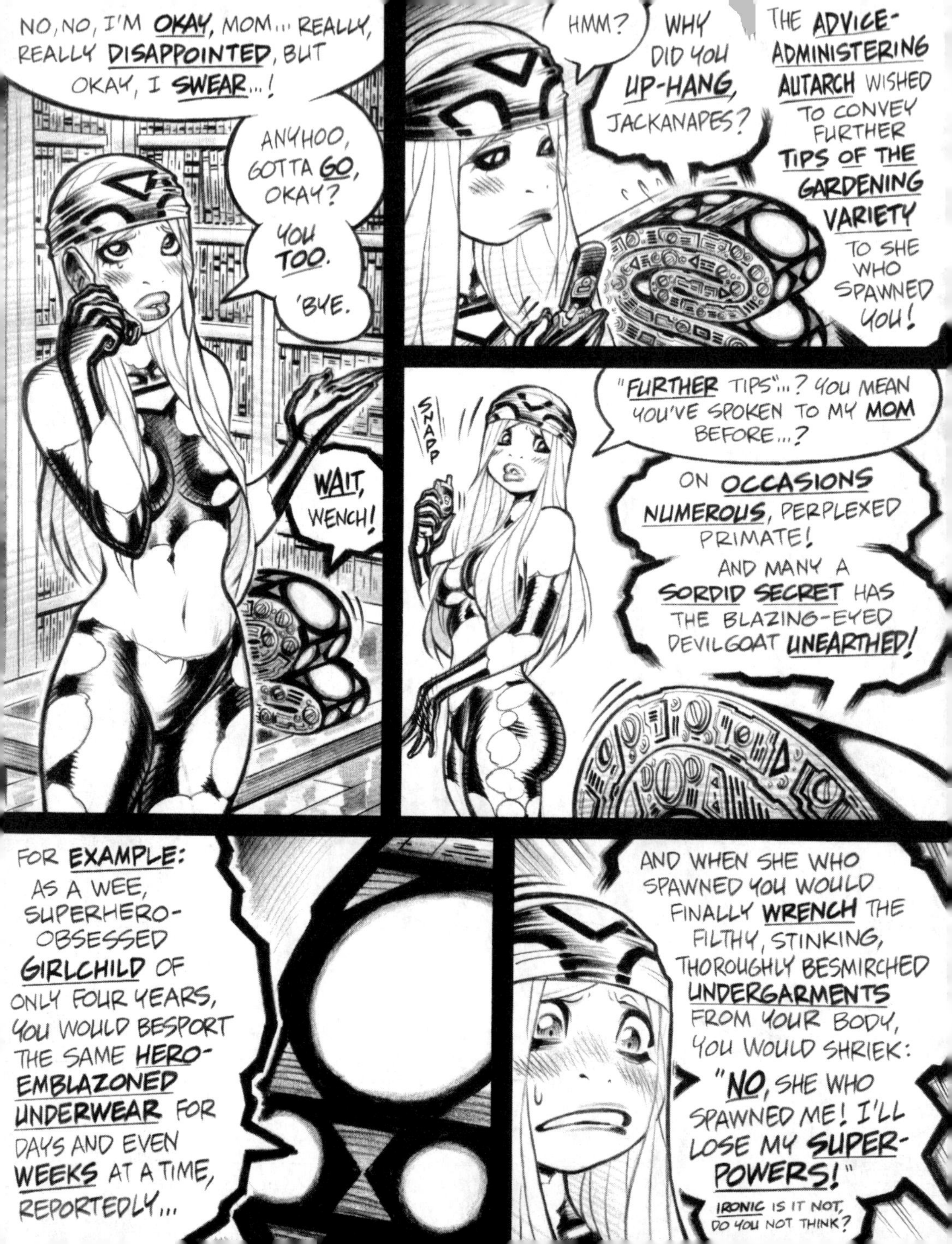
NO, NO, I'M OKAY, MOM... REALLY, REALLY DISAPPOINTED, BUT OKAY, I SWEAR...!
ANYHOO, GOTTA GO, OKAY?
YOU TOO.
'BYE.
WAIT, WENCH!
HMM?
WHY DID YOU UP-HANG, JACKANAPES?
THE ADVICE-ADMINISTERING AUTARCH WISHED TO CONVEY FURTHER TIPS OF THE GARDENING VARIETY TO SHE WHO SPAWNED YOU!
SNAPP
"FURTHER TIPS"...? YOU MEAN YOU'VE SPOKEN TO MY MOM BEFORE...?
ON OCCASIONS NUMEROUS, PERPLEXED PRIMATE!
AND MANY A SORDID SECRET HAS THE BLAZING-EYED DEVILGOAT UNEARTHED!
FOR EXAMPLE: AS A WEE, SUPERHERO-OBSESSED GIRLCHILD OF ONLY FOUR YEARS, YOU WOULD BESPORT THE SAME HERO-EMBLAZONED UNDERWEAR FOR DAYS AND EVEN WEEKS AT A TIME, REPORTEDLY...
AND WHEN SHE WHO SPAWNED YOU WOULD FINALLY WRENCH THE FILTHY, STINKING, THOROUGHLY BESMIRCHED UNDERGARMENTS FROM YOUR BODY, YOU WOULD SHRIEK:
"NO, SHE WHO SPAWNED ME! I'LL LOSE MY SUPER-POWERS!"
IRONIC IS IT NOT, DO YOU NOT THINK?

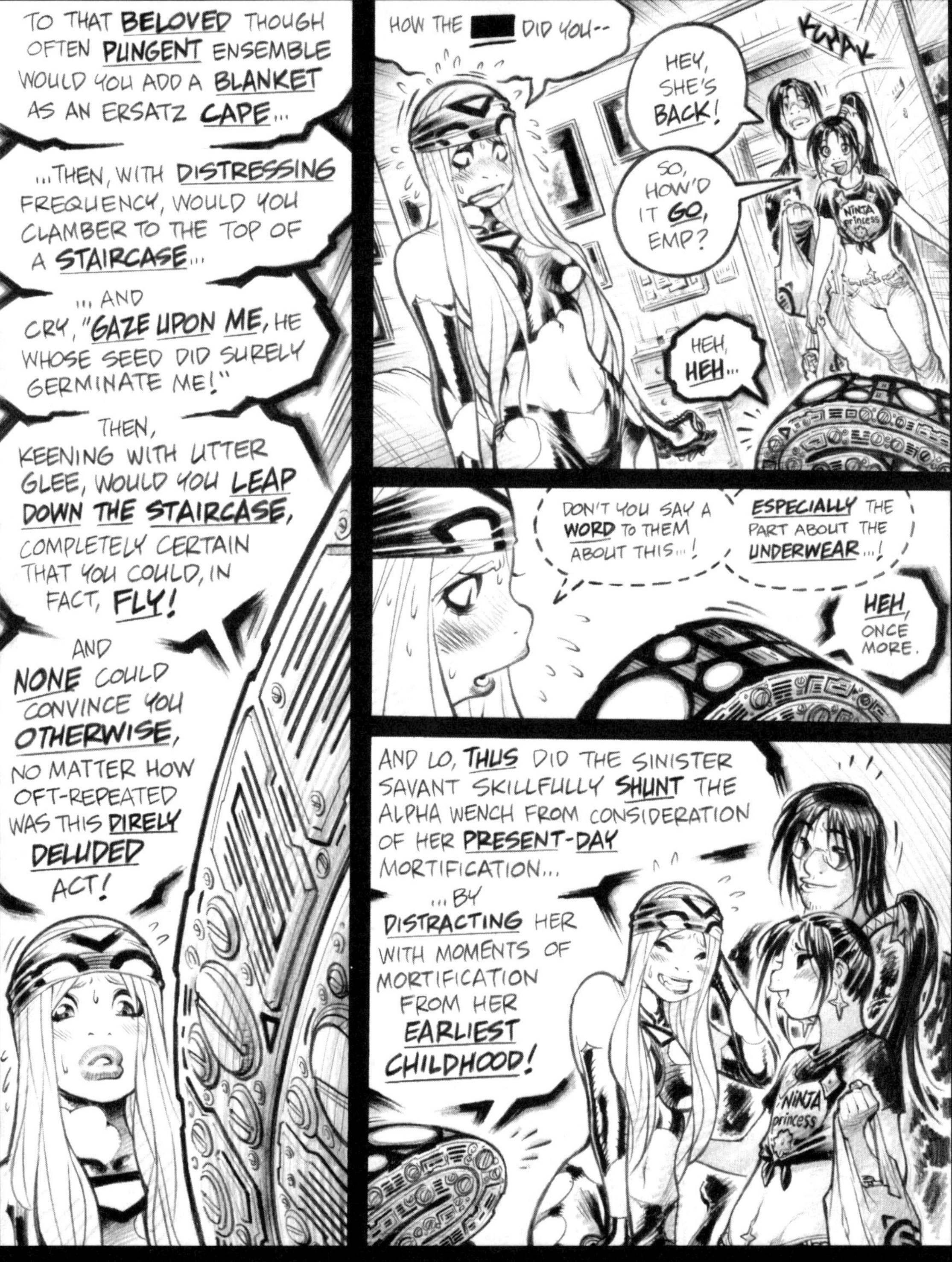
TO THAT BELOVED THOUGH OFTEN PUNGENT ENSEMBLE WOULD YOU ADD A BLANKET AS AN ERSATZ CAPE...
...THEN, WITH DISTRESSING FREQUENCY, WOULD YOU CLAMBER TO THE TOP OF A STAIRCASE...
...AND CRY, "GAZE UPON ME, HE WHOSE SEED DID SURELY GERMINATE ME!"
THEN, KEENING WITH UTTER GLEE, WOULD YOU LEAP DOWN THE STAIRCASE, COMPLETELY CERTAIN THAT YOU COULD, IN FACT, FLY!
AND NONE COULD CONVINCE YOU OTHERWISE, NO MATTER HOW OFT-REPEATED WAS THIS DIRELY DELUDED ACT!
HOW THE [redacted] DID YOU--
KWAK
HEY, SHE'S BACK!
SO, HOW'D IT GO, EMP?
NINJA princess
HEH, HEH...
DON'T YOU SAY A WORD TO THEM ABOUT THIS...!
ESPECIALLY THE PART ABOUT THE UNDERWEAR...!
HEH, ONCE MORE.
AND LO, THUS DID THE SINISTER SAVANT SKILLFULLY SHUNT THE ALPHA WENCH FROM CONSIDERATION OF HER PRESENT-DAY MORTIFICATION...
...BY DISTRACTING HER WITH MOMENTS OF MORTIFICATION FROM HER EARLIEST CHILDHOOD!
NINJA princess

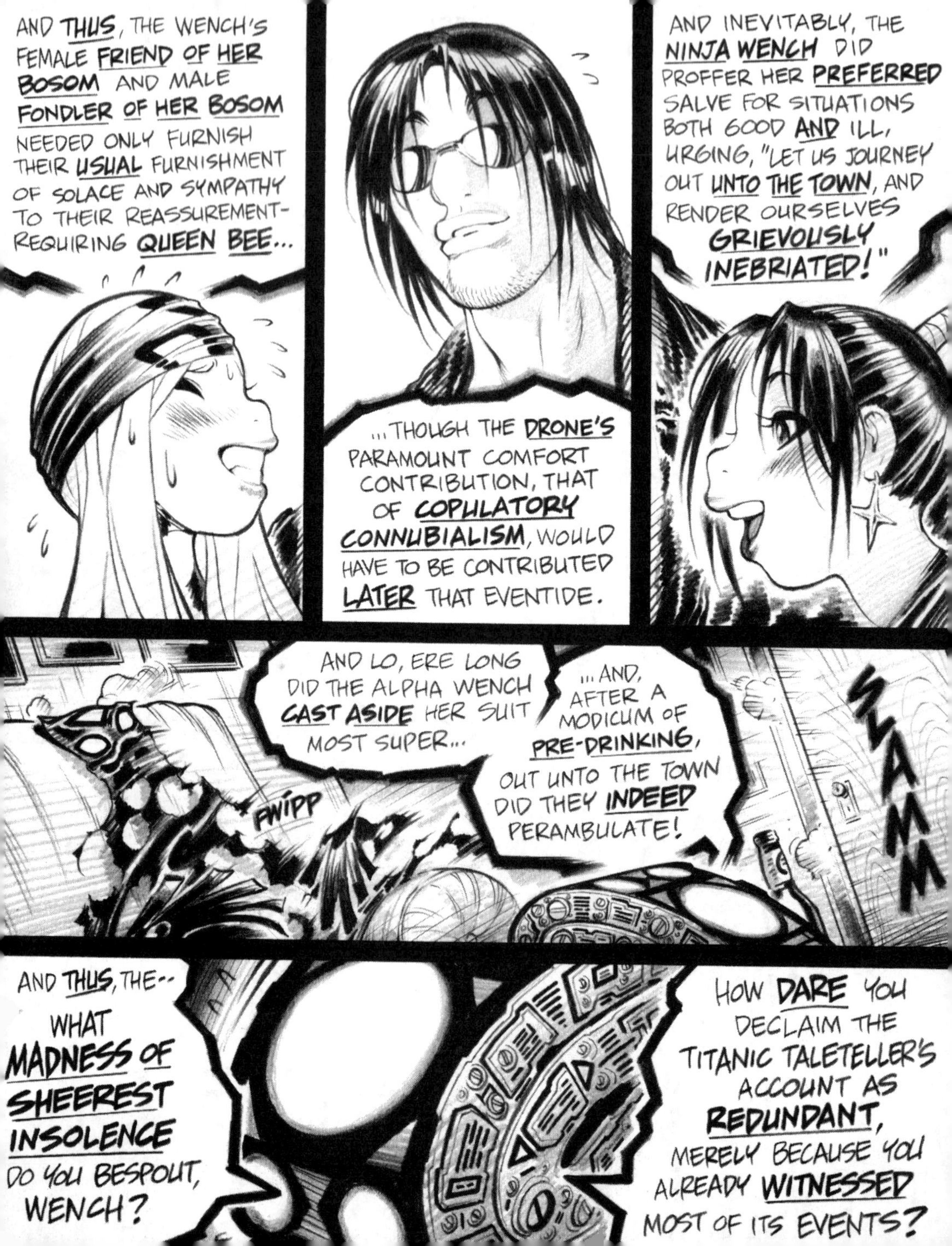
AND THUS, THE WENCH'S FEMALE FRIEND OF HER BOSOM AND MALE FONDLER OF HER BOSOM NEEDED ONLY FURNISH THEIR USUAL FURNISHMENT OF SOLACE AND SYMPATHY TO THEIR REASSUREMENT-REQUIRING QUEEN BEE...
...THOUGH THE DRONE'S PARAMOUNT COMFORT CONTRIBUTION, THAT OF COPULATORY CONNUBIALISM, WOULD HAVE TO BE CONTRIBUTED LATER THAT EVENTIDE.
AND INEVITABLY, THE NINJA WENCH DID PROFFER HER PREFERRED SALVE FOR SITUATIONS BOTH GOOD AND ILL, URGING, "LET US JOURNEY OUT UNTO THE TOWN, AND RENDER OURSELVES GRIEVOUSLY INEBRIATED!"
AND LO, ERE LONG DID THE ALPHA WENCH CAST ASIDE HER SUIT MOST SUPER...
FWIPP
...AND, AFTER A MODICUM OF PRE-DRINKING, OUT UNTO THE TOWN DID THEY INDEED PERAMBULATE!
SLAMM
AND THUS, THE--
WHAT MADNESS OF SHEEREST INSOLENCE DO YOU BESPOUT, WENCH?
HOW DARE YOU DECLAIM THE TITANIC TALETELLER'S ACCOUNT AS REDUNDANT, MERELY BECAUSE YOU ALREADY WITNESSED MOST OF ITS EVENTS?

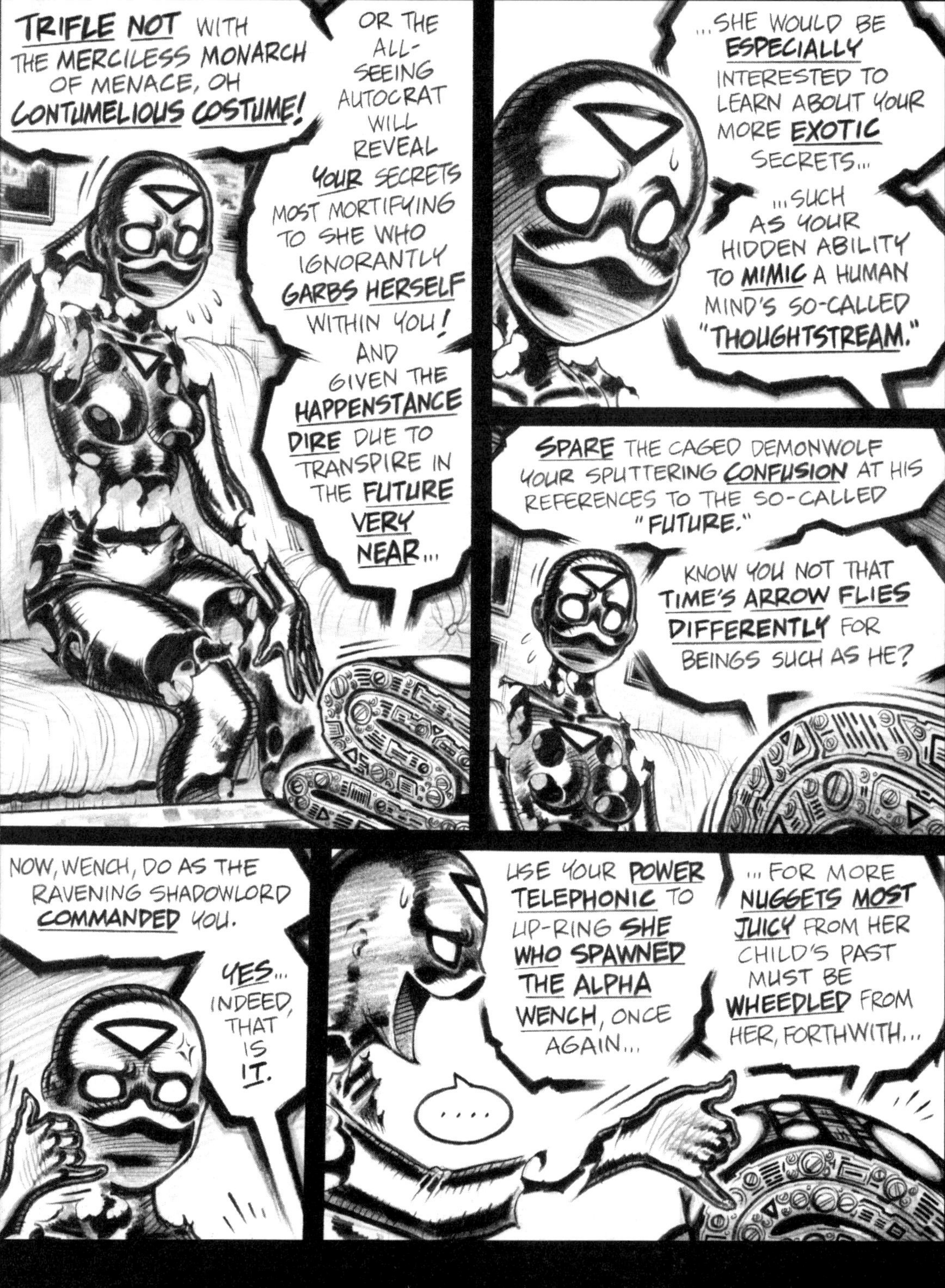
TRIFLE NOT WITH THE MERCILESS MONARCH OF MENACE, OH CONTUMELIOUS COSTUME!
OR THE ALL-SEEING AUTOCRAT WILL REVEAL YOUR SECRETS MOST MORTIFYING TO SHE WHO IGNORANTLY GARBS HERSELF WITHIN YOU! AND GIVEN THE HAPPENSTANCE DIRE DUE TO TRANSPIRE IN THE FUTURE VERY NEAR...
...SHE WOULD BE ESPECIALLY INTERESTED TO LEARN ABOUT YOUR MORE EXOTIC SECRETS...
...SUCH AS YOUR HIDDEN ABILITY TO MIMIC A HUMAN MIND'S SO-CALLED "THOUGHTSTREAM."
SPARE THE CAGED DEMONWOLF YOUR SPUTTERING CONFUSION AT HIS REFERENCES TO THE SO-CALLED "FUTURE."
KNOW YOU NOT THAT TIME'S ARROW FLIES DIFFERENTLY FOR BEINGS SUCH AS HE?
NOW, WENCH, DO AS THE RAVENING SHADOWLORD COMMANDED YOU.
YES... INDEED, THAT IS IT.
....
USE YOUR POWER TELEPHONIC TO UP-RING SHE WHO SPAWNED THE ALPHA WENCH, ONCE AGAIN...
...FOR MORE NUGGETS MOST JUICY FROM HER CHILD'S PAST MUST BE WHEEDLED FROM HER, FORTHWITH...

empowered™

When Titans Fornicate

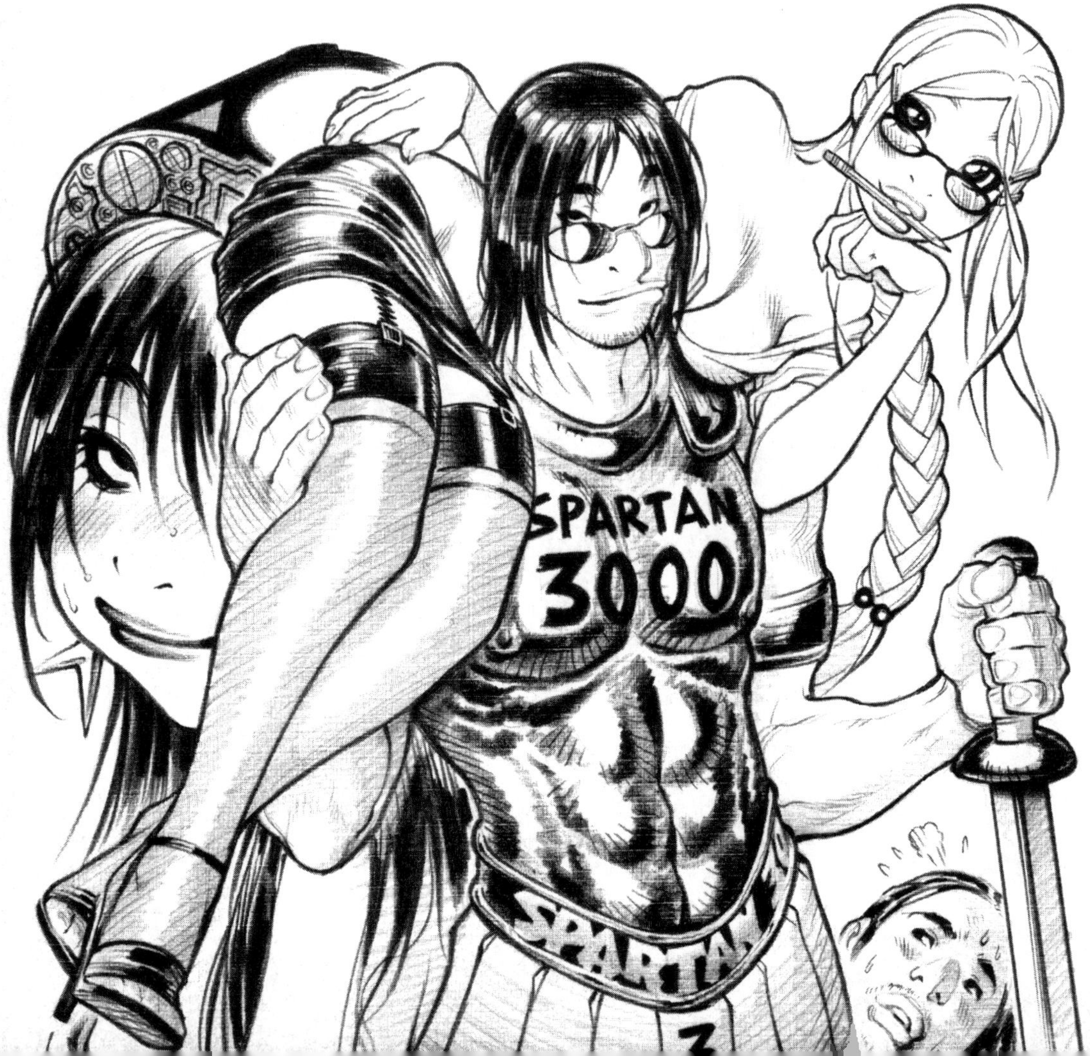
SPARTAN
3000

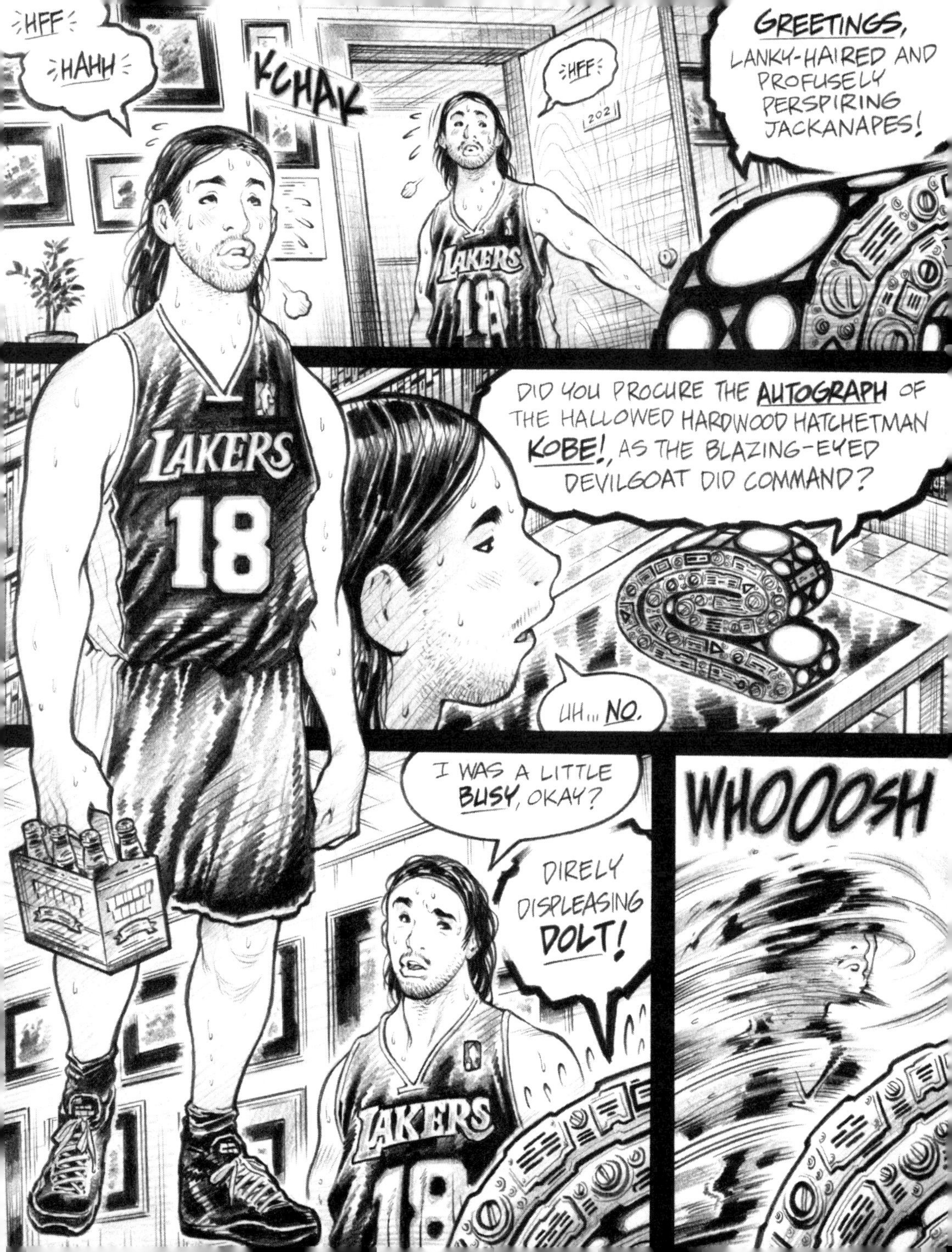
HFF
HAHH
KCHAK
HFF
202
GREETINGS, LANKY-HAIRED AND PROFUSELY PERSPIRING JACKANAPES!
DID YOU PROCURE THE AUTOGRAPH OF THE HALLOWED HARDWOOD HATCHETMAN KOBE!, AS THE BLAZING-EYED DEVILGOAT DID COMMAND?
UH... NO.
I WAS A LITTLE BUSY, OKAY?
DIRELY DISPLEASING DOLT!
WHOOOSH

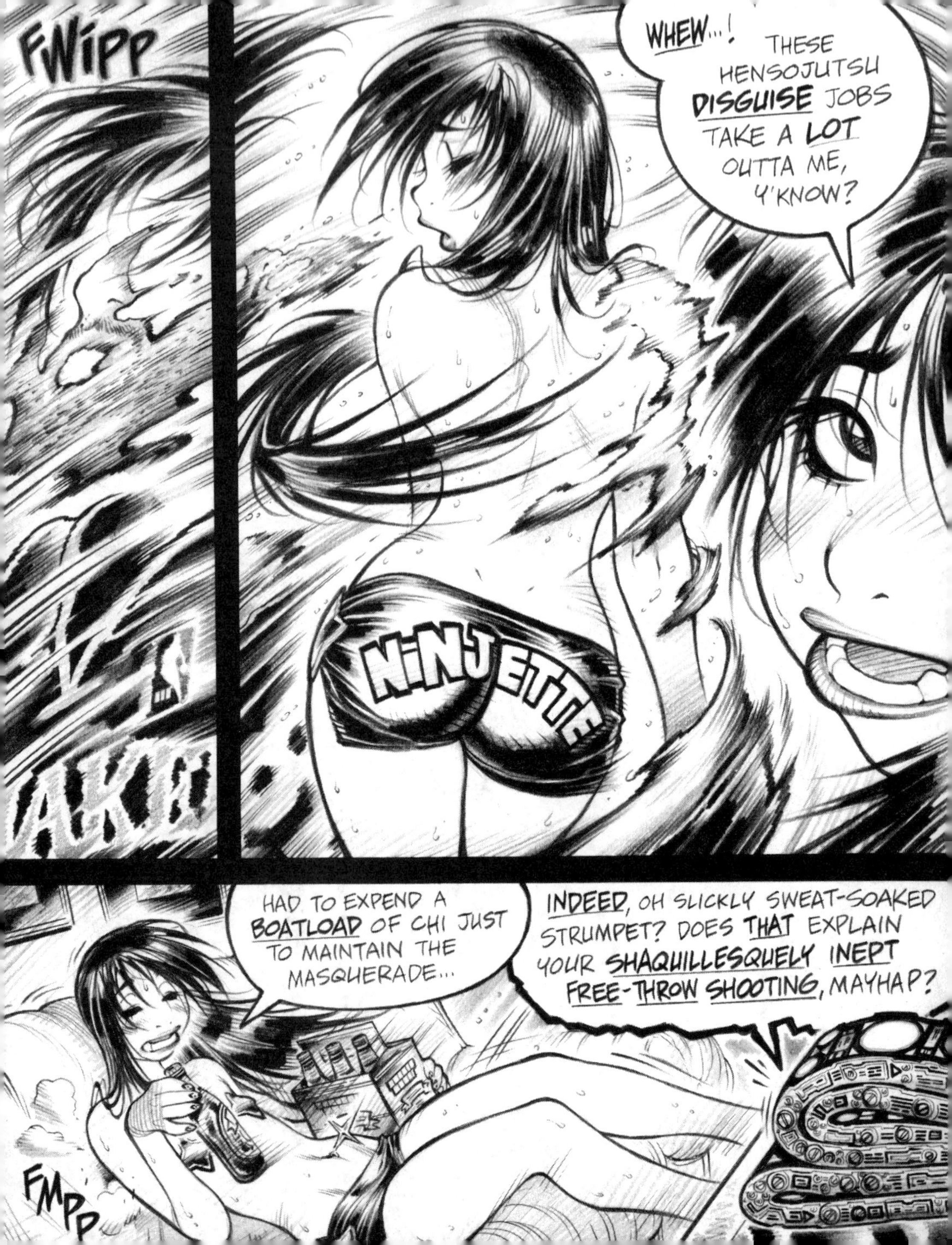
FWIPP
WHEW...! THESE HENSOJUTSU DISGUISE JOBS TAKE A LOT OUTTA ME, Y'KNOW?
NINJETTE
HAD TO EXPEND A BOATLOAD OF CHI JUST TO MAINTAIN THE MASQUERADE...
INDEED, OH SLICKLY SWEAT-SOAKED STRUMPET? DOES THAT EXPLAIN YOUR SHAQUILLESQUELY INEPT FREE-THROW SHOOTING, MAYHAP?
FMPP

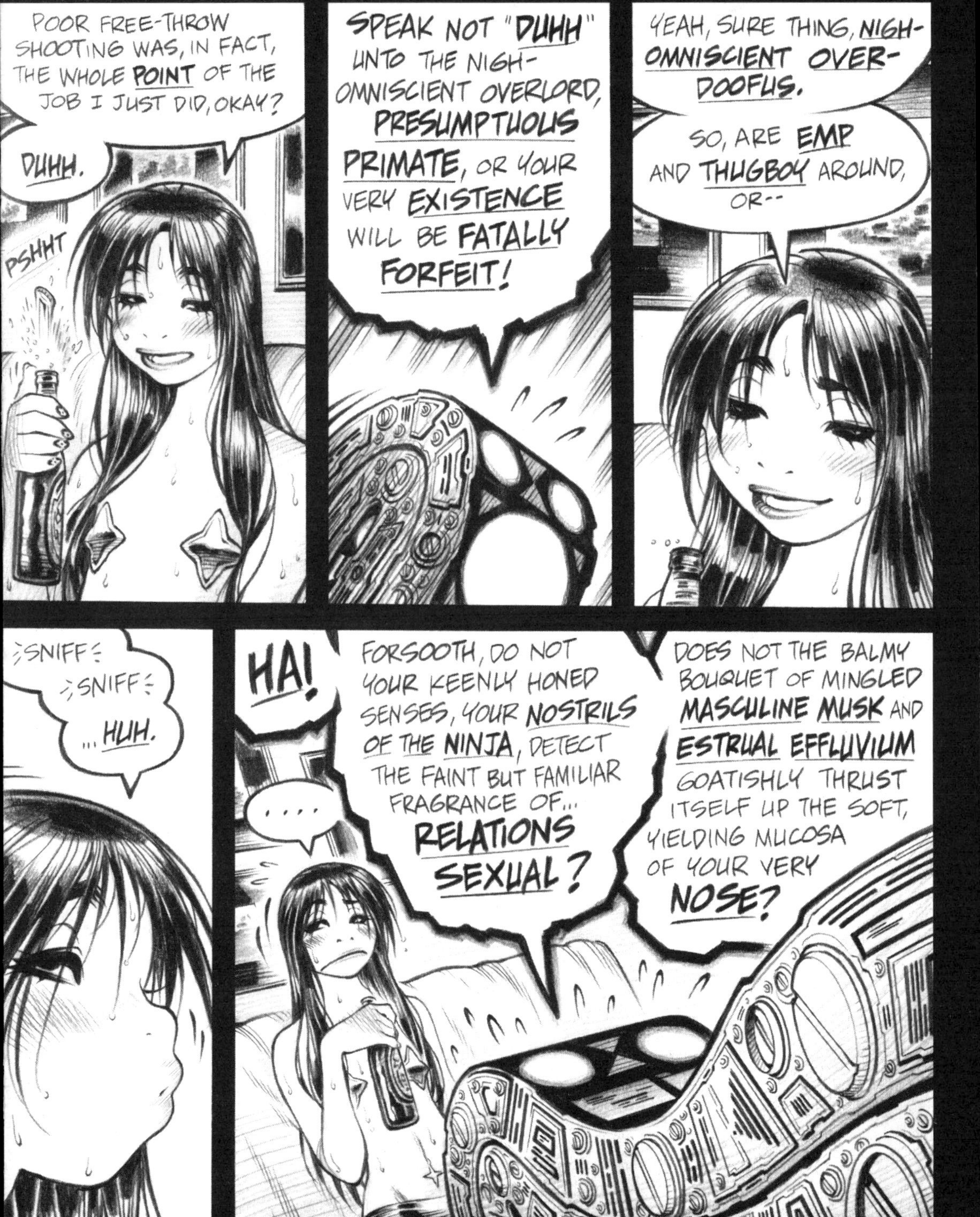
POOR FREE-THROW SHOOTING WAS, IN FACT, THE WHOLE POINT OF THE JOB I JUST DID, OKAY?
DUHH.
PSHHT
SPEAK NOT "DUHH" UNTO THE NIGH-OMNISCIENT OVERLORD, PRESUMPTUOUS PRIMATE, OR YOUR VERY EXISTENCE WILL BE FATALLY FORFEIT!
YEAH, SURE THING, NIGH-OMNISCIENT OVER-DOOFUS.
SO, ARE EMP AND THUGBOY AROUND, OR--
SNIFF
SNIFF
...HUH.
HA!
FORSOOTH, DO NOT YOUR KEENLY HONED SENSES, YOUR NOSTRILS OF THE NINJA, DETECT THE FAINT BUT FAMILIAR FRAGRANCE OF... RELATIONS SEXUAL?
DOES NOT THE BALMY BOUQUET OF MINGLED MASCULINE MUSK AND ESTRUAL EFFLUVIUM GOATISHLY THRUST ITSELF UP THE SOFT, YIELDING MUCOSA OF YOUR VERY NOSE?
....

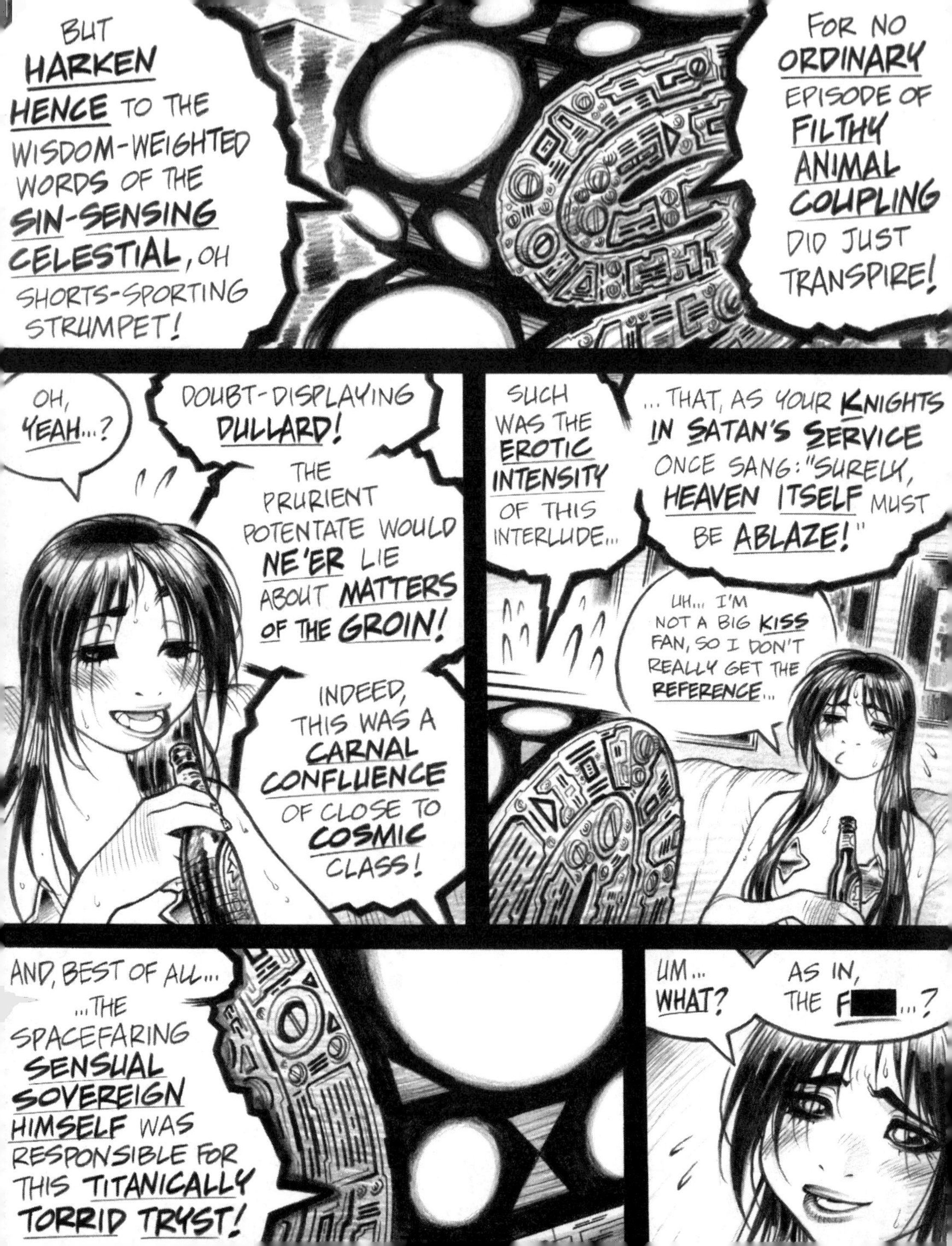

BUT HARKEN HENCE TO THE WISDOM-WEIGHTED WORDS OF THE SIN-SENSING CELESTIAL, OH SHORTS-SPORTING STRUMPET!
FOR NO ORDINARY EPISODE OF FILTHY ANIMAL COUPLING DID JUST TRANSPIRE!
OH, YEAH...?
DOUBT-DISPLAYING DULLARD!
THE PRURIENT POTENTATE WOULD NE'ER LIE ABOUT MATTERS OF THE GROIN!
INDEED, THIS WAS A CARNAL CONFLUENCE OF CLOSE TO COSMIC CLASS!
SUCH WAS THE EROTIC INTENSITY OF THIS INTERLUDE...
...THAT, AS YOUR KNIGHTS IN SATAN'S SERVICE ONCE SANG: "SURELY, HEAVEN ITSELF MUST BE ABLAZE!"
UH... I'M NOT A BIG KISS FAN, SO I DON'T REALLY GET THE REFERENCE...
AND, BEST OF ALL...
...THE SPACEFARING SENSUAL SOVEREIGN HIMSELF WAS RESPONSIBLE FOR THIS TITANICALLY TORRID TRYST!
UM... WHAT?
AS IN, THE F[redacted]...?

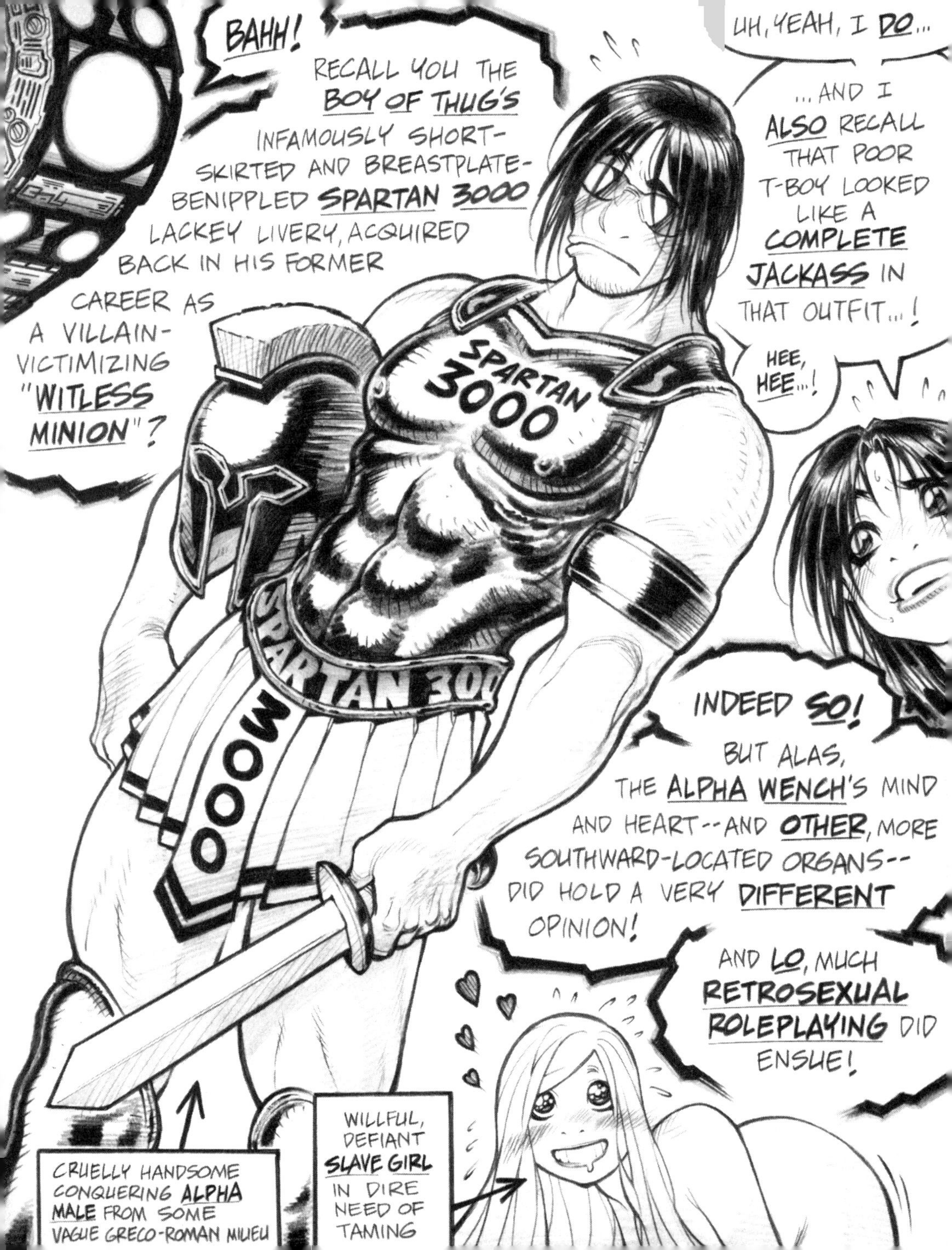
BAHH!
RECALL YOU THE BOY OF THUG'S INFAMOUSLY SHORT-SKIRTED AND BREASTPLATE-BENIPPLED SPARTAN 3000 LACKEY LIVERY, ACQUIRED BACK IN HIS FORMER CAREER AS A VILLAIN-VICTIMIZING "WITLESS MINION"?
UH, YEAH, I DO...
...AND I ALSO RECALL THAT POOR T-BOY LOOKED LIKE A COMPLETE JACKASS IN THAT OUTFIT...!
HEE, HEE...!
SPARTAN 3000
SPARTAN 3000
3000
INDEED SO!
BUT ALAS, THE ALPHA WENCH'S MIND AND HEART--AND OTHER, MORE SOUTHWARD-LOCATED ORGANS--DID HOLD A VERY DIFFERENT OPINION!
AND LO, MUCH RETROSEXUAL ROLEPLAYING DID ENSUE!
CRUELLY HANDSOME CONQUERING ALPHA MALE FROM SOME VAGUE GRECO-ROMAN MILIEU
WILLFUL, DEFIANT SLAVE GIRL IN DIRE NEED OF TAMING

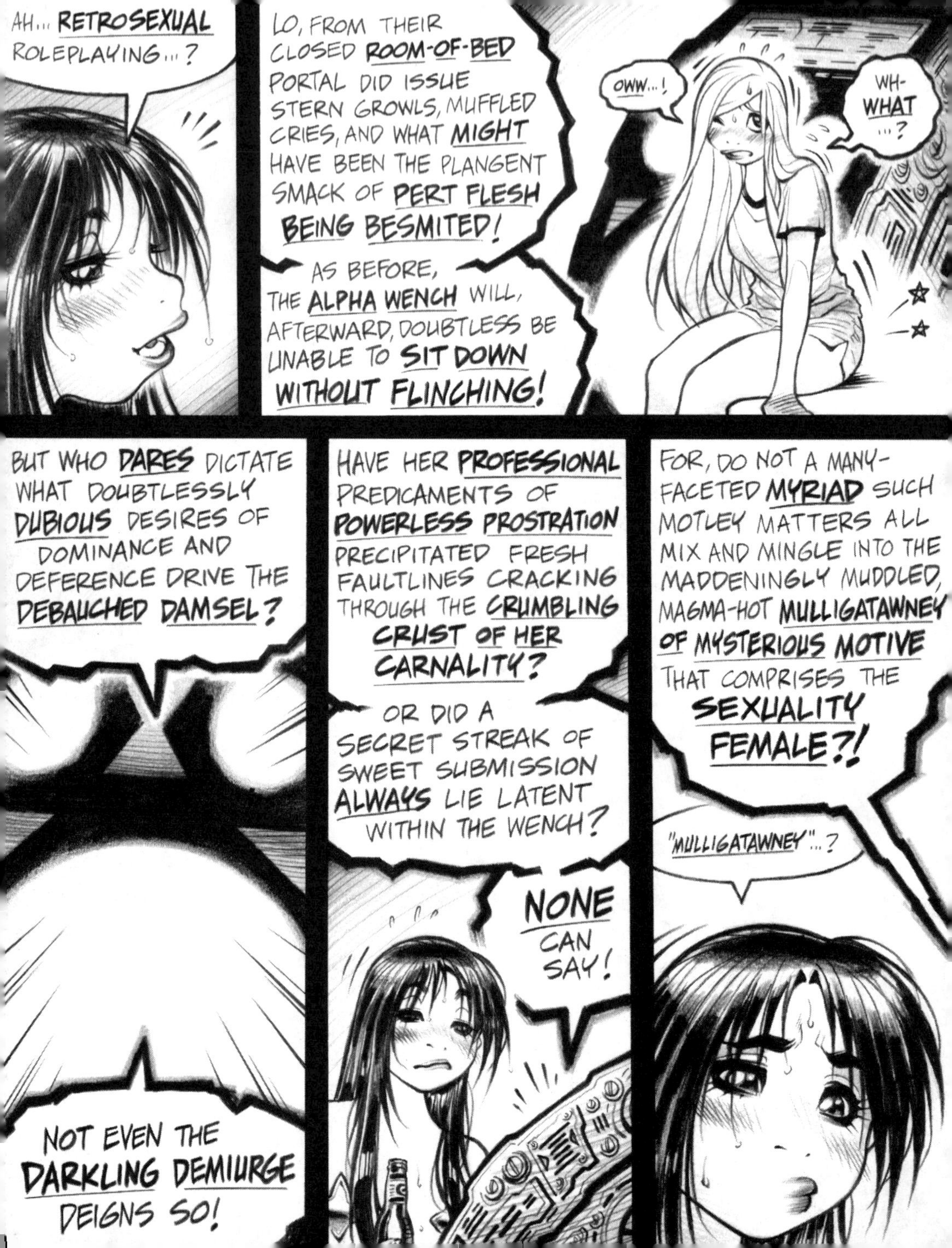
AH... RETROSEXUAL ROLEPLAYING...?
LO, FROM THEIR CLOSED ROOM-OF-BED PORTAL DID ISSUE STERN GROWLS, MUFFLED CRIES, AND WHAT MIGHT HAVE BEEN THE PLANGENT SMACK OF PERT FLESH BEING BESMITED!
AS BEFORE, THE ALPHA WENCH WILL, AFTERWARD, DOUBTLESS BE UNABLE TO SIT DOWN WITHOUT FLINCHING!
OWW...!
WH-WHAT...?
BUT WHO DARES DICTATE WHAT DOUBTLESSLY DUBIOUS DESIRES OF DOMINANCE AND DEFERENCE DRIVE THE DEBAUCHED DAMSEL?
NOT EVEN THE DARKLING DEMIURGE DEIGNS SO!
HAVE HER PROFESSIONAL PREDICAMENTS OF POWERLESS PROSTRATION PRECIPITATED FRESH FAULTLINES CRACKING THROUGH THE CRUMBLING CRUST OF HER CARNALITY?
OR DID A SECRET STREAK OF SWEET SUBMISSION ALWAYS LIE LATENT WITHIN THE WENCH?
NONE CAN SAY!
FOR, DO NOT A MANY-FACETED MYRIAD SUCH MOTLEY MATTERS ALL MIX AND MINGLE INTO THE MADDENINGLY MUDDLED, MAGMA-HOT MULLIGATAWNEY OF MYSTERIOUS MOTIVE THAT COMPRISES THE SEXUALITY FEMALE?!
"MULLIGATAWNEY"...?

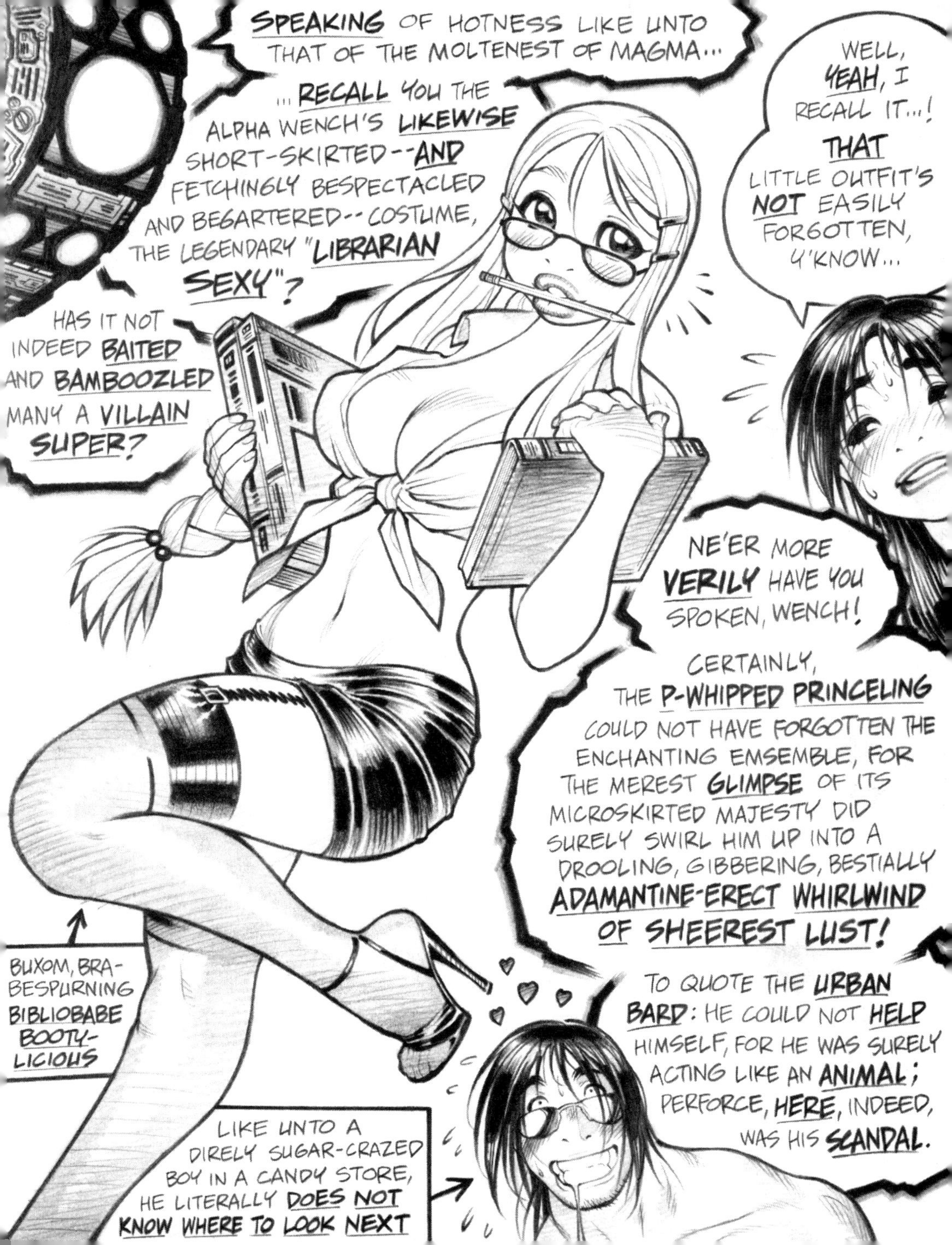

SPEAKING OF HOTNESS LIKE UNTO THAT OF THE MOLTENEST OF MAGMA...
...RECALL YOU THE ALPHA WENCH'S LIKEWISE SHORT-SKIRTED--AND FETCHINGLY BESPECTACLED AND BEGARTERED--COSTUME, THE LEGENDARY "LIBRARIAN SEXY"?
HAS IT NOT INDEED BAITED AND BAMBOOZLED MANY A VILLAIN SUPER?
WELL, YEAH, I RECALL IT...! THAT LITTLE OUTFIT'S NOT EASILY FORGOTTEN, Y'KNOW...
NE'ER MORE VERILY HAVE YOU SPOKEN, WENCH!
CERTAINLY, THE P-WHIPPED PRINCELING COULD NOT HAVE FORGOTTEN THE ENCHANTING EMSEMBLE, FOR THE MEREST GLIMPSE OF ITS MICROSKIRTED MAJESTY DID SURELY SWIRL HIM UP INTO A DROOLING, GIBBERING, BESTIALLY ADAMANTINE-ERECT WHIRLWIND OF SHEEREST LUST!
BUXOM, BRA-BESPURNING BIBLIOBABE BOOTY-LICIOUS
TO QUOTE THE URBAN BARD: HE COULD NOT HELP HIMSELF, FOR HE WAS SURELY ACTING LIKE AN ANIMAL; PERFORCE, HERE, INDEED, WAS HIS SCANDAL.
LIKE UNTO A DIRELY SUGAR-CRAZED BOY IN A CANDY STORE, HE LITERALLY DOES NOT KNOW WHERE TO LOOK NEXT

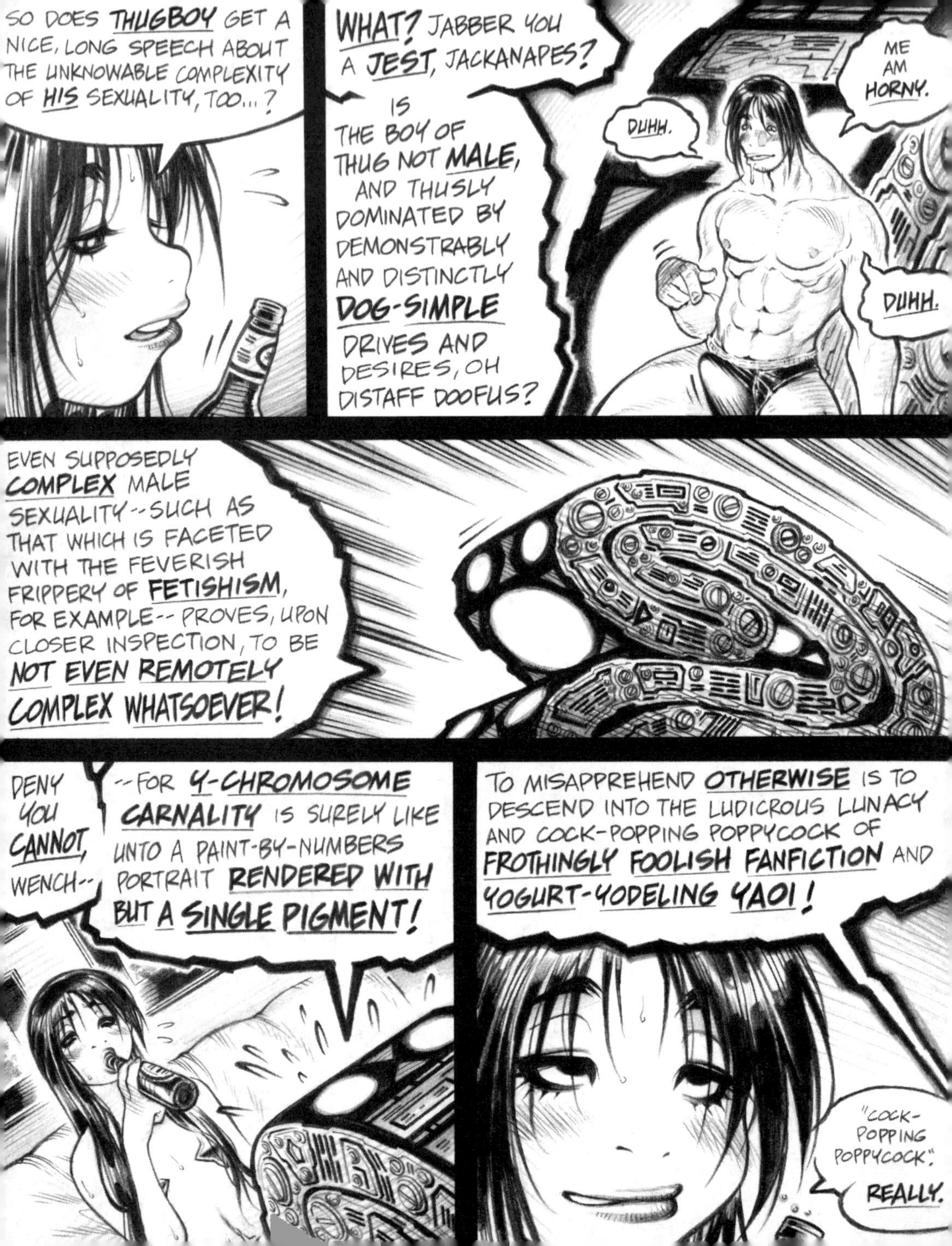
SO DOES THUGBOY GET A NICE, LONG SPEECH ABOUT THE UNKNOWABLE COMPLEXITY OF HIS SEXUALITY, TOO...?
WHAT? JABBER YOU A JEST, JACKANAPES?
IS THE BOY OF THUG NOT MALE, AND THUSLY DOMINATED BY DEMONSTRABLY AND DISTINCTLY DOG-SIMPLE DRIVES AND DESIRES, OH DISTAFF DOOFUS?
DUHH.
ME AM HORNY.
DUHH.
EVEN SUPPOSEDLY COMPLEX MALE SEXUALITY--SUCH AS THAT WHICH IS FACETED WITH THE FEVERISH FRIPPERY OF FETISHISM, FOR EXAMPLE--PROVES, UPON CLOSER INSPECTION, TO BE NOT EVEN REMOTELY COMPLEX WHATSOEVER!
DENY YOU CANNOT, WENCH--
--FOR Y-CHROMOSOME CARNALITY IS SURELY LIKE UNTO A PAINT-BY-NUMBERS PORTRAIT RENDERED WITH BUT A SINGLE PIGMENT!
TO MISAPPREHEND OTHERWISE IS TO DESCEND INTO THE LUDICROUS LUNACY AND COCK-POPPING POPPYCOCK OF FROTHINGLY FOOLISH FANFICTION AND YOGURT-YODELING YAOI!
"COCK-POPPING POPPYCOCK". REALLY.

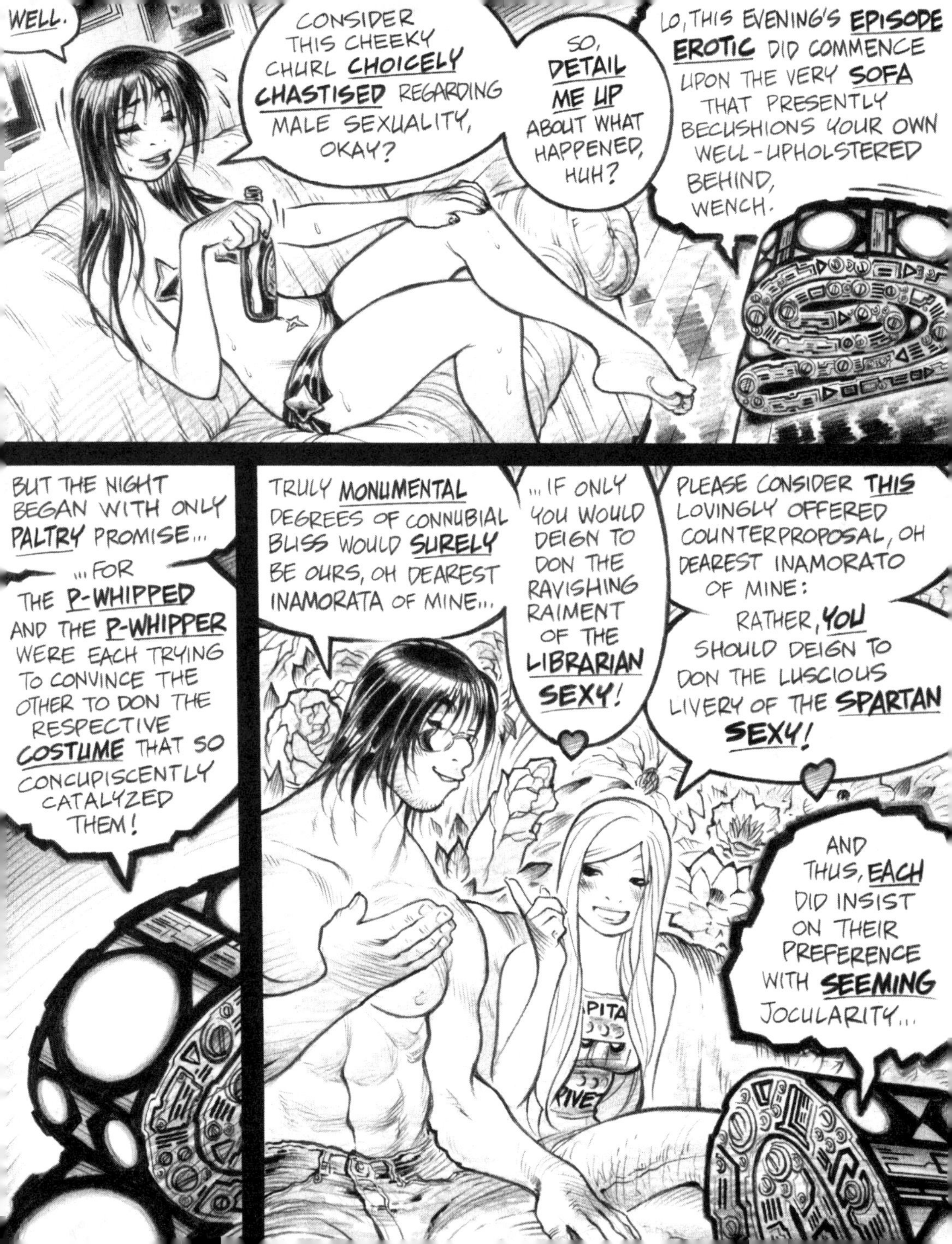
WELL.
CONSIDER THIS CHEEKY CHURL CHOICELY CHASTISED REGARDING MALE SEXUALITY, OKAY?
SO, DETAIL ME UP ABOUT WHAT HAPPENED, HUH?
LO, THIS EVENING'S EPISODE EROTIC DID COMMENCE UPON THE VERY SOFA THAT PRESENTLY BECUSHIONS YOUR OWN WELL-UPHOLSTERED BEHIND, WENCH.
BUT THE NIGHT BEGAN WITH ONLY PALTRY PROMISE...
...FOR THE P-WHIPPED AND THE P-WHIPPER WERE EACH TRYING TO CONVINCE THE OTHER TO DON THE RESPECTIVE COSTUME THAT SO CONCUPISCENTLY CATALYZED THEM!
TRULY MONUMENTAL DEGREES OF CONNUBIAL BLISS WOULD SURELY BE OURS, OH DEAREST INAMORATA OF MINE...
...IF ONLY YOU WOULD DEIGN TO DON THE RAVISHING RAIMENT OF THE LIBRARIAN SEXY!
PLEASE CONSIDER THIS LOVINGLY OFFERED COUNTERPROPOSAL, OH DEAREST INAMORATO OF MINE:
RATHER, YOU SHOULD DEIGN TO DON THE LUSCIOUS LIVERY OF THE SPARTAN SEXY!
AND THUS, EACH DID INSIST ON THEIR PREFERENCE WITH SEEMING JOCULARITY...

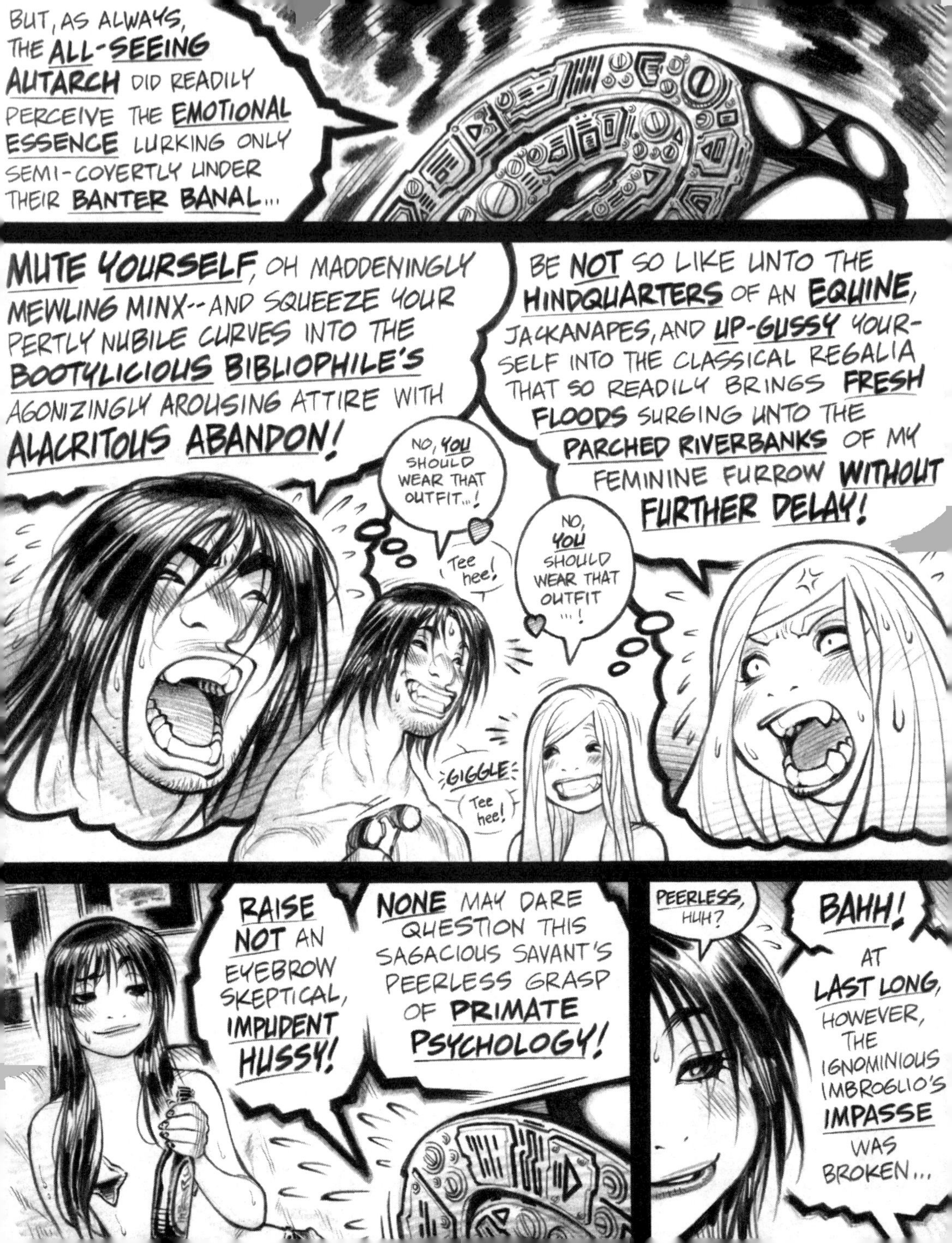

BUT, AS ALWAYS, THE ALL-SEEING AUTARCH DID READILY PERCEIVE THE EMOTIONAL ESSENCE LURKING ONLY SEMI-COVERTLY UNDER THEIR BANTER BANAL...
MUTE YOURSELF, OH MADDENINGLY MEWLING MINX--AND SQUEEZE YOUR PERTLY NUBILE CURVES INTO THE BOOTYLICIOUS BIBLIOPHILE'S AGONIZINGLY AROUSING ATTIRE WITH ALACRITOUS ABANDON!
BE NOT SO LIKE UNTO THE HINDQUARTERS OF AN EQUINE, JACKANAPES, AND UP-GUSSY YOURSELF INTO THE CLASSICAL REGALIA THAT SO READILY BRINGS FRESH FLOODS SURGING UNTO THE PARCHED RIVERBANKS OF MY FEMININE FURROW WITHOUT FURTHER DELAY!
NO, YOU SHOULD WEAR THAT OUTFIT...!
Tee hee!
NO, YOU SHOULD WEAR THAT OUTFIT...!
GIGGLE
Tee hee!
RAISE NOT AN EYEBROW SKEPTICAL, IMPUDENT HUSSY!
NONE MAY DARE QUESTION THIS SAGACIOUS SAVANT'S PEERLESS GRASP OF PRIMATE PSYCHOLOGY!
PEERLESS, HUH?
BAHH!
AT LAST LONG, HOWEVER, THE IGNOMINIOUS IMBROGLIO'S IMPASSE WAS BROKEN...

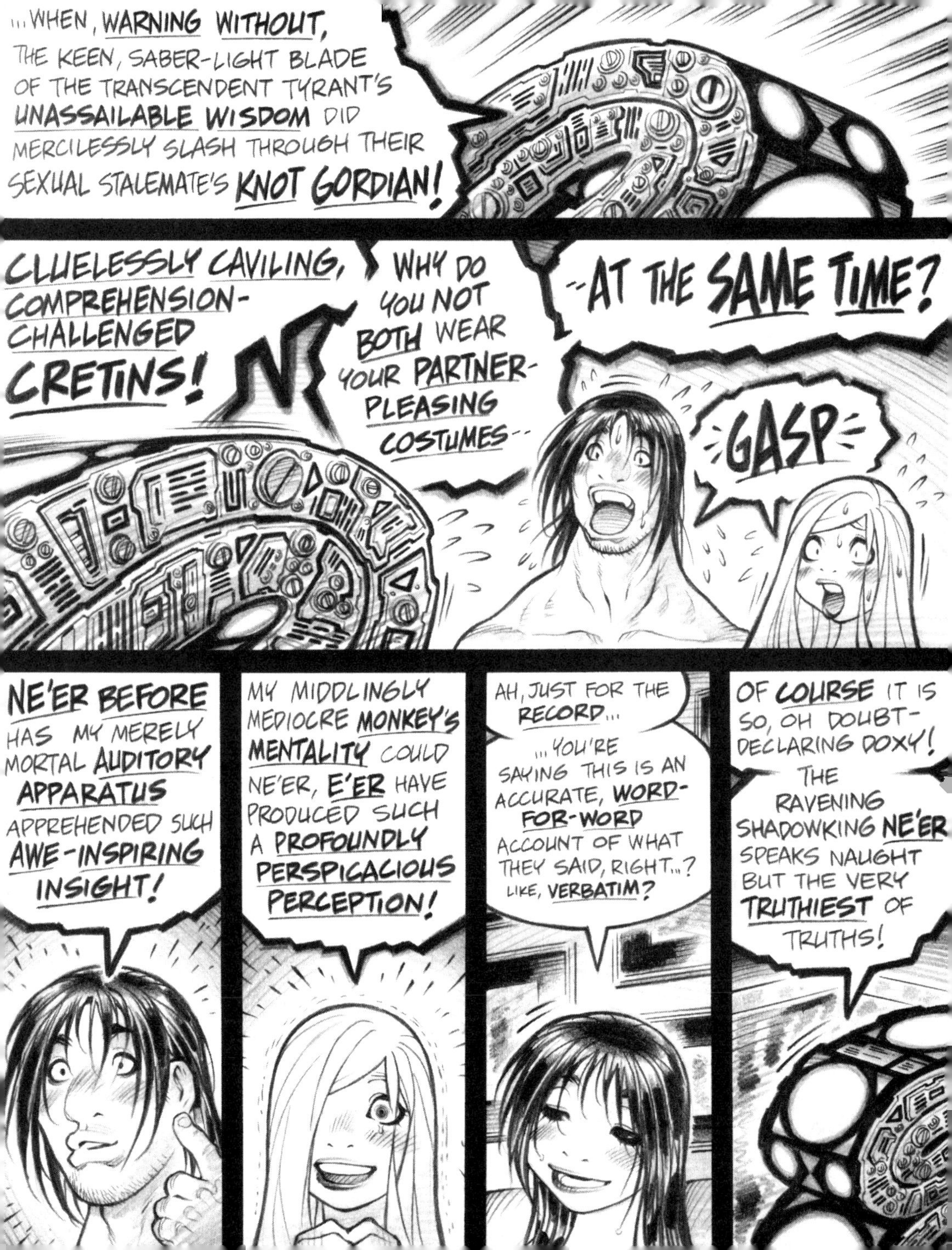
...WHEN, WARNING WITHOUT, THE KEEN, SABER-LIGHT BLADE OF THE TRANSCENDENT TYRANT'S UNASSAILABLE WISDOM DID MERCILESSLY SLASH THROUGH THEIR SEXUAL STALEMATE'S KNOT GORDIAN!
CLUELESSLY CAVILING, COMPREHENSION-CHALLENGED CRETINS!
WHY DO YOU NOT BOTH WEAR YOUR PARTNER-PLEASING COSTUMES--
--AT THE SAME TIME?
GASP
NE'ER BEFORE HAS MY MERELY MORTAL AUDITORY APPARATUS APPREHENDED SUCH AWE-INSPIRING INSIGHT!
MY MIDDLINGLY MEDIOCRE MONKEY'S MENTALITY COULD NE'ER, E'ER HAVE PRODUCED SUCH A PROFOUNDLY PERSPICACIOUS PERCEPTION!
AH, JUST FOR THE RECORD...
...YOU'RE SAYING THIS IS AN ACCURATE, WORD-FOR-WORD ACCOUNT OF WHAT THEY SAID, RIGHT...? LIKE, VERBATIM?
OF COURSE IT IS SO, OH DOUBT-DECLARING DOXY!
THE RAVENING SHADOWKING NE'ER SPEAKS NAUGHT BUT THE VERY TRUTHIEST OF TRUTHS!

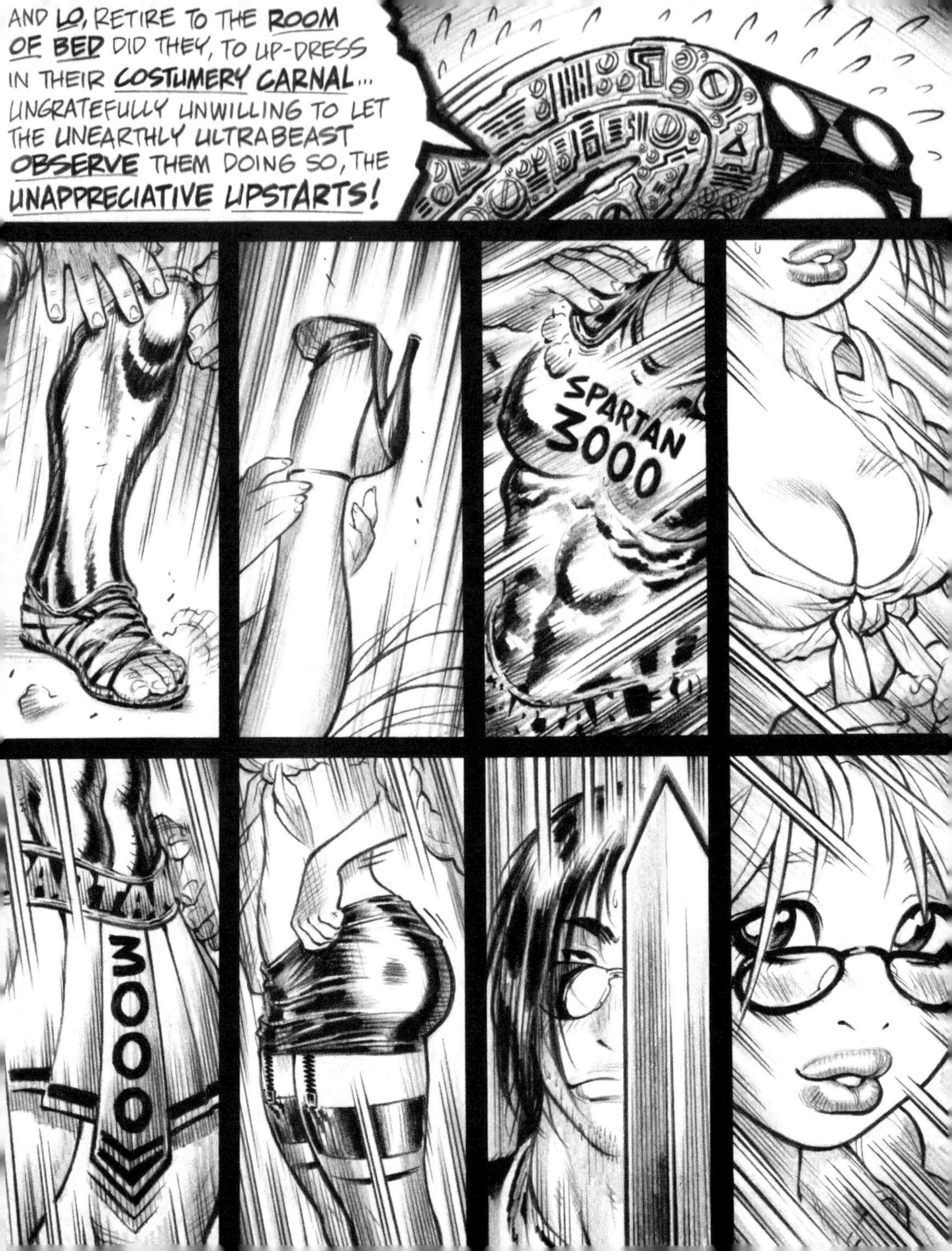
AND LO, RETIRE TO THE ROOM OF BED DID THEY, TO UP-DRESS IN THEIR COSTUMERY CARNAL... UNGRATEFULLY UNWILLING TO LET THE UNEARTHLY ULTRABEAST OBSERVE THEM DOING SO, THE UNAPPRECIATIVE UPSTARTS!
SPARTAN 3000
3000

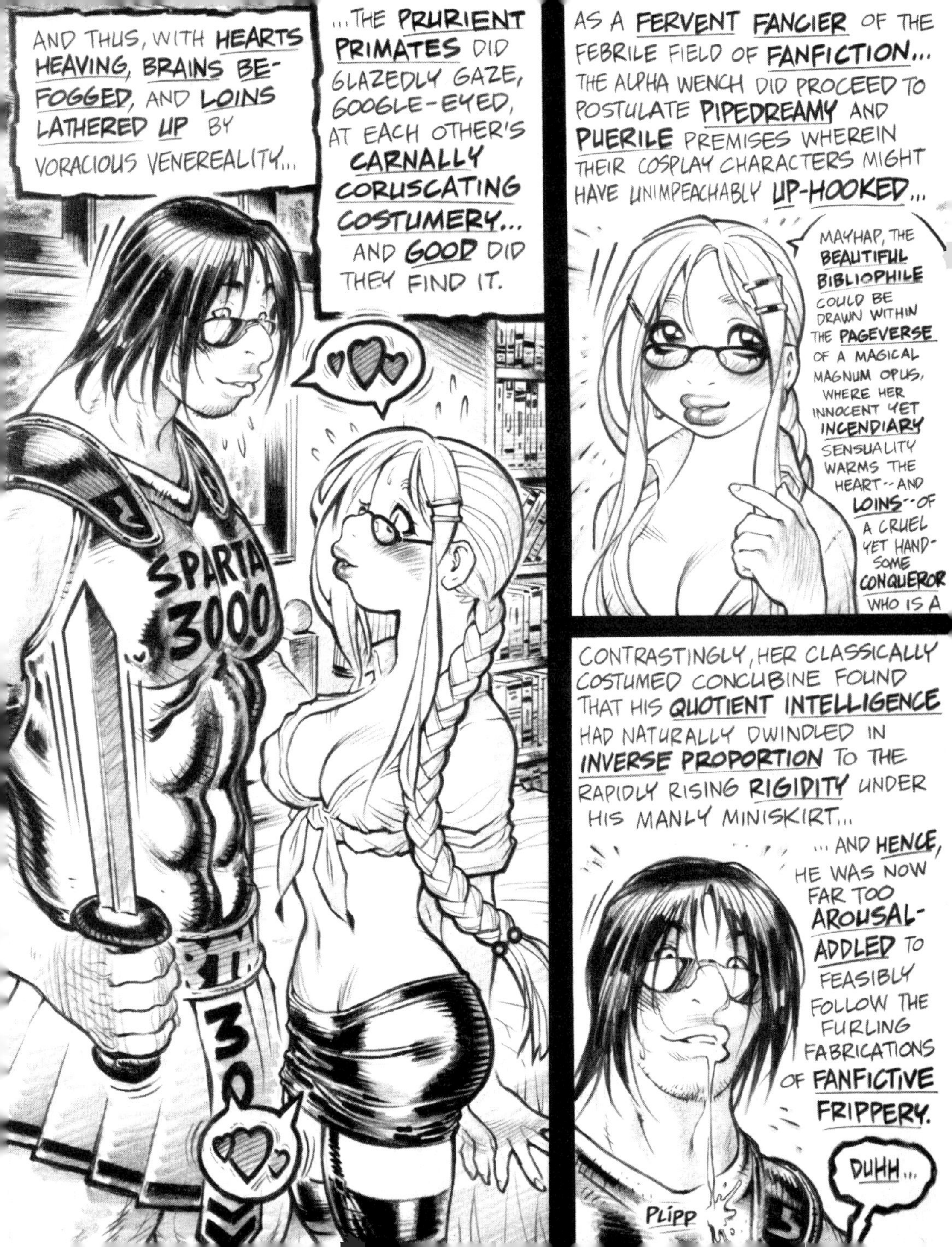

AND THUS, WITH HEARTS HEAVING, BRAINS BE-FOGGED, AND LOINS LATHERED UP BY VORACIOUS VENEREALITY...
...THE PRURIENT PRIMATES DID GLAZEDLY GAZE, GOOGLE-EYED, AT EACH OTHER'S CARNALLY CORUSCATING COSTUMERY... AND GOOD DID THEY FIND IT.
SPARTA 3000
AS A FERVENT FANCIER OF THE FEBRILE FIELD OF FANFICTION... THE ALPHA WENCH DID PROCEED TO POSTULATE PIPEDREAMY AND PUERILE PREMISES WHEREIN THEIR COSPLAY CHARACTERS MIGHT HAVE UNIMPEACHABLY UP-HOOKED...
MAYHAP, THE BEAUTIFUL BIBLIOPHILE COULD BE DRAWN WITHIN THE PAGEVERSE OF A MAGICAL MAGNUM OPUS, WHERE HER INNOCENT YET INCENDIARY SENSUALITY WARMS THE HEART--AND LOINS--OF A CRUEL YET HAND-SOME CONQUEROR WHO IS A
CONTRASTINGLY, HER CLASSICALLY COSTUMED CONCUBINE FOUND THAT HIS QUOTIENT INTELLIGENCE HAD NATURALLY DWINDLED IN INVERSE PROPORTION TO THE RAPIDLY RISING RIGIDITY UNDER HIS MANLY MINISKIRT...
...AND HENCE, HE WAS NOW FAR TOO AROUSAL-ADDLED TO FEASIBLY FOLLOW THE FURLING FABRICATIONS OF FANFICTIVE FRIPPERY.
PLIPP
DUHH...

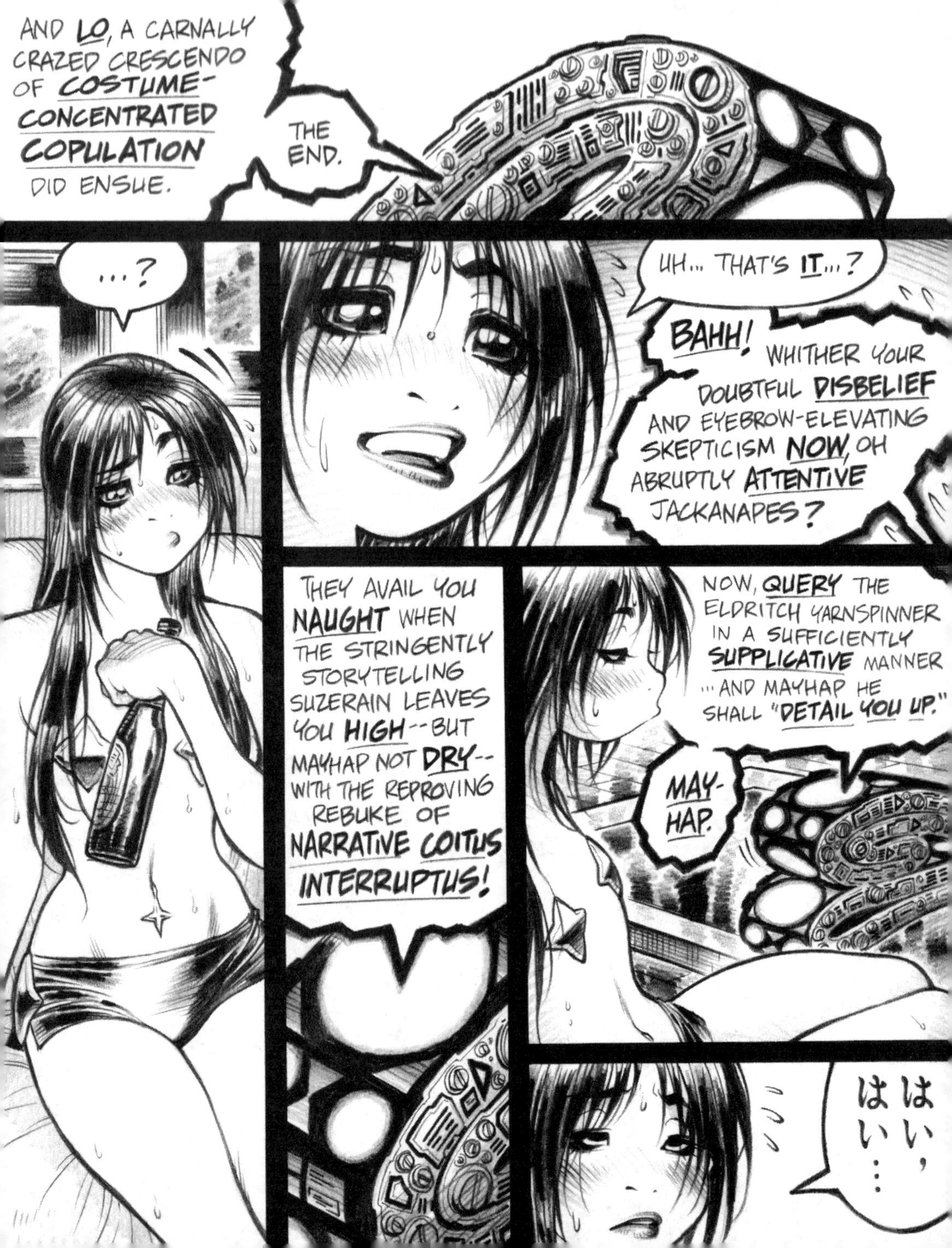

AND LO, A CARNALLY CRAZED CRESCENDO OF COSTUME-CONCENTRATED COPULATION DID ENSUE.
THE END.
...?
UH... THAT'S IT...?
BAHH! WHITHER YOUR DOUBTFUL DISBELIEF AND EYEBROW-ELEVATING SKEPTICISM NOW, OH ABRUPTLY ATTENTIVE JACKANAPES?
THEY AVAIL YOU NAUGHT WHEN THE STRINGENTLY STORYTELLING SUZERAIN LEAVES YOU HIGH--BUT MAYHAP NOT DRY--WITH THE REPROVING REBUKE OF NARRATIVE COITUS INTERRUPTUS!
NOW, QUERY THE ELDRITCH YARNSPINNER IN A SUFFICIENTLY SUPPLICATIVE MANNER ...AND MAYHAP HE SHALL "DETAIL YOU UP."
MAY-HAP.
はい，はい…

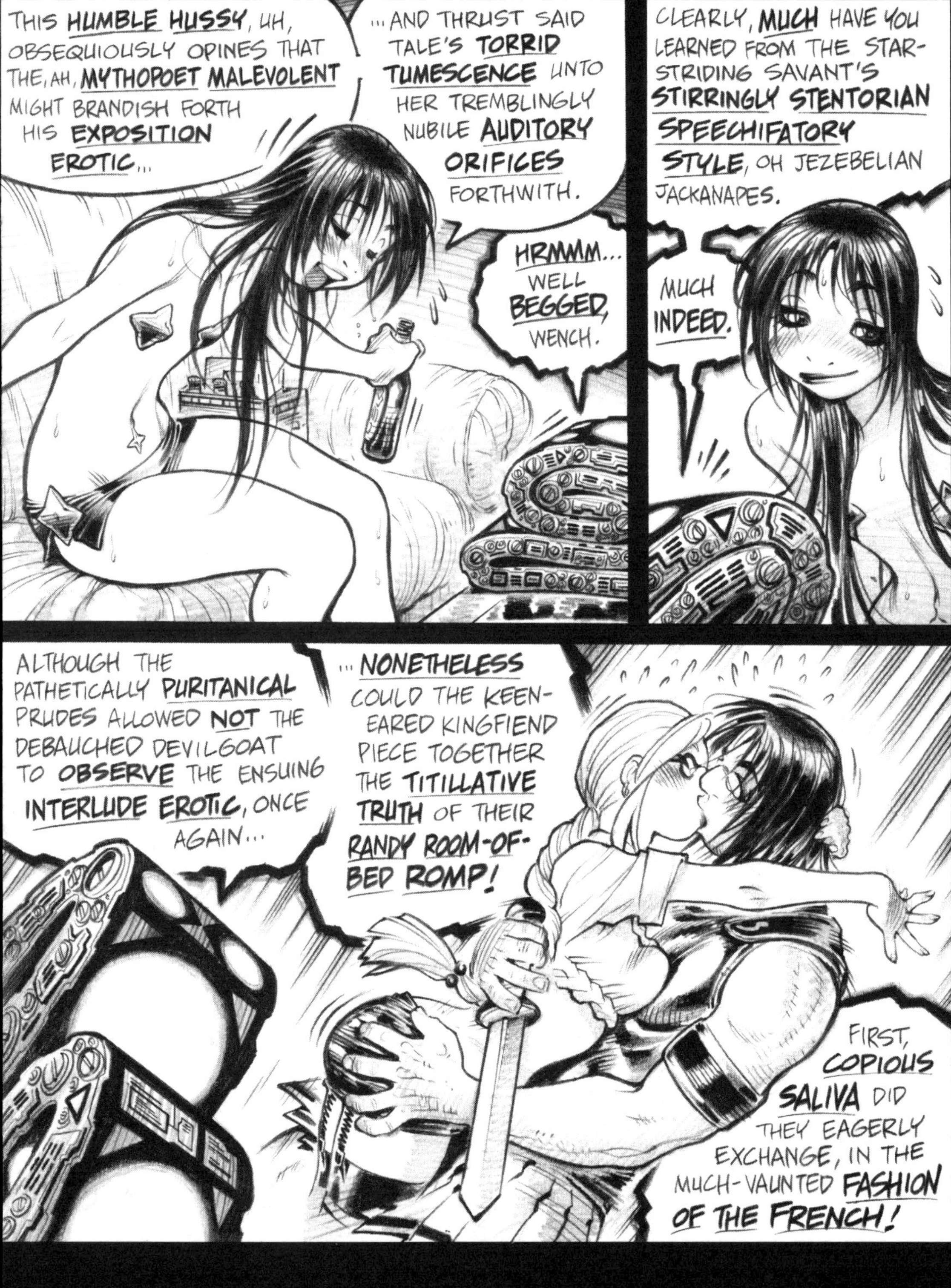
THIS HUMBLE HUSSY, UH, OBSEQUIOUSLY OPINES THAT THE, AH, MYTHOPOET MALEVOLENT MIGHT BRANDISH FORTH HIS EXPOSITION EROTIC...
...AND THRUST SAID TALE'S TORRID TUMESCENCE UNTO HER TREMBLINGLY NUBILE AUDITORY ORIFICES FORTHWITH.
HRMMM... WELL BEGGED, WENCH.
CLEARLY, MUCH HAVE YOU LEARNED FROM THE STAR-STRIDING SAVANT'S STIRRINGLY STENTORIAN SPEECHIFATORY STYLE, OH JEZEBELIAN JACKANAPES.
MUCH INDEED.
ALTHOUGH THE PATHETICALLY PURITANICAL PRUDES ALLOWED NOT THE DEBAUCHED DEVILGOAT TO OBSERVE THE ENSUING INTERLUDE EROTIC, ONCE AGAIN...
...NONETHELESS COULD THE KEEN-EARED KINGFIEND PIECE TOGETHER THE TITILLATIVE TRUTH OF THEIR RANDY ROOM-OF-BED ROMP!
FIRST, COPIOUS SALIVA DID THEY EAGERLY EXCHANGE, IN THE MUCH-VAUNTED FASHION OF THE FRENCH!

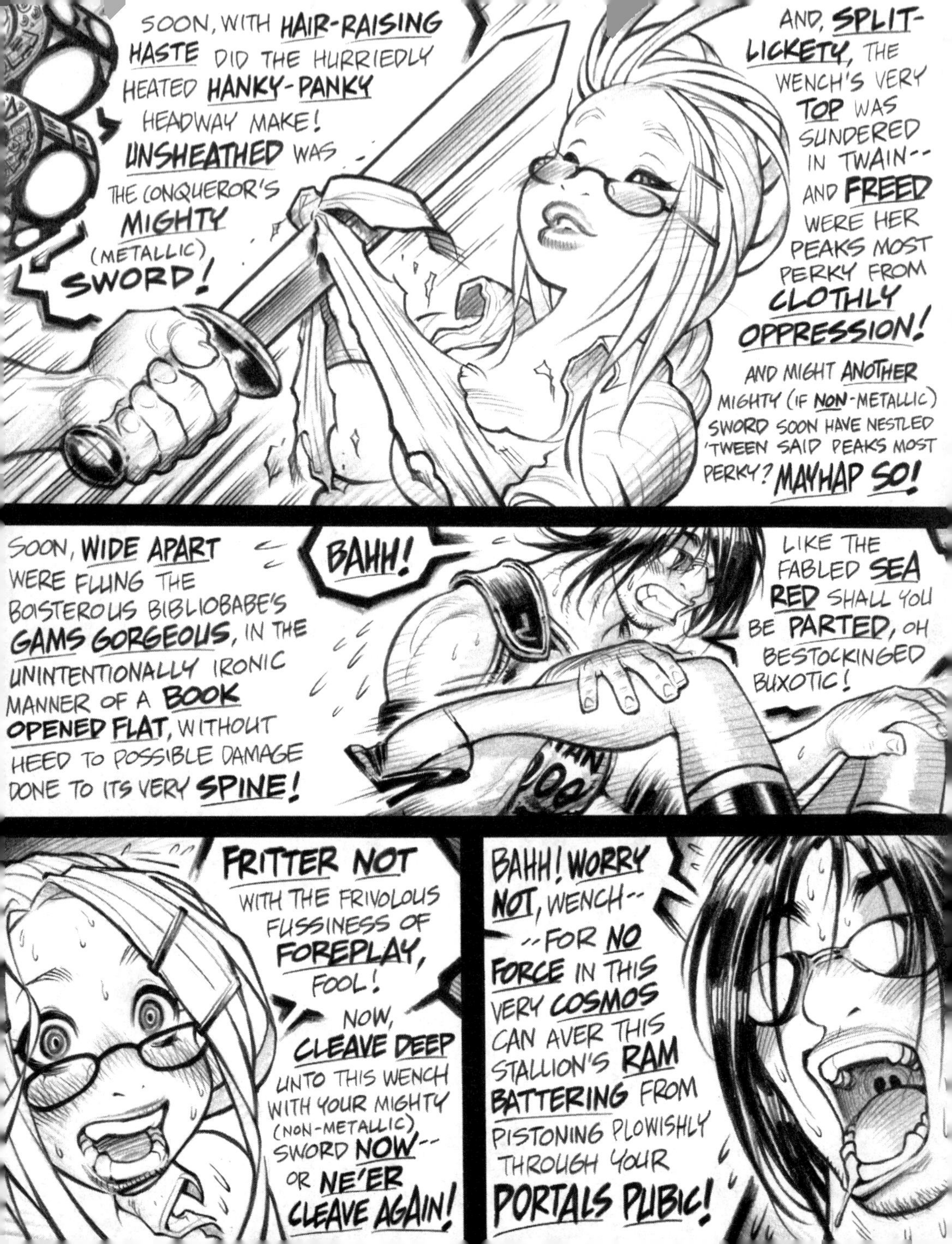
SOON, WITH HAIR-RAISING HASTE DID THE HURRIEDLY HEATED HANKY-PANKY HEADWAY MAKE! UNSHEATHED WAS THE CONQUEROR'S MIGHTY (METALLIC) SWORD!
AND, SPLIT-LICKETY, THE WENCH'S VERY TOP WAS SUNDERED IN TWAIN-- AND FREED WERE HER PEAKS MOST PERKY FROM CLOTHLY OPPRESSION!
AND MIGHT ANOTHER MIGHTY (IF NON-METALLIC) SWORD SOON HAVE NESTLED 'TWEEN SAID PEAKS MOST PERKY? MAYHAP SO!
SOON, WIDE APART WERE FLUNG THE BOISTEROUS BIBLIOBABE'S GAMS GORGEOUS, IN THE UNINTENTIONALLY IRONIC MANNER OF A BOOK OPENED FLAT, WITHOUT HEED TO POSSIBLE DAMAGE DONE TO ITS VERY SPINE!
BAHH!
LIKE THE FABLED SEA RED SHALL YOU BE PARTED, OH BESTOCKINGED BUXOTIC!
FRITTER NOT WITH THE FRIVOLOUS FUSSINESS OF FOREPLAY, FOOL!
NOW, CLEAVE DEEP UNTO THIS WENCH WITH YOUR MIGHTY (NON-METALLIC) SWORD NOW-- OR NE'ER CLEAVE AGAIN!
BAHH! WORRY NOT, WENCH--
--FOR NO FORCE IN THIS VERY COSMOS CAN AVER THIS STALLION'S RAM BATTERING FROM PISTONING PLOWISHLY THROUGH YOUR PORTALS PUBIC!

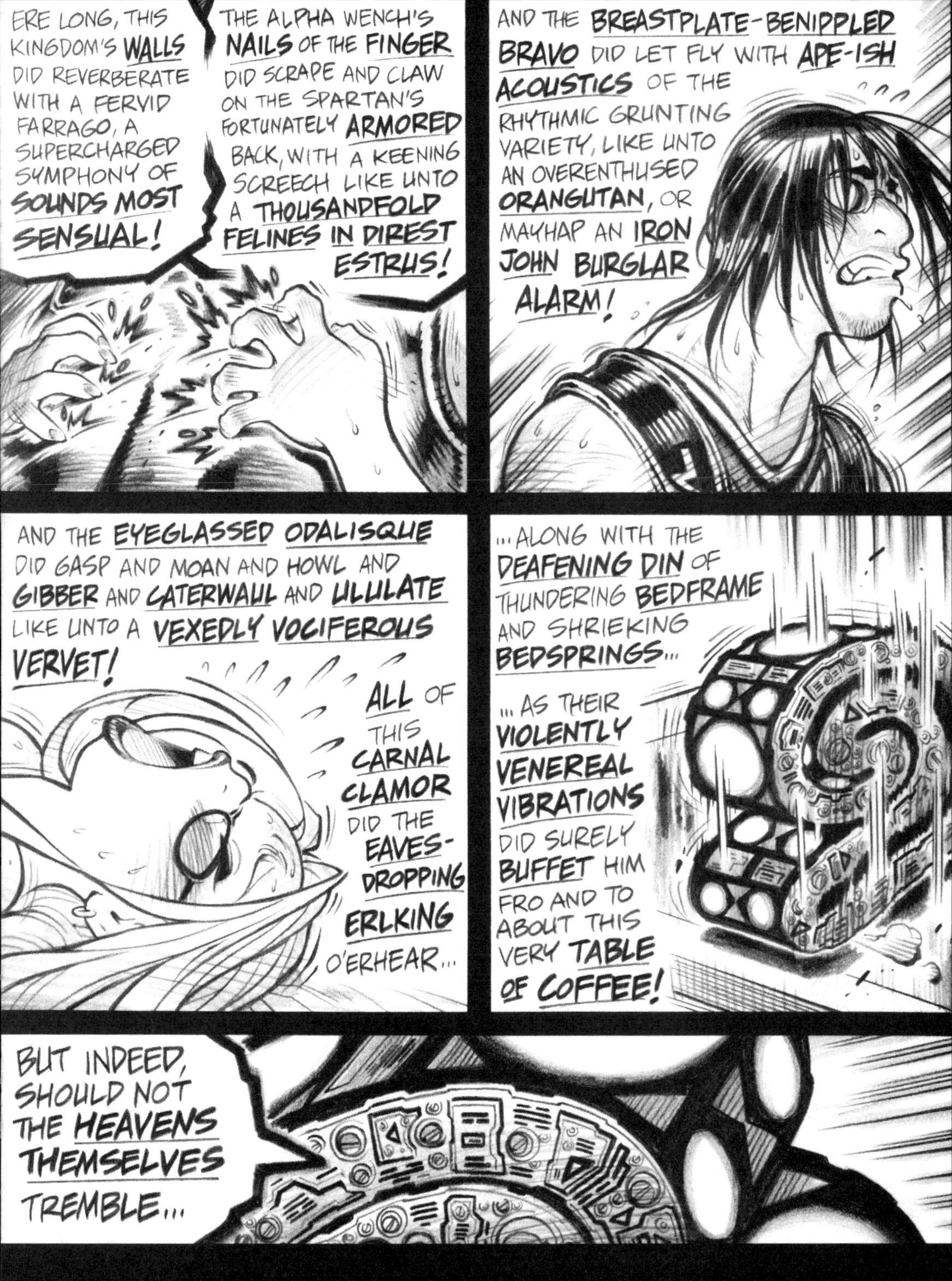
ERE LONG, THIS KINGDOM'S WALLS DID REVERBERATE WITH A FERVID FARRAGO, A SUPERCHARGED SYMPHONY OF SOUNDS MOST SENSUAL!
THE ALPHA WENCH'S NAILS OF THE FINGER DID SCRAPE AND CLAW ON THE SPARTAN'S FORTUNATELY ARMORED BACK, WITH A KEENING SCREECH LIKE UNTO A THOUSANDFOLD FELINES IN DIREST ESTRUS!
AND THE BREASTPLATE-BENIPPLED BRAVO DID LET FLY WITH APE-ISH ACOUSTICS OF THE RHYTHMIC GRUNTING VARIETY, LIKE UNTO AN OVERENTHUSED ORANGUTAN, OR MAYHAP AN IRON JOHN BURGLAR ALARM!
AND THE EYEGLASSED ODALISQUE DID GASP AND MOAN AND HOWL AND GIBBER AND CATERWAUL AND ULULATE LIKE UNTO A VEXEDLY VOCIFEROUS VERVET!
ALL OF THIS CARNAL CLAMOR DID THE EAVES-DROPPING ERLKING O'ERHEAR...
...ALONG WITH THE DEAFENING DIN OF THUNDERING BEDFRAME AND SHRIEKING BEDSPRINGS...
...AS THEIR VIOLENTLY VENEREAL VIBRATIONS DID SURELY BUFFET HIM FRO AND TO ABOUT THIS VERY TABLE OF COFFEE!
BUT INDEED, SHOULD NOT THE HEAVENS THEMSELVES TREMBLE...

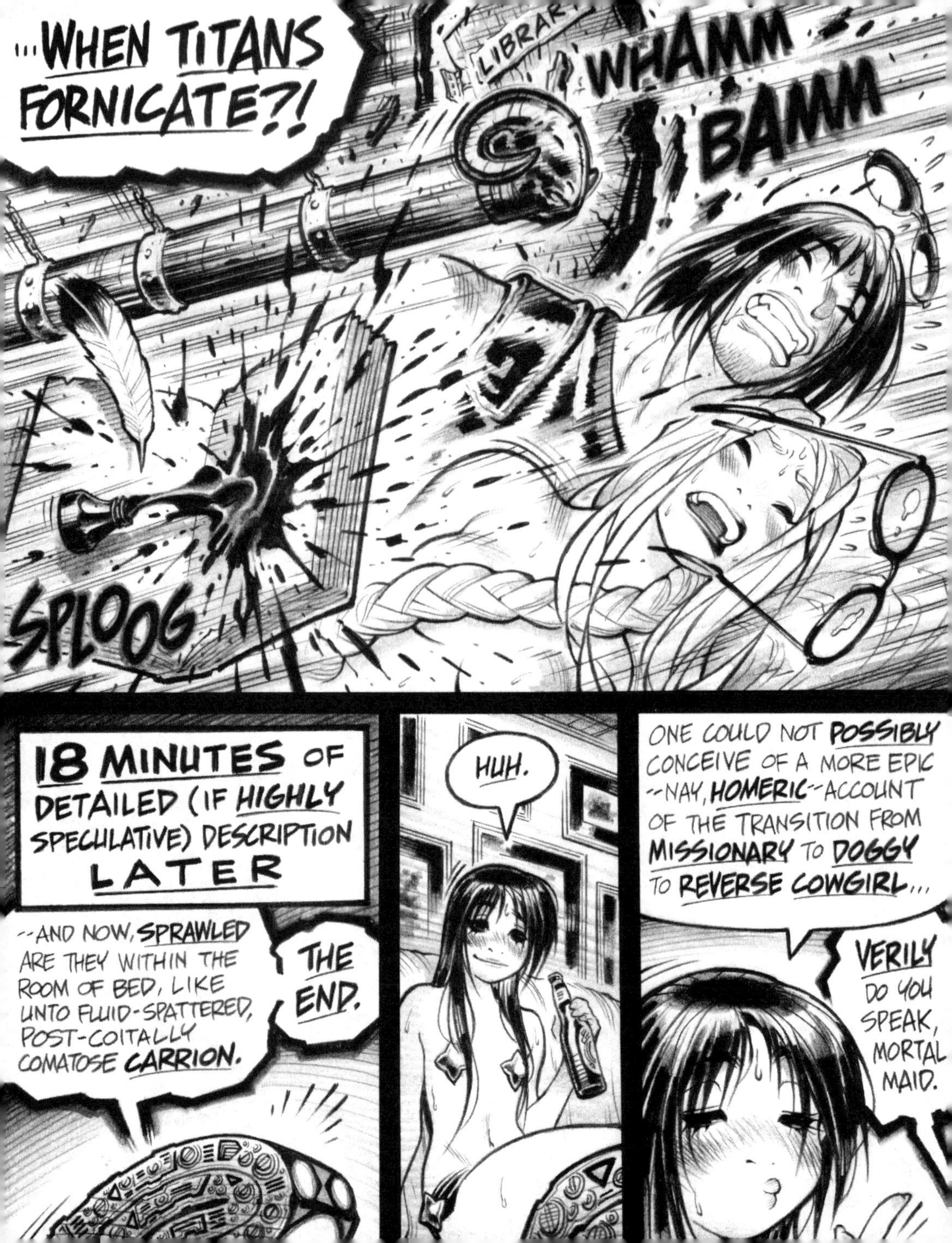
...WHEN TITANS FORNICATE?!
LIBRAR
WHAMM BAMM
SPLOOG
18 MINUTES OF DETAILED (IF HIGHLY SPECULATIVE) DESCRIPTION LATER
--AND NOW, SPRAWLED ARE THEY WITHIN THE ROOM OF BED, LIKE UNTO FLUID-SPATTERED, POST-COITALLY COMATOSE CARRION.
THE END.
HUH.
ONE COULD NOT POSSIBLY CONCEIVE OF A MORE EPIC --NAY, HOMERIC-- ACCOUNT OF THE TRANSITION FROM MISSIONARY TO DOGGY TO REVERSE COWGIRL...
VERILY DO YOU SPEAK, MORTAL MAID.

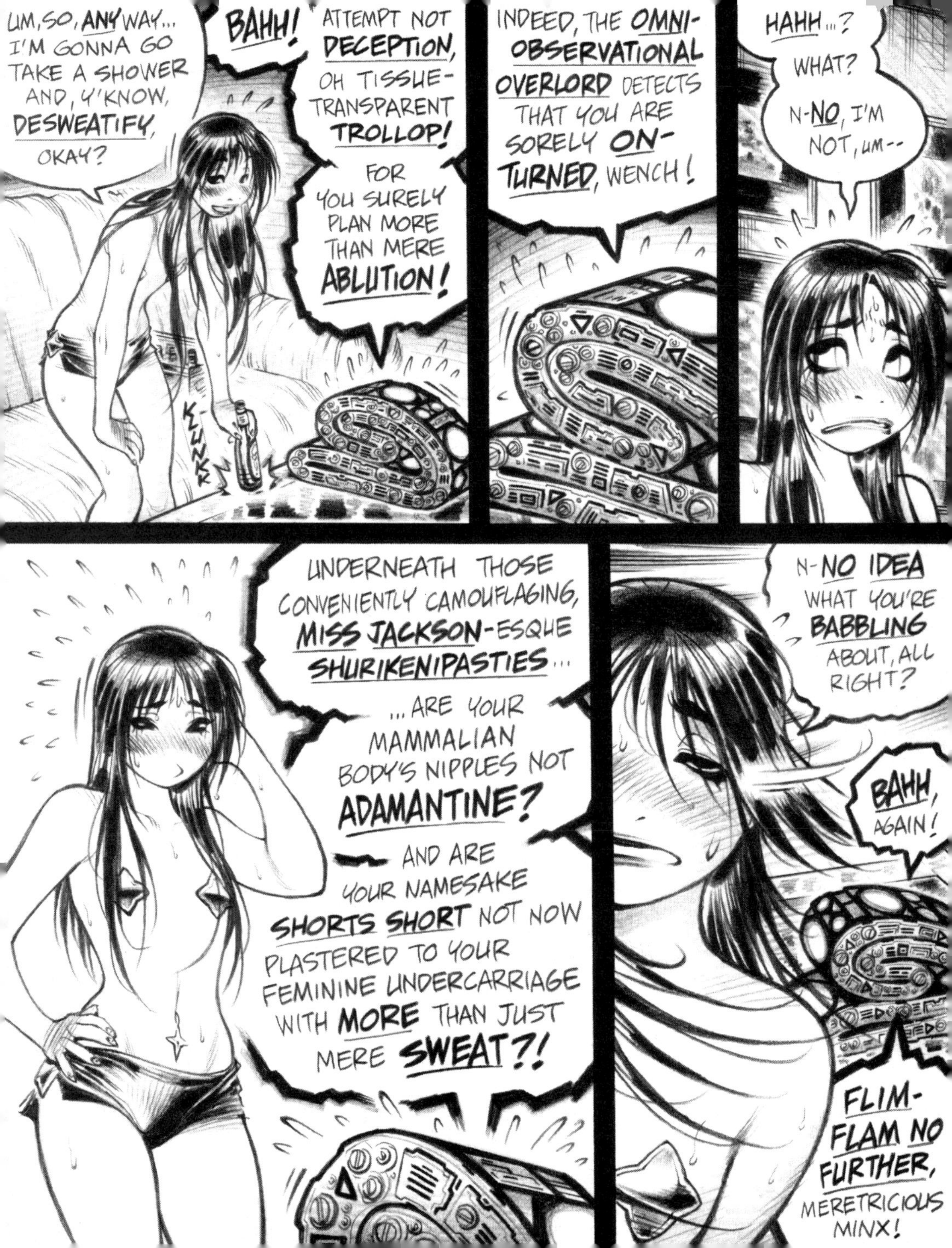
UM, SO, ANYWAY... I'M GONNA GO TAKE A SHOWER AND, Y'KNOW, DESWEATIFY, OKAY?
BAHH!
ATTEMPT NOT DECEPTION, OH TISSUE-TRANSPARENT TROLLOP!
FOR YOU SURELY PLAN MORE THAN MERE ABLUTION!
KLUNKK
INDEED, THE OMNI-OBSERVATIONAL OVERLORD DETECTS THAT YOU ARE SORELY ON-TURNED, WENCH!
HAHH...?
WHAT?
N-NO, I'M NOT, UM--
UNDERNEATH THOSE CONVENIENTLY CAMOUFLAGING, MISS JACKSON-ESQUE SHURIKENIPASTIES...
...ARE YOUR MAMMALIAN BODY'S NIPPLES NOT ADAMANTINE?
AND ARE YOUR NAMESAKE SHORTS SHORT NOT NOW PLASTERED TO YOUR FEMININE UNDERCARRIAGE WITH MORE THAN JUST MERE SWEAT?!
N-NO IDEA WHAT YOU'RE BABBLING ABOUT, ALL RIGHT?
BAHH, AGAIN!
FLIM-FLAM NO FURTHER, MERETRICIOUS MINX!

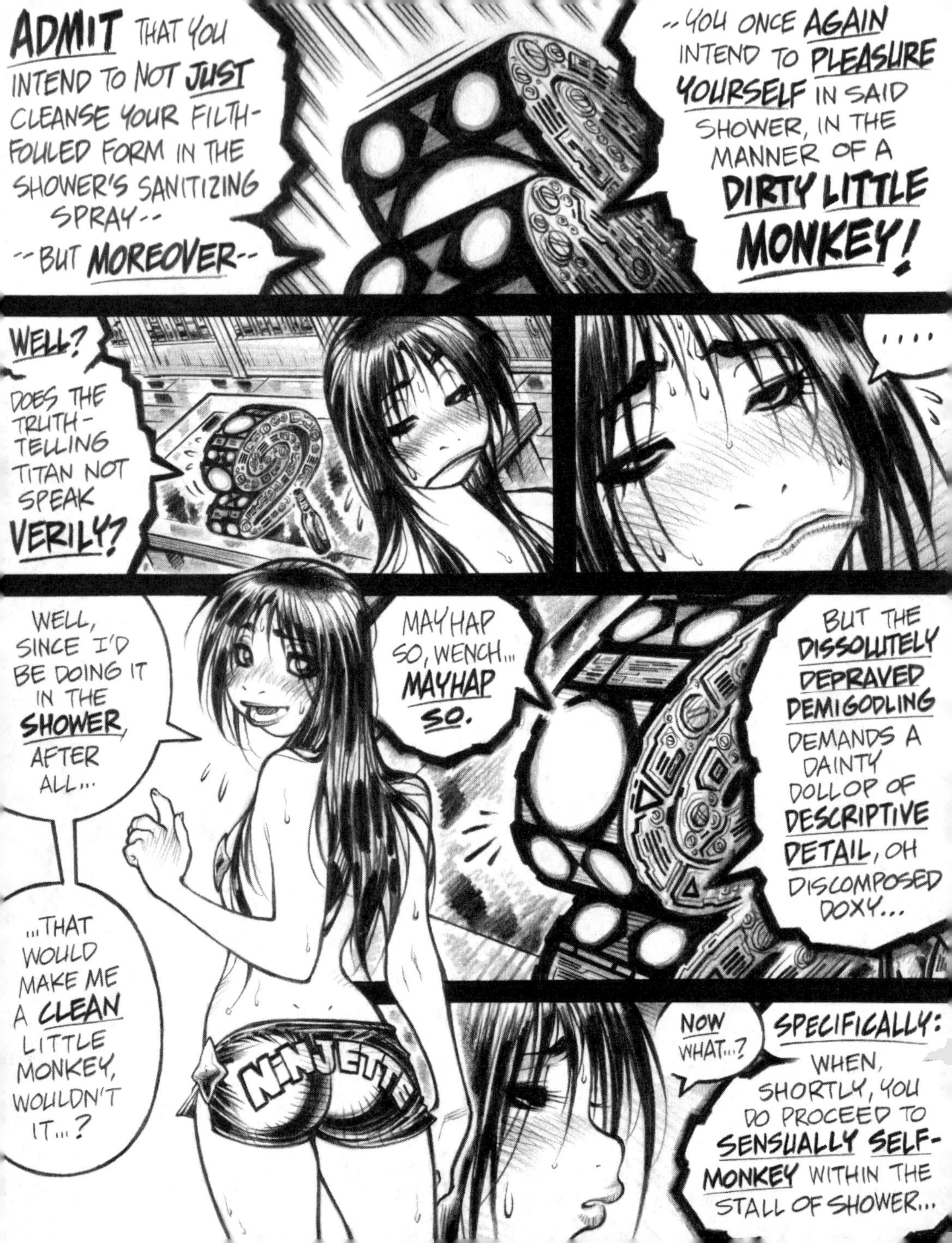

ADMIT THAT YOU INTEND TO NOT JUST CLEANSE YOUR FILTH-FOULED FORM IN THE SHOWER'S SANITIZING SPRAY--
--BUT MOREOVER--
--YOU ONCE AGAIN INTEND TO PLEASURE YOURSELF IN SAID SHOWER, IN THE MANNER OF A DIRTY LITTLE MONKEY!
WELL?
DOES THE TRUTH-TELLING TITAN NOT SPEAK VERILY?
....
WELL, SINCE I'D BE DOING IT IN THE SHOWER, AFTER ALL...
...THAT WOULD MAKE ME A CLEAN LITTLE MONKEY, WOULDN'T IT...?
NINJETTE
MAYHAP SO, WENCH... MAYHAP SO.
BUT THE DISSOLUTELY DEPRAVED DEMIGODLING DEMANDS A DAINTY DOLLOP OF DESCRIPTIVE DETAIL, OH DISCOMPOSED DOXY...
NOW WHAT...?
SPECIFICALLY:
WHEN, SHORTLY, YOU DO PROCEED TO SENSUALLY SELF-MONKEY WITHIN THE STALL OF SHOWER...

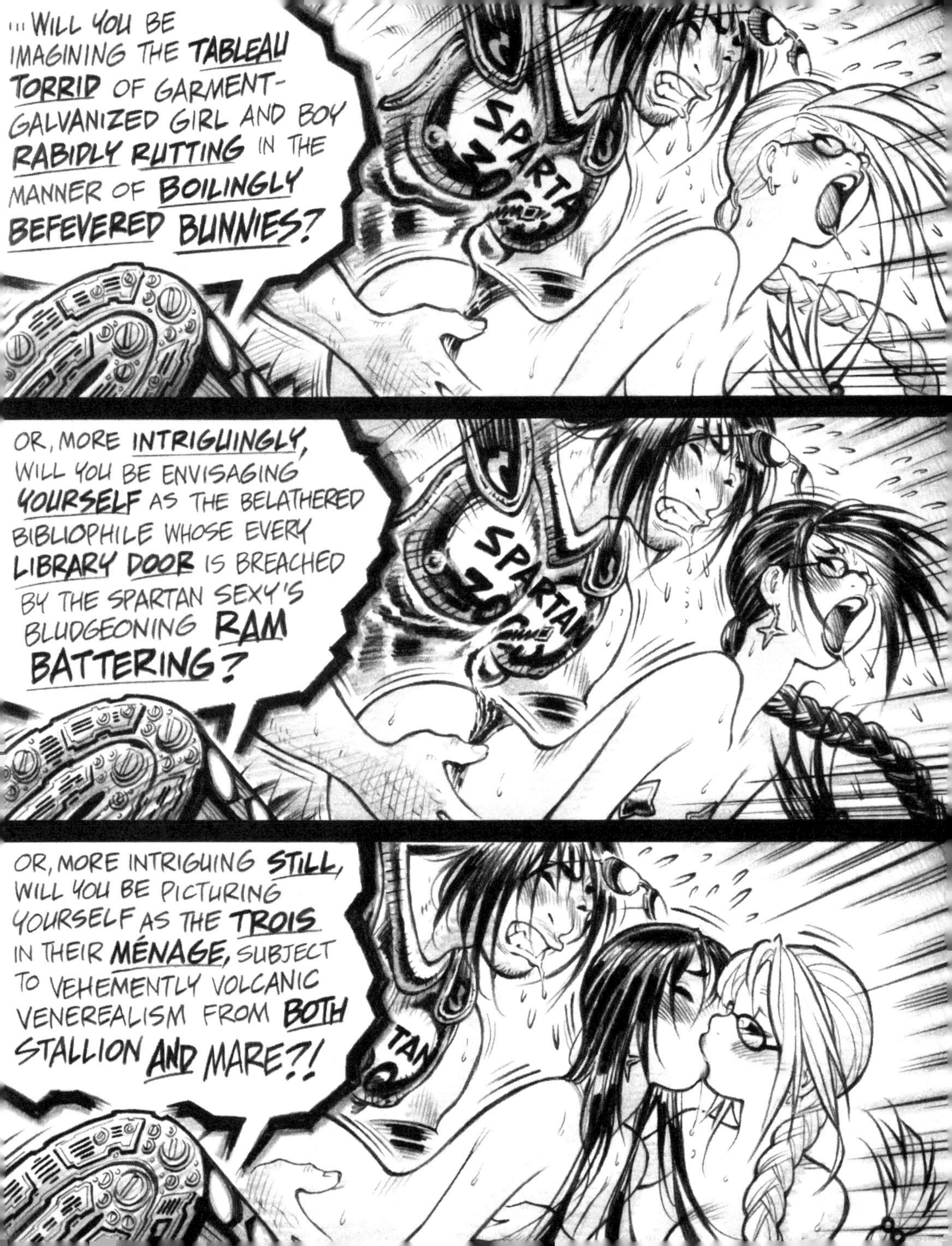
...WILL YOU BE IMAGINING THE TABLEAU TORRID OF GARMENT-GALVANIZED GIRL AND BOY RABIDLY RUTTING IN THE MANNER OF BOILINGLY BEFEVERED BUNNIES?
OR, MORE INTRIGUINGLY, WILL YOU BE ENVISAGING YOURSELF AS THE BELATHERED BIBLIOPHILE WHOSE EVERY LIBRARY DOOR IS BREACHED BY THE SPARTAN SEXY'S BLUDGEONING RAM BATTERING?
OR, MORE INTRIGUING STILL, WILL YOU BE PICTURING YOURSELF AS THE TROIS IN THEIR MÉNAGE, SUBJECT TO VEHEMENTLY VOLCANIC VENEREALISM FROM BOTH STALLION AND MARE?!

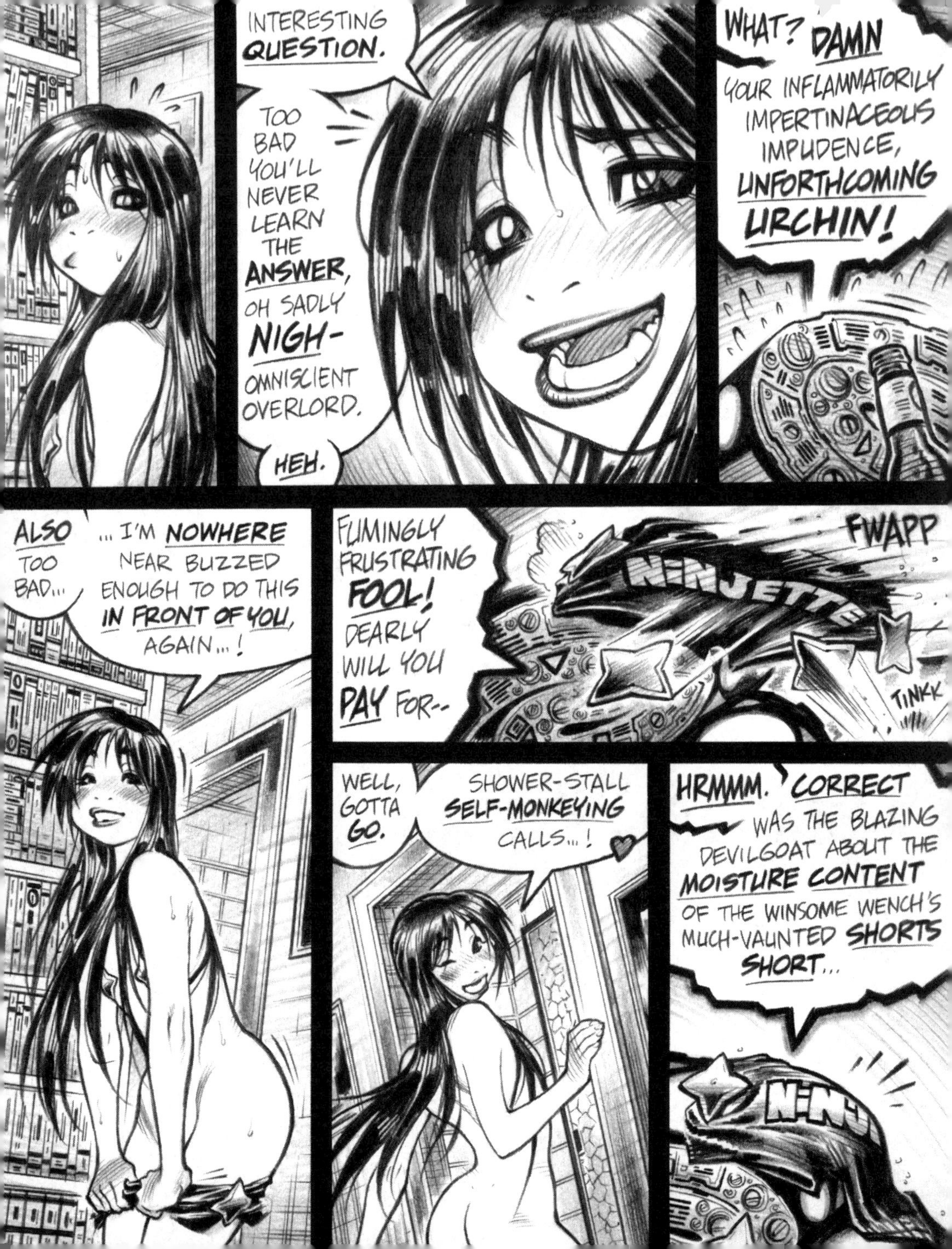
INTERESTING QUESTION.
TOO BAD YOU'LL NEVER LEARN THE ANSWER, OH SADLY NIGH-OMNISCIENT OVERLORD.
HEH.
WHAT? DAMN YOUR INFLAMMATORILY IMPERTINACEOUS IMPUDENCE, UNFORTHCOMING URCHIN!
ALSO TOO BAD...
...I'M NOWHERE NEAR BUZZED ENOUGH TO DO THIS IN FRONT OF YOU, AGAIN...!
FUMINGLY FRUSTRATING FOOL! DEARLY WILL YOU PAY FOR--
FWAPP
NINJETTE
TINKK
WELL, GOTTA GO.
SHOWER-STALL SELF-MONKEYING CALLS...!
HRMMM. CORRECT WAS THE BLAZING DEVILGOAT ABOUT THE MOISTURE CONTENT OF THE WINSOME WENCH'S MUCH-VAUNTED SHORTS SHORT...

Empowered™

I Know How Much You Love Blondes

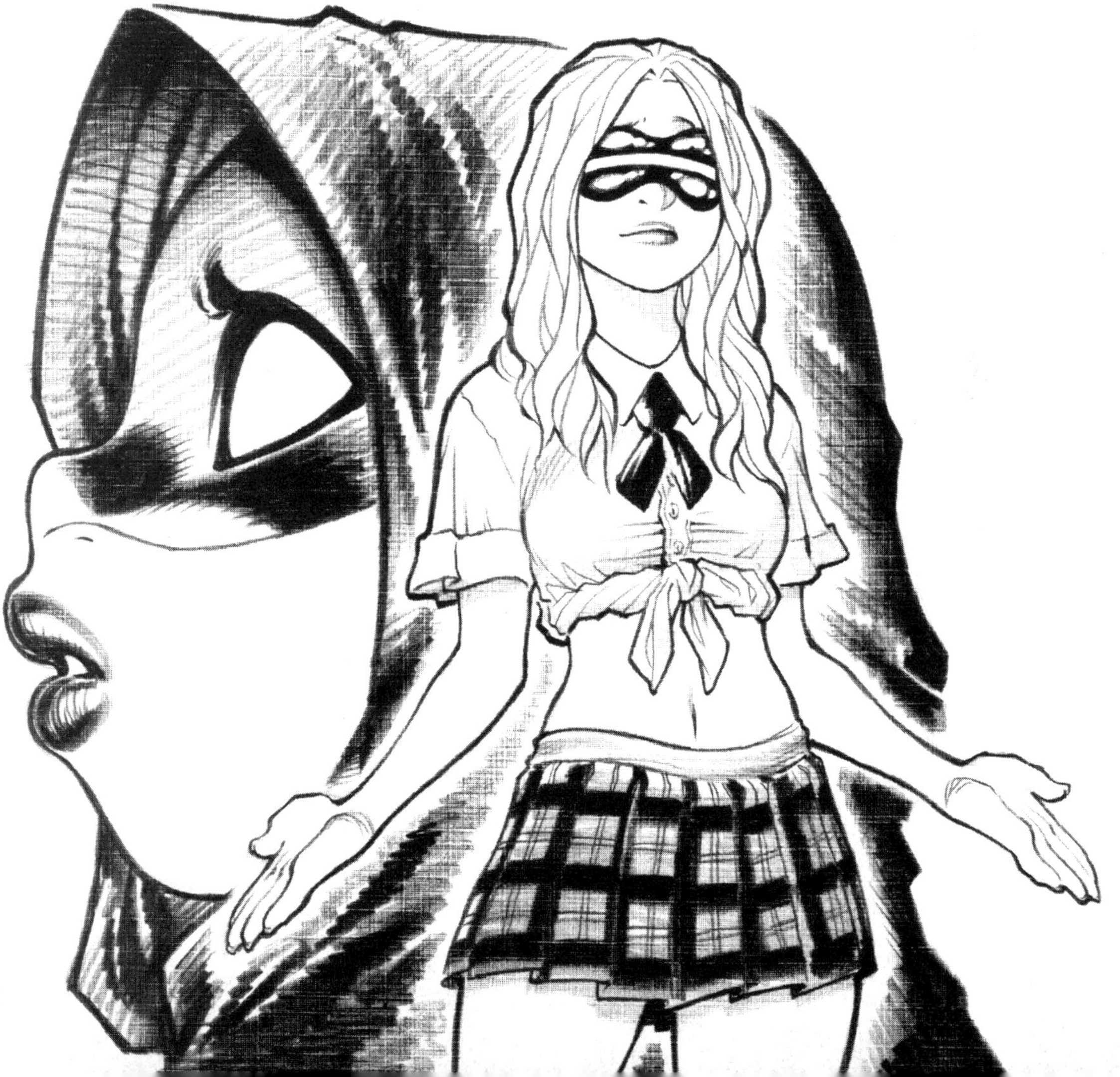

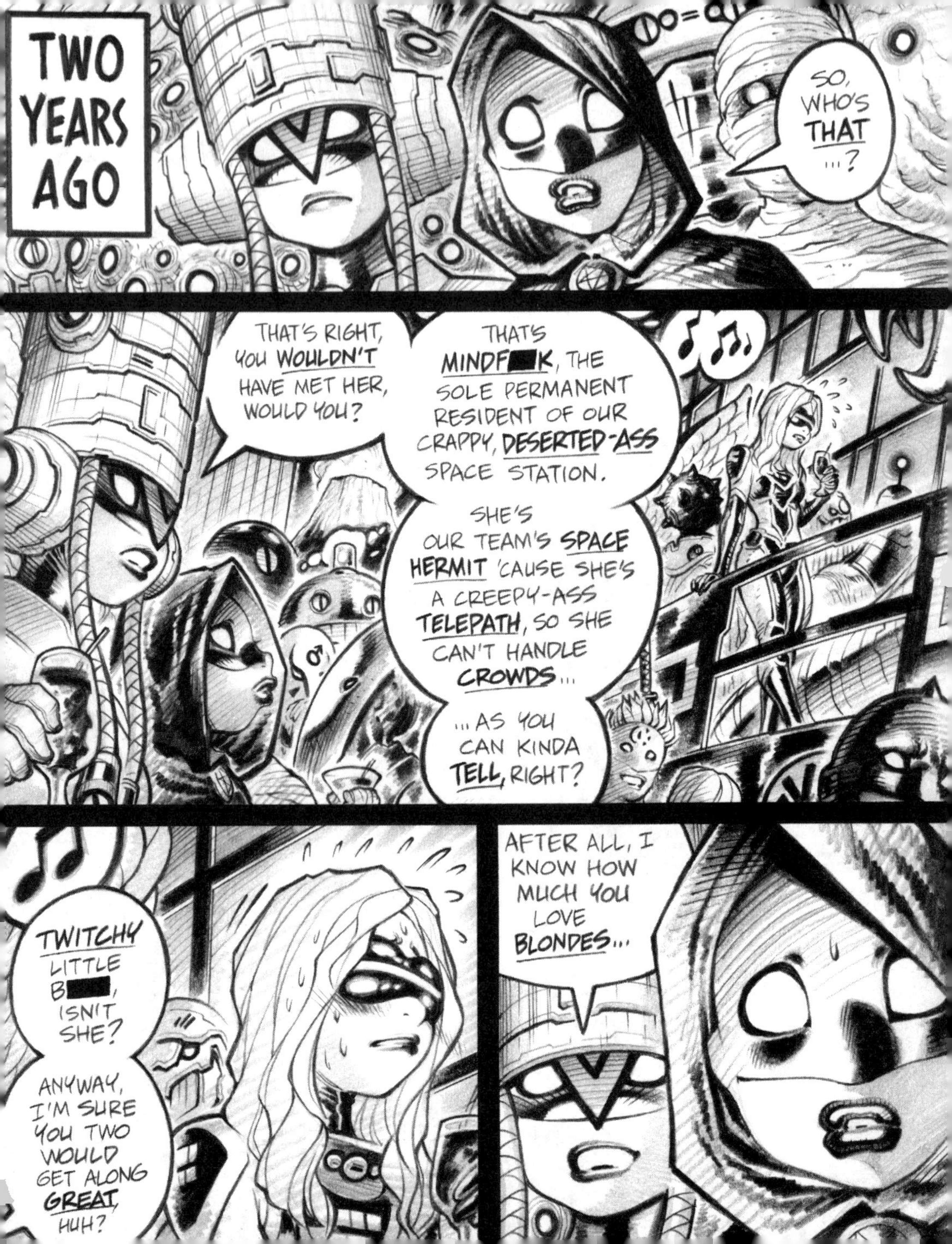
TWO YEARS AGO
SO, WHO'S THAT ...?
THAT'S RIGHT, YOU WOULDN'T HAVE MET HER, WOULD YOU?
THAT'S MINDF[redacted]K, THE SOLE PERMANENT RESIDENT OF OUR CRAPPY, DESERTED-ASS SPACE STATION.
SHE'S OUR TEAM'S SPACE HERMIT 'CAUSE SHE'S A CREEPY-ASS TELEPATH, SO SHE CAN'T HANDLE CROWDS...
...AS YOU CAN KINDA TELL, RIGHT?
TWITCHY LITTLE B[redacted], ISN'T SHE?
ANYWAY, I'M SURE YOU TWO WOULD GET ALONG GREAT, HUH?
AFTER ALL, I KNOW HOW MUCH YOU LOVE BLONDES...

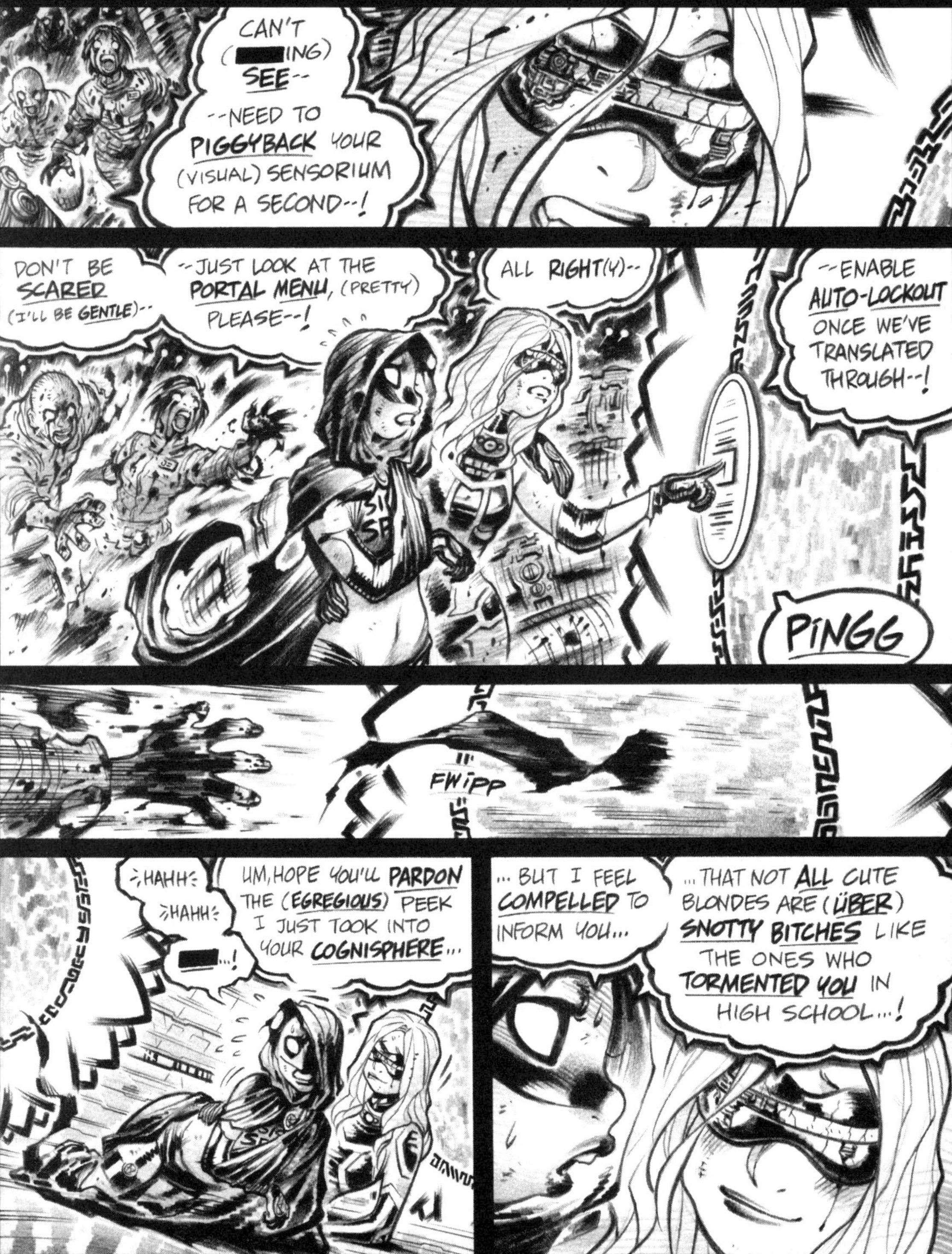
CAN'T ([redacted]ING) SEE-- --NEED TO PIGGYBACK YOUR (VISUAL) SENSORIUM FOR A SECOND--!
DON'T BE SCARED (I'LL BE GENTLE)--
--JUST LOOK AT THE PORTAL MENU, (PRETTY) PLEASE--!
ALL RIGHT(Y)--
--ENABLE AUTO-LOCKOUT ONCE WE'VE TRANSLATED THROUGH--!
PINGG
FWIPP
HAHH
HAHH
[redacted]...!
UM, HOPE YOU'LL PARDON THE (EGREGIOUS) PEEK I JUST TOOK INTO YOUR COGNISPHERE...
... BUT I FEEL COMPELLED TO INFORM YOU...
...THAT NOT ALL CUTE BLONDES ARE (ÜBER) SNOTTY BITCHES LIKE THE ONES WHO TORMENTED YOU IN HIGH SCHOOL...!

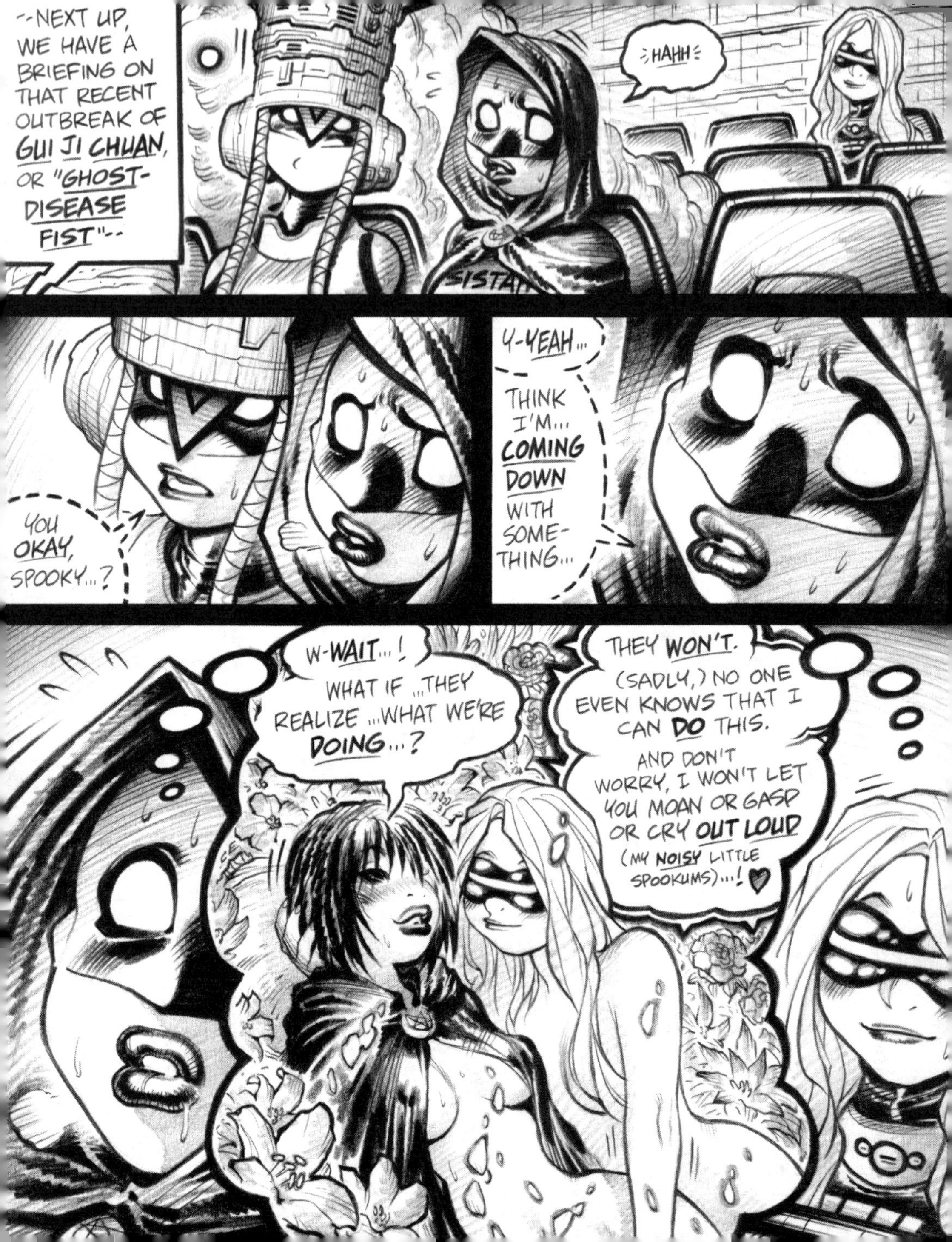

--NEXT UP, WE HAVE A BRIEFING ON THAT RECENT OUTBREAK OF GUI JI CHUAN, OR "GHOST-DISEASE FIST"--
HAHH
YOU OKAY, SPOOKY...?
Y-YEAH...
THINK I'M... COMING DOWN WITH SOME-THING...
W-WAIT...! WHAT IF ...THEY REALIZE ...WHAT WE'RE DOING...?
THEY WON'T.
(SADLY,) NO ONE EVEN KNOWS THAT I CAN DO THIS.
AND DON'T WORRY, I WON'T LET YOU MOAN OR GASP OR CRY OUT LOUD (MY NOISY LITTLE SPOOKUMS)...! ♥

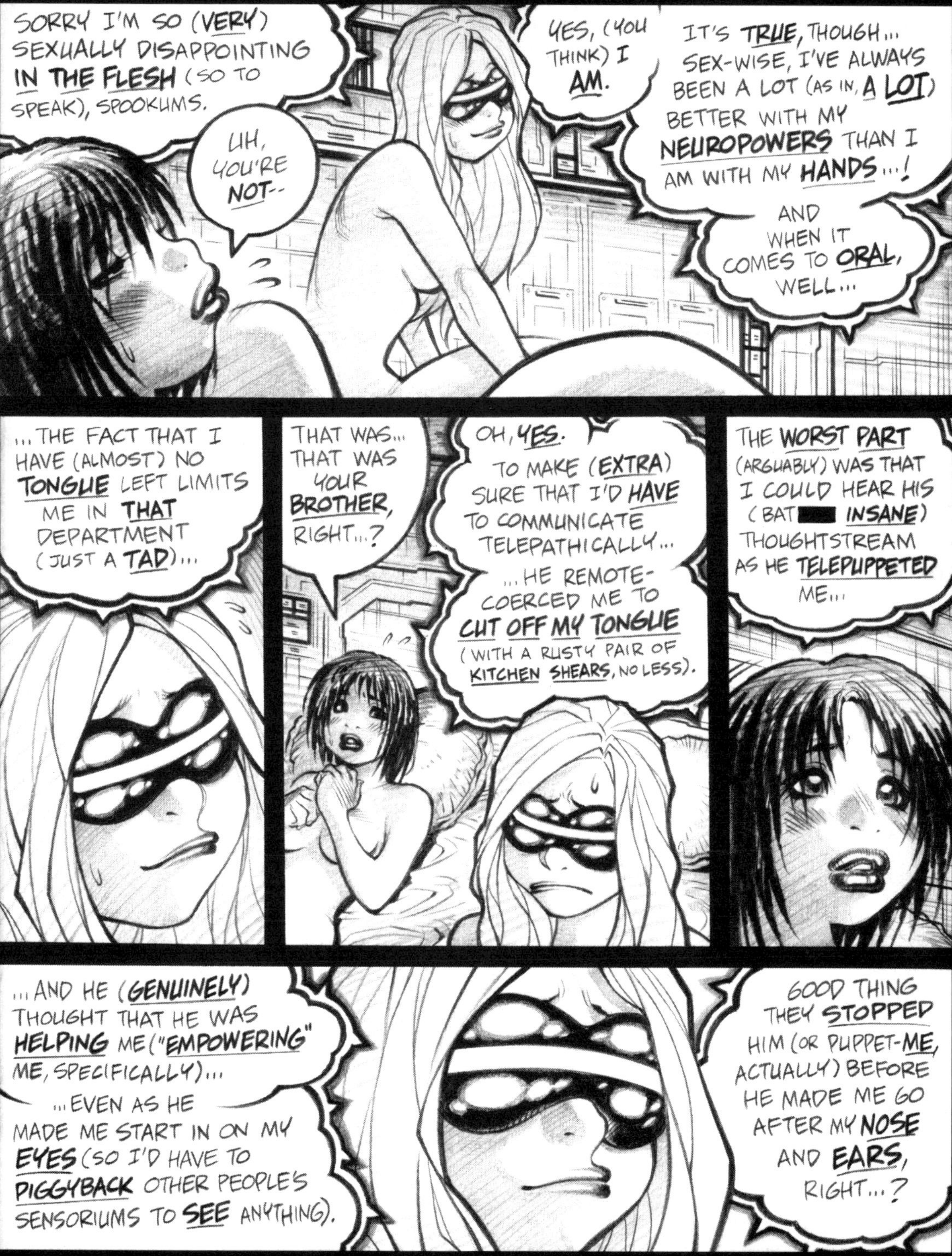
SORRY I'M SO (VERY) SEXUALLY DISAPPOINTING IN THE FLESH (SO TO SPEAK), SPOOKUMS.
UH, YOU'RE NOT--
YES, (YOU THINK) I AM.
IT'S TRUE, THOUGH... SEX-WISE, I'VE ALWAYS BEEN A LOT (AS IN, A LOT) BETTER WITH MY NEUROPOWERS THAN I AM WITH MY HANDS...!
AND WHEN IT COMES TO ORAL, WELL...
...THE FACT THAT I HAVE (ALMOST) NO TONGUE LEFT LIMITS ME IN THAT DEPARTMENT (JUST A TAD)...
THAT WAS... THAT WAS YOUR BROTHER, RIGHT...?
OH, YES.
TO MAKE (EXTRA) SURE THAT I'D HAVE TO COMMUNICATE TELEPATHICALLY...
...HE REMOTE-COERCED ME TO CUT OFF MY TONGUE (WITH A RUSTY PAIR OF KITCHEN SHEARS, NO LESS).
THE WORST PART (ARGUABLY) WAS THAT I COULD HEAR HIS (BAT [redacted] INSANE) THOUGHTSTREAM AS HE TELEPUPPETED ME...
...AND HE (GENUINELY) THOUGHT THAT HE WAS HELPING ME ("EMPOWERING" ME, SPECIFICALLY)...
...EVEN AS HE MADE ME START IN ON MY EYES (SO I'D HAVE TO PIGGYBACK OTHER PEOPLE'S SENSORIUMS TO SEE ANYTHING).
GOOD THING THEY STOPPED HIM (OR PUPPET-ME, ACTUALLY) BEFORE HE MADE ME GO AFTER MY NOSE AND EARS, RIGHT...?

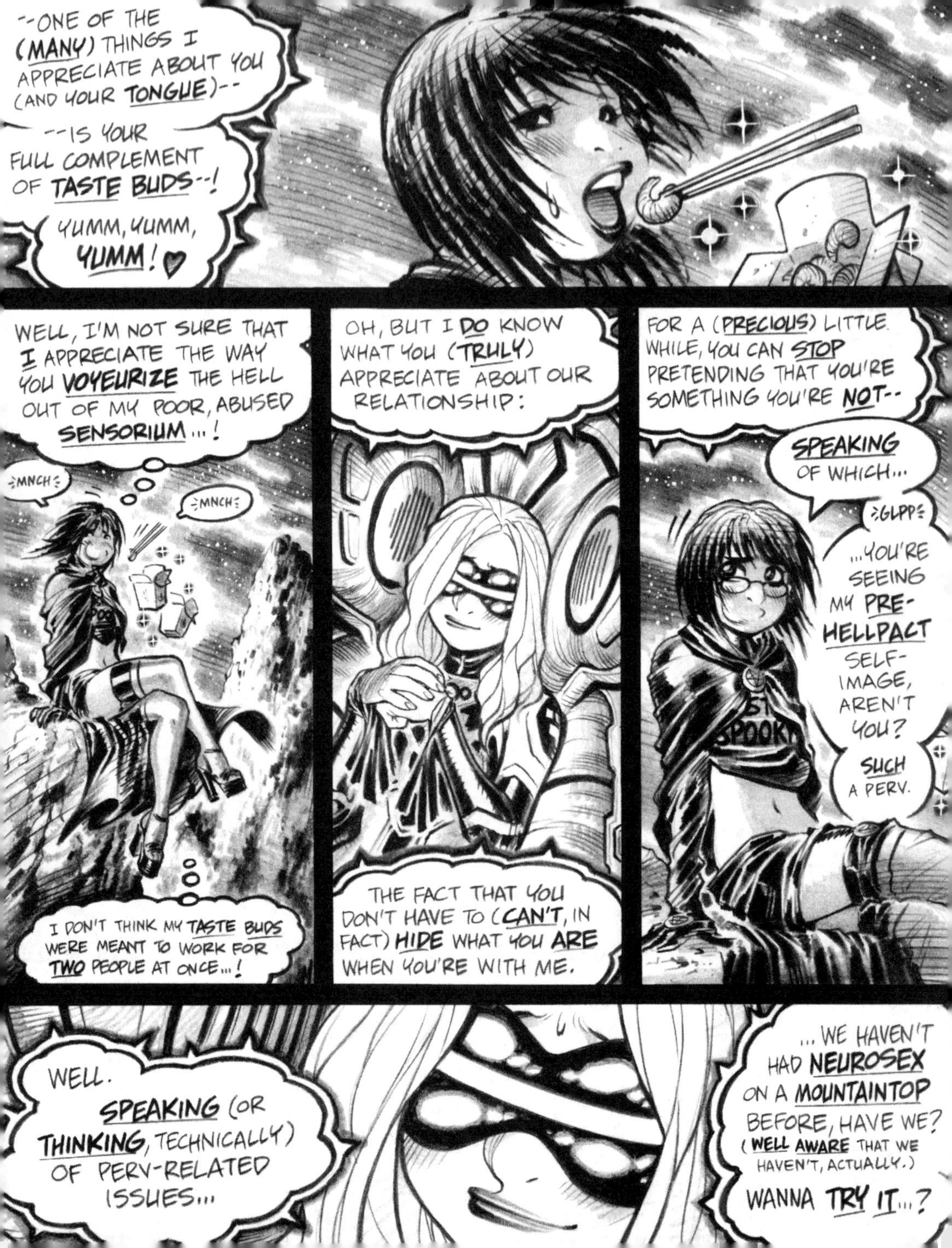
--ONE OF THE (MANY) THINGS I APPRECIATE ABOUT YOU (AND YOUR TONGUE)--
--IS YOUR FULL COMPLEMENT OF TASTE BUDS--!
YUMM, YUMM, YUMM! ♥
WELL, I'M NOT SURE THAT I APPRECIATE THE WAY YOU VOYEURIZE THE HELL OUT OF MY POOR, ABUSED SENSORIUM...!
MNCH
MNCH
I DON'T THINK MY TASTE BUDS WERE MEANT TO WORK FOR TWO PEOPLE AT ONCE...!
OH, BUT I DO KNOW WHAT YOU (TRULY) APPRECIATE ABOUT OUR RELATIONSHIP:
THE FACT THAT YOU DON'T HAVE TO (CAN'T, IN FACT) HIDE WHAT YOU ARE WHEN YOU'RE WITH ME.
FOR A (PRECIOUS) LITTLE WHILE, YOU CAN STOP PRETENDING THAT YOU'RE SOMETHING YOU'RE NOT--
SPEAKING OF WHICH...
GLPP
...YOU'RE SEEING MY PRE-HELLPACT SELF-IMAGE, AREN'T YOU?
SUCH A PERV.
WELL.
SPEAKING (OR THINKING, TECHNICALLY) OF PERV-RELATED ISSUES...
...WE HAVEN'T HAD NEUROSEX ON A MOUNTAINTOP BEFORE, HAVE WE?
(WELL AWARE THAT WE HAVEN'T, ACTUALLY.)
WANNA TRY IT...?

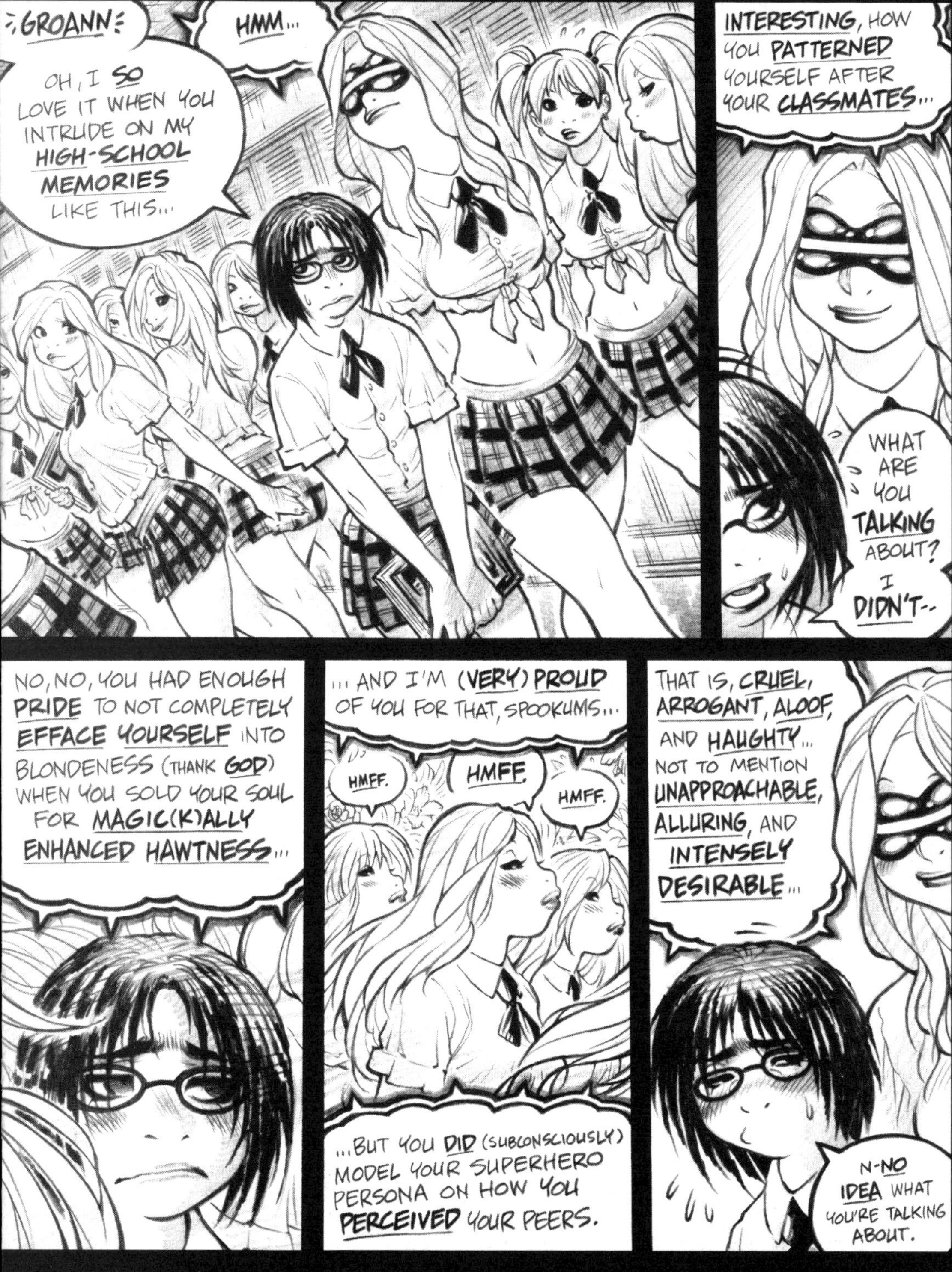

GROANN
HMM...
OH, I SO LOVE IT WHEN YOU INTRUDE ON MY HIGH-SCHOOL MEMORIES LIKE THIS...
INTERESTING, HOW YOU PATTERNED YOURSELF AFTER YOUR CLASSMATES...
WHAT ARE YOU TALKING ABOUT? I DIDN'T--
NO, NO, YOU HAD ENOUGH PRIDE TO NOT COMPLETELY EFFACE YOURSELF INTO BLONDENESS (THANK GOD) WHEN YOU SOLD YOUR SOUL FOR MAGIC(K)ALLY ENHANCED HAWTNESS...
...AND I'M (VERY) PROUD OF YOU FOR THAT, SPOOKUMS...
HMFF.
HMFF.
HMFF.
...BUT YOU DID (SUBCONSCIOUSLY) MODEL YOUR SUPERHERO PERSONA ON HOW YOU PERCEIVED YOUR PEERS.
THAT IS, CRUEL, ARROGANT, ALOOF, AND HAUGHTY... NOT TO MENTION UNAPPROACHABLE, ALLURING, AND INTENSELY DESIRABLE...
N-NO IDEA WHAT YOU'RE TALKING ABOUT.

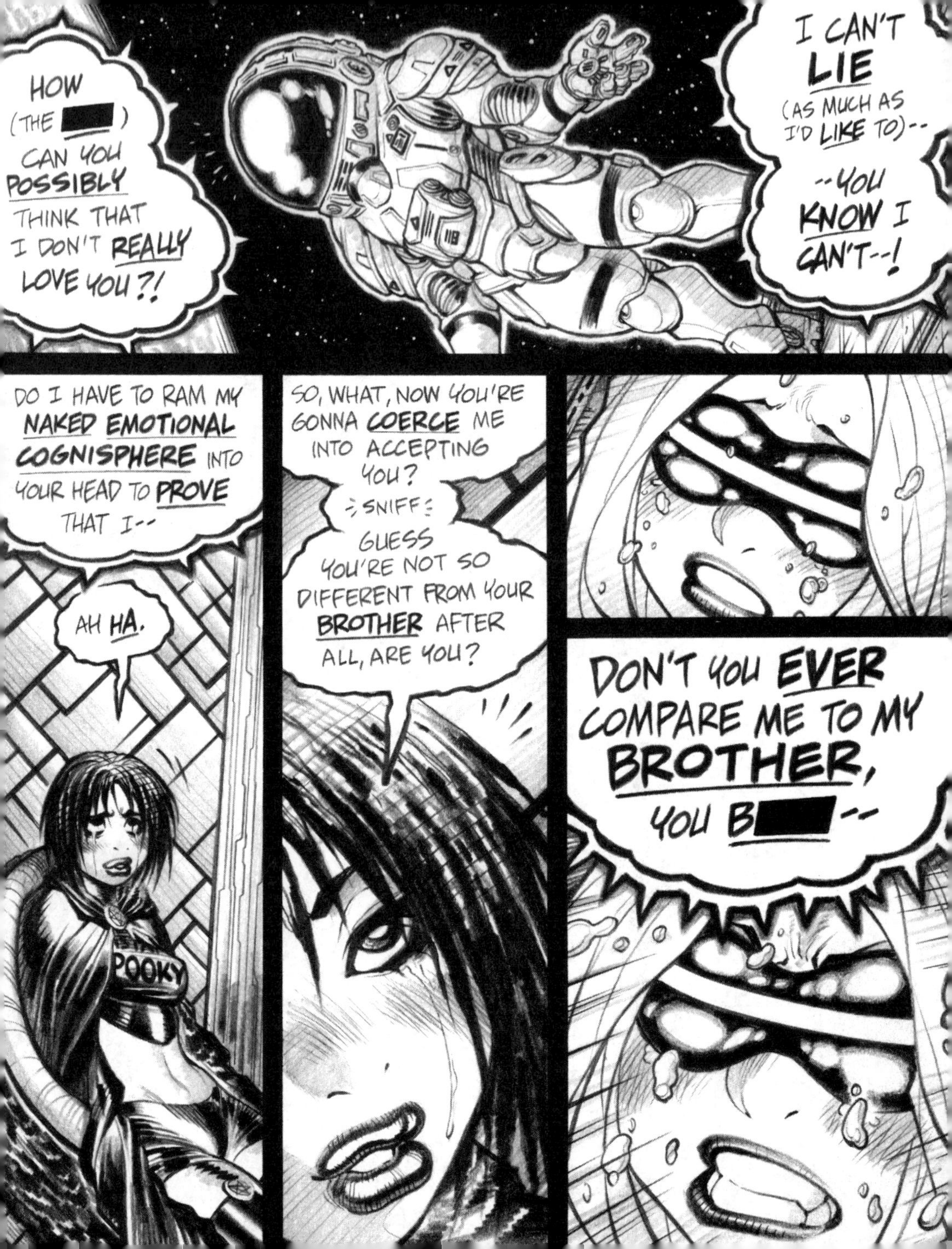
HOW (THE [redacted]) CAN YOU POSSIBLY THINK THAT I DON'T REALLY LOVE YOU?!
I CAN'T LIE (AS MUCH AS I'D LIKE TO)--
--YOU KNOW I CAN'T--!
DO I HAVE TO RAM MY NAKED EMOTIONAL COGNISPHERE INTO YOUR HEAD TO PROVE THAT I--
AH HA.
SO, WHAT, NOW YOU'RE GONNA COERCE ME INTO ACCEPTING YOU?
SNIFF
GUESS YOU'RE NOT SO DIFFERENT FROM YOUR BROTHER AFTER ALL, ARE YOU?
DON'T YOU EVER COMPARE ME TO MY BROTHER, YOU B[redacted]--
POOKY

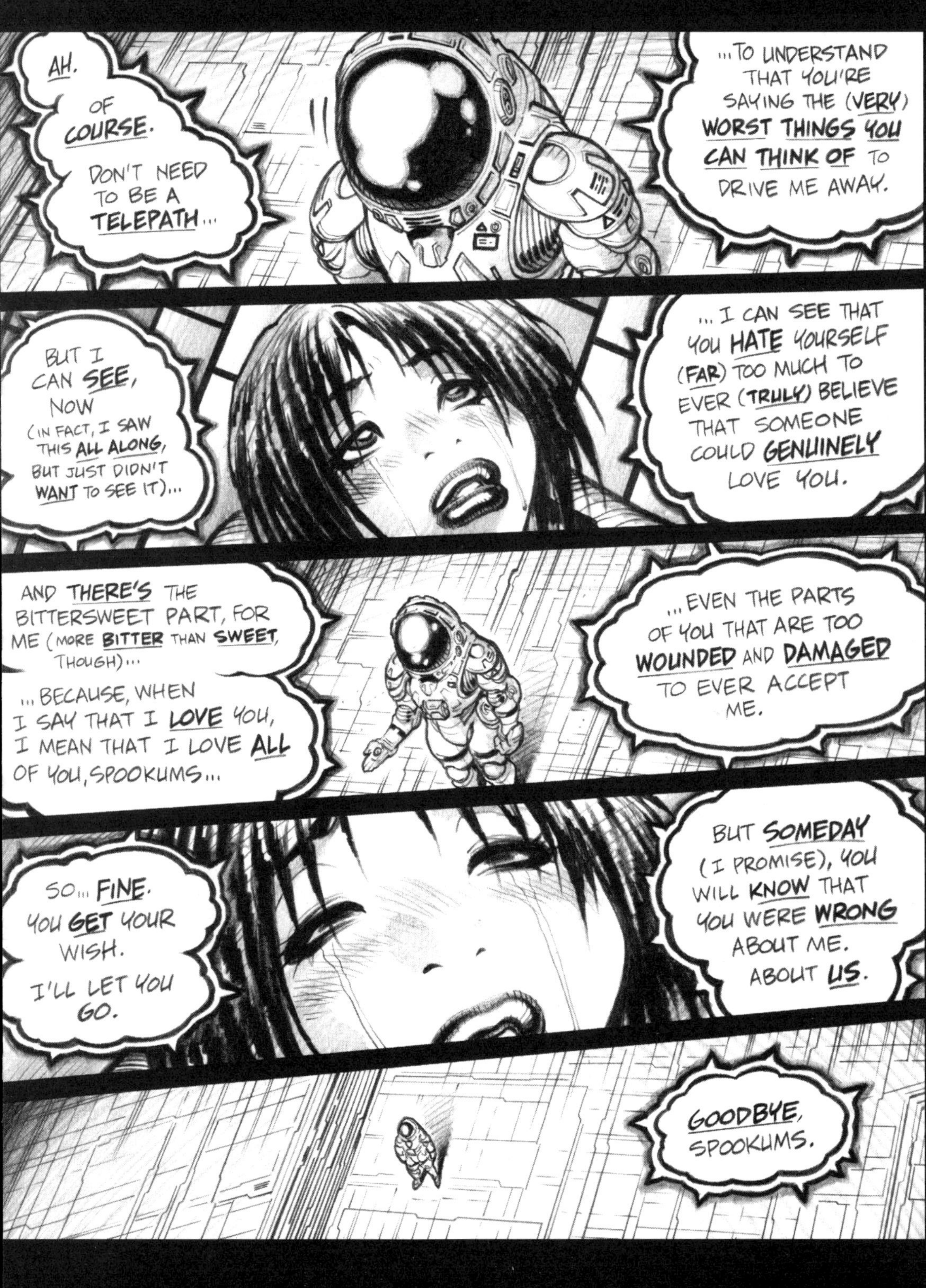
AH. OF COURSE. DON'T NEED TO BE A TELEPATH...
...TO UNDERSTAND THAT YOU'RE SAYING THE (VERY) WORST THINGS YOU CAN THINK OF TO DRIVE ME AWAY.
BUT I CAN SEE, NOW (IN FACT, I SAW THIS ALL ALONG, BUT JUST DIDN'T WANT TO SEE IT)...
...I CAN SEE THAT YOU HATE YOURSELF (FAR) TOO MUCH TO EVER (TRULY) BELIEVE THAT SOMEONE COULD GENUINELY LOVE YOU.
AND THERE'S THE BITTERSWEET PART, FOR ME (MORE BITTER THAN SWEET, THOUGH)...
...BECAUSE, WHEN I SAY THAT I LOVE YOU, I MEAN THAT I LOVE ALL OF YOU, SPOOKUMS...
...EVEN THE PARTS OF YOU THAT ARE TOO WOUNDED AND DAMAGED TO EVER ACCEPT ME.
SO... FINE. YOU GET YOUR WISH.
I'LL LET YOU GO.
BUT SOMEDAY (I PROMISE), YOU WILL KNOW THAT YOU WERE WRONG ABOUT ME.
ABOUT US.
GOODBYE, SPOOKUMS.

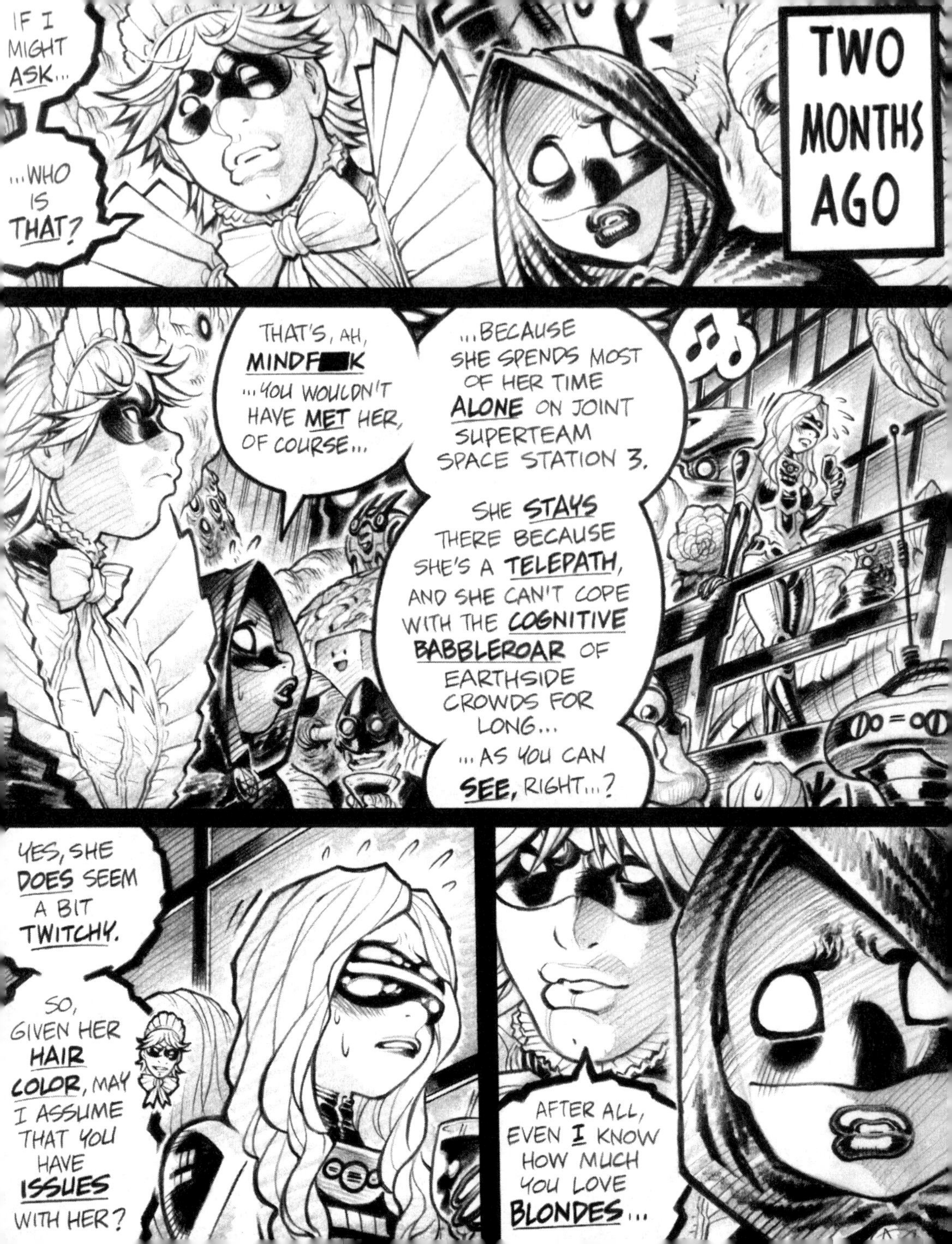
IF I MIGHT ASK...
...WHO IS THAT?
TWO MONTHS AGO
THAT'S, AH, MINDF[redacted]K ...YOU WOULDN'T HAVE MET HER, OF COURSE...
...BECAUSE SHE SPENDS MOST OF HER TIME ALONE ON JOINT SUPERTEAM SPACE STATION 3.
SHE STAYS THERE BECAUSE SHE'S A TELEPATH, AND SHE CAN'T COPE WITH THE COGNITIVE BABBLEROAR OF EARTHSIDE CROWDS FOR LONG...
...AS YOU CAN SEE, RIGHT...?
YES, SHE DOES SEEM A BIT TWITCHY.
SO, GIVEN HER HAIR COLOR, MAY I ASSUME THAT YOU HAVE ISSUES WITH HER?
AFTER ALL, EVEN I KNOW HOW MUCH YOU LOVE BLONDES...

Empowered™

Outrageouslah Erroneous

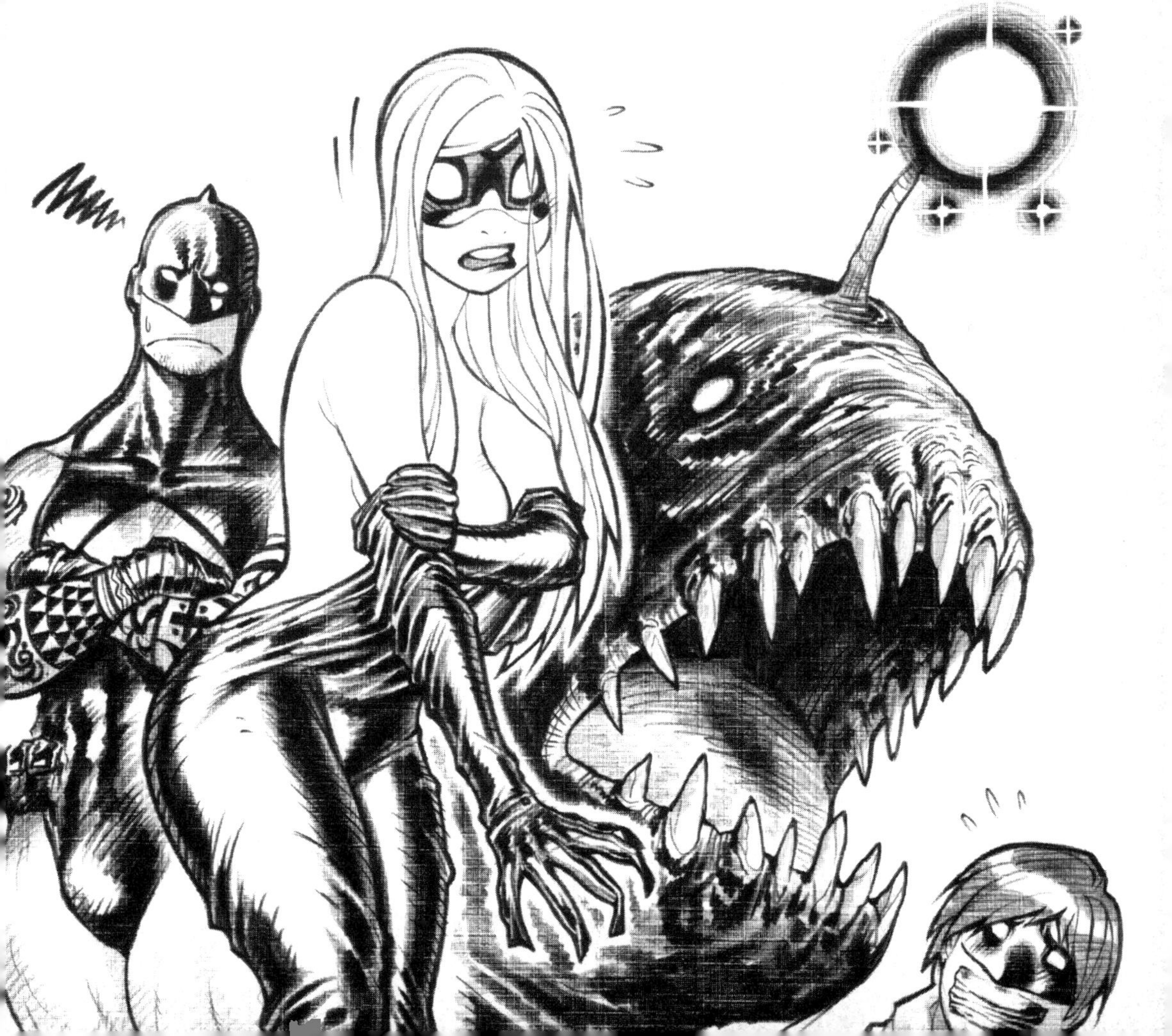

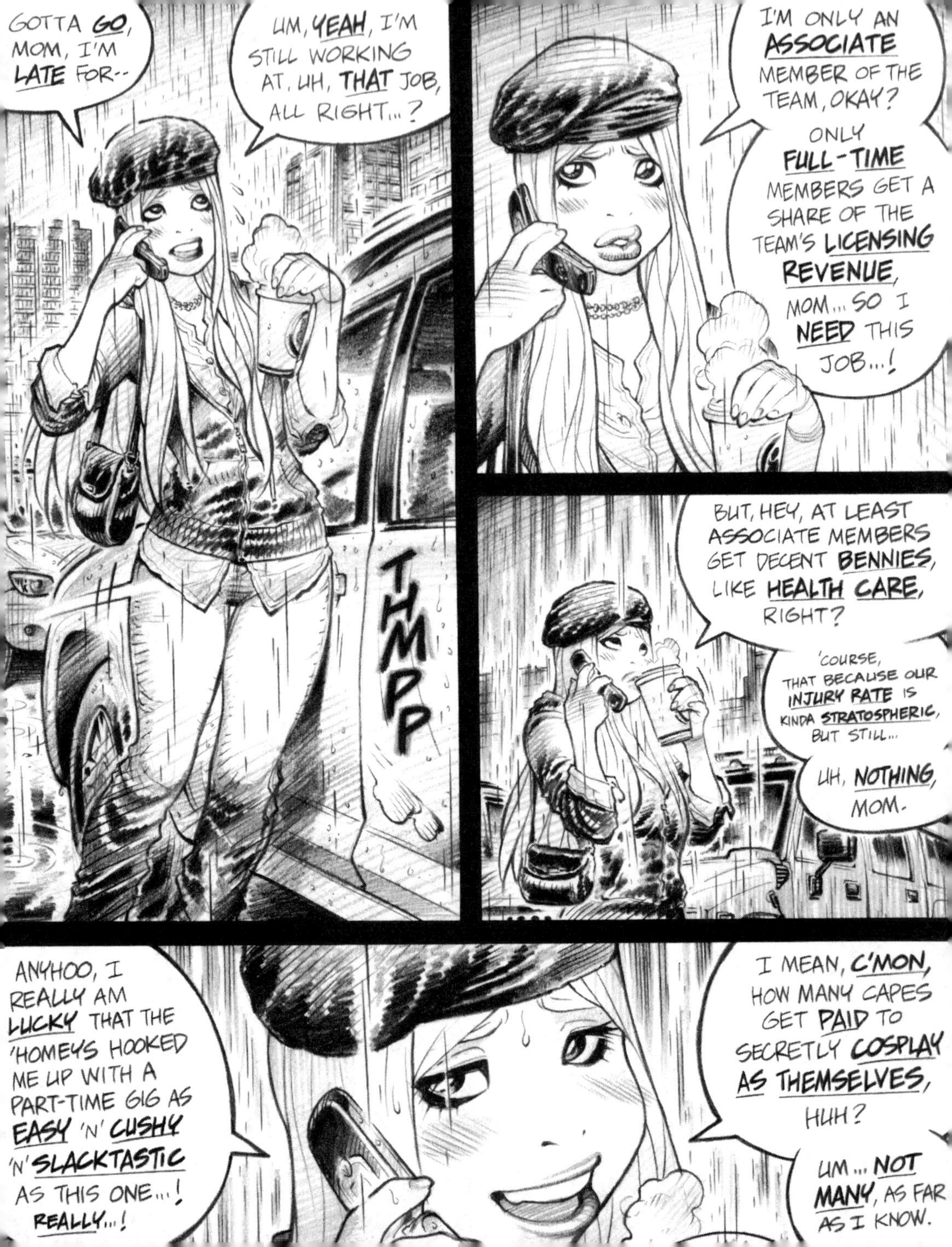
GOTTA GO, MOM, I'M LATE FOR--
UM, YEAH, I'M STILL WORKING AT, UH, THAT JOB, ALL RIGHT...?
THMPP
I'M ONLY AN ASSOCIATE MEMBER OF THE TEAM, OKAY?
ONLY FULL-TIME MEMBERS GET A SHARE OF THE TEAM'S LICENSING REVENUE, MOM... SO I NEED THIS JOB...!
BUT, HEY, AT LEAST ASSOCIATE MEMBERS GET DECENT BENNIES, LIKE HEALTH CARE, RIGHT?
'COURSE, THAT BECAUSE OUR INJURY RATE IS KINDA STRATOSPHERIC, BUT STILL...
UH, NOTHING, MOM.
ANYHOO, I REALLY AM LUCKY THAT THE 'HOMEYS HOOKED ME UP WITH A PART-TIME GIG AS EASY 'N' CUSHY 'N' SLACKTASTIC AS THIS ONE...! REALLY...!
I MEAN, C'MON, HOW MANY CAPES GET PAID TO SECRETLY COSPLAY AS THEMSELVES, HUH?
UM... NOT MANY, AS FAR AS I KNOW.

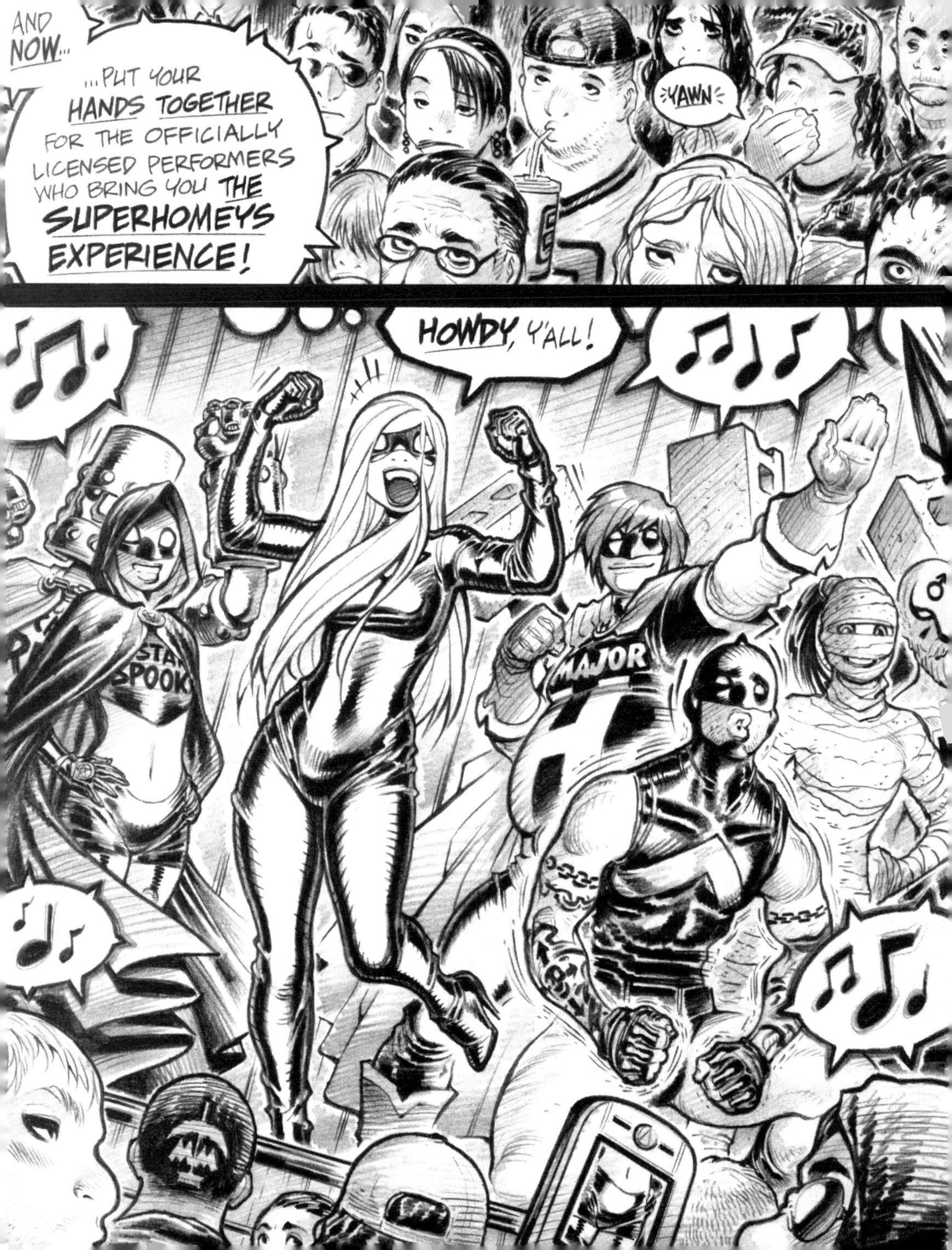
AND NOW...
...PUT YOUR HANDS TOGETHER FOR THE OFFICIALLY LICENSED PERFORMERS WHO BRING YOU THE SUPERHOMEYS EXPERIENCE!
YAWN
HOWDY, Y'ALL!
MAJOR

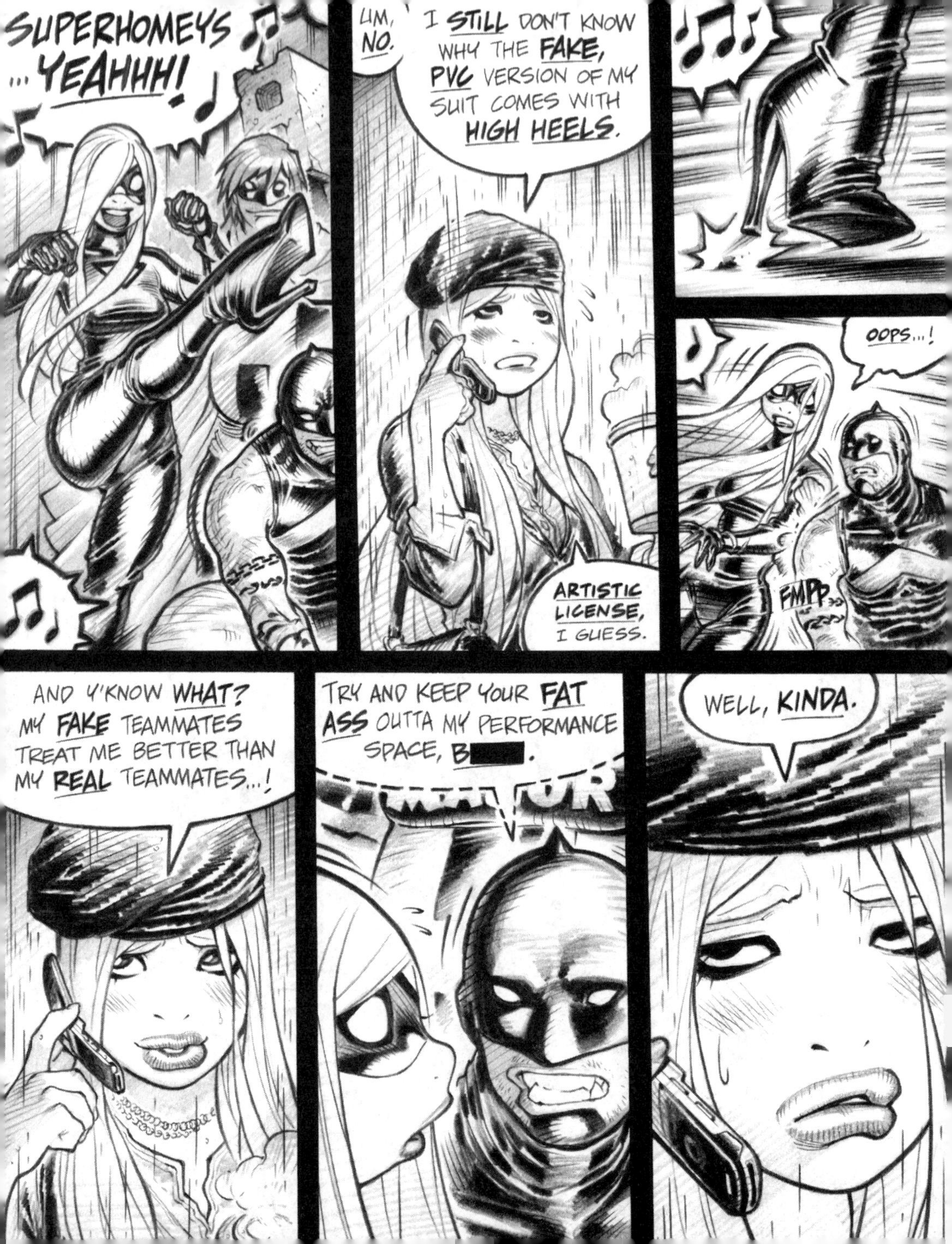
SUPERHOMEYS ...YEAHHH!
UM, NO.
I STILL DON'T KNOW WHY THE FAKE, PVC VERSION OF MY SUIT COMES WITH HIGH HEELS.
ARTISTIC LICENSE, I GUESS.
OOPS...!
FMPP
AND Y'KNOW WHAT? MY FAKE TEAMMATES TREAT ME BETTER THAN MY REAL TEAMMATES...!
TRY AND KEEP YOUR FAT ASS OUTTA MY PERFORMANCE SPACE, B[redacted].
WELL, KINDA.

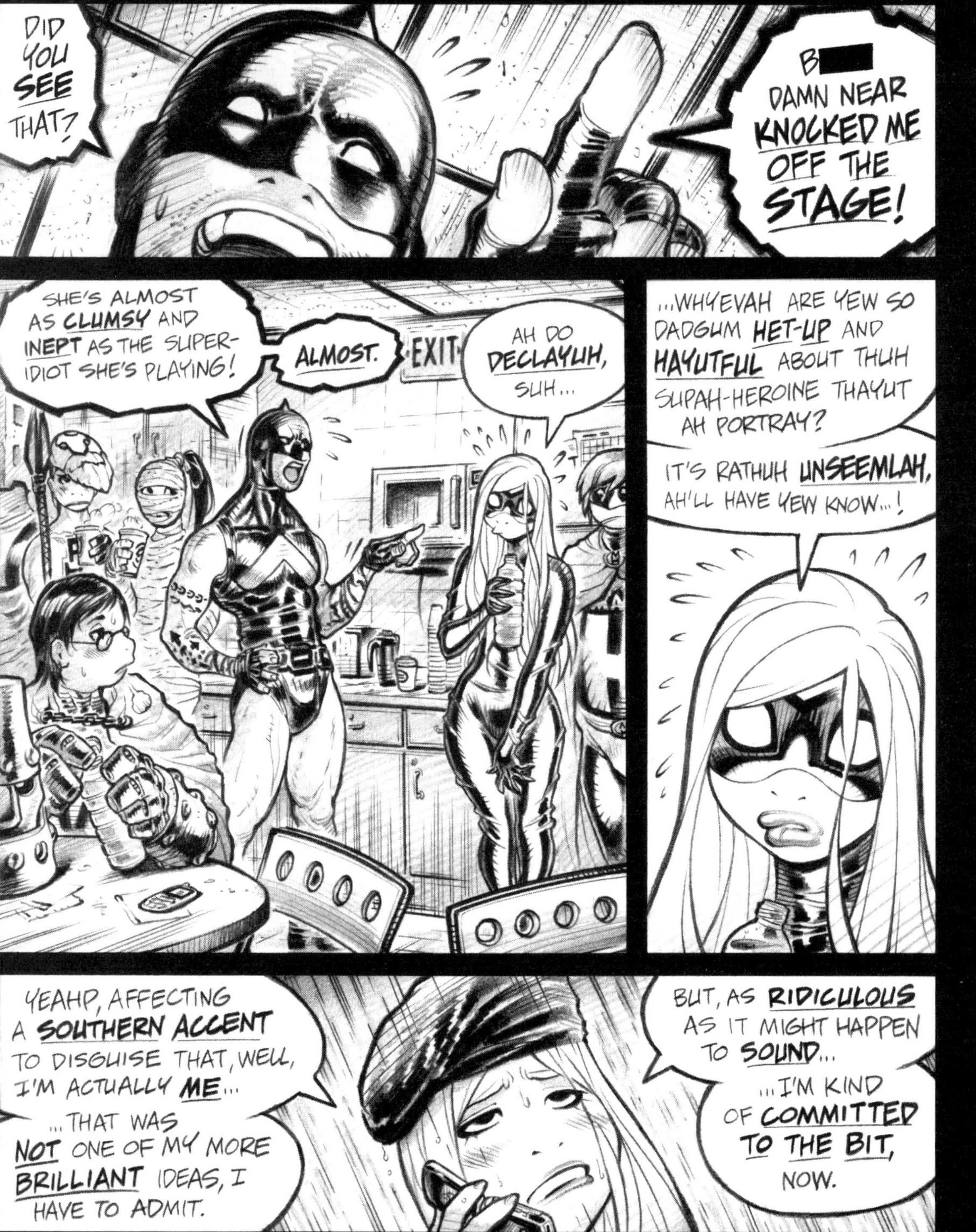
DID YOU SEE THAT?
B[redacted] DAMN NEAR KNOCKED ME OFF THE STAGE!
SHE'S ALMOST AS CLUMSY AND INEPT AS THE SUPER-IDIOT SHE'S PLAYING!
ALMOST.
EXIT
AH DO DECLAYUH, SUH...
...WHYEVAH ARE YEW SO DADGUM HET-UP AND HAYUTFUL ABOUT THUH SUPAH-HEROINE THAYUT AH PORTRAY?
IT'S RATHUH UNSEEMLAH, AH'LL HAVE YEW KNOW...!
YEAHP, AFFECTING A SOUTHERN ACCENT TO DISGUISE THAT, WELL, I'M ACTUALLY ME...
...THAT WAS NOT ONE OF MY MORE BRILLIANT IDEAS, I HAVE TO ADMIT.
BUT, AS RIDICULOUS AS IT MIGHT HAPPEN TO SOUND...
...I'M KIND OF COMMITTED TO THE BIT, NOW.

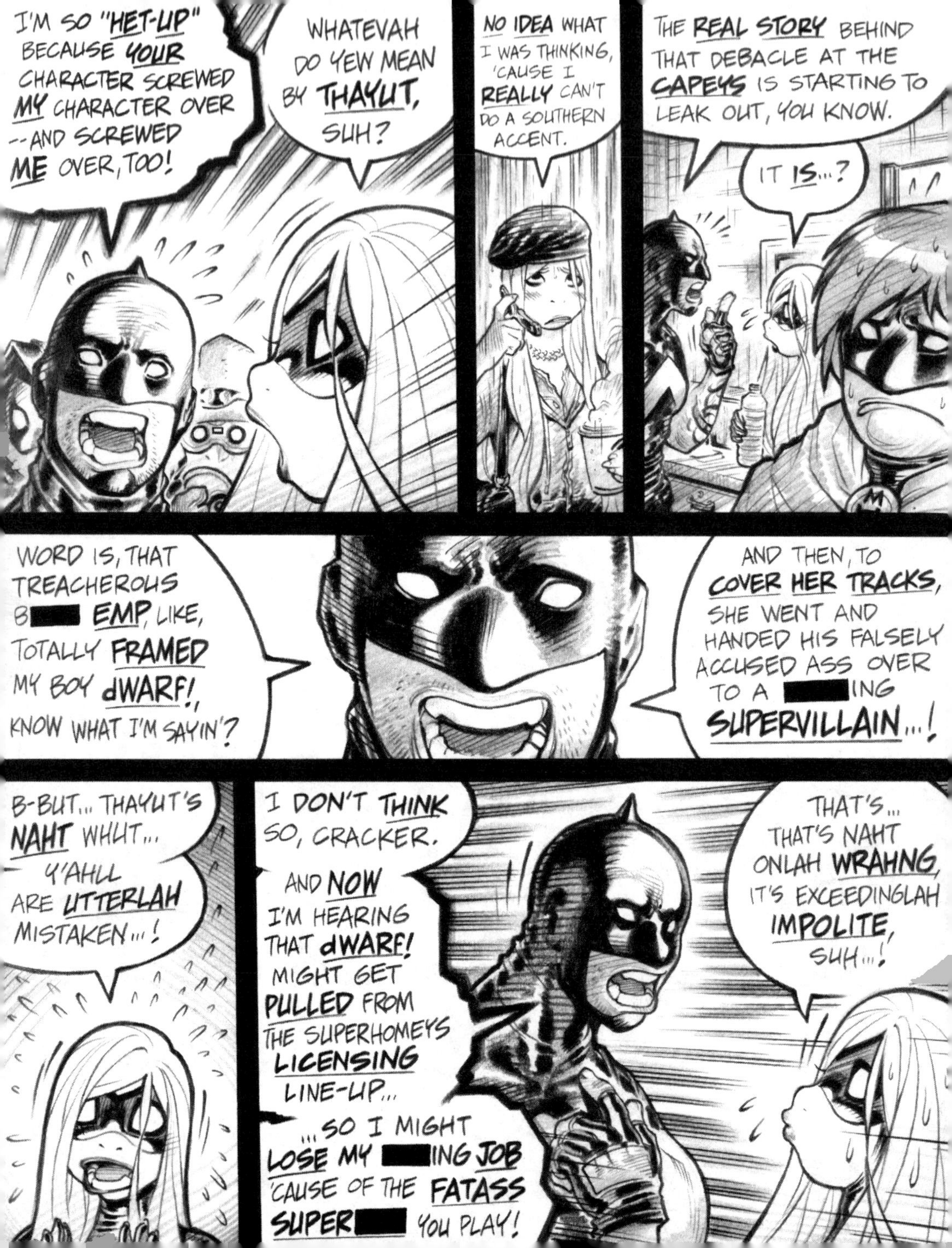
I'M SO "HET-UP" BECAUSE YOUR CHARACTER SCREWED MY CHARACTER OVER --AND SCREWED ME OVER, TOO!
WHATEVAH DO YEW MEAN BY THAYUT, SUH?
NO IDEA WHAT I WAS THINKING, 'CAUSE I REALLY CAN'T DO A SOUTHERN ACCENT.
THE REAL STORY BEHIND THAT DEBACLE AT THE CAPEYS IS STARTING TO LEAK OUT, YOU KNOW.
IT IS...?
WORD IS, THAT TREACHEROUS B[redacted] EMP, LIKE, TOTALLY FRAMED MY BOY dWARF!, KNOW WHAT I'M SAYIN'?
AND THEN, TO COVER HER TRACKS, SHE WENT AND HANDED HIS FALSELY ACCUSED ASS OVER TO A [redacted]ING SUPERVILLAIN...!
B-BUT... THAYUT'S NAHT WHUT... Y'AHLL ARE UTTERLAH MISTAKEN...!
I DON'T THINK SO, CRACKER.
THAT'S... THAT'S NAHT ONLAH WRAHNG, IT'S EXCEEDINGLAH IMPOLITE, SUH...!
AND NOW I'M HEARING THAT dWARF! MIGHT GET PULLED FROM THE SUPERHOMEYS LICENSING LINE-UP...
...SO I MIGHT LOSE MY [redacted]ING JOB 'CAUSE OF THE FATASS SUPER[redacted] YOU PLAY!

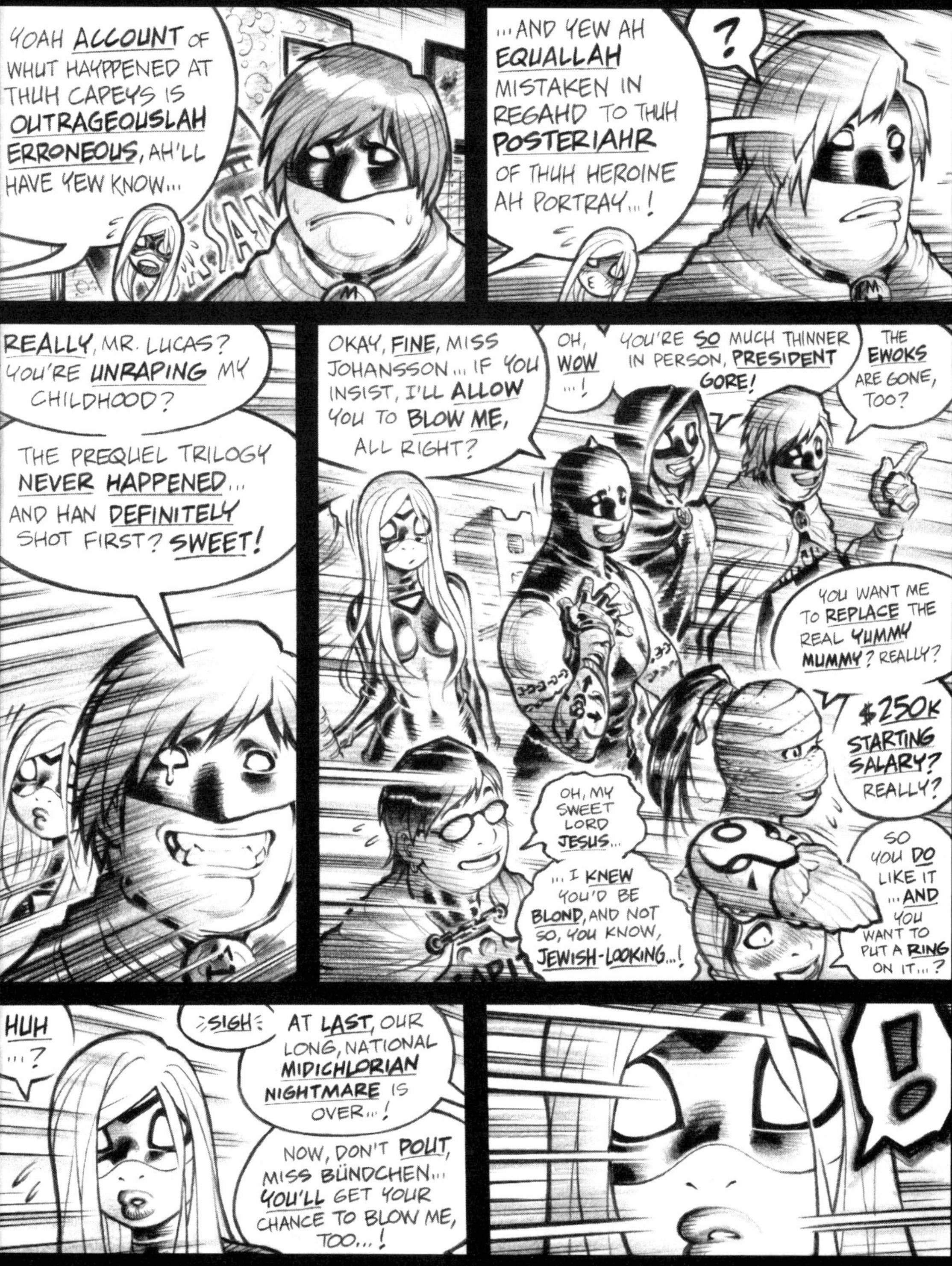
YOAH ACCOUNT OF WHUT HAYPPENED AT THUH CAPEYS IS OUTRAGEOUSLAH ERRONEOUS, AH'LL HAVE YEW KNOW...
...AND YEW AH EQUALLAH MISTAKEN IN REGAHD TO THUH POSTERIAHR OF THUH HEROINE AH PORTRAY...!
?
REALLY, MR. LUCAS? YOU'RE UNRAPING MY CHILDHOOD?
THE PREQUEL TRILOGY NEVER HAPPENED... AND HAN DEFINITELY SHOT FIRST? SWEET!
OKAY, FINE, MISS JOHANSSON... IF YOU INSIST, I'LL ALLOW YOU TO BLOW ME, ALL RIGHT?
OH, WOW ...!
YOU'RE SO MUCH THINNER IN PERSON, PRESIDENT GORE!
THE EWOKS ARE GONE, TOO?
YOU WANT ME TO REPLACE THE REAL YUMMY MUMMY? REALLY?
$250K STARTING SALARY? REALLY?
OH, MY SWEET LORD JESUS...
...I KNEW YOU'D BE BLOND, AND NOT SO, YOU KNOW, JEWISH-LOOKING...!
SO YOU DO LIKE IT ...AND YOU WANT TO PUT A RING ON IT...?
HUH ...?
SIGH
AT LAST, OUR LONG, NATIONAL MIDICHLORIAN NIGHTMARE IS OVER...!
NOW, DON'T POUT, MISS BÜNDCHEN... YOU'LL GET YOUR CHANCE TO BLOW ME, TOO...!
!

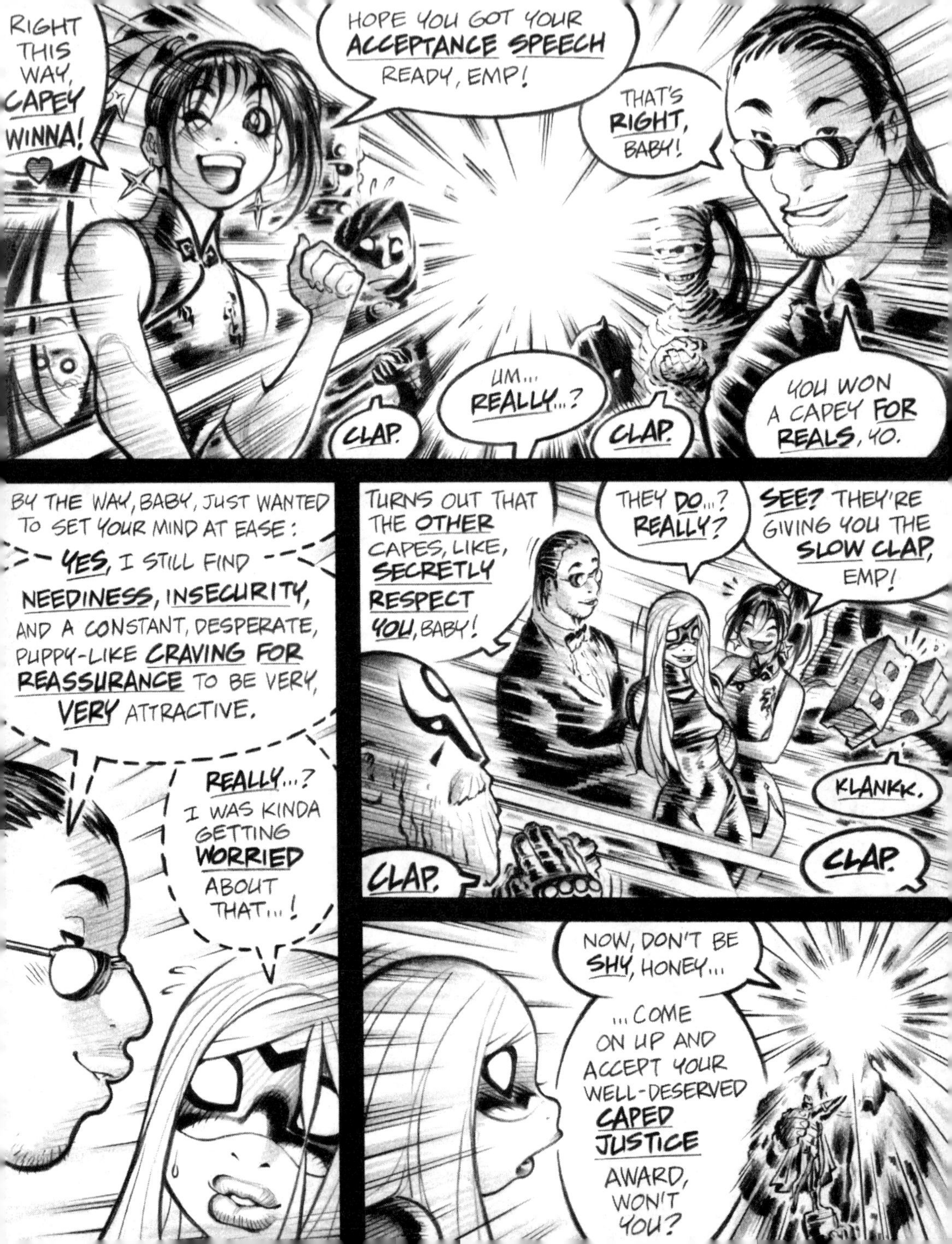

RIGHT THIS WAY, CAPEY WINNA!
HOPE YOU GOT YOUR ACCEPTANCE SPEECH READY, EMP!
THAT'S RIGHT, BABY!
UM... REALLY...?
CLAP.
CLAP.
YOU WON A CAPEY FOR REALS, YO.
BY THE WAY, BABY, JUST WANTED TO SET YOUR MIND AT EASE:
YES, I STILL FIND NEEDINESS, INSECURITY, AND A CONSTANT, DESPERATE, PUPPY-LIKE CRAVING FOR REASSURANCE TO BE VERY, VERY ATTRACTIVE.
REALLY...? I WAS KINDA GETTING WORRIED ABOUT THAT...!
TURNS OUT THAT THE OTHER CAPES, LIKE, SECRETLY RESPECT YOU, BABY!
THEY DO...? REALLY?
SEE? THEY'RE GIVING YOU THE SLOW CLAP, EMP!
KLANKK.
CLAP.
CLAP.
NOW, DON'T BE SHY, HONEY...
...COME ON UP AND ACCEPT YOUR WELL-DESERVED CAPED JUSTICE AWARD, WON'T YOU?

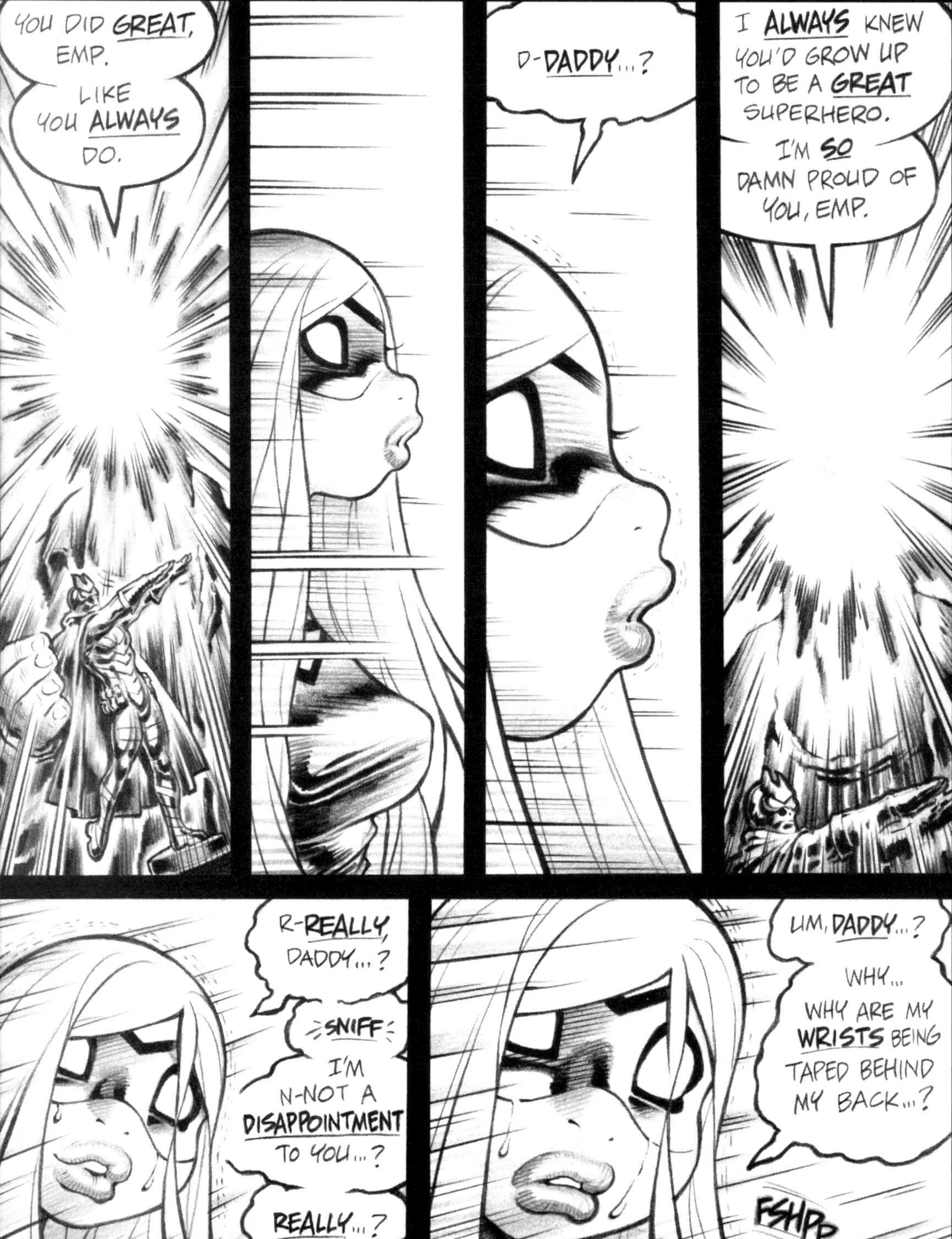
YOU DID GREAT, EMP.
LIKE YOU ALWAYS DO.
D-DADDY...?
I ALWAYS KNEW YOU'D GROW UP TO BE A GREAT SUPERHERO.
I'M SO DAMN PROUD OF YOU, EMP.
R-REALLY, DADDY...?
SNIFF
I'M N-NOT A DISAPPOINTMENT TO YOU...?
REALLY...?
UM, DADDY...?
WHY...
WHY ARE MY WRISTS BEING TAPED BEHIND MY BACK...?
FSHPP

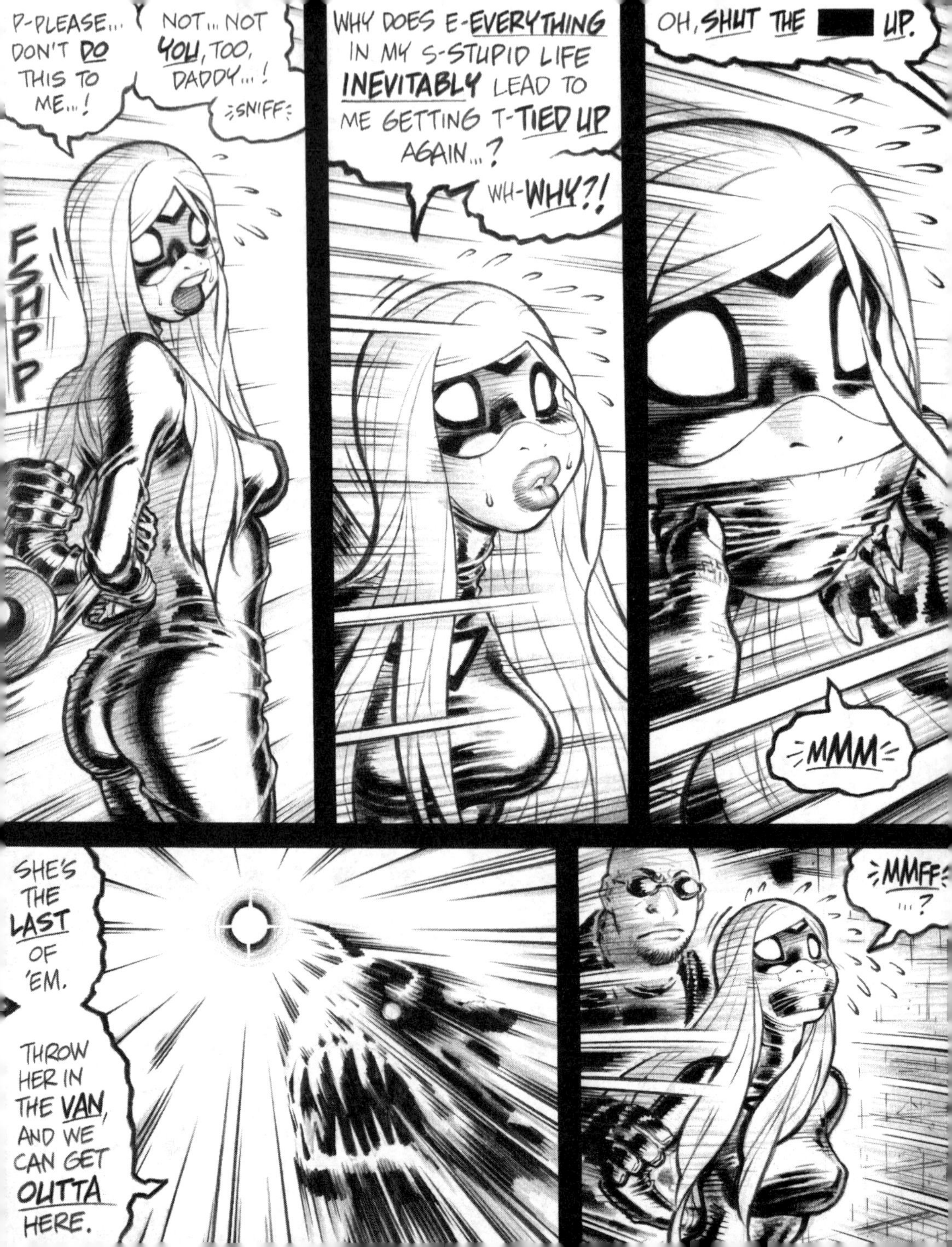
P-PLEASE... DON'T DO THIS TO ME...!
NOT... NOT YOU, TOO, DADDY...!
SNIFF
FSHPP
WHY DOES E-EVERYTHING IN MY S-STUPID LIFE INEVITABLY LEAD TO ME GETTING T-TIED UP AGAIN...?
WH-WHY?!
OH, SHUT THE [redacted] UP.
MMM
SHE'S THE LAST OF 'EM.
THROW HER IN THE VAN, AND WE CAN GET OUTTA HERE.
MMFF ...?

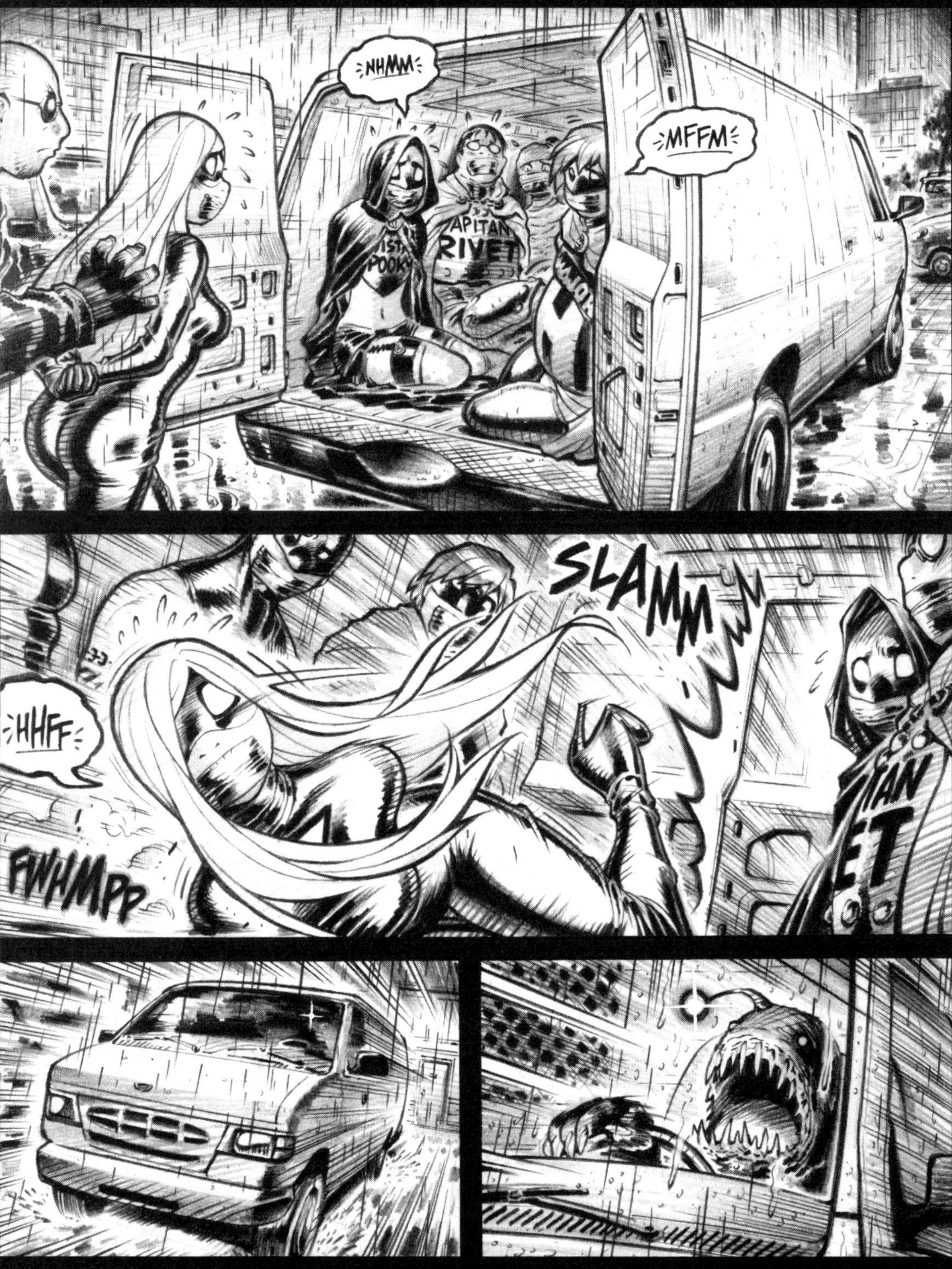
NHMM
MFFM
1ST
POOKY
APITAN
RIVET
SLAMM
HHFF
FWHMPP
TAN
ET

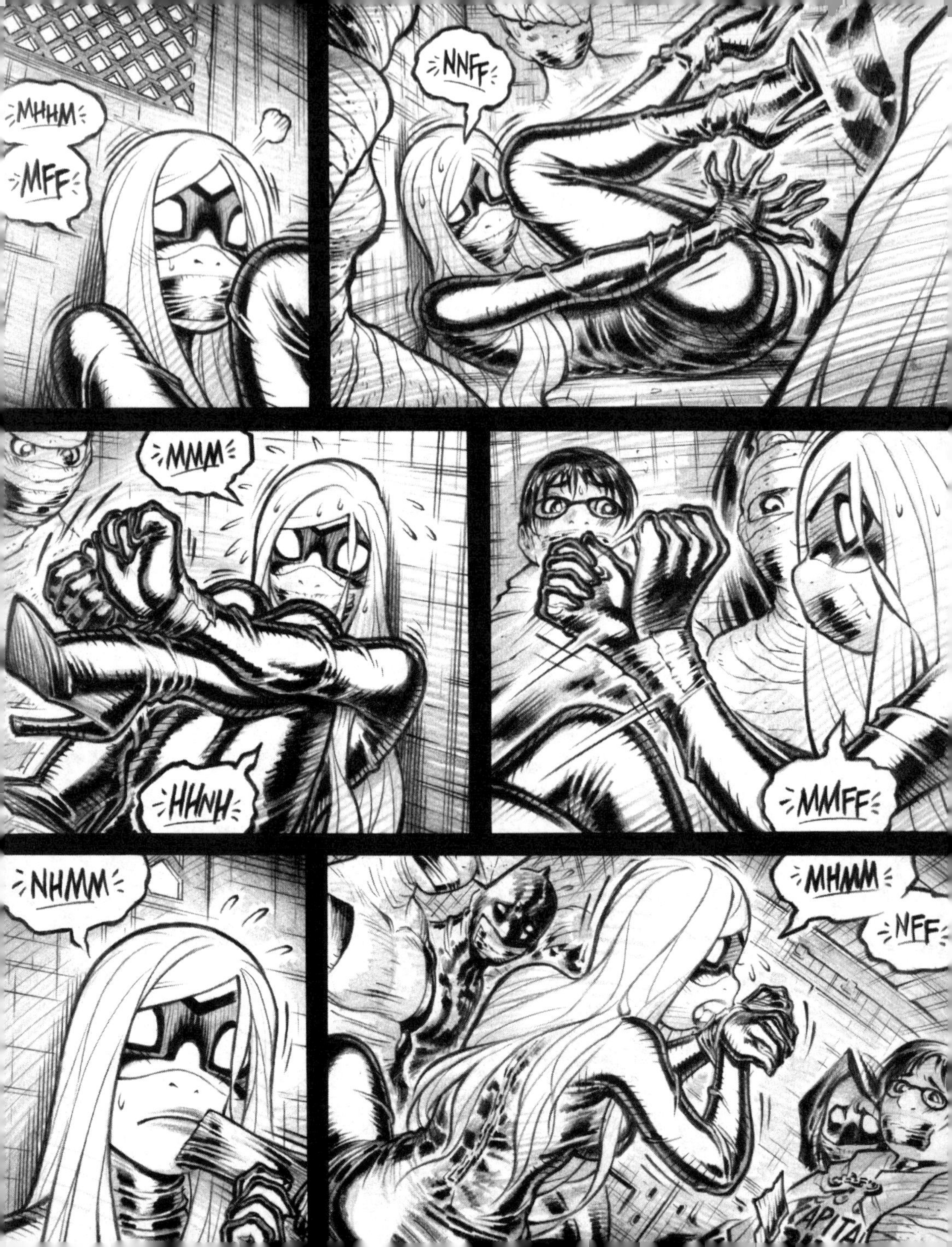
MHHM
MFF
NNFF
MMM
HHNH
MMFF
NHMM
MHMM
NFF

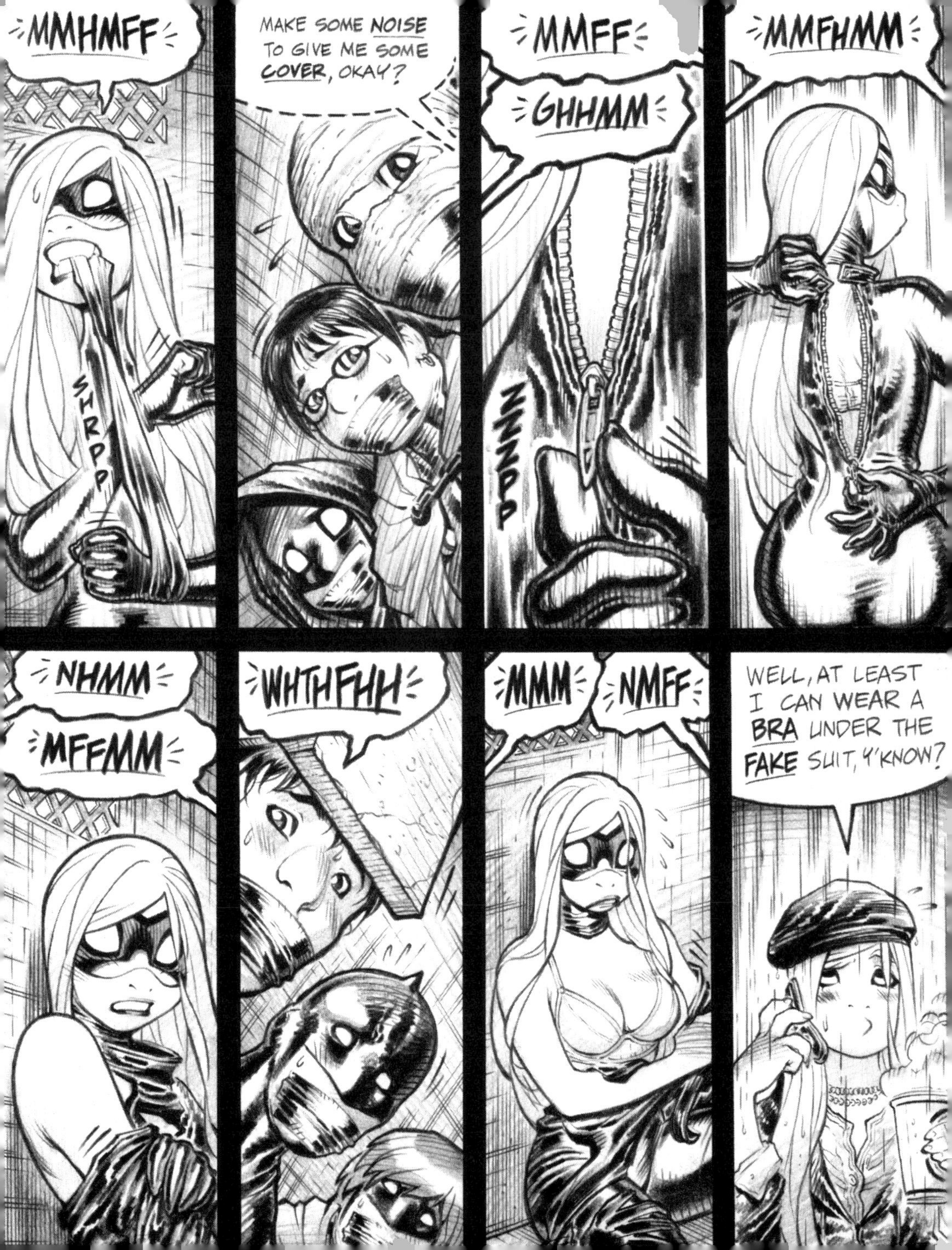
MMHMFF
SHRPP
MAKE SOME NOISE TO GIVE ME SOME COVER, OKAY?
MMFF
GHHMM
ZZZPP
MMFHMM
NHMM
MFFMM
WHTHFHH
MMM
NMFF
WELL, AT LEAST I CAN WEAR A BRA UNDER THE FAKE SUIT, Y'KNOW?

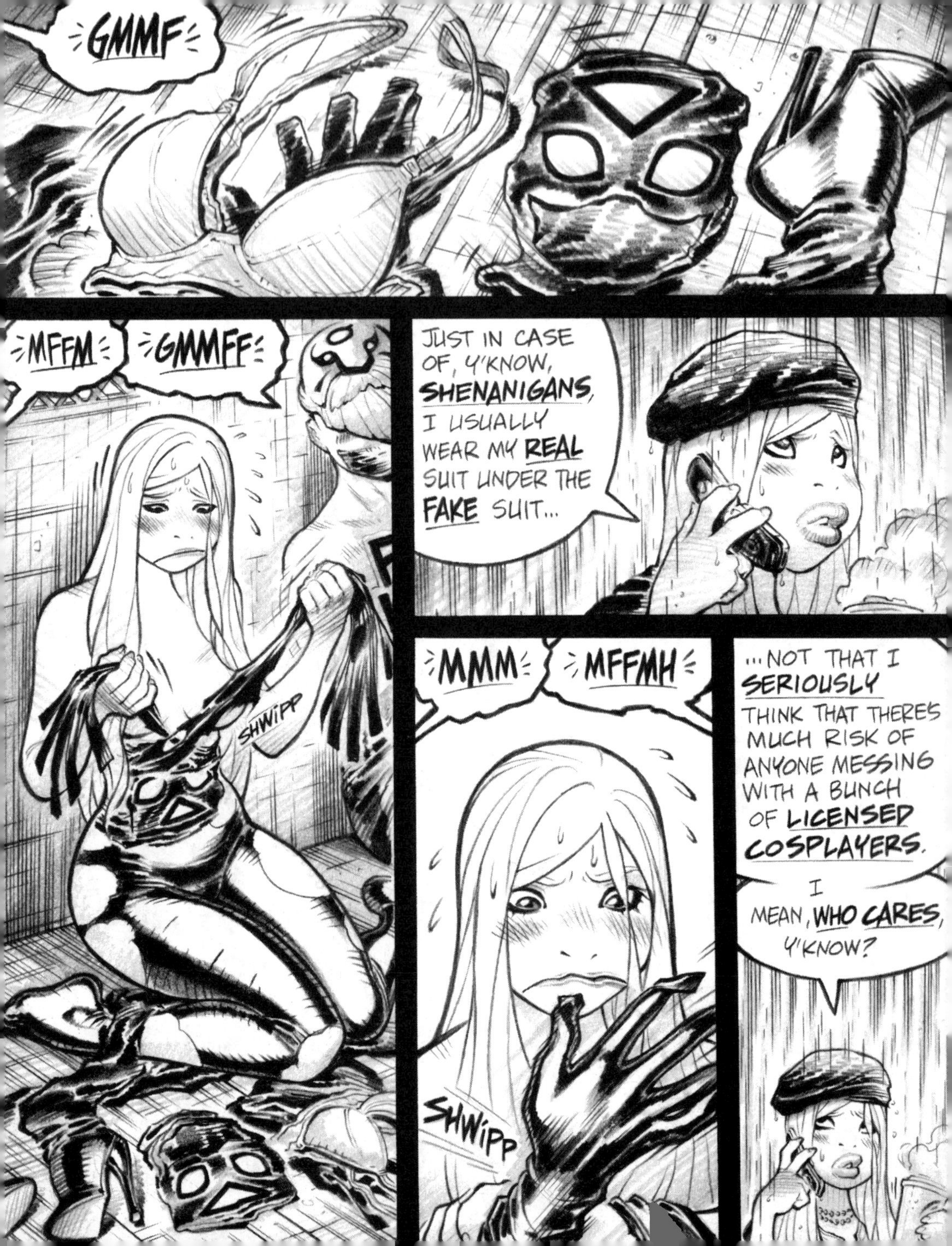
GMMF
MFFM
GMMFF
JUST IN CASE OF, Y'KNOW, SHENANIGANS, I USUALLY WEAR MY REAL SUIT UNDER THE FAKE SUIT...
SHWIPP
MMM
MFFMH
...NOT THAT I SERIOUSLY THINK THAT THERE'S MUCH RISK OF ANYONE MESSING WITH A BUNCH OF LICENSED COSPLAYERS.
I MEAN, WHO CARES, Y'KNOW?
SHWIPP

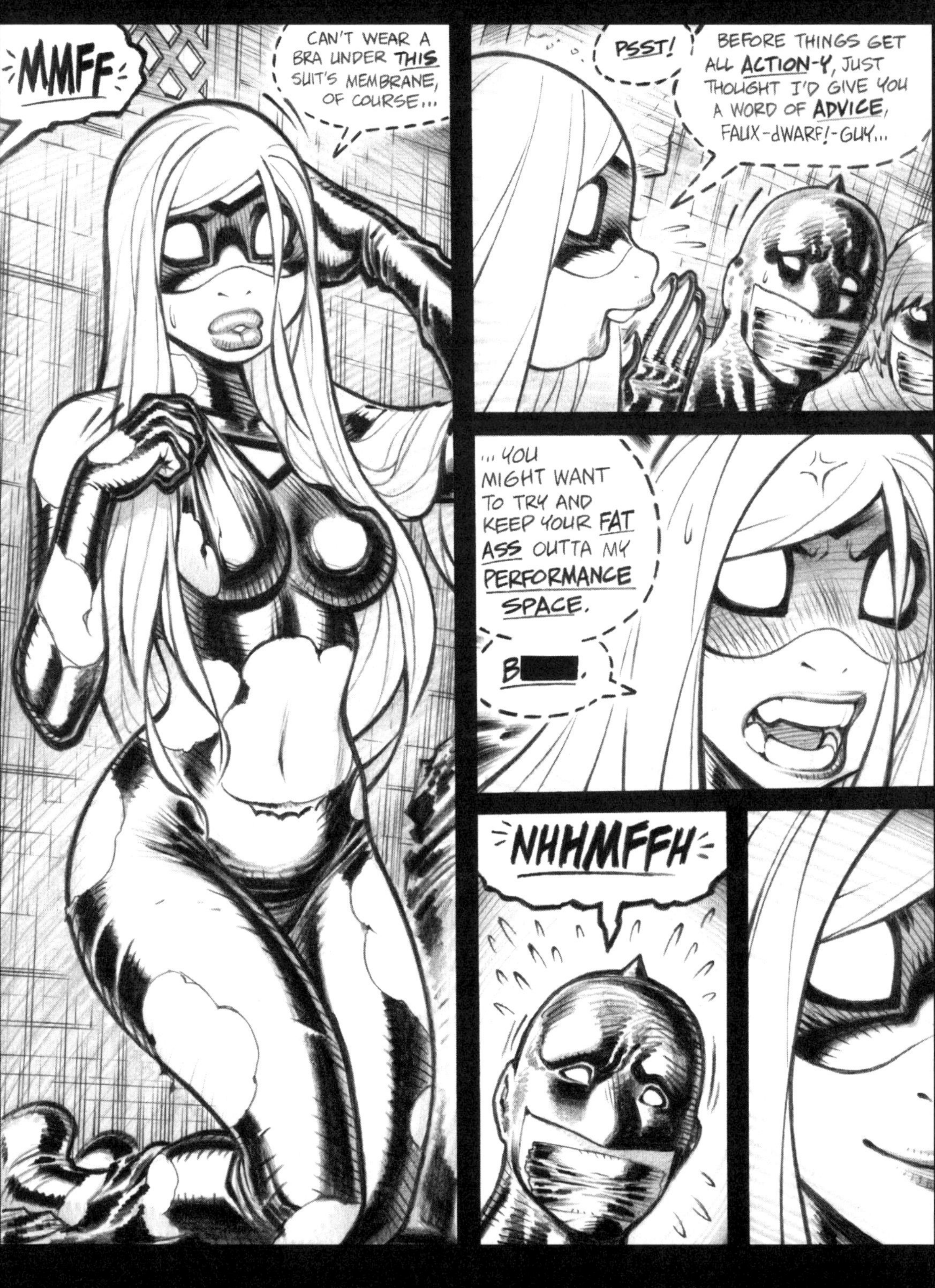
MMFF
CAN'T WEAR A BRA UNDER THIS SUIT'S MEMBRANE, OF COURSE...
PSST!
BEFORE THINGS GET ALL ACTION-Y, JUST THOUGHT I'D GIVE YOU A WORD OF ADVICE, FAUX-dWARF!-GUY...
...YOU MIGHT WANT TO TRY AND KEEP YOUR FAT ASS OUTTA MY PERFORMANCE SPACE.
B[redacted].
NHHMFFH

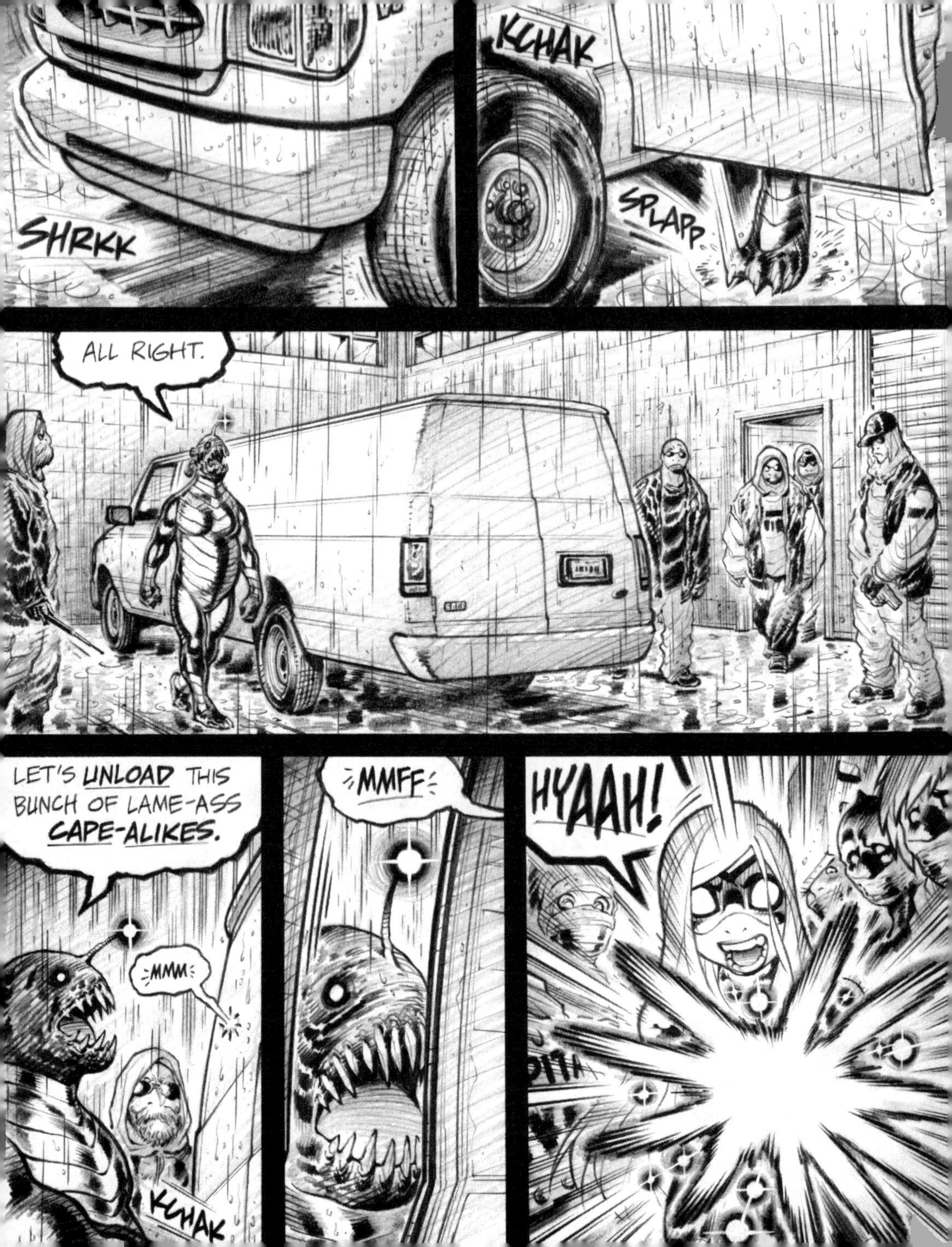
SHRKK
KCHAK
SPLAPP
ALL RIGHT.
LET'S UNLOAD THIS BUNCH OF LAME-ASS CAPE-ALIKES.
MMM
KCHAK
MMFF
HYAAH!

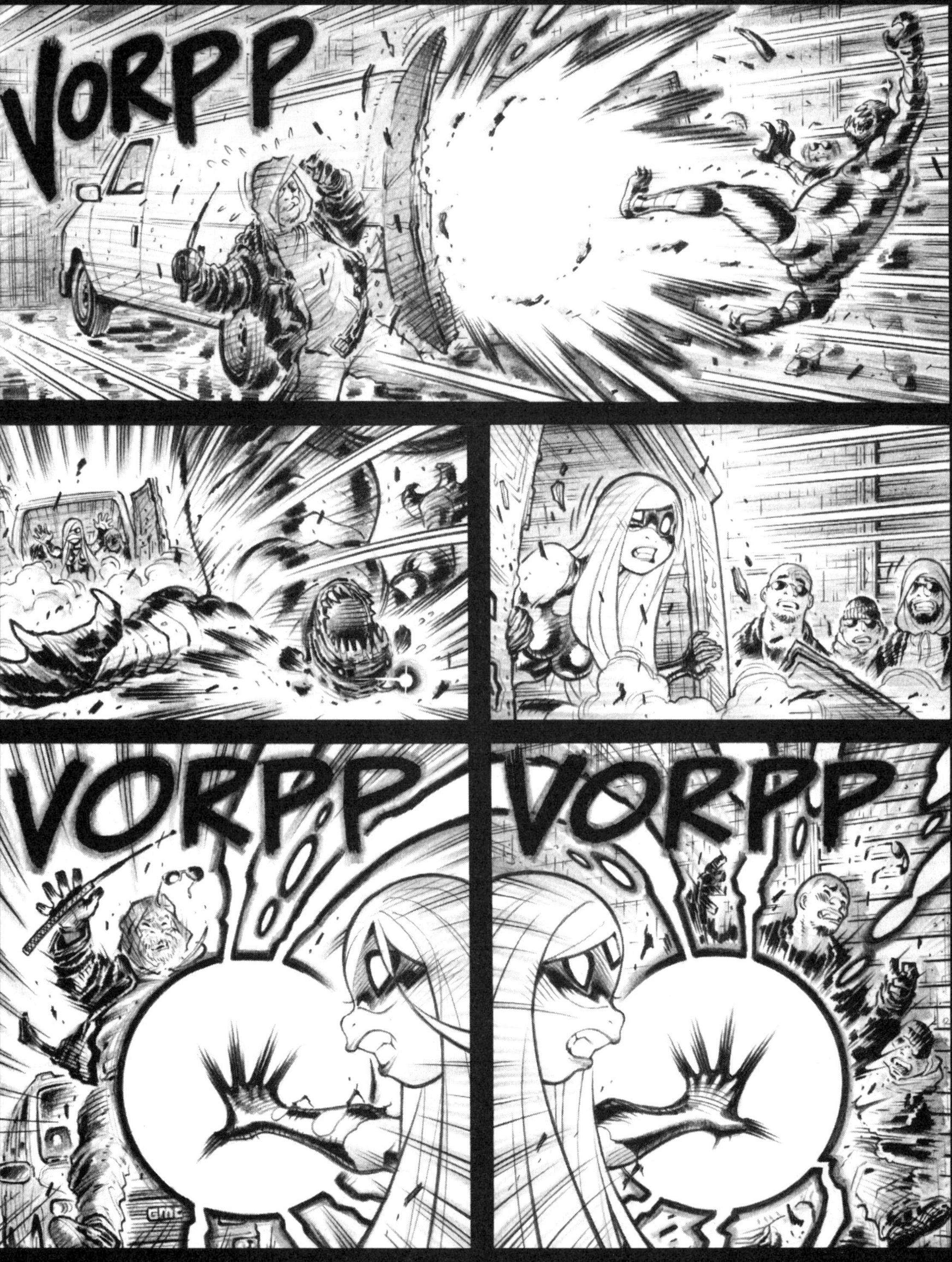
VORPP
VORPP
GMC
VORPP

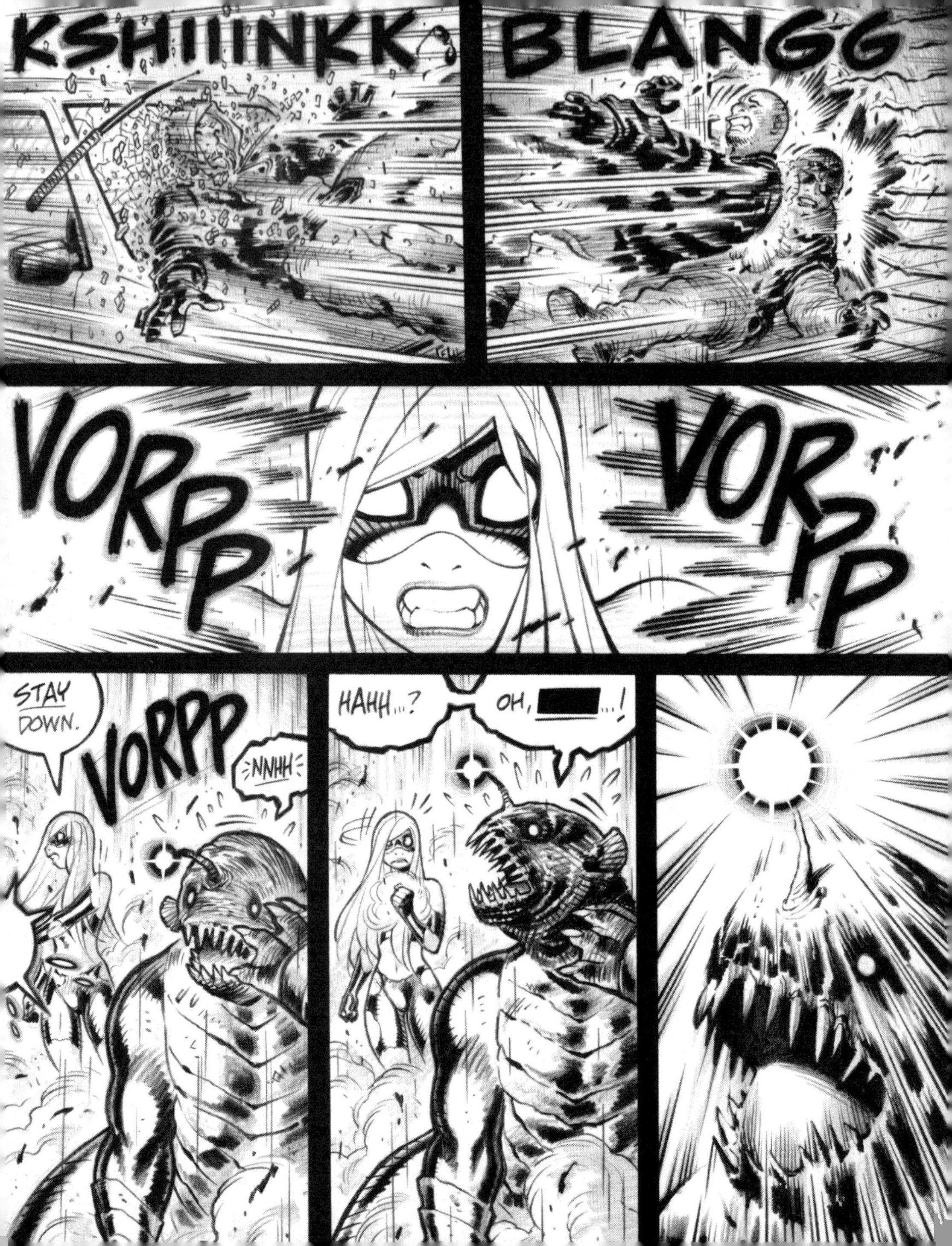
KSHIIINKK
BLANGG
VORPP
VORPP
STAY DOWN.
VORPP
NNHH
HAHH...?
OH, [redacted]...!

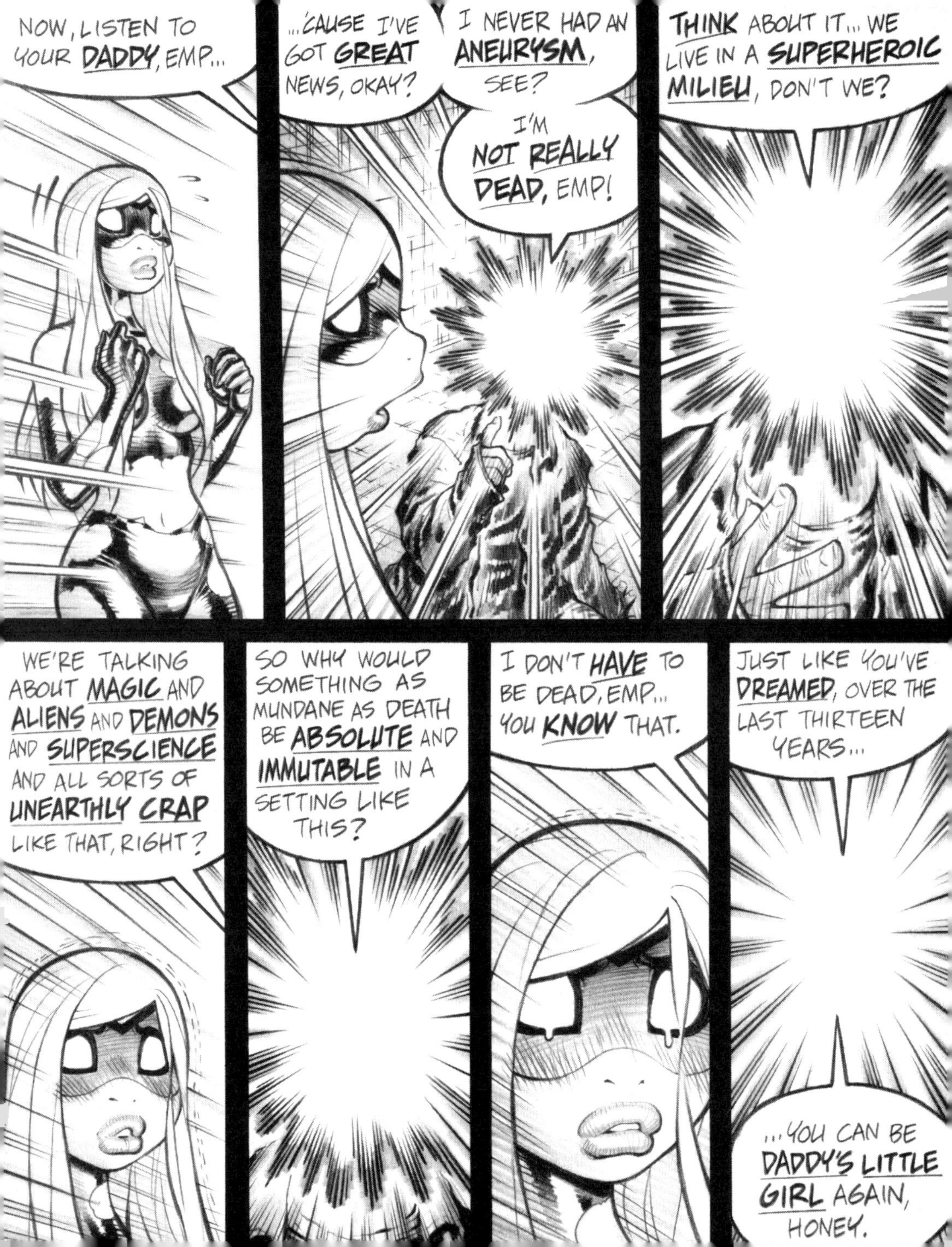
NOW, LISTEN TO YOUR DADDY, EMP...
...'CAUSE I'VE GOT GREAT NEWS, OKAY?
I NEVER HAD AN ANEURYSM, SEE?
I'M NOT REALLY DEAD, EMP!
THINK ABOUT IT... WE LIVE IN A SUPERHEROIC MILIEU, DON'T WE?
WE'RE TALKING ABOUT MAGIC AND ALIENS AND DEMONS AND SUPERSCIENCE AND ALL SORTS OF UNEARTHLY CRAP LIKE THAT, RIGHT?
SO WHY WOULD SOMETHING AS MUNDANE AS DEATH BE ABSOLUTE AND IMMUTABLE IN A SETTING LIKE THIS?
I DON'T HAVE TO BE DEAD, EMP... YOU KNOW THAT.
JUST LIKE YOU'VE DREAMED, OVER THE LAST THIRTEEN YEARS...
...YOU CAN BE DADDY'S LITTLE GIRL AGAIN, HONEY.

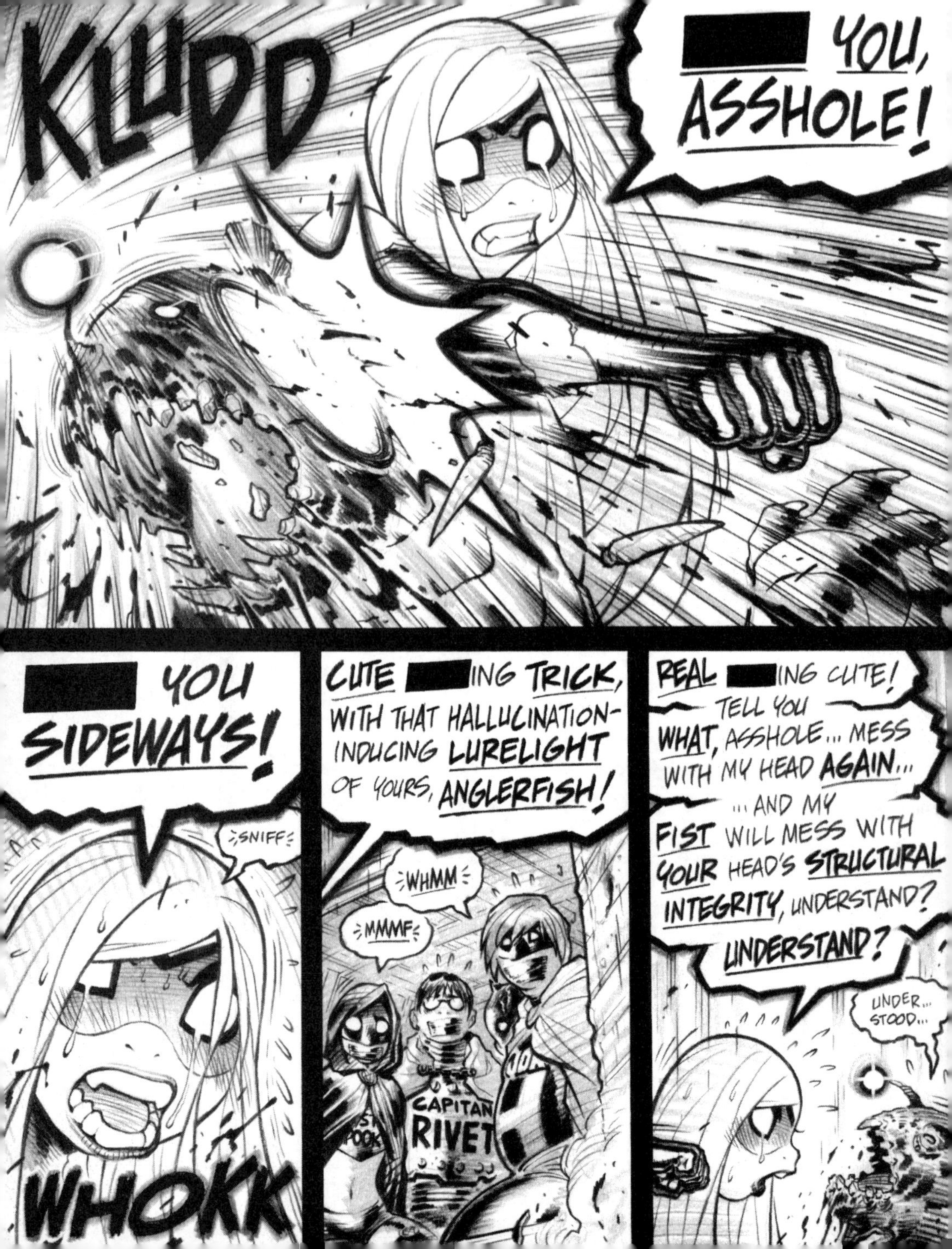
KLUDD
[redacted] YOU, ASSHOLE!
[redacted] YOU SIDEWAYS!
SNIFF
WHOKK
CUTE [redacted]ING TRICK, WITH THAT HALLUCINATION-INDUCING LURELIGHT OF YOURS, ANGLERFISH!
WHMM
MMMF
CAPITAN RIVET
REAL [redacted]ING CUTE! TELL YOU WHAT, ASSHOLE... MESS WITH MY HEAD AGAIN...
...AND MY FIST WILL MESS WITH YOUR HEAD'S STRUCTURAL INTEGRITY, UNDERSTAND?
UNDERSTAND?
UNDER... STOOD...

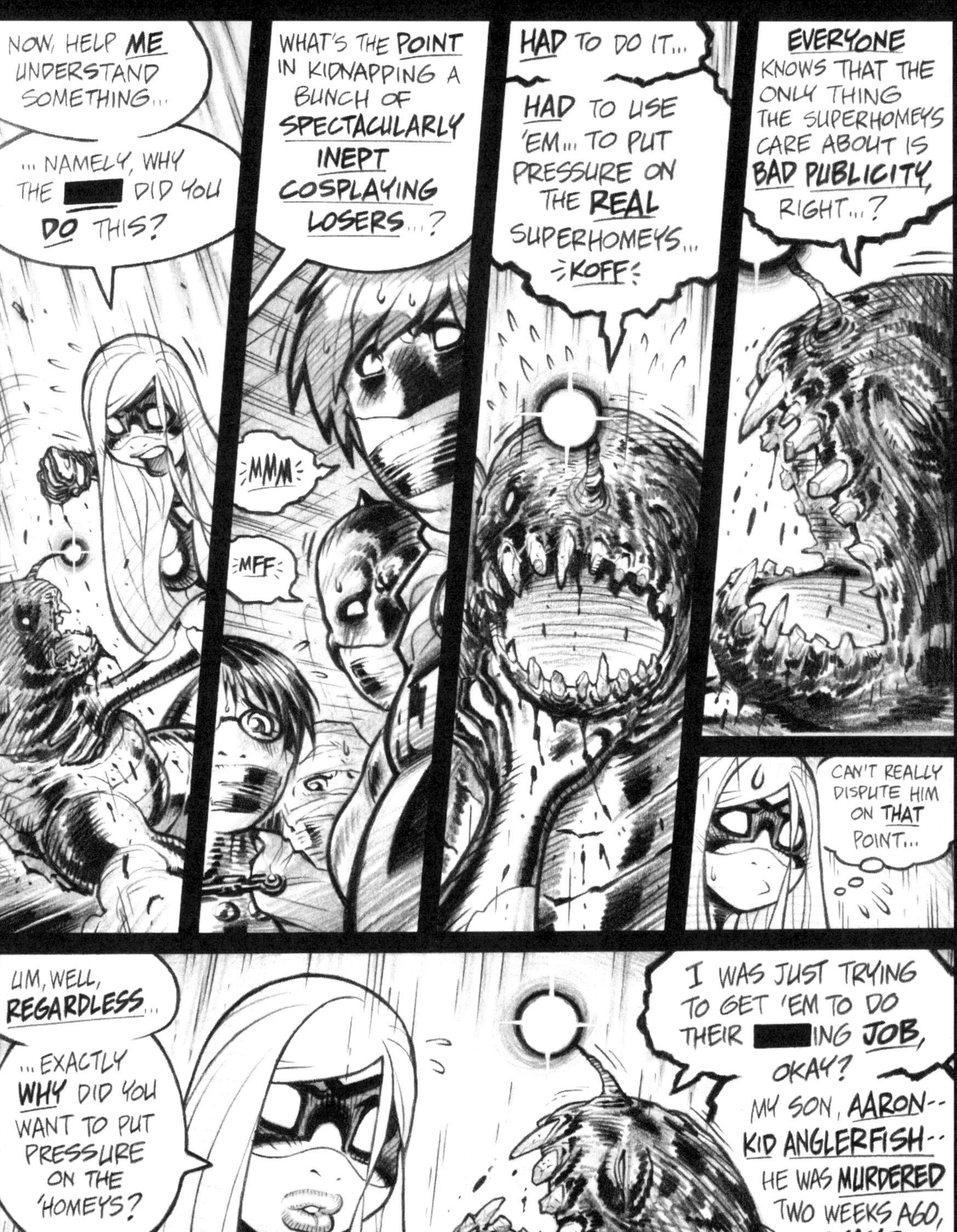
NOW, HELP ME UNDERSTAND SOMETHING...
...NAMELY, WHY THE [redacted] DID YOU DO THIS?
WHAT'S THE POINT IN KIDNAPPING A BUNCH OF SPECTACULARLY INEPT COSPLAYING LOSERS...?
MMM
MFF
HAD TO DO IT...
HAD TO USE 'EM... TO PUT PRESSURE ON THE REAL SUPERHOMEYS... KOFF
EVERYONE KNOWS THAT THE ONLY THING THE SUPERHOMEYS CARE ABOUT IS BAD PUBLICITY, RIGHT...?
CAN'T REALLY DISPUTE HIM ON THAT POINT...
UM, WELL, REGARDLESS...
...EXACTLY WHY DID YOU WANT TO PUT PRESSURE ON THE 'HOMEYS?
I WAS JUST TRYING TO GET 'EM TO DO THEIR [redacted]ING JOB, OKAY?
MY SON, AARON-- KID ANGLERFISH-- HE WAS MURDERED TWO WEEKS AGO, OKAY?

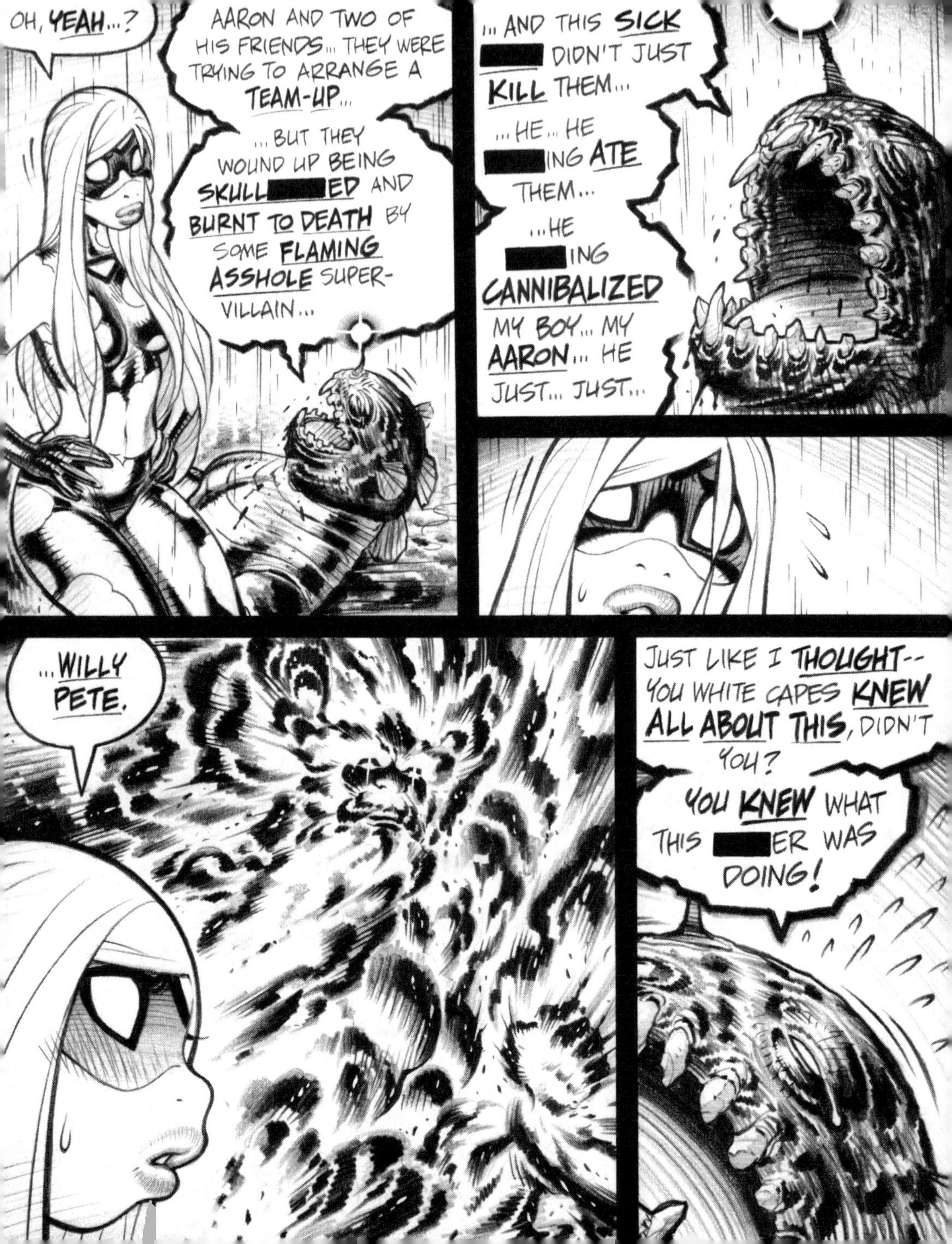
OH, YEAH...?
AARON AND TWO OF HIS FRIENDS... THEY WERE TRYING TO ARRANGE A TEAM-UP...
...BUT THEY WOUND UP BEING SKULL[redacted]ED AND BURNT TO DEATH BY SOME FLAMING ASSHOLE SUPER-VILLAIN...
...AND THIS SICK [redacted] DIDN'T JUST KILL THEM...
...HE... HE [redacted]ING ATE THEM...
...HE [redacted]ING CANNIBALIZED MY BOY... MY AARON... HE JUST... JUST...
...WILLY PETE.
JUST LIKE I THOUGHT-- YOU WHITE CAPES KNEW ALL ABOUT THIS, DIDN'T YOU?
YOU KNEW WHAT THIS [redacted]ER WAS DOING!

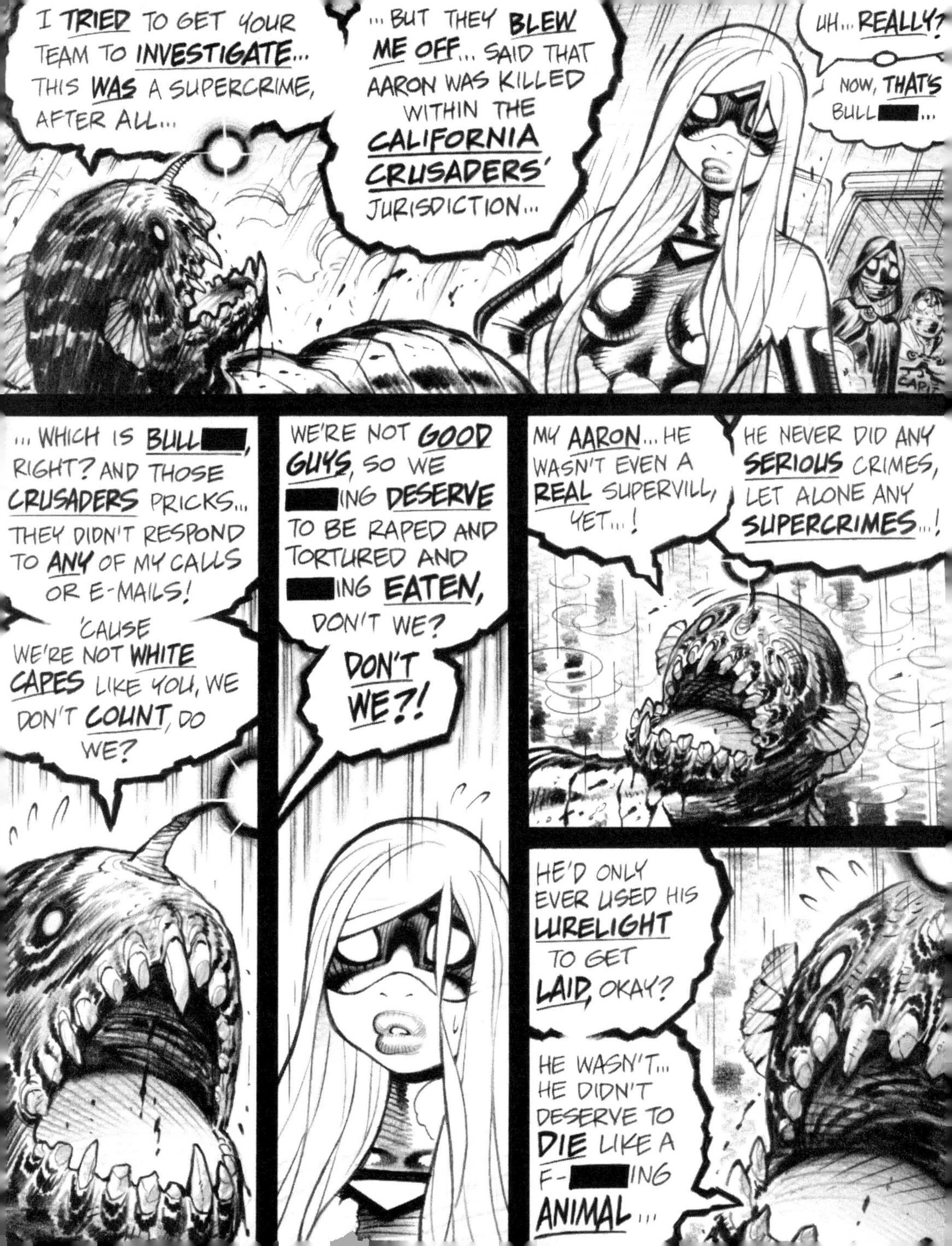
I TRIED TO GET YOUR TEAM TO INVESTIGATE... THIS WAS A SUPERCRIME, AFTER ALL...
...BUT THEY BLEW ME OFF... SAID THAT AARON WAS KILLED WITHIN THE CALIFORNIA CRUSADERS' JURISDICTION...
UH... REALLY?
NOW, THAT'S BULL[redacted]...
...WHICH IS BULL[redacted], RIGHT? AND THOSE CRUSADERS PRICKS... THEY DIDN'T RESPOND TO ANY OF MY CALLS OR E-MAILS!
'CAUSE WE'RE NOT WHITE CAPES LIKE YOU, WE DON'T COUNT, DO WE?
WE'RE NOT GOOD GUYS, SO WE [redacted]ING DESERVE TO BE RAPED AND TORTURED AND [redacted]ING EATEN, DON'T WE?
DON'T WE?!
MY AARON... HE WASN'T EVEN A REAL SUPERVILL, YET...!
HE NEVER DID ANY SERIOUS CRIMES, LET ALONE ANY SUPERCRIMES...!
HE'D ONLY EVER USED HIS LURELIGHT TO GET LAID, OKAY?
HE WASN'T... HE DIDN'T DESERVE TO DIE LIKE A F-[redacted]ING ANIMAL...

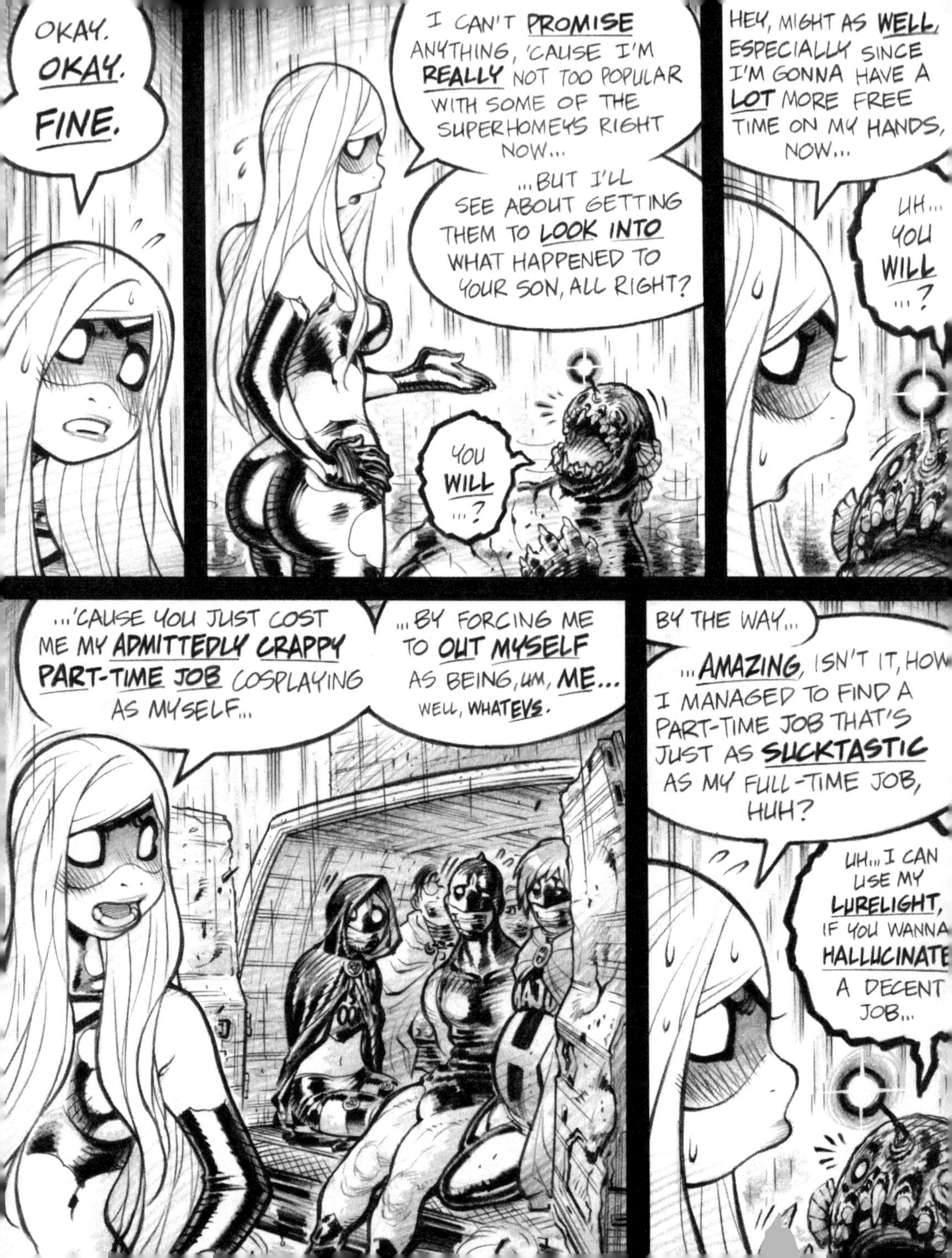
OKAY. OKAY. FINE.
I CAN'T PROMISE ANYTHING, 'CAUSE I'M REALLY NOT TOO POPULAR WITH SOME OF THE SUPERHOMEYS RIGHT NOW...
...BUT I'LL SEE ABOUT GETTING THEM TO LOOK INTO WHAT HAPPENED TO YOUR SON, ALL RIGHT?
YOU WILL...?
HEY, MIGHT AS WELL, ESPECIALLY SINCE I'M GONNA HAVE A LOT MORE FREE TIME ON MY HANDS, NOW...
UH... YOU WILL...?
...'CAUSE YOU JUST COST ME MY ADMITTEDLY CRAPPY PART-TIME JOB COSPLAYING AS MYSELF...
...BY FORCING ME TO OUT MYSELF AS BEING, UM, ME... WELL, WHATEVS.
BY THE WAY...
...AMAZING, ISN'T IT, HOW I MANAGED TO FIND A PART-TIME JOB THAT'S JUST AS SUCKTASTIC AS MY FULL-TIME JOB, HUH?
UH... I CAN USE MY LURELIGHT, IF YOU WANNA HALLUCINATE A DECENT JOB...

empowered™

The Powaaah of the Duct Side

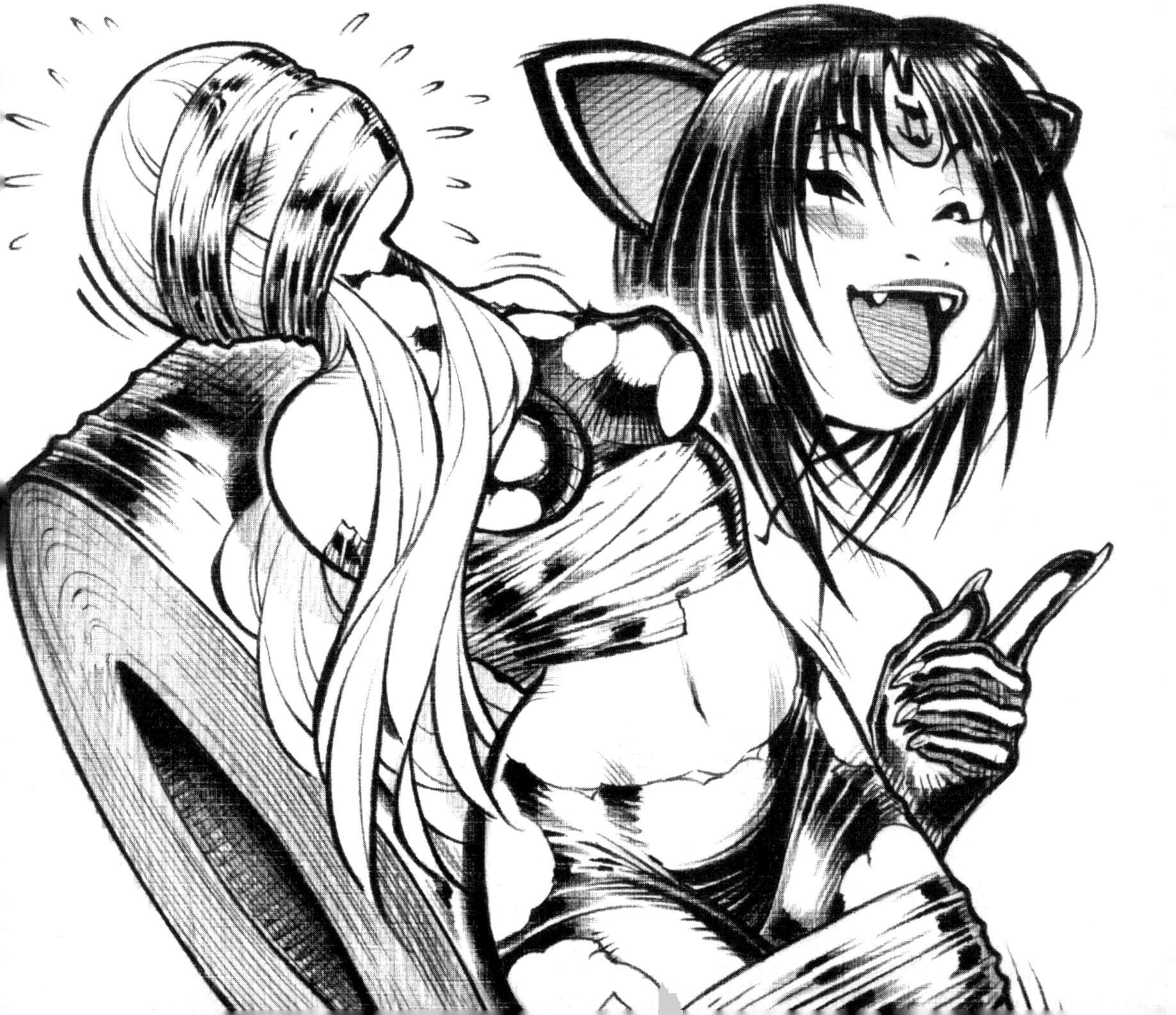

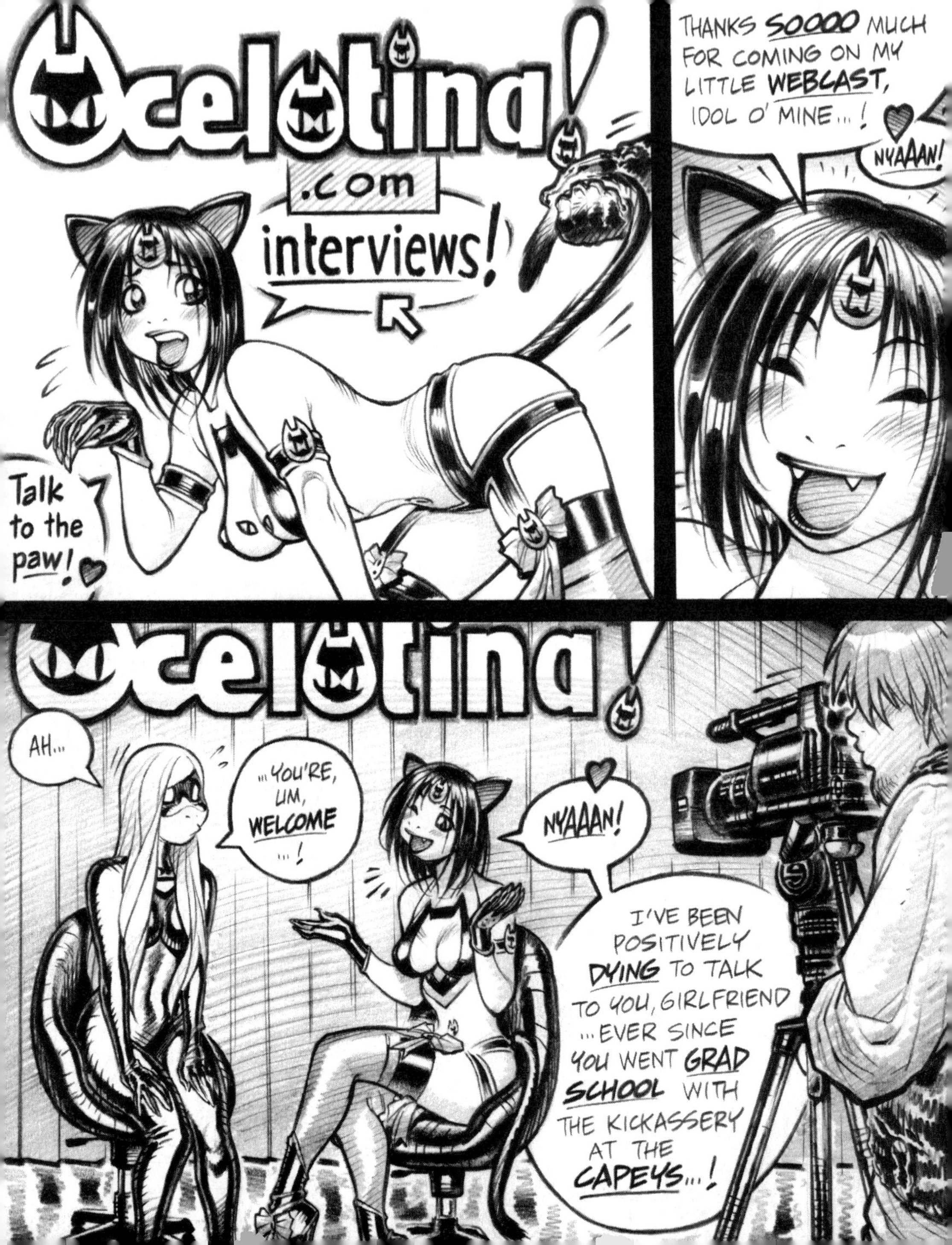
Ocelotina!
.com
interviews!
Talk to the paw!
THANKS SOOOO MUCH FOR COMING ON MY LITTLE WEBCAST, IDOL O' MINE...!
NYAAAN!
Ocelotina!
AH...
...YOU'RE, UM, WELCOME...!
NYAAAN!
I'VE BEEN POSITIVELY DYING TO TALK TO YOU, GIRLFRIEND ...EVER SINCE YOU WENT GRAD SCHOOL WITH THE KICKASSERY AT THE CAPEYS...!

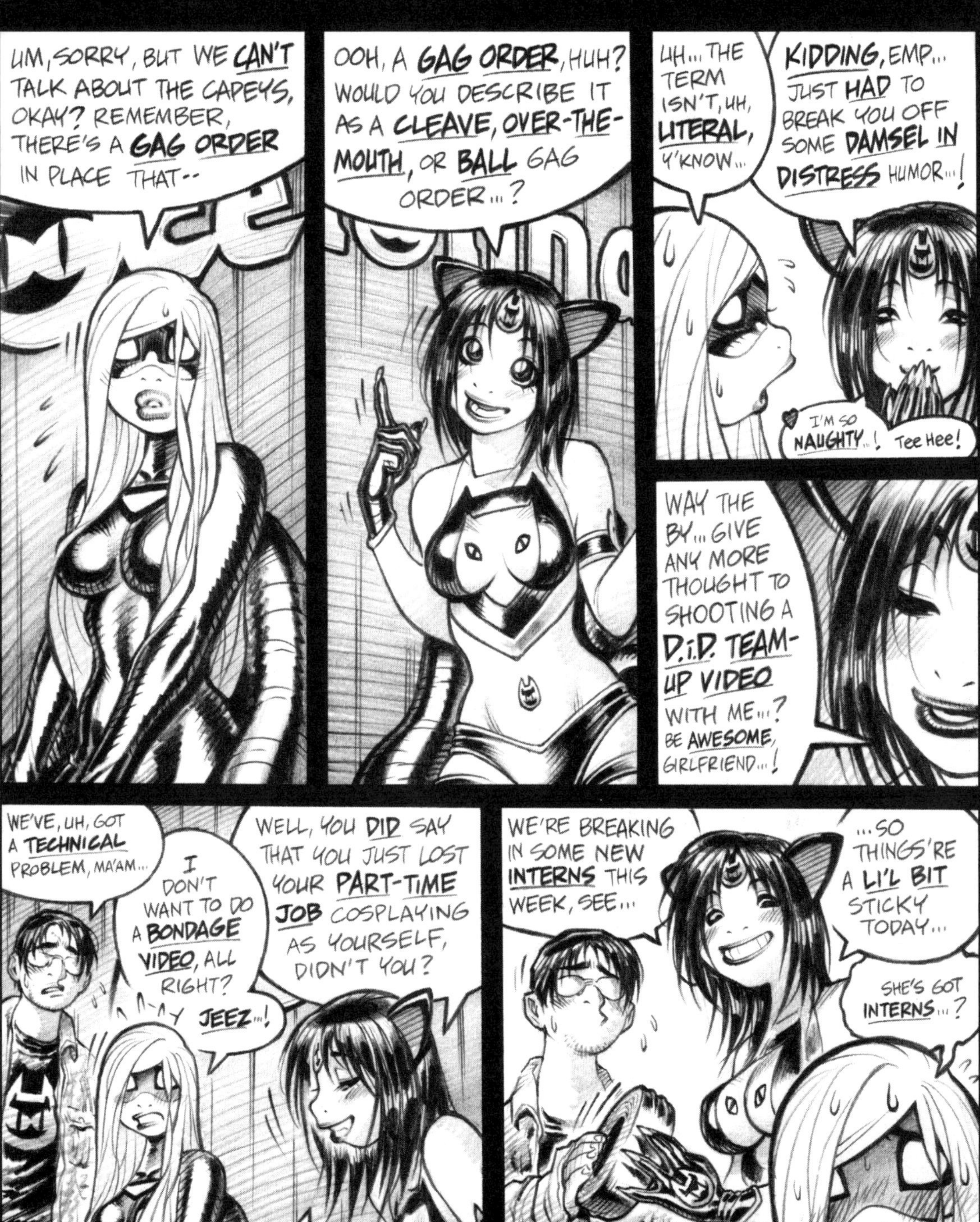
UM, SORRY, BUT WE CAN'T TALK ABOUT THE CAPEYS, OKAY? REMEMBER, THERE'S A GAG ORDER IN PLACE THAT--
OOH, A GAG ORDER, HUH? WOULD YOU DESCRIBE IT AS A CLEAVE, OVER-THE-MOUTH, OR BALL GAG ORDER...?
UH... THE TERM ISN'T, UH, LITERAL, Y'KNOW...
KIDDING, EMP... JUST HAD TO BREAK YOU OFF SOME DAMSEL IN DISTRESS HUMOR...!
I'M SO NAUGHTY...! Tee Hee!
WAY THE BY... GIVE ANY MORE THOUGHT TO SHOOTING A D.i.D. TEAM-UP VIDEO WITH ME...? BE AWESOME, GIRLFRIEND...!
WE'VE, UH, GOT A TECHNICAL PROBLEM, MA'AM...
I DON'T WANT TO DO A BONDAGE VIDEO, ALL RIGHT?
JEEZ...!
WELL, YOU DID SAY THAT YOU JUST LOST YOUR PART-TIME JOB COSPLAYING AS YOURSELF, DIDN'T YOU?
'SCUSE ME FOR A SEC, 'KAY?
WE'RE BREAKING IN SOME NEW INTERNS THIS WEEK, SEE...
...SO THINGS'RE A LI'L BIT STICKY TODAY...
SHE'S GOT INTERNS...?

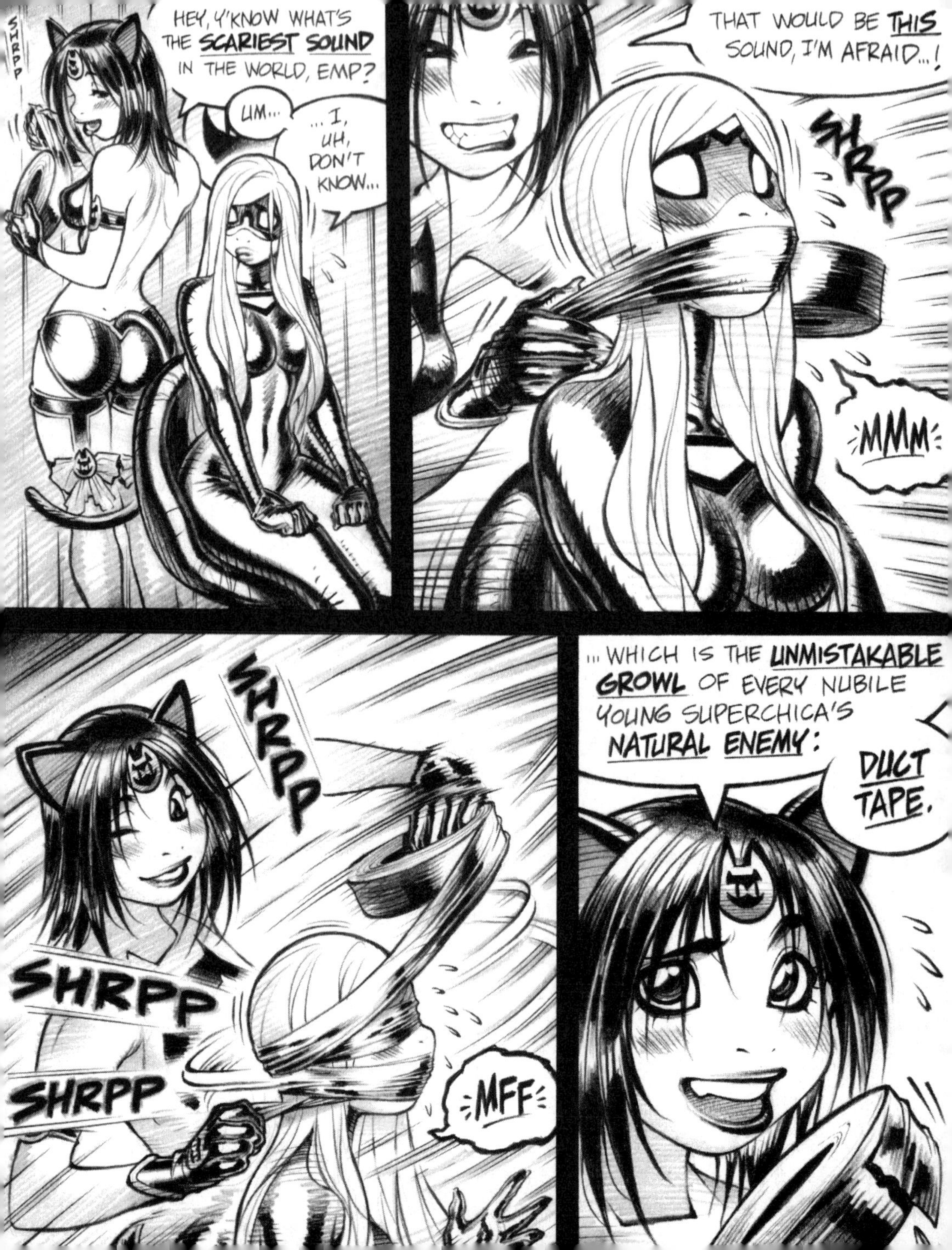
SHRPP
HEY, Y'KNOW WHAT'S THE SCARIEST SOUND IN THE WORLD, EMP?
UM...
...I, UH, DON'T KNOW...
THAT WOULD BE THIS SOUND, I'M AFRAID...!
SHRPP
MMM
SHRPP
SHRPP
SHRPP
MFF
...WHICH IS THE UNMISTAKABLE GROWL OF EVERY NUBILE YOUNG SUPERCHICA'S NATURAL ENEMY:
DUCT TAPE.

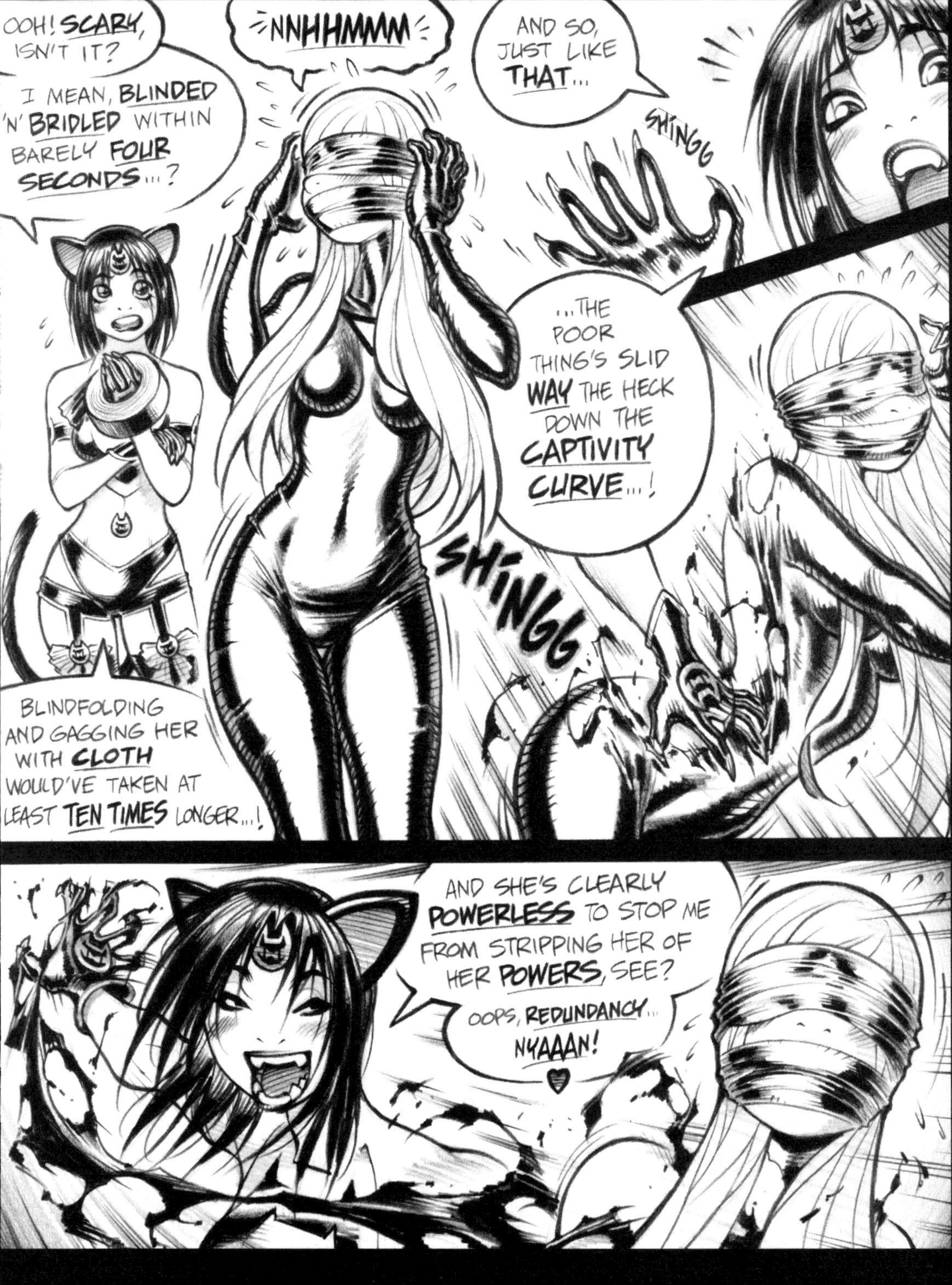
OOH! SCARY, ISN'T IT?
I MEAN, BLINDED 'N' BRIDLED WITHIN BARELY FOUR SECONDS...?
NNHHMMM
AND SO, JUST LIKE THAT...
SHINGG
...THE POOR THING'S SLID WAY THE HECK DOWN THE CAPTIVITY CURVE...!
SHINGG
BLINDFOLDING AND GAGGING HER WITH CLOTH WOULD'VE TAKEN AT LEAST TEN TIMES LONGER...!
AND SHE'S CLEARLY POWERLESS TO STOP ME FROM STRIPPING HER OF HER POWERS, SEE?
OOPS, REDUNDANCY... NYAAAN!

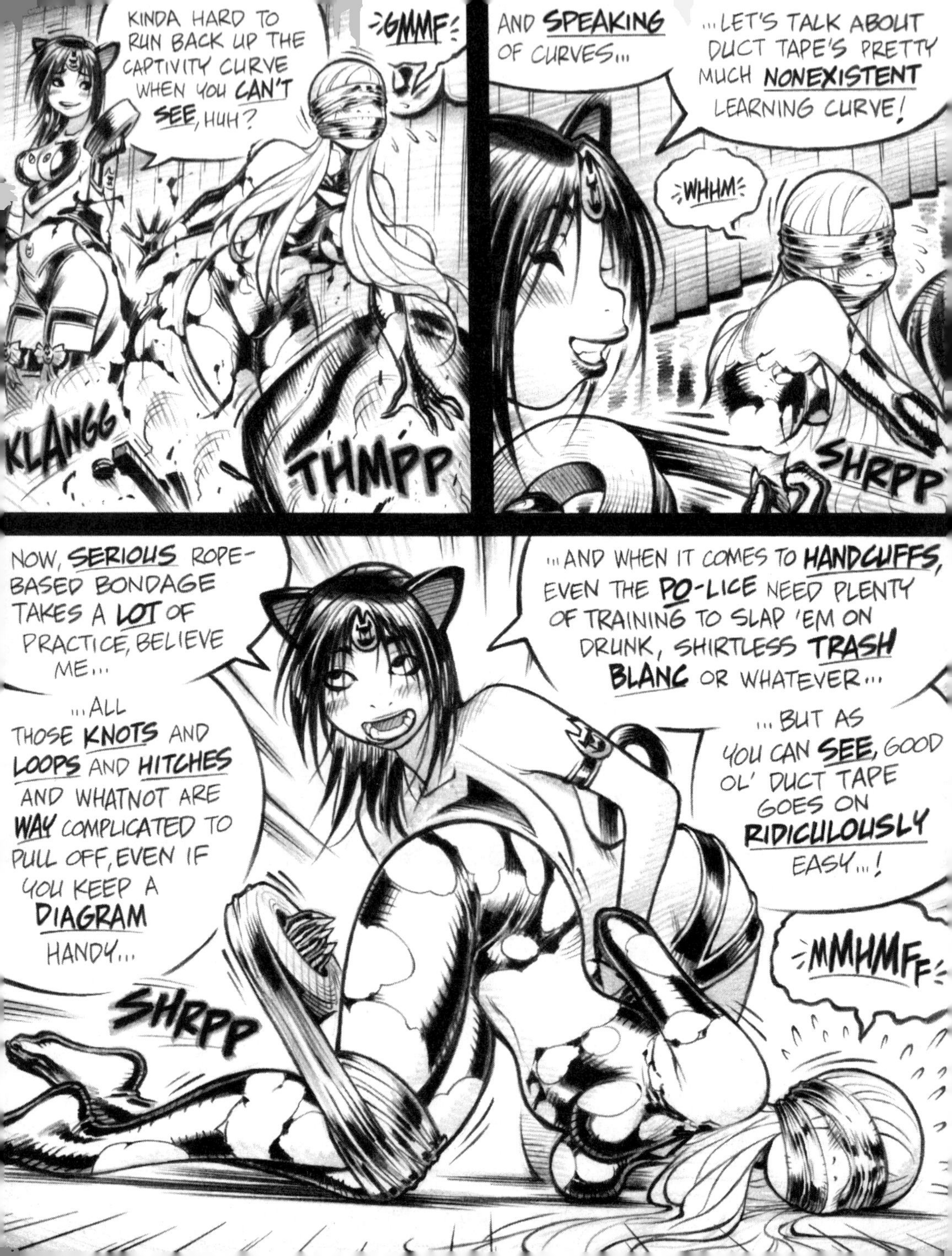
KINDA HARD TO RUN BACK UP THE CAPTIVITY CURVE WHEN YOU CAN'T SEE, HUH?
GMMF
KLANGG
THMPP
AND SPEAKING OF CURVES...
...LET'S TALK ABOUT DUCT TAPE'S PRETTY MUCH NONEXISTENT LEARNING CURVE!
WHHM
SHRPP
NOW, SERIOUS ROPE-BASED BONDAGE TAKES A LOT OF PRACTICE, BELIEVE ME...
...ALL THOSE KNOTS AND LOOPS AND HITCHES AND WHATNOT ARE WAY COMPLICATED TO PULL OFF, EVEN IF YOU KEEP A DIAGRAM HANDY...
...AND WHEN IT COMES TO HANDCUFFS, EVEN THE PO-LICE NEED PLENTY OF TRAINING TO SLAP 'EM ON DRUNK, SHIRTLESS TRASH BLANC OR WHATEVER...
...BUT AS YOU CAN SEE, GOOD OL' DUCT TAPE GOES ON RIDICULOUSLY EASY...!
MMHMFF
SHRPP

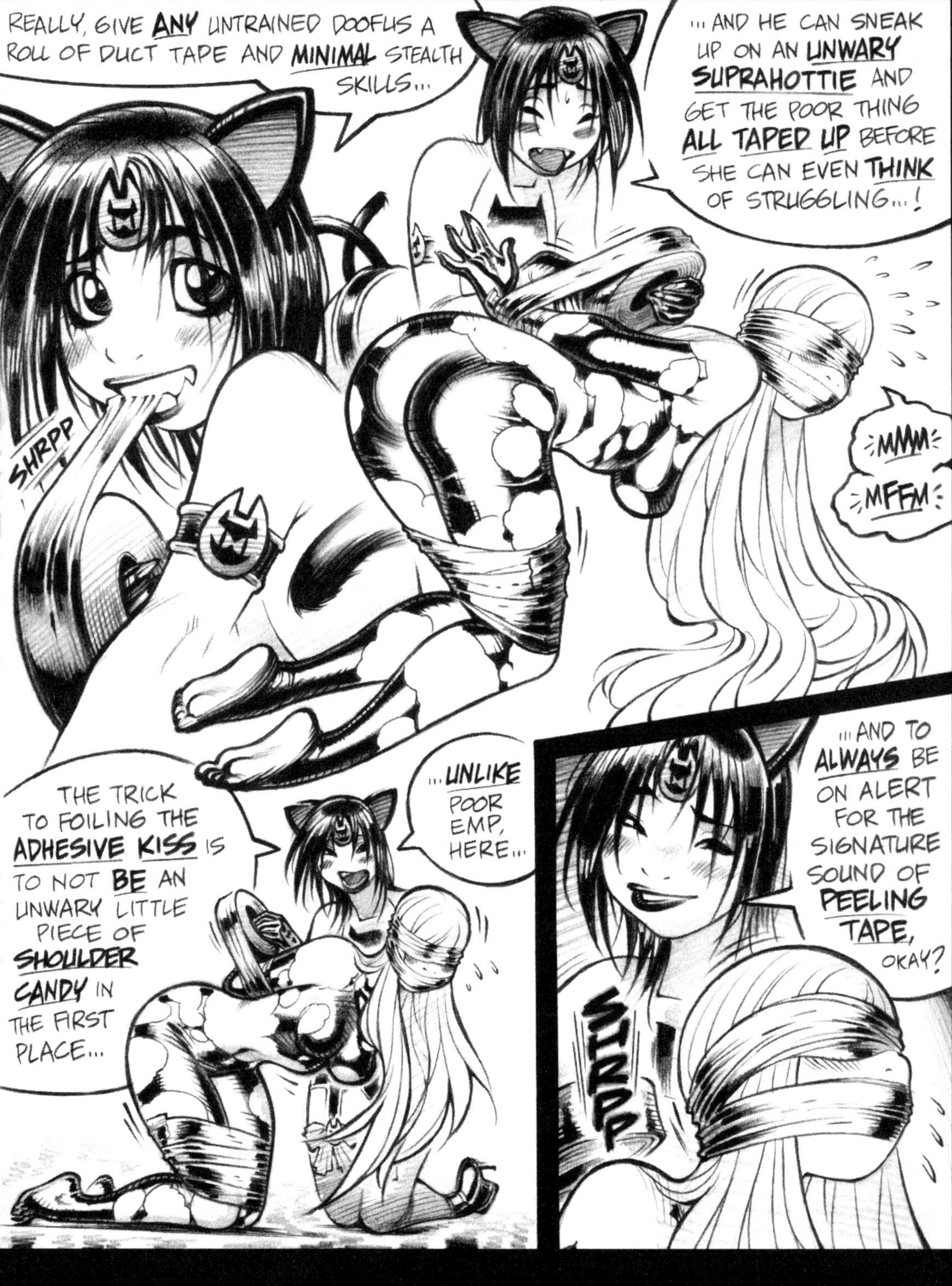

REALLY, GIVE ANY UNTRAINED DOOFUS A ROLL OF DUCT TAPE AND MINIMAL STEALTH SKILLS...
...AND HE CAN SNEAK UP ON AN UNWARY SUPRAHOTTIE AND GET THE POOR THING ALL TAPED UP BEFORE SHE CAN EVEN THINK OF STRUGGLING...!
SHRPP
MMM
MFFM
THE TRICK TO FOILING THE ADHESIVE KISS IS TO NOT BE AN UNWARY LITTLE PIECE OF SHOULDER CANDY IN THE FIRST PLACE...
...UNLIKE POOR EMP, HERE...
...AND TO ALWAYS BE ON ALERT FOR THE SIGNATURE SOUND OF PEELING TAPE, OKAY?
SHRPP

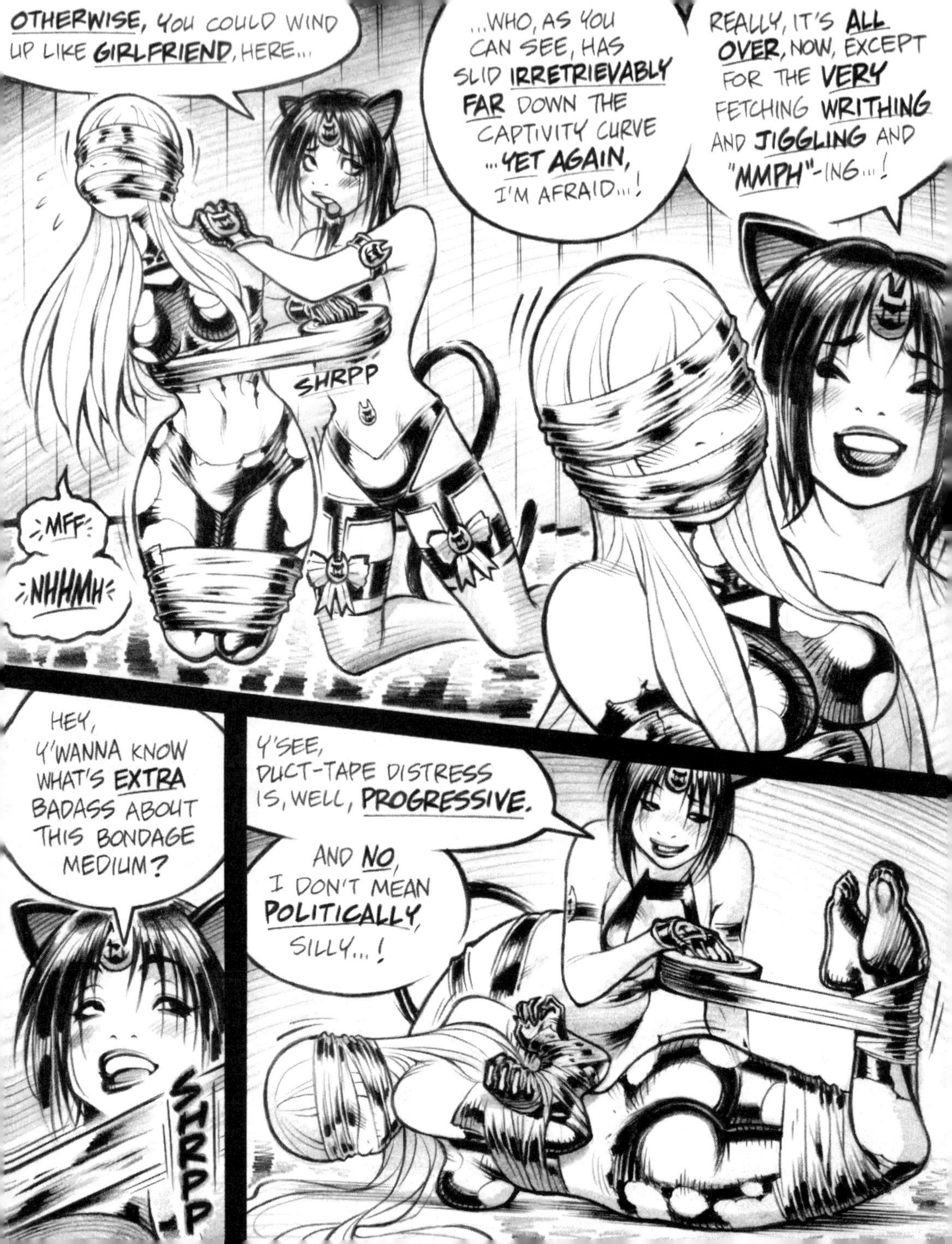
OTHERWISE, YOU COULD WIND UP LIKE GIRLFRIEND, HERE...
...WHO, AS YOU CAN SEE, HAS SLID IRRETRIEVABLY FAR DOWN THE CAPTIVITY CURVE ...YET AGAIN, I'M AFRAID...!
SHRPP
MFF
NHHMH
REALLY, IT'S ALL OVER, NOW, EXCEPT FOR THE VERY FETCHING WRITHING AND JIGGLING AND "MMPH"-ING...!
HEY, Y'WANNA KNOW WHAT'S EXTRA BADASS ABOUT THIS BONDAGE MEDIUM?
SHRPP
Y'SEE, DUCT-TAPE DISTRESS IS, WELL, PROGRESSIVE.
AND NO, I DON'T MEAN POLITICALLY, SILLY...!

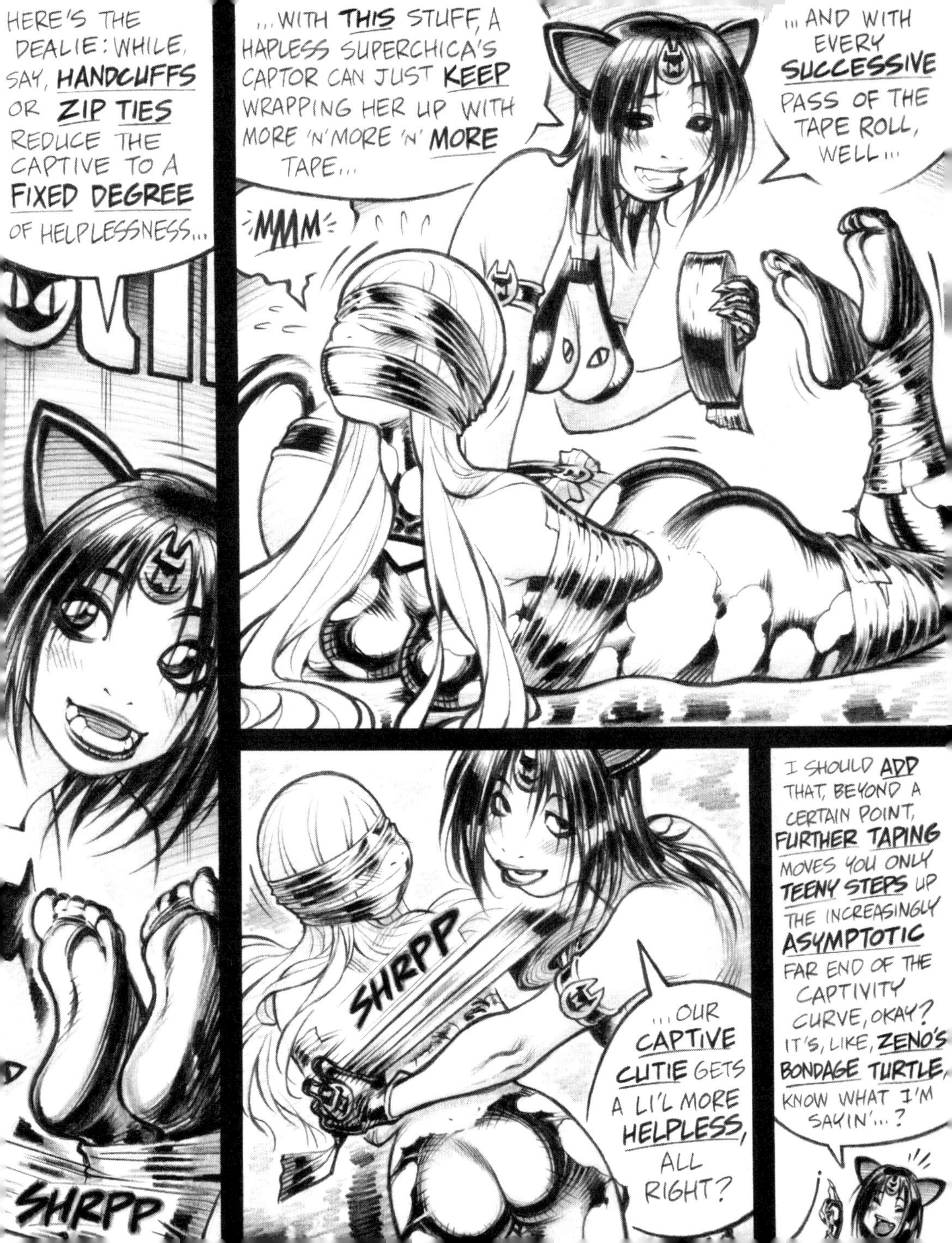
HERE'S THE DEALIE: WHILE, SAY, HANDCUFFS OR ZIP TIES REDUCE THE CAPTIVE TO A FIXED DEGREE OF HELPLESSNESS...
SHRPP
...WITH THIS STUFF, A HAPLESS SUPERCHICA'S CAPTOR CAN JUST KEEP WRAPPING HER UP WITH MORE 'N' MORE 'N' MORE TAPE...
...AND WITH EVERY SUCCESSIVE PASS OF THE TAPE ROLL, WELL...
MMM
SHRPP
...OUR CAPTIVE CUTIE GETS A LI'L MORE HELPLESS, ALL RIGHT?
I SHOULD ADD THAT, BEYOND A CERTAIN POINT, FURTHER TAPING MOVES YOU ONLY TEENY STEPS UP THE INCREASINGLY ASYMPTOTIC FAR END OF THE CAPTIVITY CURVE, OKAY? IT'S, LIKE, ZENO'S BONDAGE TURTLE, KNOW WHAT I'M SAYIN'...?

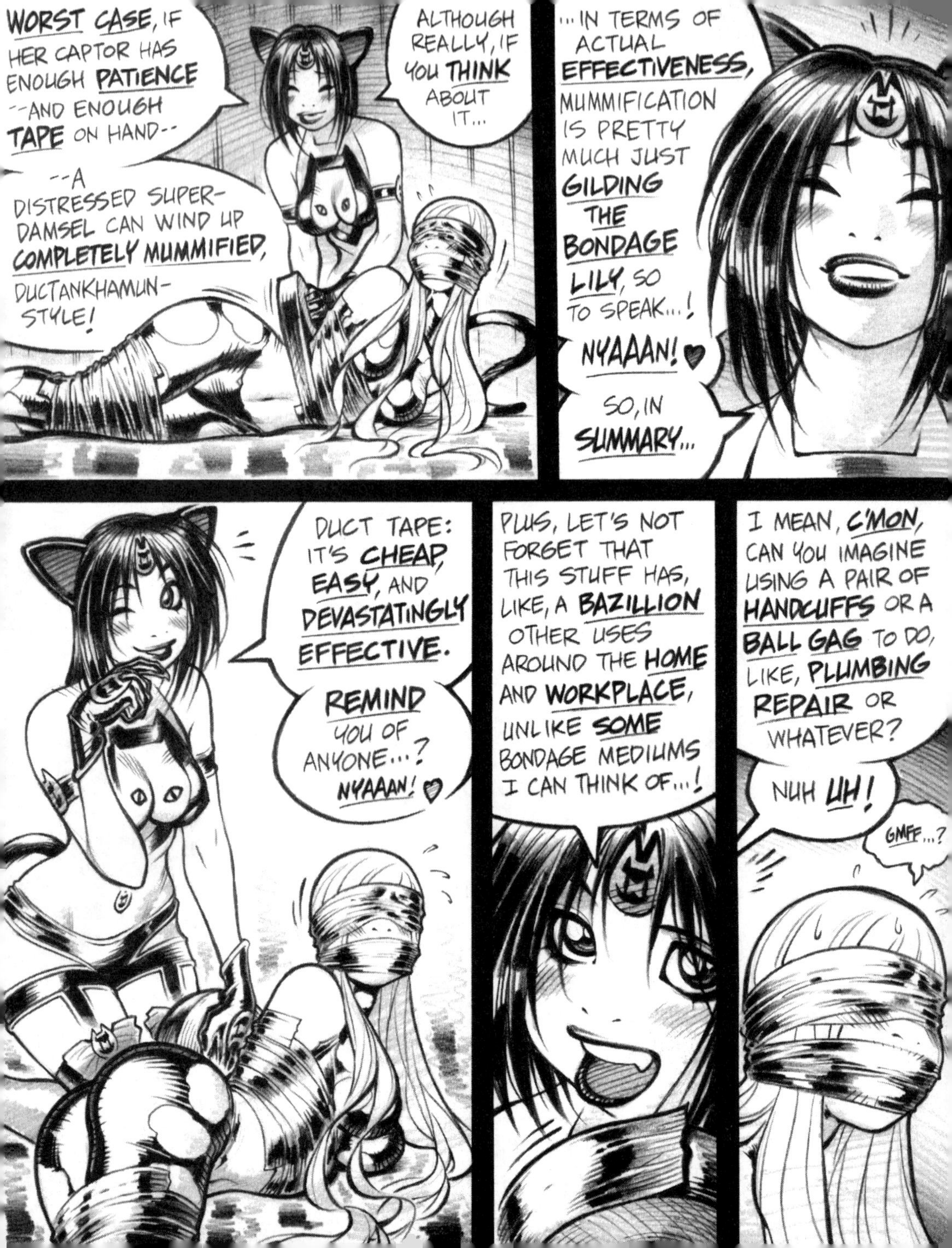
WORST CASE, IF HER CAPTOR HAS ENOUGH PATIENCE --AND ENOUGH TAPE ON HAND--
ALTHOUGH REALLY, IF YOU THINK ABOUT IT...
--A DISTRESSED SUPER-DAMSEL CAN WIND UP COMPLETELY MUMMIFIED, DUCTANKHAMUN-STYLE!
...IN TERMS OF ACTUAL EFFECTIVENESS, MUMMIFICATION IS PRETTY MUCH JUST GILDING THE BONDAGE LILY, SO TO SPEAK...!
NYAAAN! ♥
SO, IN SUMMARY...
DUCT TAPE: IT'S CHEAP, EASY, AND DEVASTATINGLY EFFECTIVE.
REMIND YOU OF ANYONE...? NYAAAN! ♥
PLUS, LET'S NOT FORGET THAT THIS STUFF HAS, LIKE, A BAZILLION OTHER USES AROUND THE HOME AND WORKPLACE, UNLIKE SOME BONDAGE MEDIUMS I CAN THINK OF...!
I MEAN, C'MON, CAN YOU IMAGINE USING A PAIR OF HANDCUFFS OR A BALL GAG TO DO, LIKE, PLUMBING REPAIR OR WHATEVER?
NUH UH!
GMFF...?

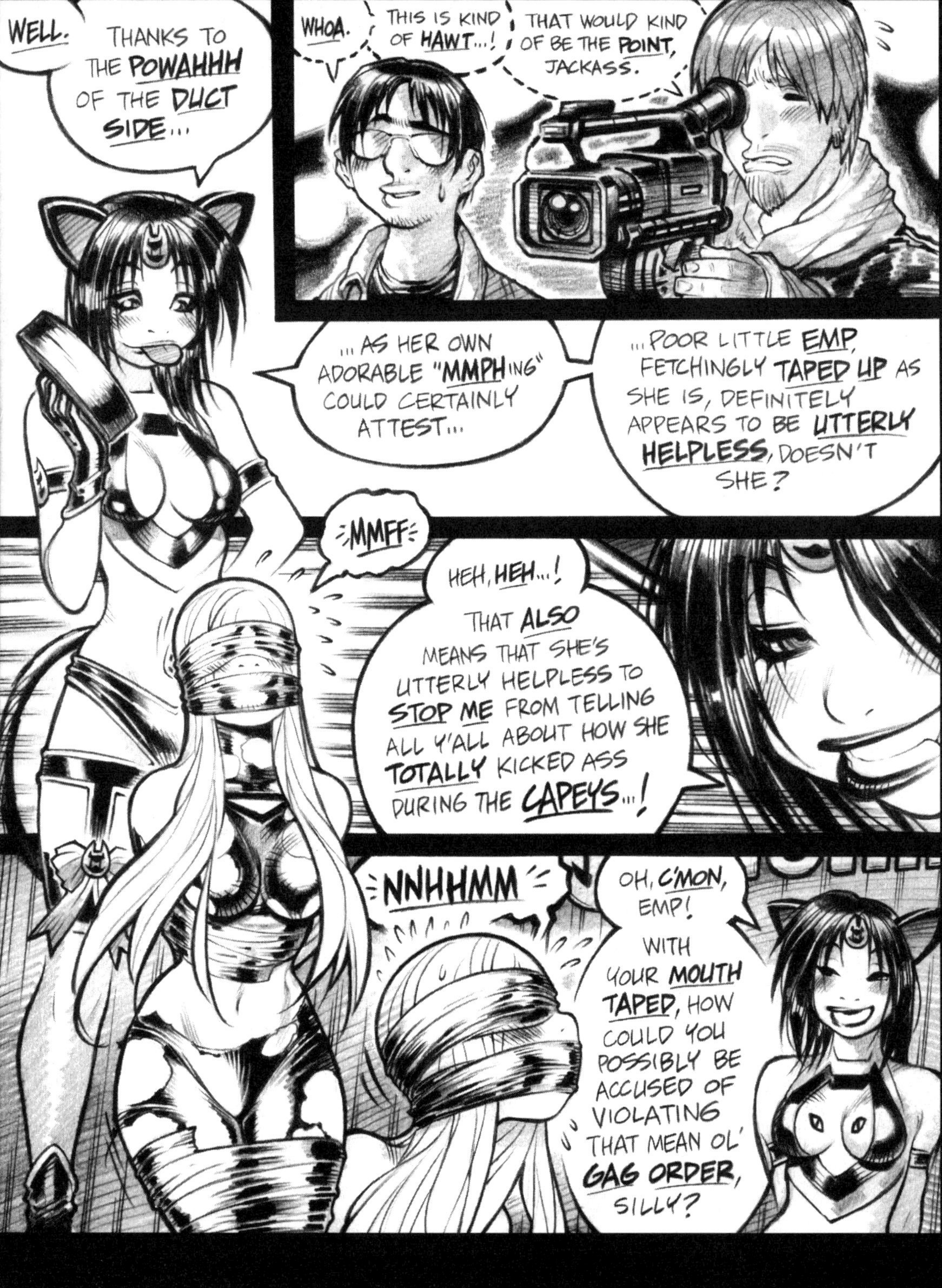
WELL. THANKS TO THE POWAHHH OF THE DUCT SIDE...
WHOA.
THIS IS KIND OF HAWT...!
THAT WOULD KIND OF BE THE POINT, JACKASS.
...AS HER OWN ADORABLE "MMPHING" COULD CERTAINLY ATTEST...
...POOR LITTLE EMP, FETCHINGLY TAPED UP AS SHE IS, DEFINITELY APPEARS TO BE UTTERLY HELPLESS, DOESN'T SHE?
MMFF
HEH, HEH...! THAT ALSO MEANS THAT SHE'S UTTERLY HELPLESS TO STOP ME FROM TELLING ALL Y'ALL ABOUT HOW SHE TOTALLY KICKED ASS DURING THE CAPEYS...!
NNHHMM
OH, C'MON, EMP! WITH YOUR MOUTH TAPED, HOW COULD YOU POSSIBLY BE ACCUSED OF VIOLATING THAT MEAN OL' GAG ORDER, SILLY?

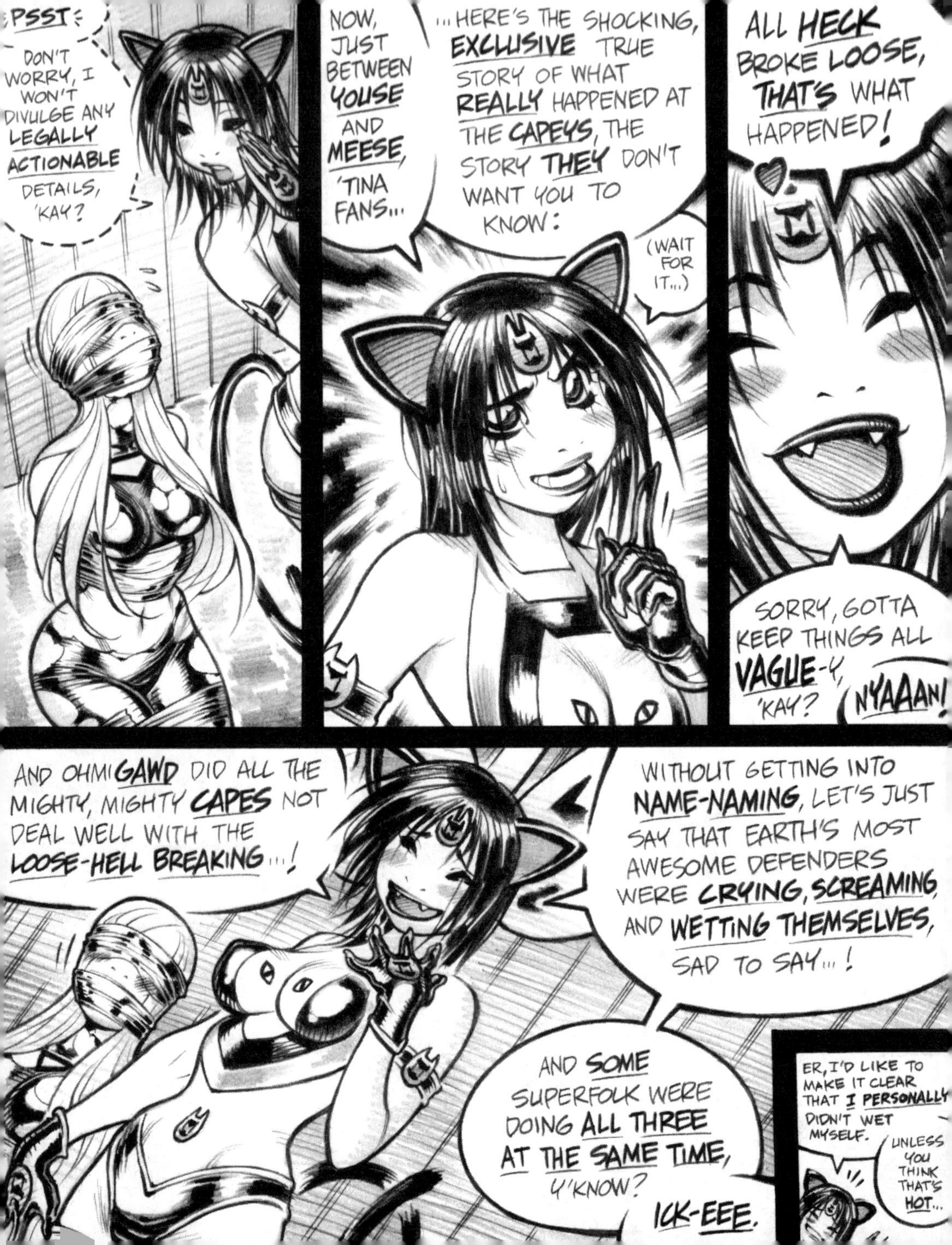
PSST
DON'T WORRY, I WON'T DIVULGE ANY LEGALLY ACTIONABLE DETAILS, 'KAY?
NOW, JUST BETWEEN YOUSE AND MEESE, 'TINA FANS...
...HERE'S THE SHOCKING, EXCLUSIVE TRUE STORY OF WHAT REALLY HAPPENED AT THE CAPEYS, THE STORY THEY DON'T WANT YOU TO KNOW:
(WAIT FOR IT...)
ALL HECK BROKE LOOSE, THAT'S WHAT HAPPENED!
SORRY, GOTTA KEEP THINGS ALL VAGUE-Y, 'KAY?
NYAAAN!
AND OHMIGAWD DID ALL THE MIGHTY, MIGHTY CAPES NOT DEAL WELL WITH THE LOOSE-HELL BREAKING...!
WITHOUT GETTING INTO NAME-NAMING, LET'S JUST SAY THAT EARTH'S MOST AWESOME DEFENDERS WERE CRYING, SCREAMING, AND WETTING THEMSELVES, SAD TO SAY...!
AND SOME SUPERFOLK WERE DOING ALL THREE AT THE SAME TIME, Y'KNOW?
ICK-EEE.
ER, I'D LIKE TO MAKE IT CLEAR THAT I PERSONALLY DIDN'T WET MYSELF.
UNLESS YOU THINK THAT'S HOT...

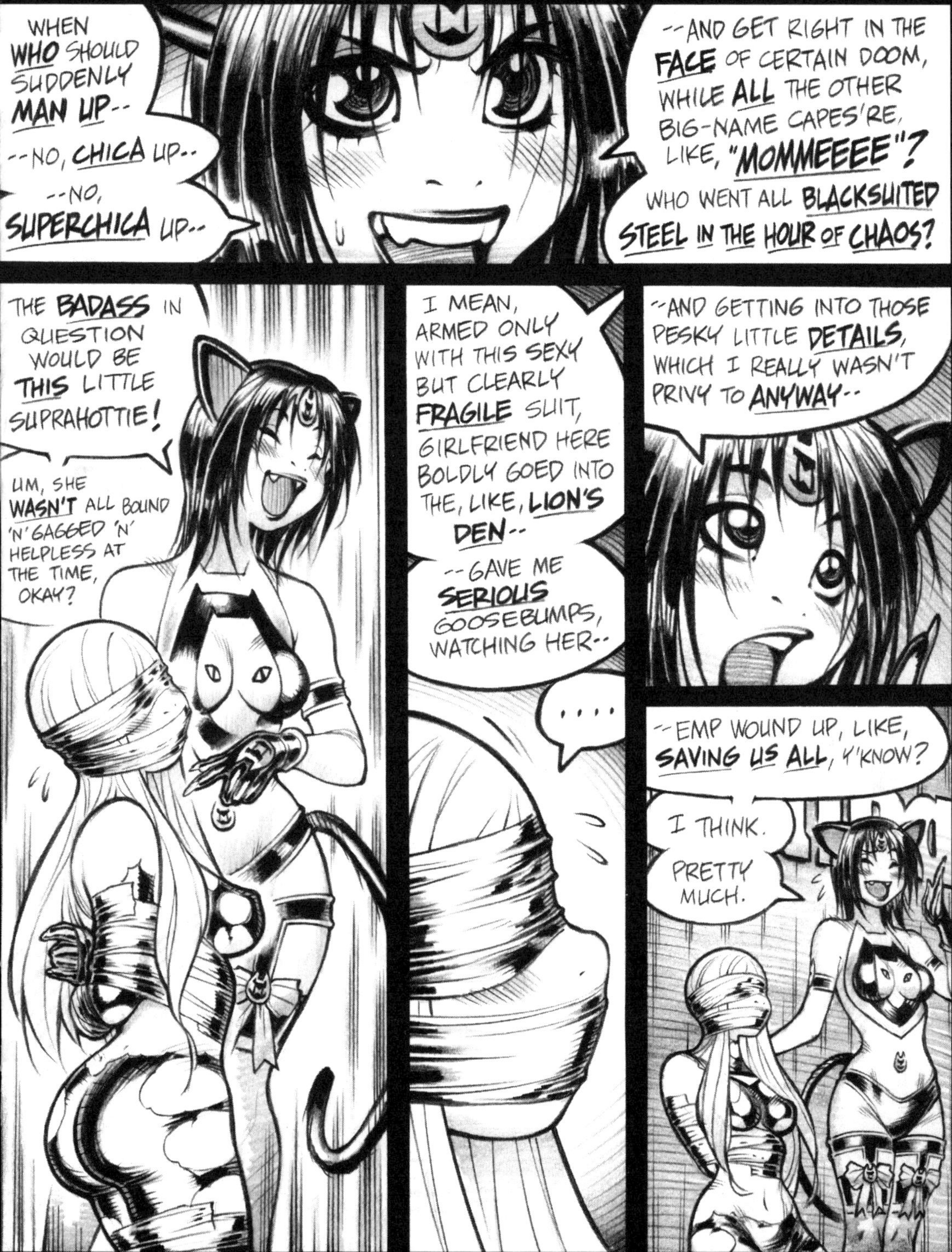
WHEN WHO SHOULD SUDDENLY MAN UP--
--NO, CHICA UP--
--NO, SUPERCHICA UP--
--AND GET RIGHT IN THE FACE OF CERTAIN DOOM, WHILE ALL THE OTHER BIG-NAME CAPES'RE, LIKE, "MOMMEEEE"?
WHO WENT ALL BLACKSUITED STEEL IN THE HOUR OF CHAOS?
THE BADASS IN QUESTION WOULD BE THIS LITTLE SUPRAHOTTIE!
UM, SHE WASN'T ALL BOUND 'N' GAGGED 'N' HELPLESS AT THE TIME, OKAY?
I MEAN, ARMED ONLY WITH THIS SEXY BUT CLEARLY FRAGILE SUIT, GIRLFRIEND HERE BOLDLY GOED INTO THE, LIKE, LION'S DEN--
--GAVE ME SERIOUS GOOSEBUMPS, WATCHING HER--
....
--AND GETTING INTO THOSE PESKY LITTLE DETAILS, WHICH I REALLY WASN'T PRIVY TO ANYWAY--
--EMP WOUND UP, LIKE, SAVING US ALL, Y'KNOW?
I THINK.
PRETTY MUCH.

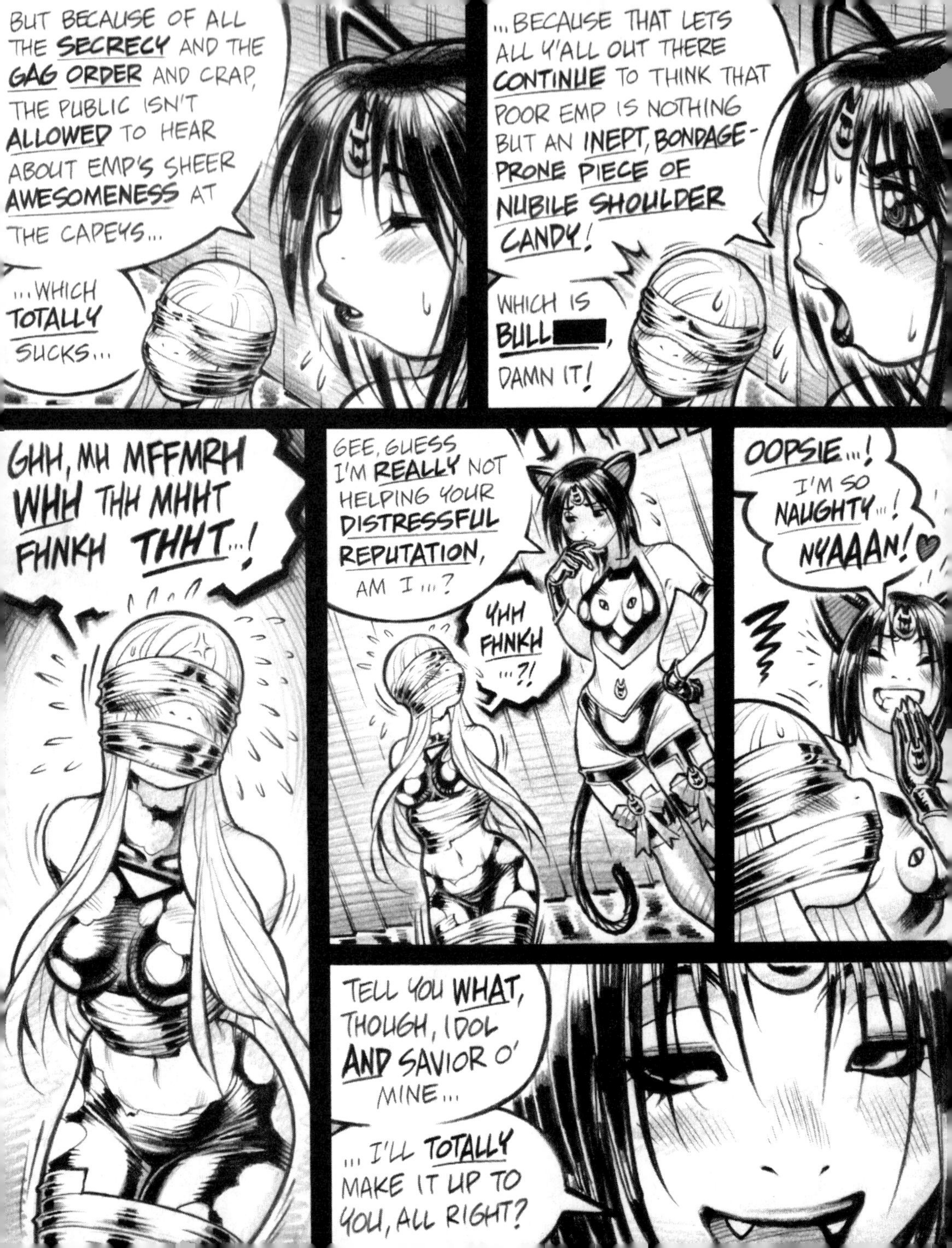
BUT BECAUSE OF ALL THE SECRECY AND THE GAG ORDER AND CRAP, THE PUBLIC ISN'T ALLOWED TO HEAR ABOUT EMP'S SHEER AWESOMENESS AT THE CAPEYS...
...WHICH TOTALLY SUCKS...
...BECAUSE THAT LETS ALL Y'ALL OUT THERE CONTINUE TO THINK THAT POOR EMP IS NOTHING BUT AN INEPT, BONDAGE-PRONE PIECE OF NUBILE SHOULDER CANDY!
WHICH IS BULL[redacted], DAMN IT!
GHH, MH MFFMRH WHH THH MHHT FHNKH THHT...!
GEE, GUESS I'M REALLY NOT HELPING YOUR DISTRESSFUL REPUTATION, AM I...?
YHH FHNKH...?!
OOPSIE...! I'M SO NAUGHTY...! NYAAAN!♥
TELL YOU WHAT, THOUGH, IDOL AND SAVIOR O' MINE...
...I'LL TOTALLY MAKE IT UP TO YOU, ALL RIGHT?

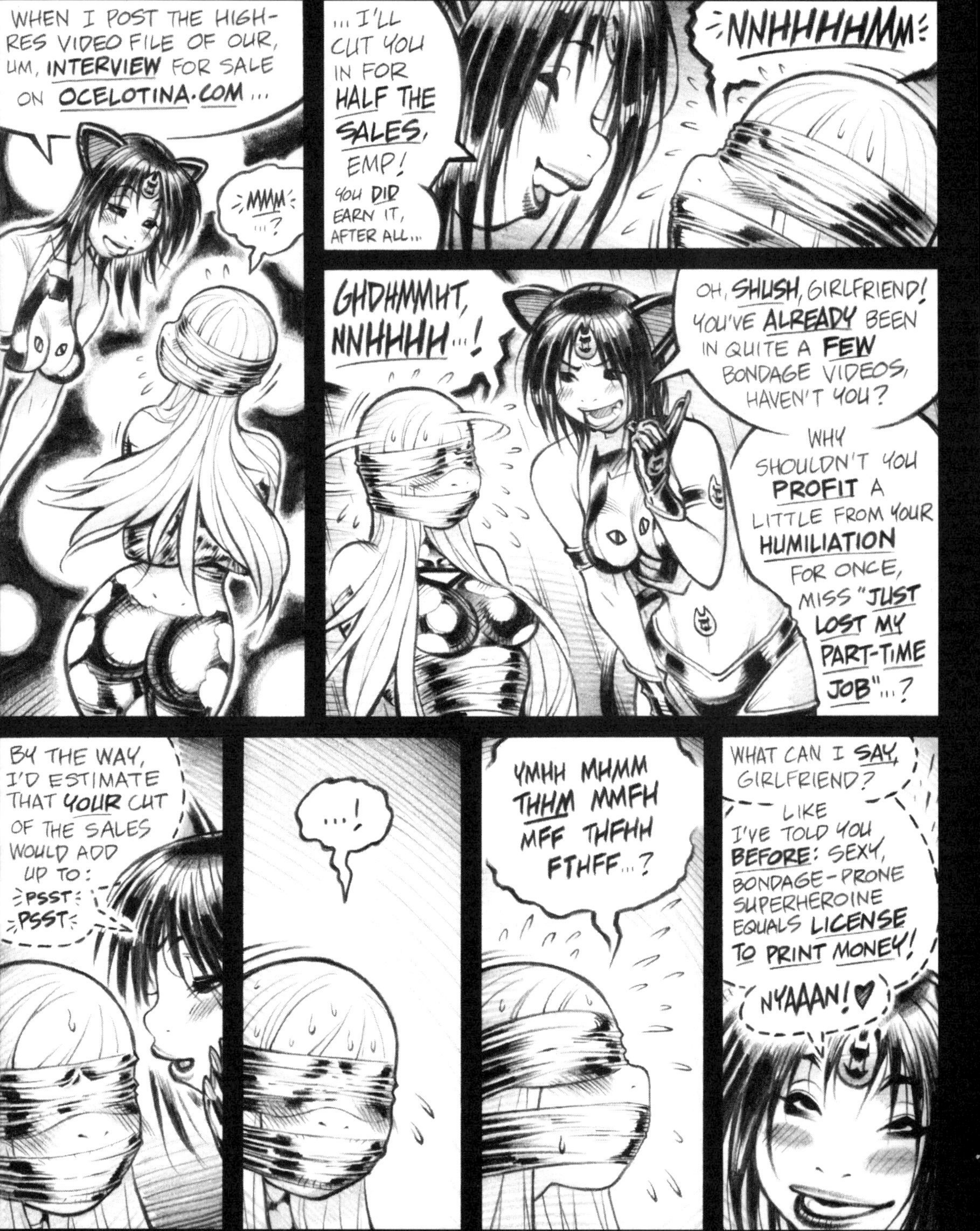
WHEN I POST THE HIGH-RES VIDEO FILE OF OUR, UM, INTERVIEW FOR SALE ON OCELOTINA.COM ...
MMM ...?
... I'LL CUT YOU IN FOR HALF THE SALES, EMP! YOU DID EARN IT, AFTER ALL...
NNHHHHHMM
GHDHMMHT, NNHHHH...!
OH, SHUSH, GIRLFRIEND! YOU'VE ALREADY BEEN IN QUITE A FEW BONDAGE VIDEOS, HAVEN'T YOU?
WHY SHOULDN'T YOU PROFIT A LITTLE FROM YOUR HUMILIATION FOR ONCE, MISS "JUST LOST MY PART-TIME JOB"...?
BY THE WAY, I'D ESTIMATE THAT YOUR CUT OF THE SALES WOULD ADD UP TO:
PSST PSST
...!
YMHH MHMM THHM MMFH MFF THFHH FTHFF...?
WHAT CAN I SAY, GIRLFRIEND?
LIKE I'VE TOLD YOU BEFORE: SEXY, BONDAGE-PRONE SUPERHEROINE EQUALS LICENSE TO PRINT MONEY!
NYAAAN! ♥

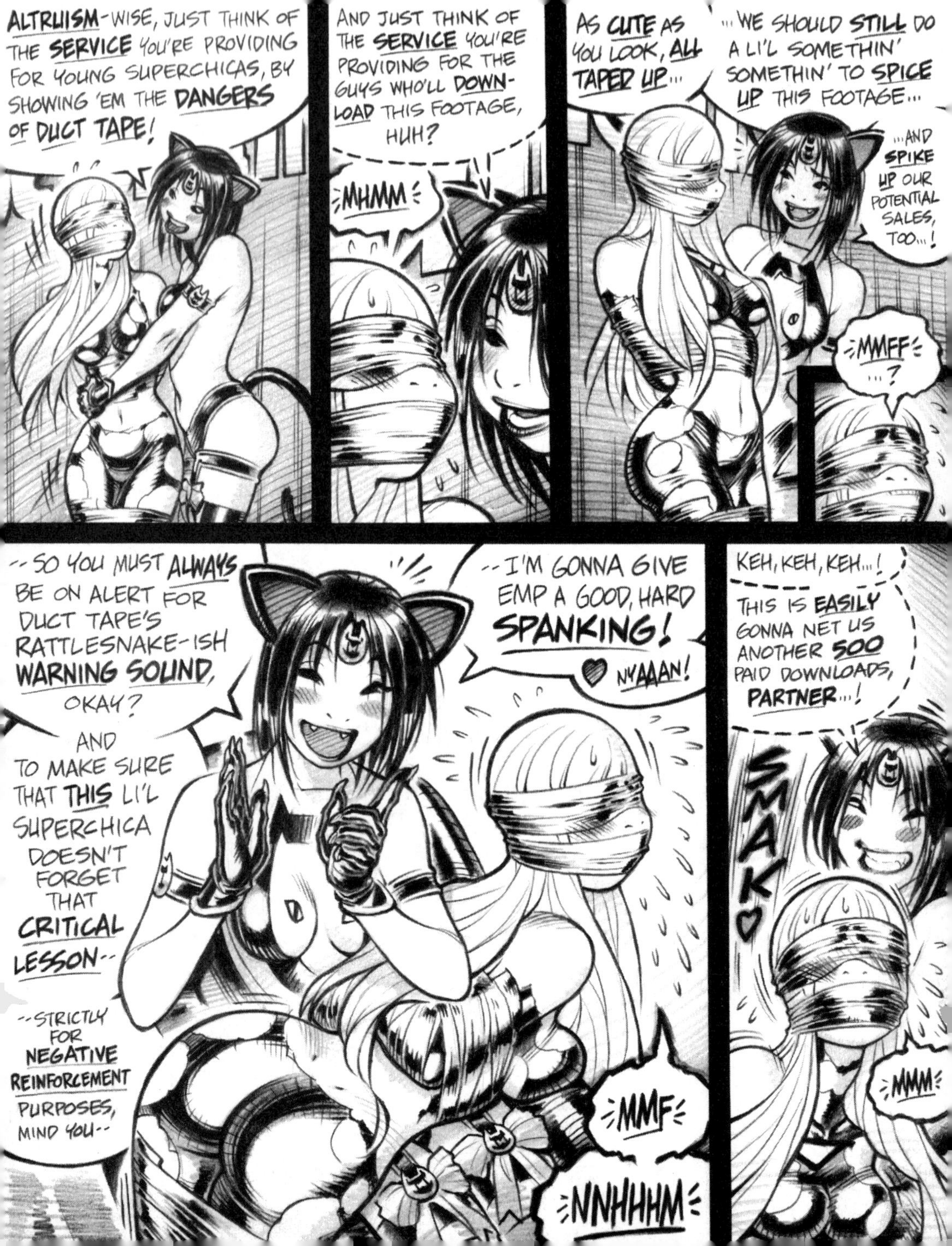
ALTRUISM-WISE, JUST THINK OF THE SERVICE YOU'RE PROVIDING FOR YOUNG SUPERCHICAS, BY SHOWING 'EM THE DANGERS OF DUCT TAPE!
AND JUST THINK OF THE SERVICE YOU'RE PROVIDING FOR THE GUYS WHO'LL DOWNLOAD THIS FOOTAGE, HUH?
MHMM
AS CUTE AS YOU LOOK, ALL TAPED UP...
...WE SHOULD STILL DO A LI'L SOMETHIN' SOMETHIN' TO SPICE UP THIS FOOTAGE...
...AND SPIKE UP OUR POTENTIAL SALES, TOO...!
MMFF...?
--SO YOU MUST ALWAYS BE ON ALERT FOR DUCT TAPE'S RATTLESNAKE-ISH WARNING SOUND, OKAY?
AND TO MAKE SURE THAT THIS LI'L SUPERCHICA DOESN'T FORGET THAT CRITICAL LESSON--
--STRICTLY FOR NEGATIVE REINFORCEMENT PURPOSES, MIND YOU--
--I'M GONNA GIVE EMP A GOOD, HARD SPANKING! ♥ NYAAAN!
MMF
NNHHHM
KEH, KEH, KEH...!
THIS IS EASILY GONNA NET US ANOTHER 500 PAID DOWNLOADS, PARTNER...!
SMAK♥
MMM

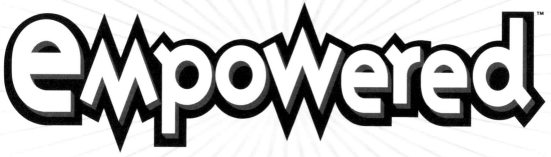

Empowered™

Problems with the Equipment

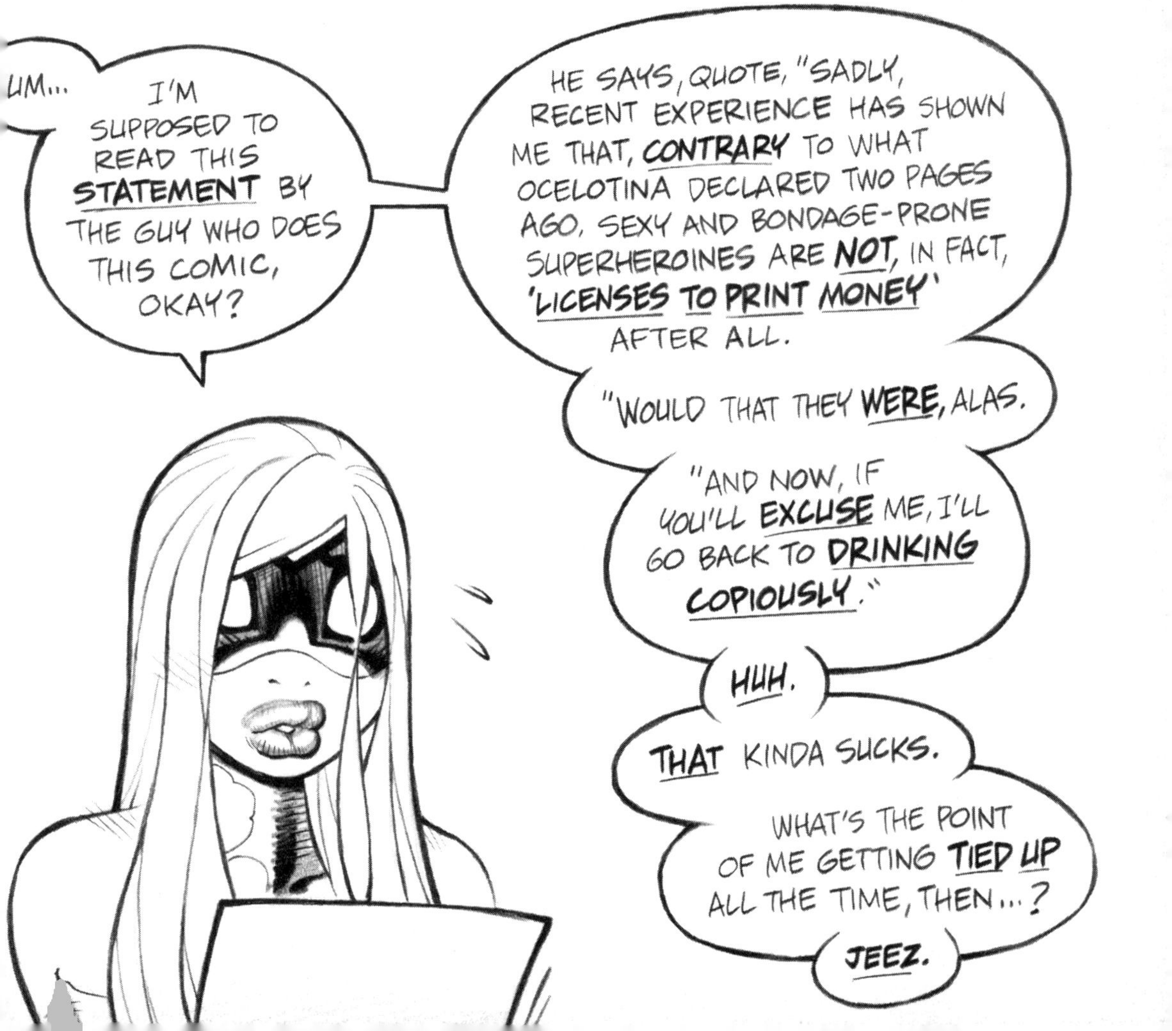
UM...
I'M SUPPOSED TO READ THIS STATEMENT BY THE GUY WHO DOES THIS COMIC, OKAY?
HE SAYS, QUOTE, "SADLY, RECENT EXPERIENCE HAS SHOWN ME THAT, CONTRARY TO WHAT OCELOTINA DECLARED TWO PAGES AGO, SEXY AND BONDAGE-PRONE SUPERHEROINES ARE NOT, IN FACT, 'LICENSES TO PRINT MONEY' AFTER ALL.
"WOULD THAT THEY WERE, ALAS.
"AND NOW, IF YOU'LL EXCUSE ME, I'LL GO BACK TO DRINKING COPIOUSLY."
HUH.
THAT KINDA SUCKS.
WHAT'S THE POINT OF ME GETTING TIED UP ALL THE TIME, THEN...?
JEEZ.

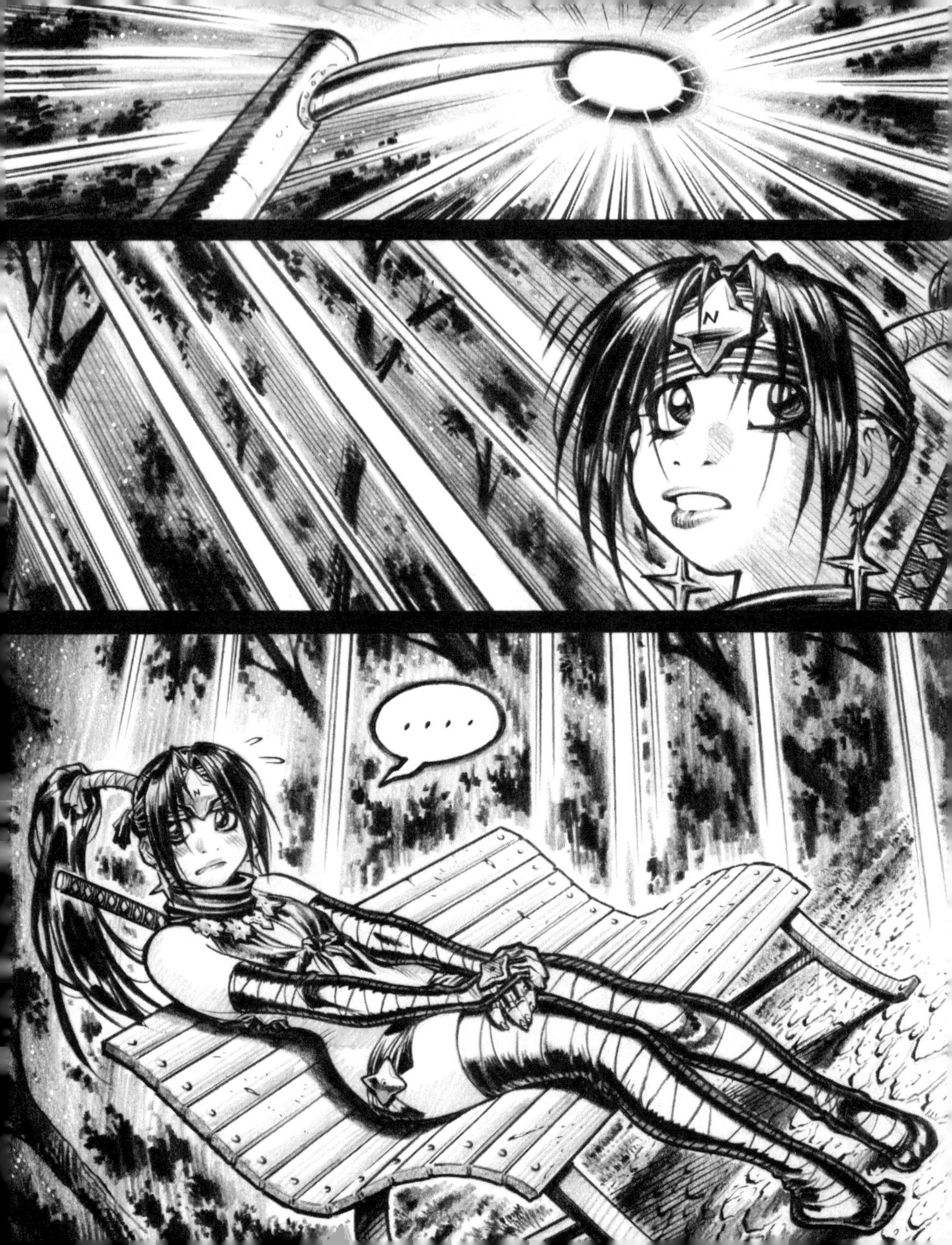
....

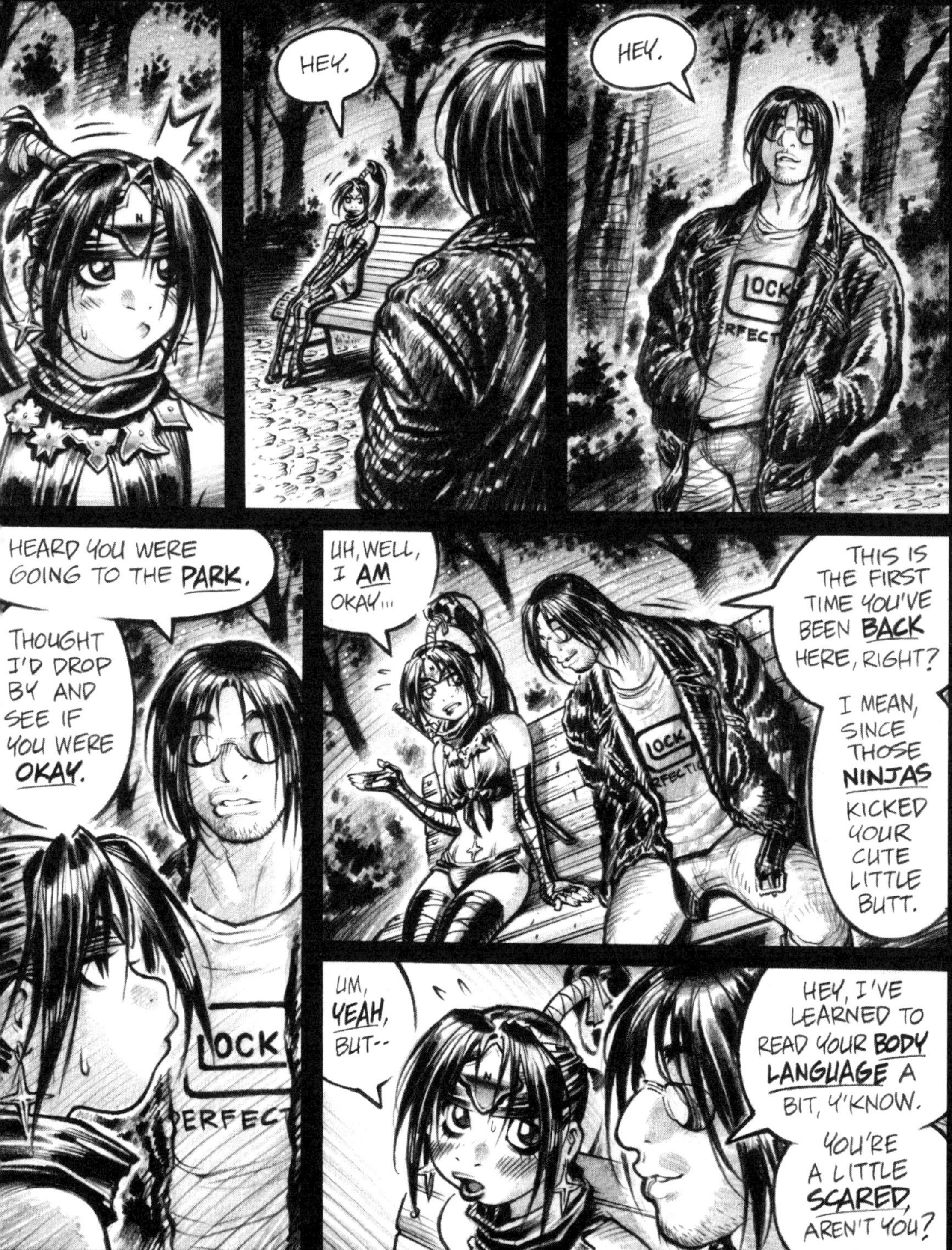

HEY.
HEY.
HEARD YOU WERE GOING TO THE PARK.
THOUGHT I'D DROP BY AND SEE IF YOU WERE OKAY.
LOCK
PERFECT
UH, WELL, I AM OKAY...
THIS IS THE FIRST TIME YOU'VE BEEN BACK HERE, RIGHT?
I MEAN, SINCE THOSE NINJAS KICKED YOUR CUTE LITTLE BUTT.
UM, YEAH, BUT--
HEY, I'VE LEARNED TO READ YOUR BODY LANGUAGE A BIT, Y'KNOW.
YOU'RE A LITTLE SCARED, AREN'T YOU?

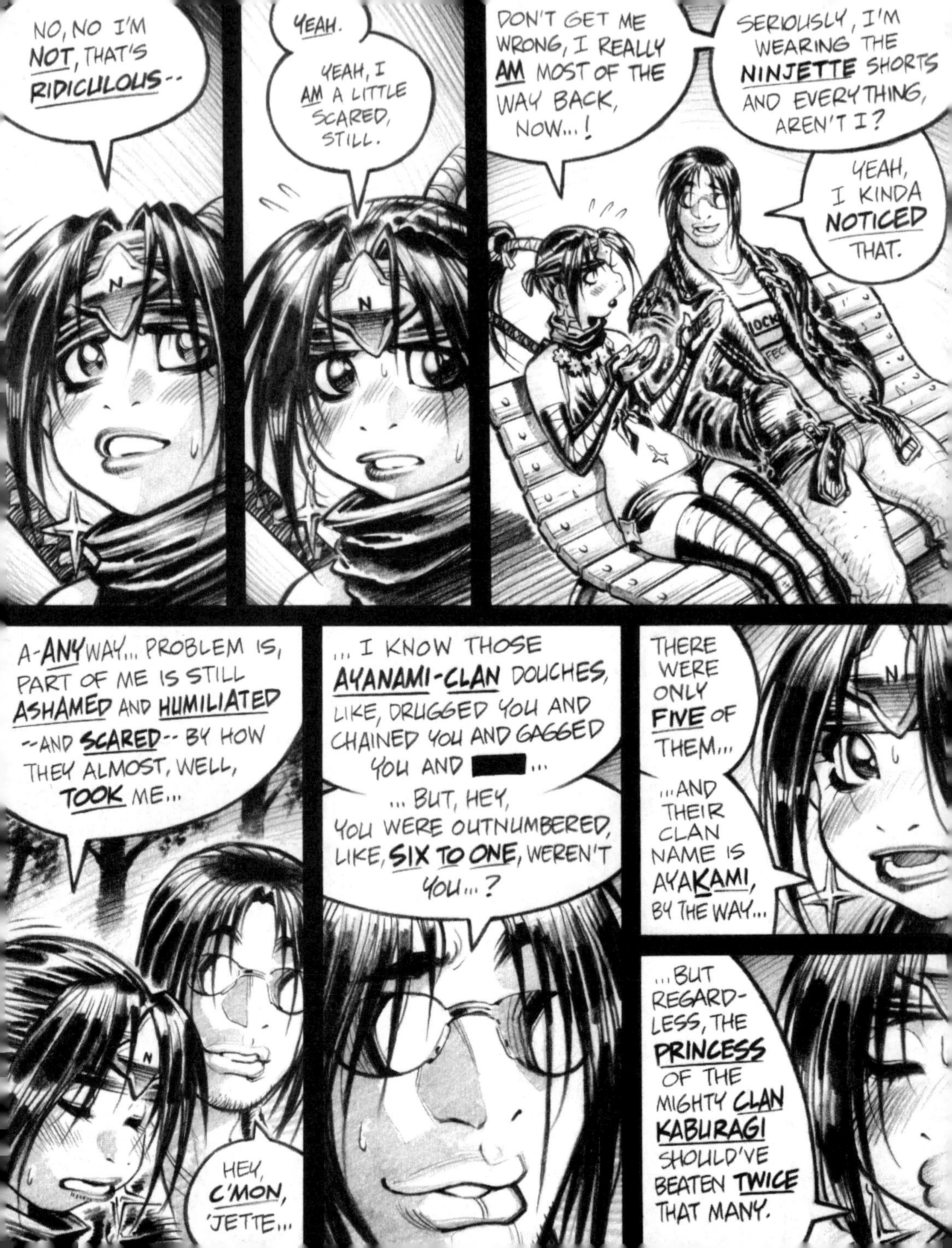

NO, NO I'M NOT, THAT'S RIDICULOUS--
YEAH.
YEAH, I AM A LITTLE SCARED, STILL.
DON'T GET ME WRONG, I REALLY AM MOST OF THE WAY BACK, NOW...!
SERIOUSLY, I'M WEARING THE NINJETTE SHORTS AND EVERYTHING, AREN'T I?
YEAH, I KINDA NOTICED THAT.
A-ANYWAY... PROBLEM IS, PART OF ME IS STILL ASHAMED AND HUMILIATED --AND SCARED-- BY HOW THEY ALMOST, WELL, TOOK ME...
HEY, C'MON, 'JETTE...
...I KNOW THOSE AYANAMI-CLAN DOUCHES, LIKE, DRUGGED YOU AND CHAINED YOU AND GAGGED YOU AND [redacted]...
...BUT, HEY, YOU WERE OUTNUMBERED, LIKE, SIX TO ONE, WEREN'T YOU...?
THERE WERE ONLY FIVE OF THEM...
...AND THEIR CLAN NAME IS AYAKAMI, BY THE WAY...
...BUT REGARDLESS, THE PRINCESS OF THE MIGHTY CLAN KABURAGI SHOULD'VE BEATEN TWICE THAT MANY.

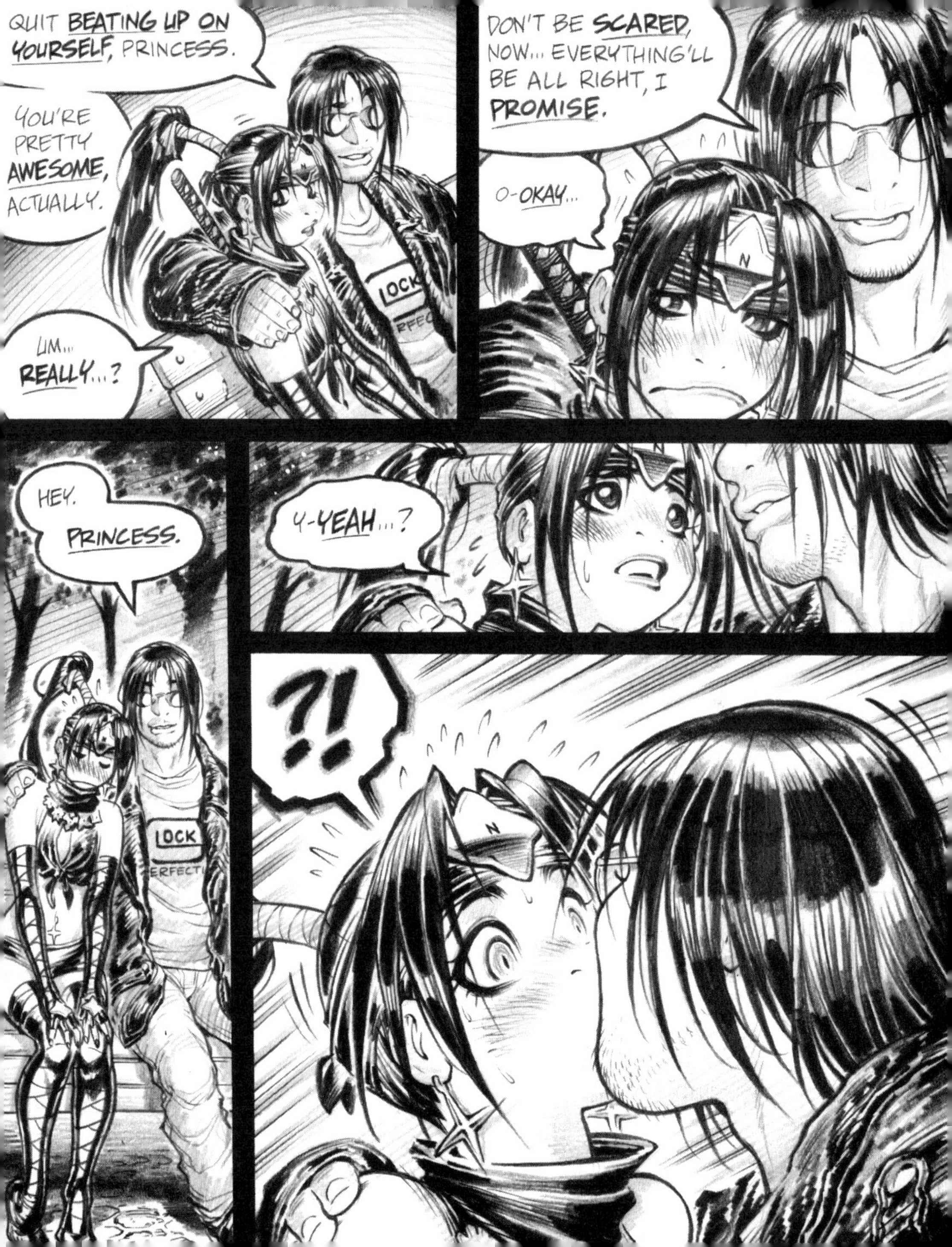
QUIT BEATING UP ON YOURSELF, PRINCESS.
YOU'RE PRETTY AWESOME, ACTUALLY.
UM... REALLY...?
LOCK
DON'T BE SCARED, NOW... EVERYTHING'LL BE ALL RIGHT, I PROMISE.
O-OKAY...
HEY. PRINCESS.
Y-YEAH...?
LOCK
?!

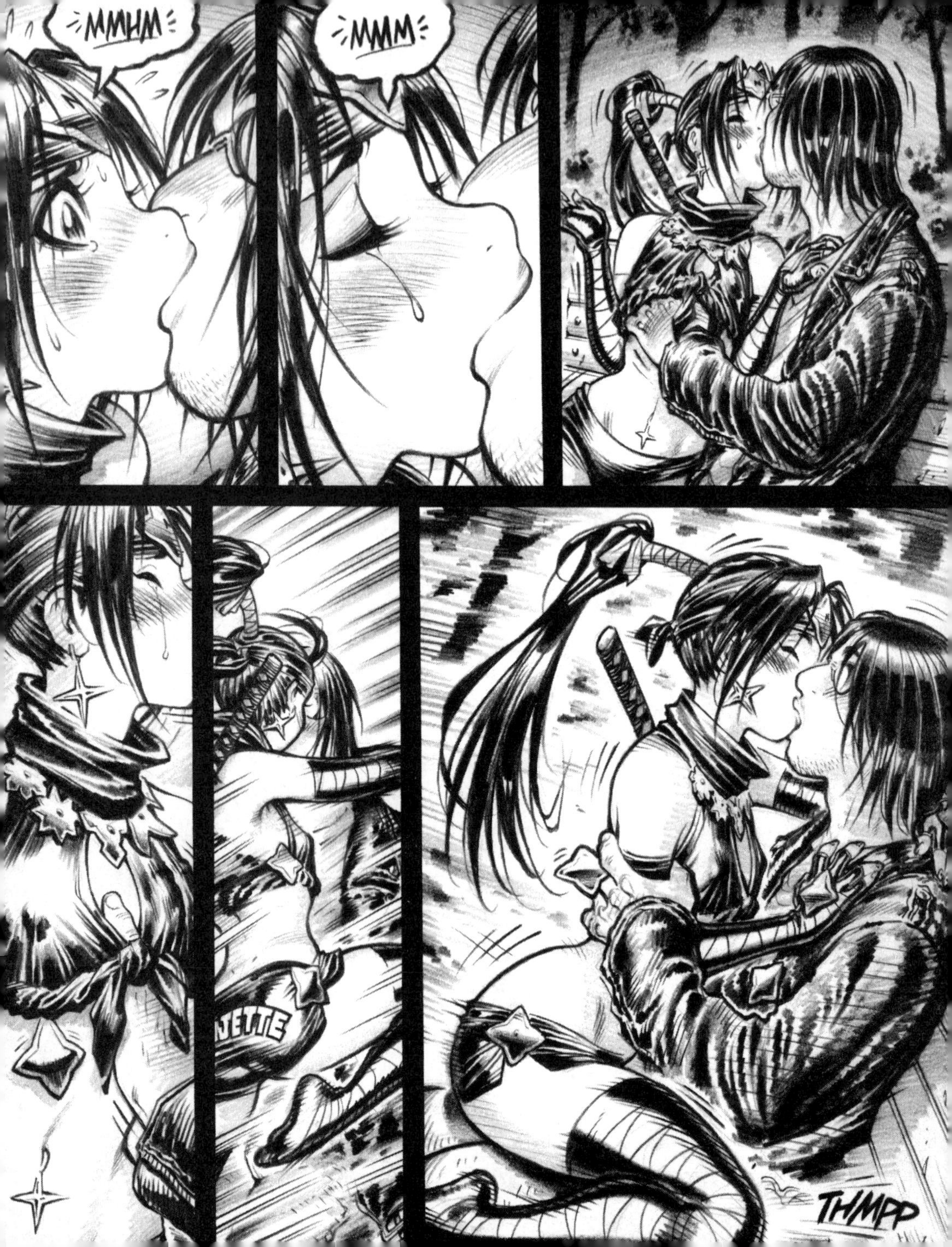
MMHM
MMM
JETTE
THMPP

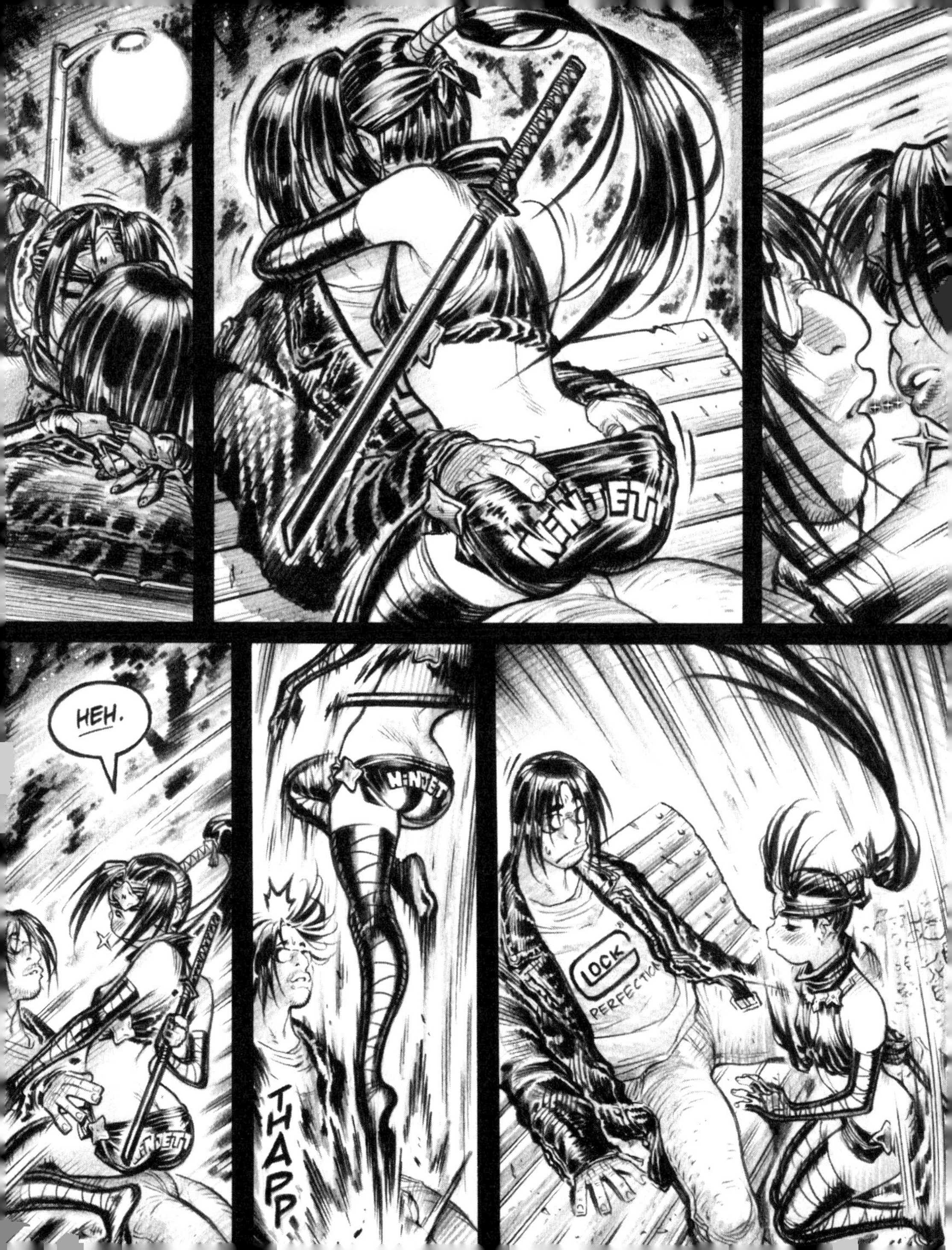
HEH.
THAPP

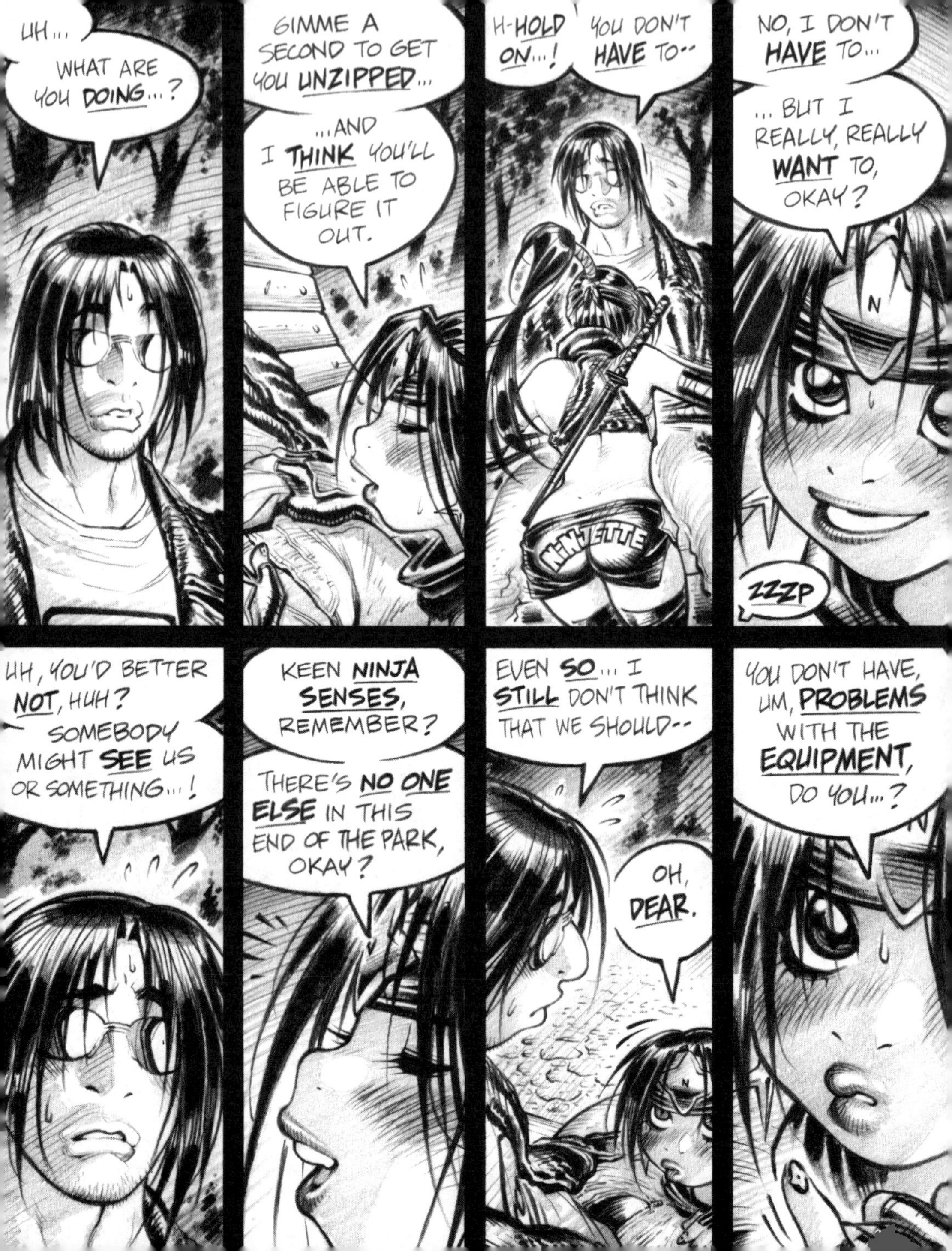
UH...
WHAT ARE YOU DOING...?
GIMME A SECOND TO GET YOU UNZIPPED...
...AND I THINK YOU'LL BE ABLE TO FIGURE IT OUT.
H-HOLD ON...!
YOU DON'T HAVE TO--
NINJETTE
NO, I DON'T HAVE TO...
...BUT I REALLY, REALLY WANT TO, OKAY?
ZZZP
UH, YOU'D BETTER NOT, HUH?
SOMEBODY MIGHT SEE US OR SOMETHING...!
KEEN NINJA SENSES, REMEMBER?
THERE'S NO ONE ELSE IN THIS END OF THE PARK, OKAY?
EVEN SO... I STILL DON'T THINK THAT WE SHOULD--
OH, DEAR.
YOU DON'T HAVE, UM, PROBLEMS WITH THE EQUIPMENT, DO YOU...?

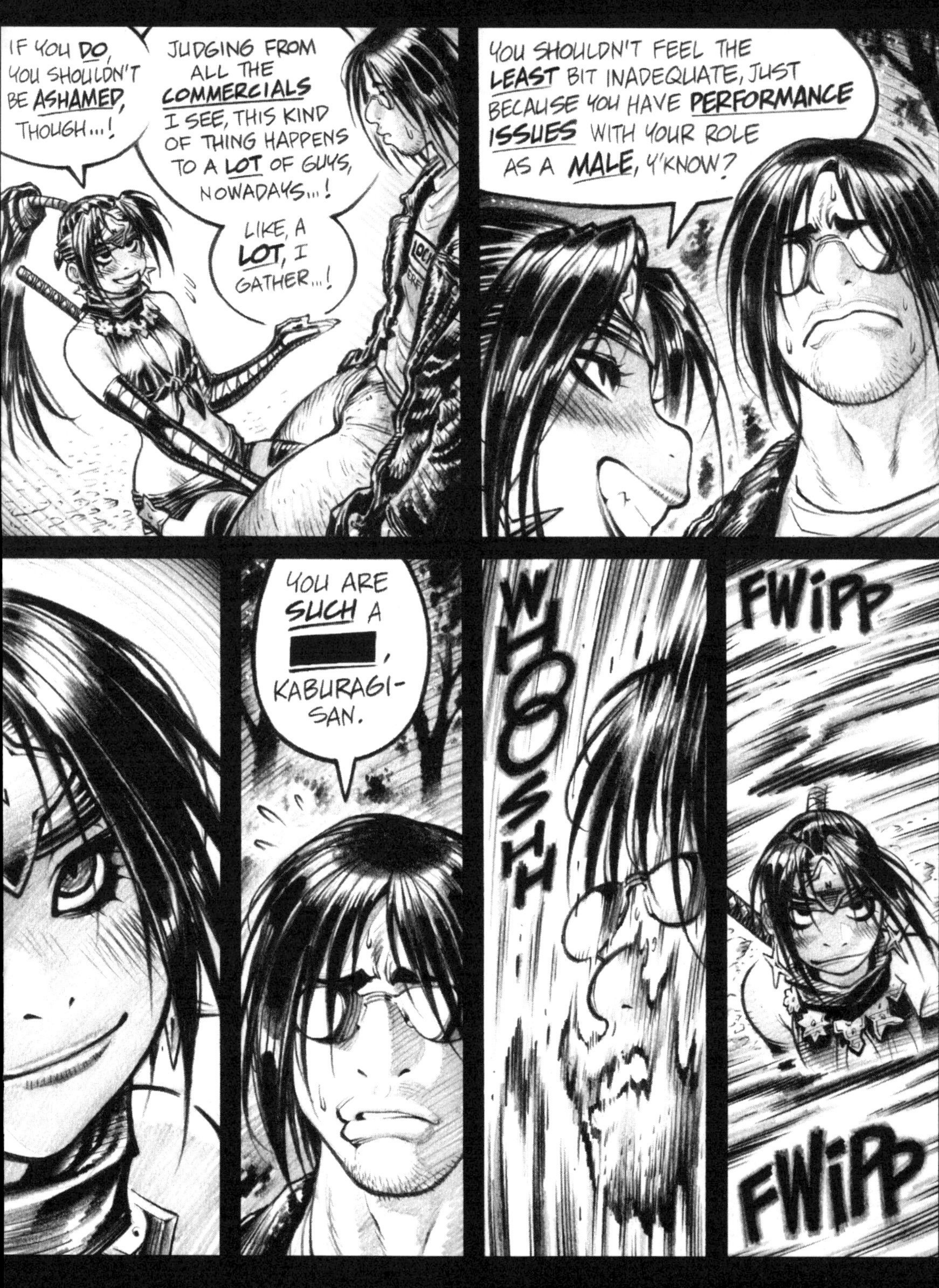
IF YOU DO, YOU SHOULDN'T BE ASHAMED, THOUGH...!
JUDGING FROM ALL THE COMMERCIALS I SEE, THIS KIND OF THING HAPPENS TO A LOT OF GUYS, NOWADAYS...!
LIKE, A LOT, I GATHER...!
YOU SHOULDN'T FEEL THE LEAST BIT INADEQUATE, JUST BECAUSE YOU HAVE PERFORMANCE ISSUES WITH YOUR ROLE AS A MALE, Y'KNOW?
YOU ARE SUCH A [redacted], KABURAGI-SAN.
WHOOSH
FWIPP
FWIPP

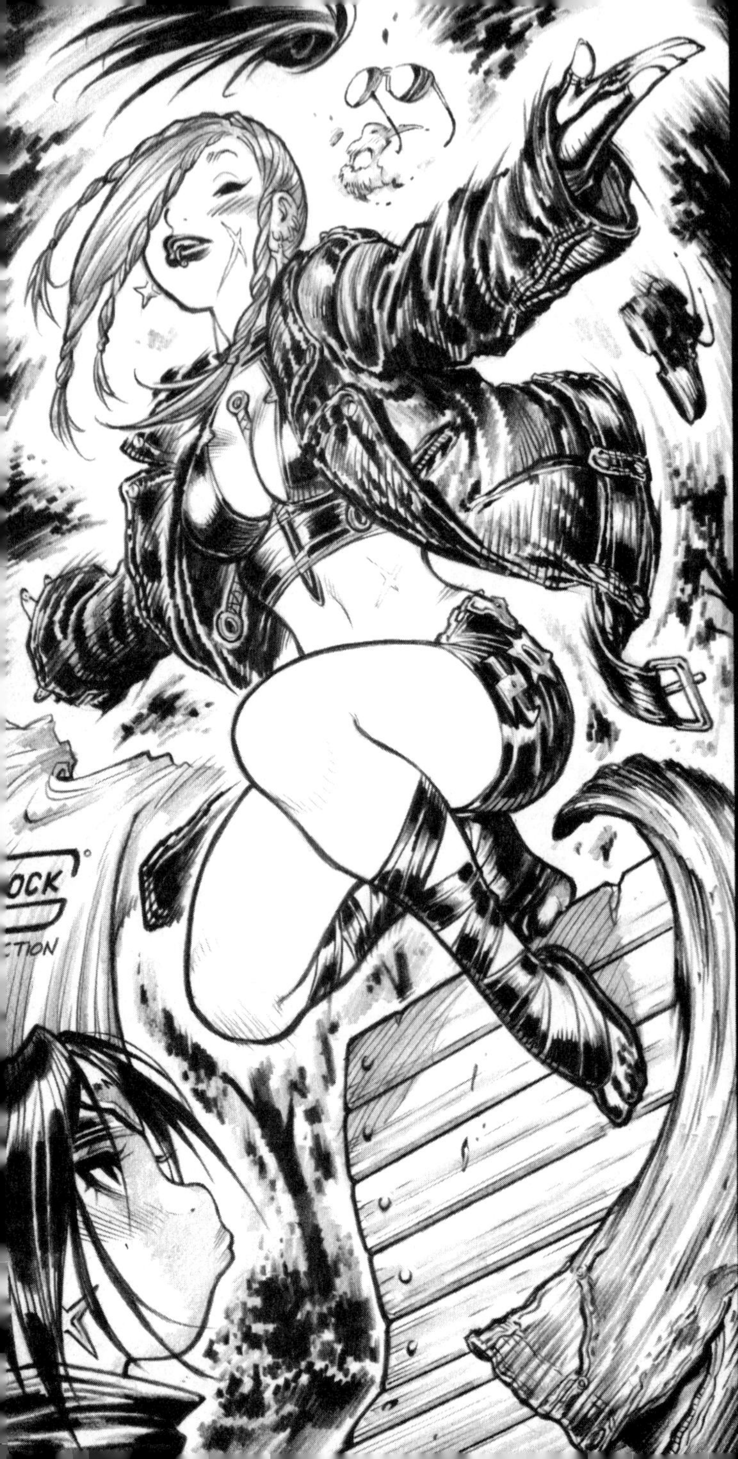

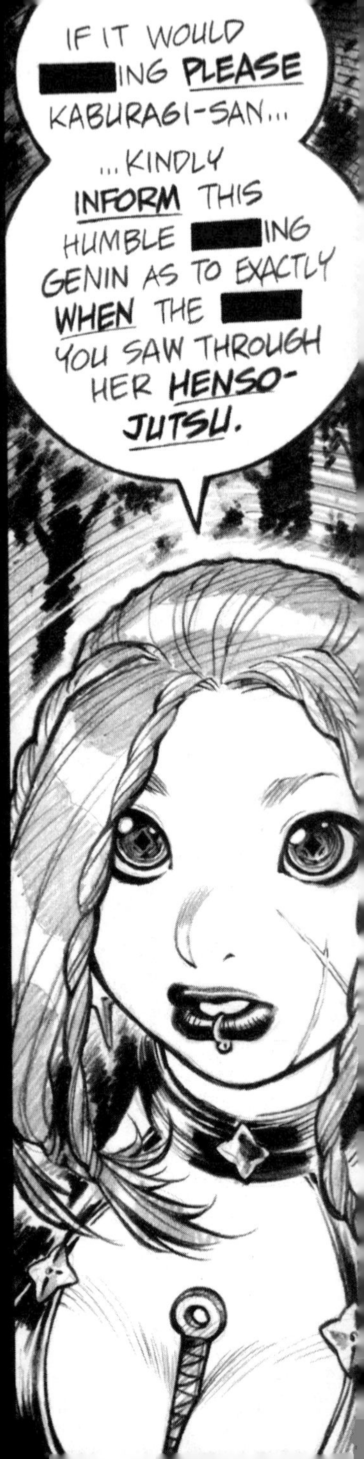
IF IT WOULD [redacted]ING PLEASE KABURAGI-SAN... ...KINDLY INFORM THIS HUMBLE [redacted]ING GENIN AS TO EXACTLY WHEN THE [redacted] YOU SAW THROUGH HER HENSO-JUTSU.

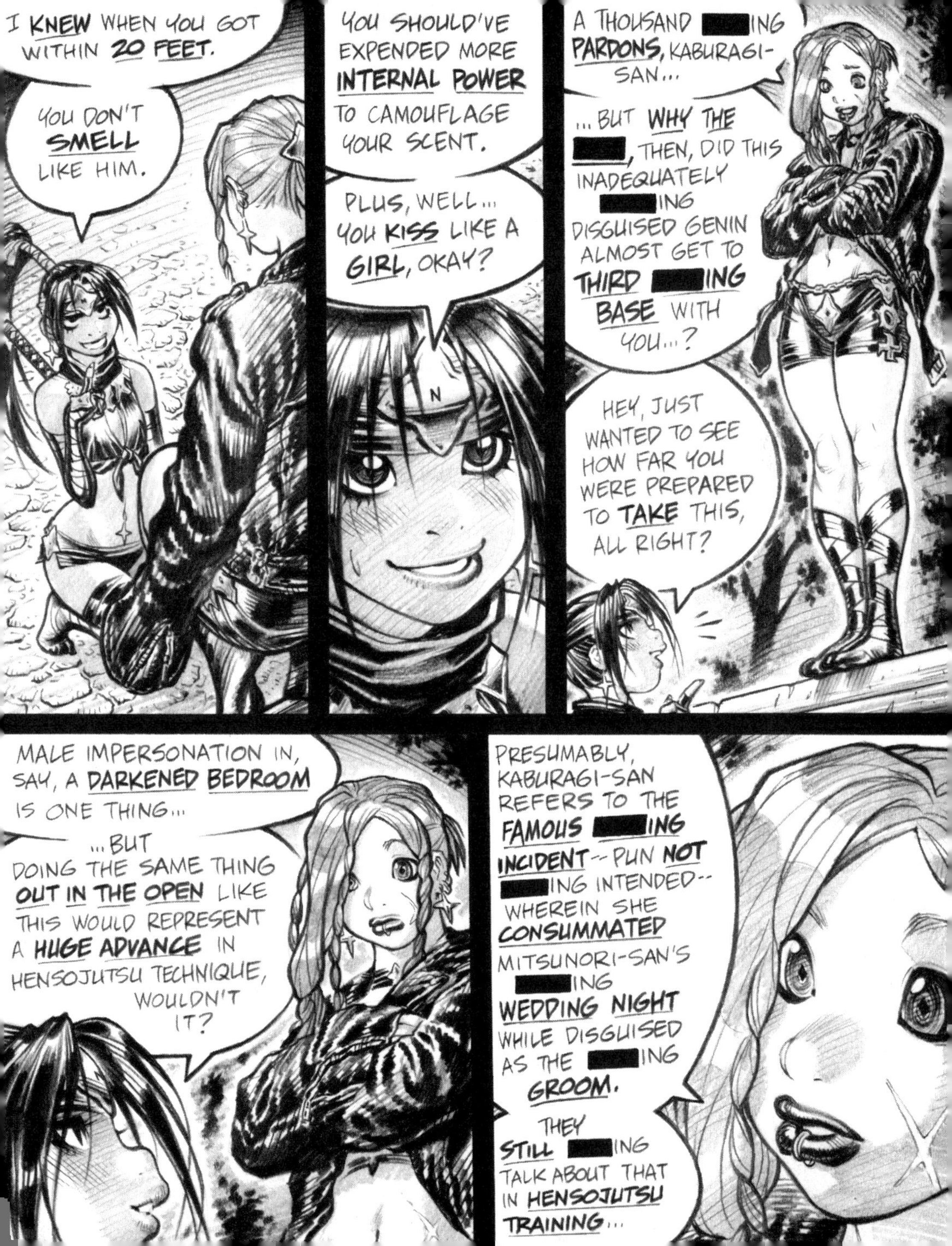
I KNEW WHEN YOU GOT WITHIN 20 FEET.
YOU DON'T SMELL LIKE HIM.
YOU SHOULD'VE EXPENDED MORE INTERNAL POWER TO CAMOUFLAGE YOUR SCENT.
PLUS, WELL... YOU KISS LIKE A GIRL, OKAY?
A THOUSAND [redacted]ING PARDONS, KABURAGI-SAN...
...BUT WHY THE [redacted], THEN, DID THIS INADEQUATELY [redacted]ING DISGUISED GENIN ALMOST GET TO THIRD [redacted]ING BASE WITH YOU...?
HEY, JUST WANTED TO SEE HOW FAR YOU WERE PREPARED TO TAKE THIS, ALL RIGHT?
MALE IMPERSONATION IN, SAY, A DARKENED BEDROOM IS ONE THING...
...BUT DOING THE SAME THING OUT IN THE OPEN LIKE THIS WOULD REPRESENT A HUGE ADVANCE IN HENSOJUTSU TECHNIQUE, WOULDN'T IT?
PRESUMABLY, KABURAGI-SAN REFERS TO THE FAMOUS [redacted]ING INCIDENT-- PUN NOT [redacted]ING INTENDED-- WHEREIN SHE CONSUMMATED MITSUNORI-SAN'S [redacted]ING WEDDING NIGHT WHILE DISGUISED AS THE [redacted]ING GROOM.
THEY STILL [redacted]ING TALK ABOUT THAT IN HENSOJUTSU TRAINING...

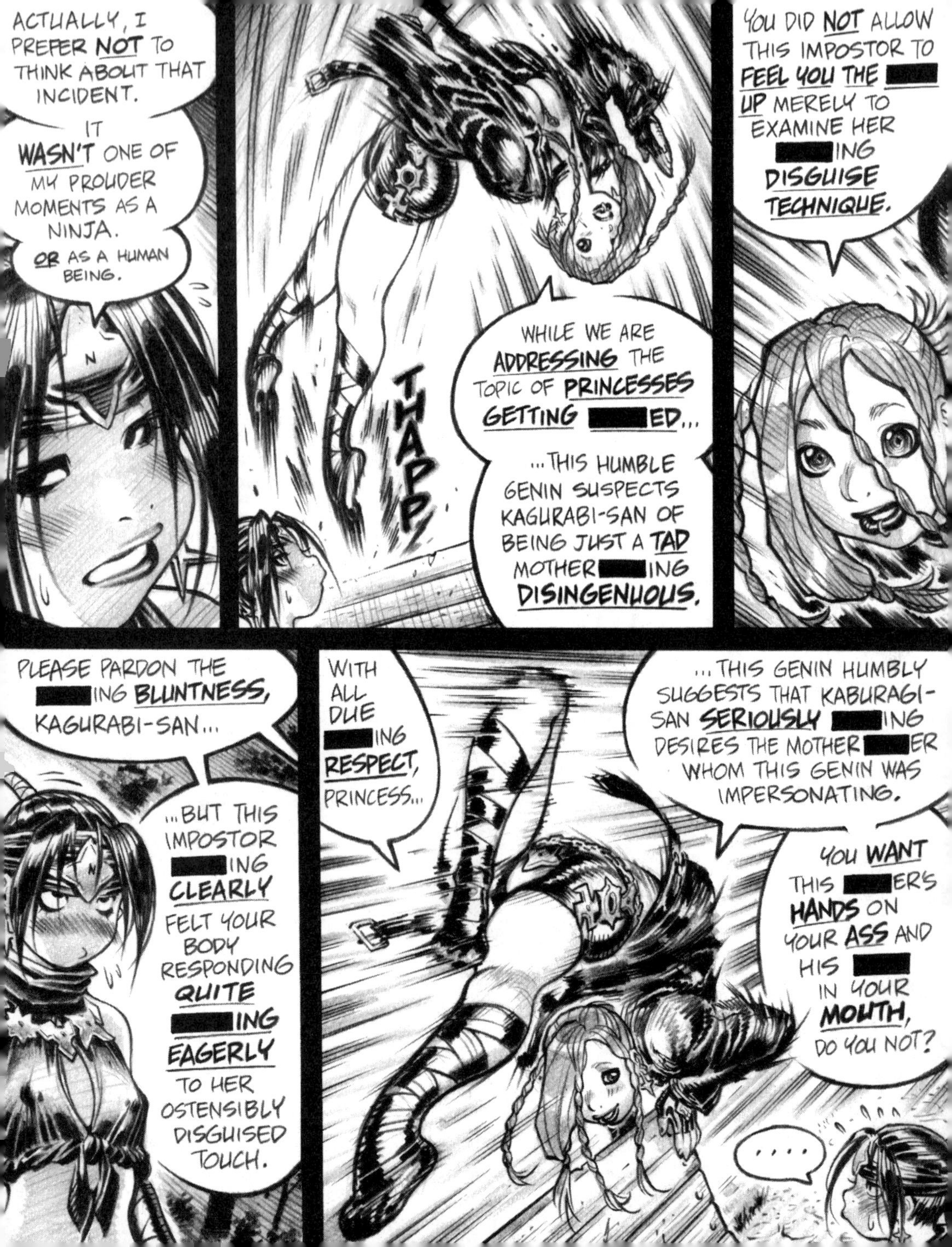
ACTUALLY, I PREFER NOT TO THINK ABOUT THAT INCIDENT.
IT WASN'T ONE OF MY PROUDER MOMENTS AS A NINJA.
OR AS A HUMAN BEING.
THAPP
WHILE WE ARE ADDRESSING THE TOPIC OF PRINCESSES GETTING [redacted]ED...
...THIS HUMBLE GENIN SUSPECTS KAGURABI-SAN OF BEING JUST A TAD MOTHER[redacted]ING DISINGENUOUS.
YOU DID NOT ALLOW THIS IMPOSTOR TO FEEL YOU THE [redacted] UP MERELY TO EXAMINE HER [redacted]ING DISGUISE TECHNIQUE.
PLEASE PARDON THE [redacted]ING BLUNTNESS, KAGURABI-SAN...
...BUT THIS IMPOSTOR [redacted]ING CLEARLY FELT YOUR BODY RESPONDING QUITE [redacted]ING EAGERLY TO HER OSTENSIBLY DISGUISED TOUCH.
WITH ALL DUE [redacted]ING RESPECT, PRINCESS...
...THIS GENIN HUMBLY SUGGESTS THAT KABURAGI-SAN SERIOUSLY [redacted]ING DESIRES THE MOTHER[redacted]ER WHOM THIS GENIN WAS IMPERSONATING.
YOU WANT THIS [redacted]ER'S HANDS ON YOUR ASS AND HIS [redacted] IN YOUR MOUTH, DO YOU NOT?
....

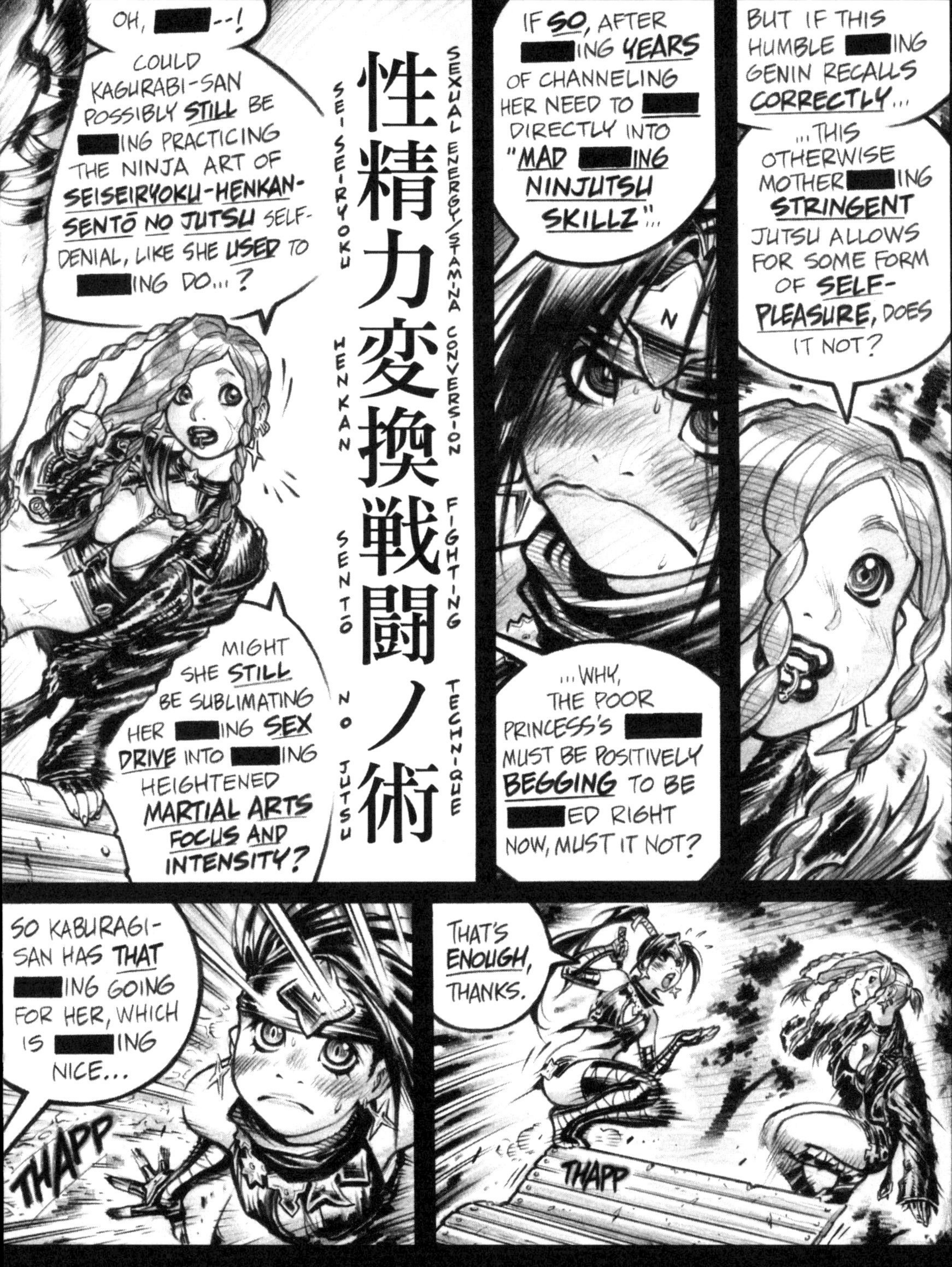
OH, [redacted]--!
COULD KAGURABI-SAN POSSIBLY STILL BE [redacted]ING PRACTICING THE NINJA ART OF SEISEIRYOKU-HENKAN-SENTŌ NO JUTSU SELF-DENIAL, LIKE SHE USED TO [redacted]ING DO...?
性精力変換戦闘ノ術
SEI-SEIRYOKU HENKAN SENTŌ NO JUTSU
SEXUAL ENERGY/STAMINA CONVERSION FIGHTING TECHNIQUE
MIGHT SHE STILL BE SUBLIMATING HER [redacted]ING SEX DRIVE INTO [redacted]ING HEIGHTENED MARTIAL ARTS FOCUS AND INTENSITY?
IF SO, AFTER [redacted]ING YEARS OF CHANNELING HER NEED TO [redacted] DIRECTLY INTO "MAD [redacted]ING NINJUTSU SKILLZ"...
N
...WHY, THE POOR PRINCESS'S [redacted] MUST BE POSITIVELY BEGGING TO BE [redacted]ED RIGHT NOW, MUST IT NOT?
BUT IF THIS HUMBLE [redacted]ING GENIN RECALLS CORRECTLY...
...THIS OTHERWISE MOTHER[redacted]ING STRINGENT JUTSU ALLOWS FOR SOME FORM OF SELF-PLEASURE, DOES IT NOT?
SO KABURAGI-SAN HAS THAT [redacted]ING GOING FOR HER, WHICH IS [redacted]ING NICE...
THAPP
THAT'S ENOUGH, THANKS.
THAPP

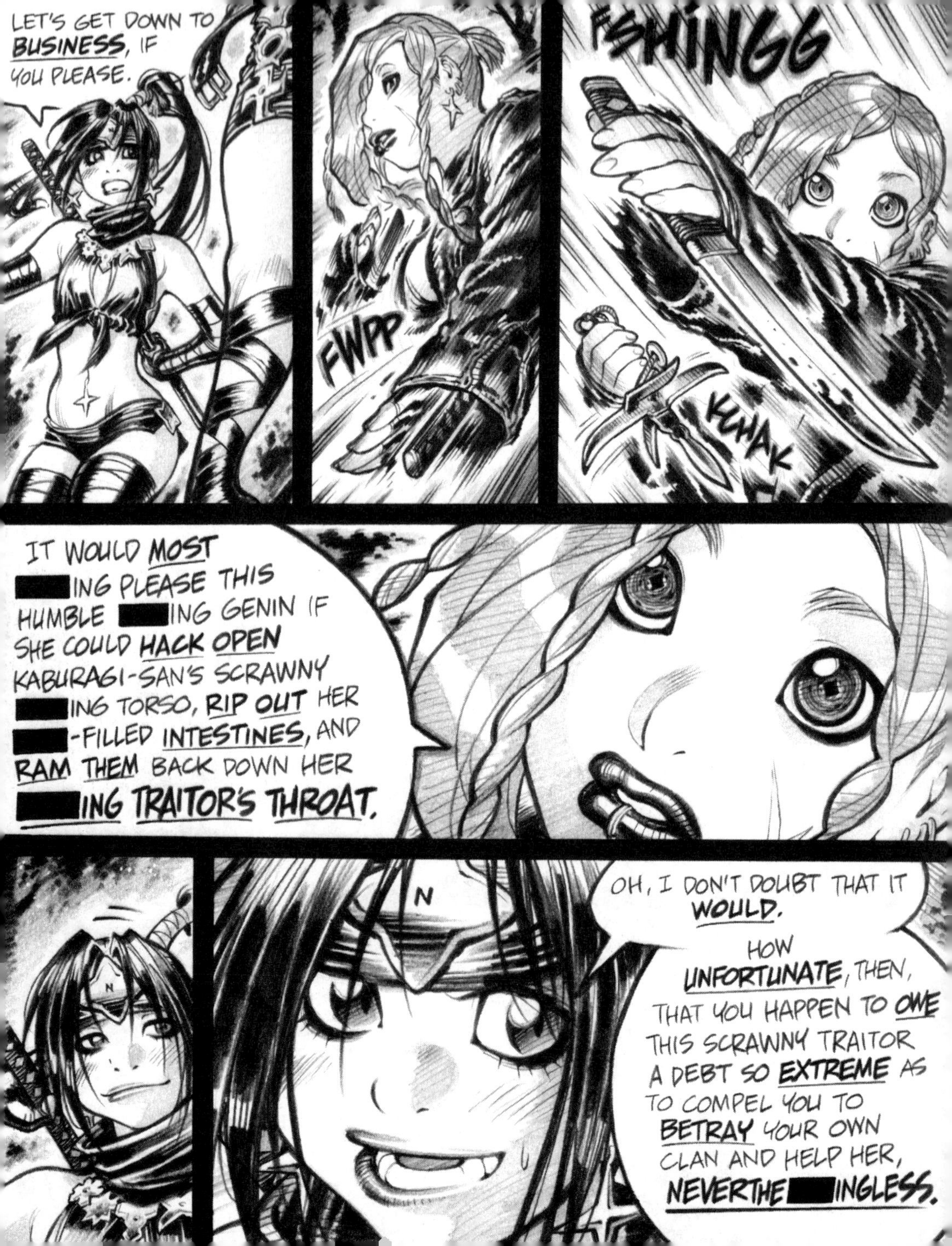
LET'S GET DOWN TO **BUSINESS**, IF YOU PLEASE.
FWPP
FSHINGG
KWAK
IT WOULD **MOST** [redacted]ING PLEASE THIS HUMBLE [redacted]ING GENIN IF SHE COULD **HACK OPEN** KABURAGI-SAN'S SCRAWNY [redacted]ING TORSO, **RIP OUT** HER [redacted]-FILLED **INTESTINES**, AND **RAM THEM** BACK DOWN HER [redacted]**ING TRAITOR'S THROAT.**
N
OH, I DON'T DOUBT THAT IT **WOULD.**
HOW **UNFORTUNATE**, THEN, THAT YOU HAPPEN TO **OWE** THIS SCRAWNY TRAITOR A DEBT SO **EXTREME** AS TO COMPEL YOU TO **BETRAY** YOUR OWN CLAN AND HELP HER, **NEVERTHE**[redacted]**INGLESS.**

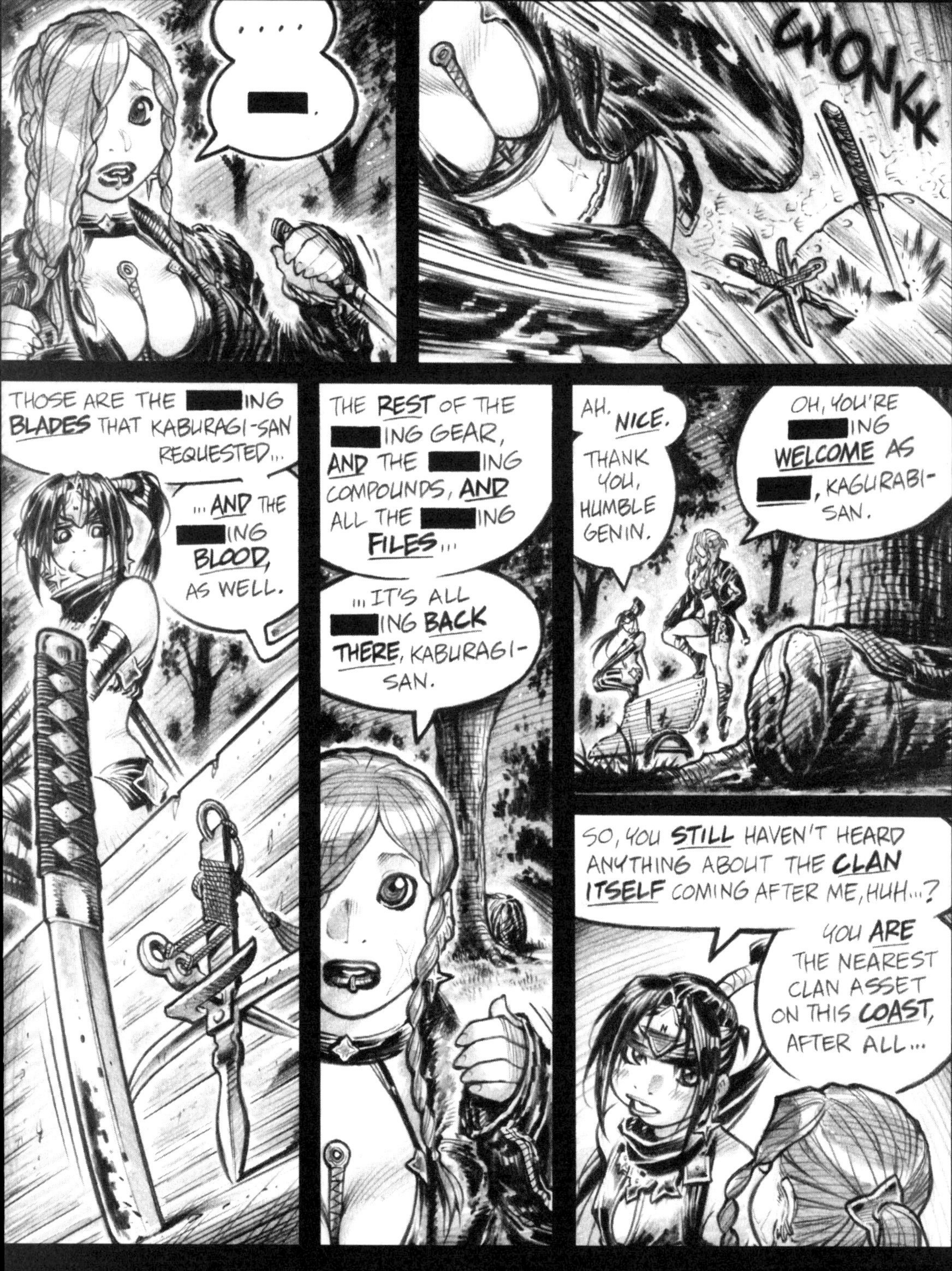
....
[redacted].
CHONKK
THOSE ARE THE [redacted]ING BLADES THAT KABURAGI-SAN REQUESTED...
...AND THE [redacted]ING BLOOD, AS WELL.
THE REST OF THE [redacted]ING GEAR, AND THE [redacted]ING COMPOUNDS, AND ALL THE [redacted]ING FILES...
...IT'S ALL [redacted]ING BACK THERE, KABURAGI-SAN.
AH. NICE. THANK YOU, HUMBLE GENIN.
OH, YOU'RE [redacted]ING WELCOME AS [redacted], KAGURABI-SAN.
SO, YOU STILL HAVEN'T HEARD ANYTHING ABOUT THE CLAN ITSELF COMING AFTER ME, HUH...?
YOU ARE THE NEAREST CLAN ASSET ON THIS COAST, AFTER ALL...

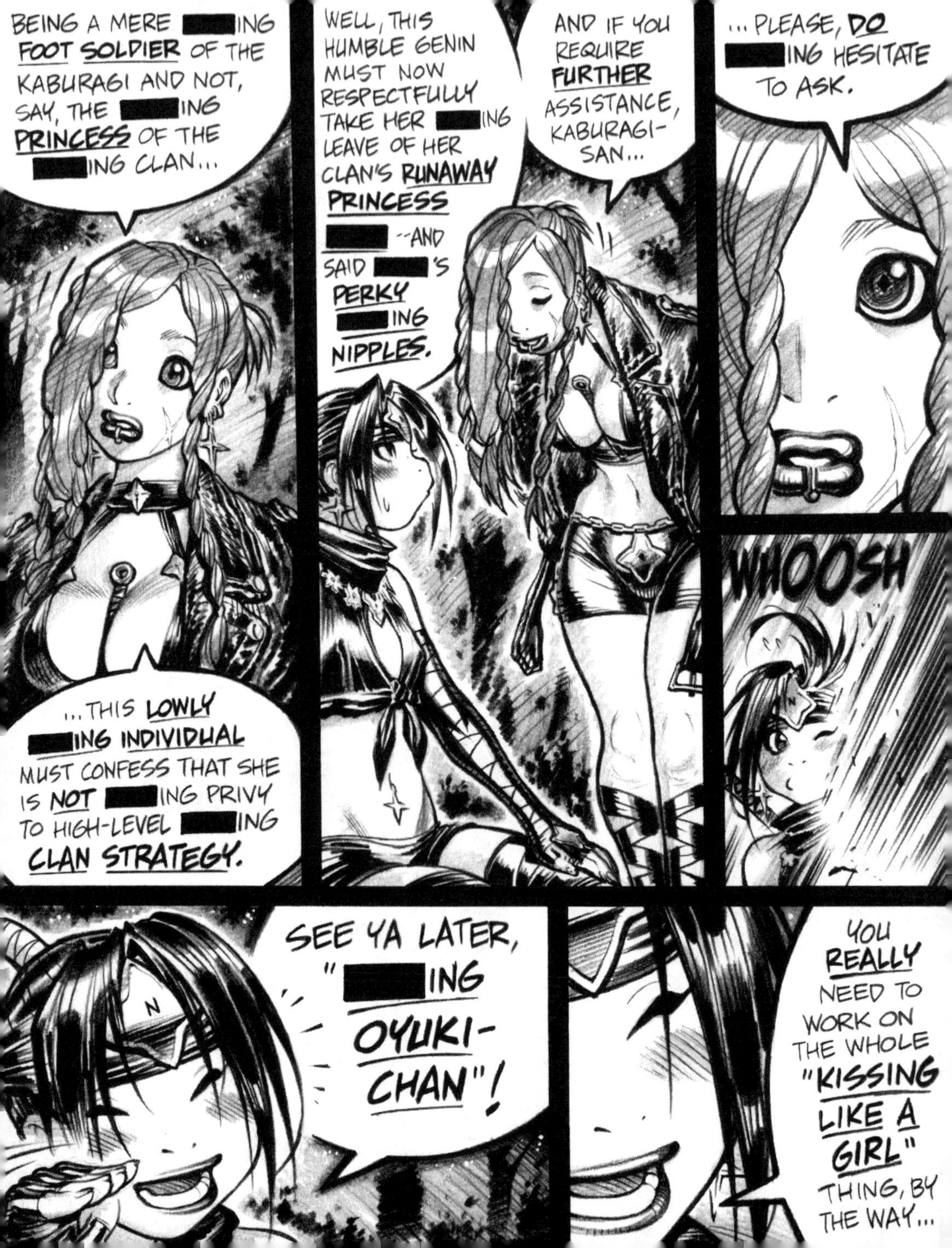
BEING A MERE [redacted]ING FOOT SOLDIER OF THE KABURAGI AND NOT, SAY, THE [redacted]ING PRINCESS OF THE [redacted]ING CLAN...
...THIS LOWLY [redacted]ING INDIVIDUAL MUST CONFESS THAT SHE IS NOT [redacted]ING PRIVY TO HIGH-LEVEL [redacted]ING CLAN STRATEGY.
WELL, THIS HUMBLE GENIN MUST NOW RESPECTFULLY TAKE HER [redacted]ING LEAVE OF HER CLAN'S RUNAWAY PRINCESS [redacted]--AND SAID [redacted]'S PERKY [redacted]ING NIPPLES.
AND IF YOU REQUIRE FURTHER ASSISTANCE, KABURAGI-SAN...
...PLEASE, DO [redacted]ING HESITATE TO ASK.
WHOOSH
SEE YA LATER, "[redacted]ING OYUKI-CHAN"!
YOU REALLY NEED TO WORK ON THE WHOLE "KISSING LIKE A GIRL" THING, BY THE WAY...

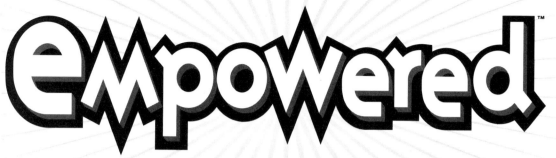

Empowered™

Upon My Back, the Monkey of Worry

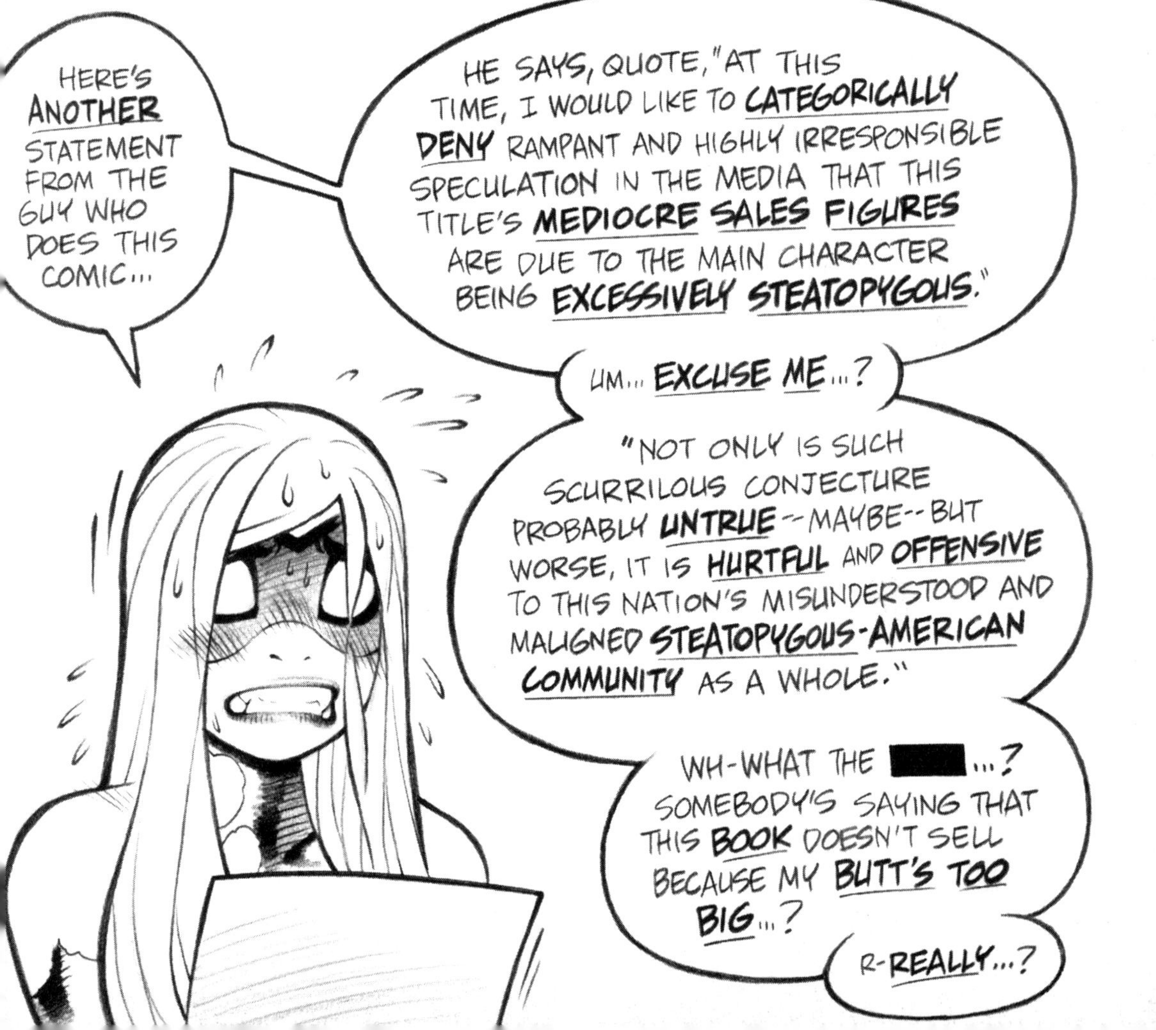
HERE'S ANOTHER STATEMENT FROM THE GUY WHO DOES THIS COMIC...
HE SAYS, QUOTE, "AT THIS TIME, I WOULD LIKE TO CATEGORICALLY DENY RAMPANT AND HIGHLY IRRESPONSIBLE SPECULATION IN THE MEDIA THAT THIS TITLE'S MEDIOCRE SALES FIGURES ARE DUE TO THE MAIN CHARACTER BEING EXCESSIVELY STEATOPYGOUS."
UM... EXCUSE ME...?
"NOT ONLY IS SUCH SCURRILOUS CONJECTURE PROBABLY UNTRUE--MAYBE--BUT WORSE, IT IS HURTFUL AND OFFENSIVE TO THIS NATION'S MISUNDERSTOOD AND MALIGNED STEATOPYGOUS-AMERICAN COMMUNITY AS A WHOLE."
WH-WHAT THE [redacted]...? SOMEBODY'S SAYING THAT THIS BOOK DOESN'T SELL BECAUSE MY BUTT'S TOO BIG...?
R-REALLY...?

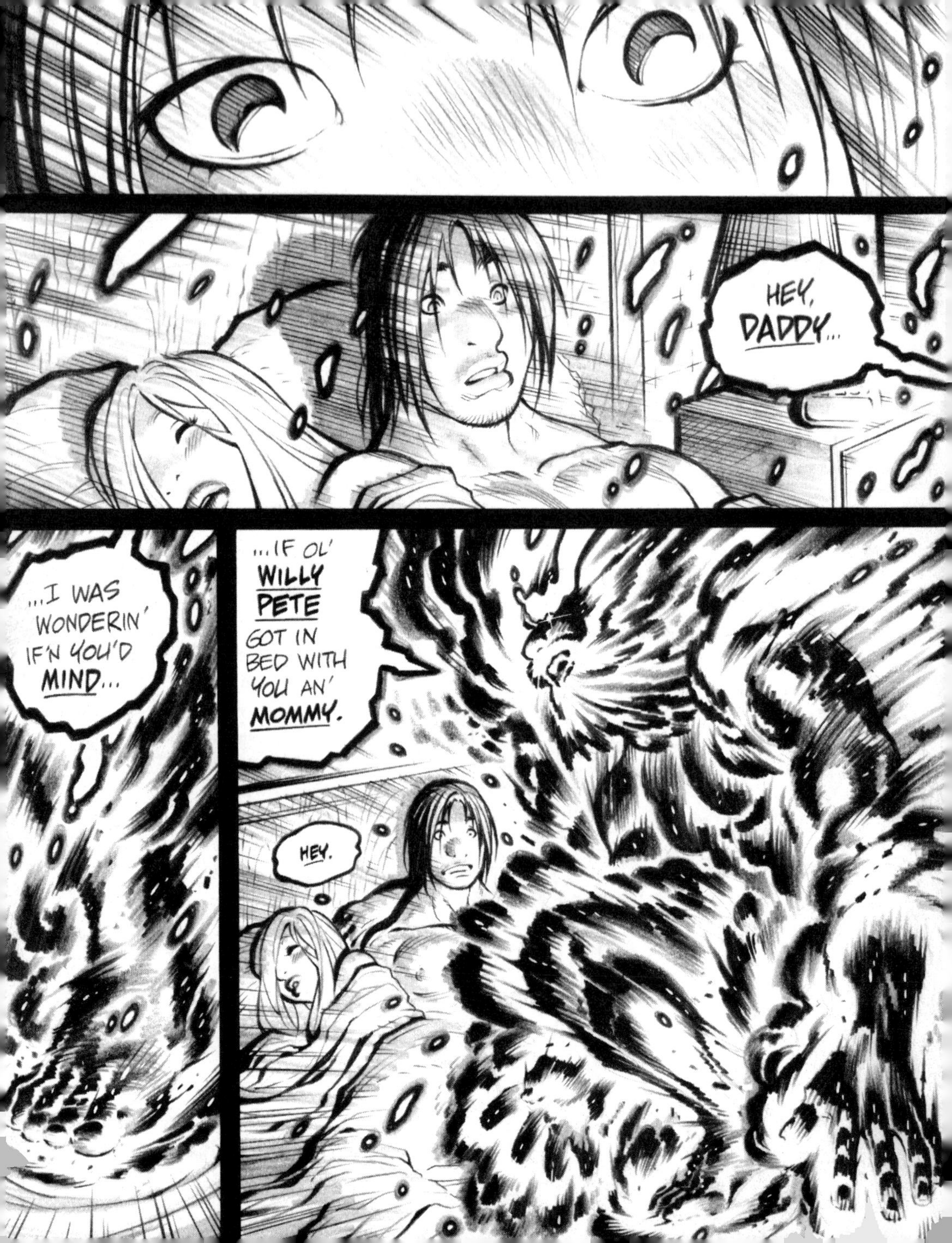
HEY, DADDY...
...I WAS WONDERIN' IF'N YOU'D MIND...
...IF OL' WILLY PETE GOT IN BED WITH YOU AN' MOMMY.
HEY.

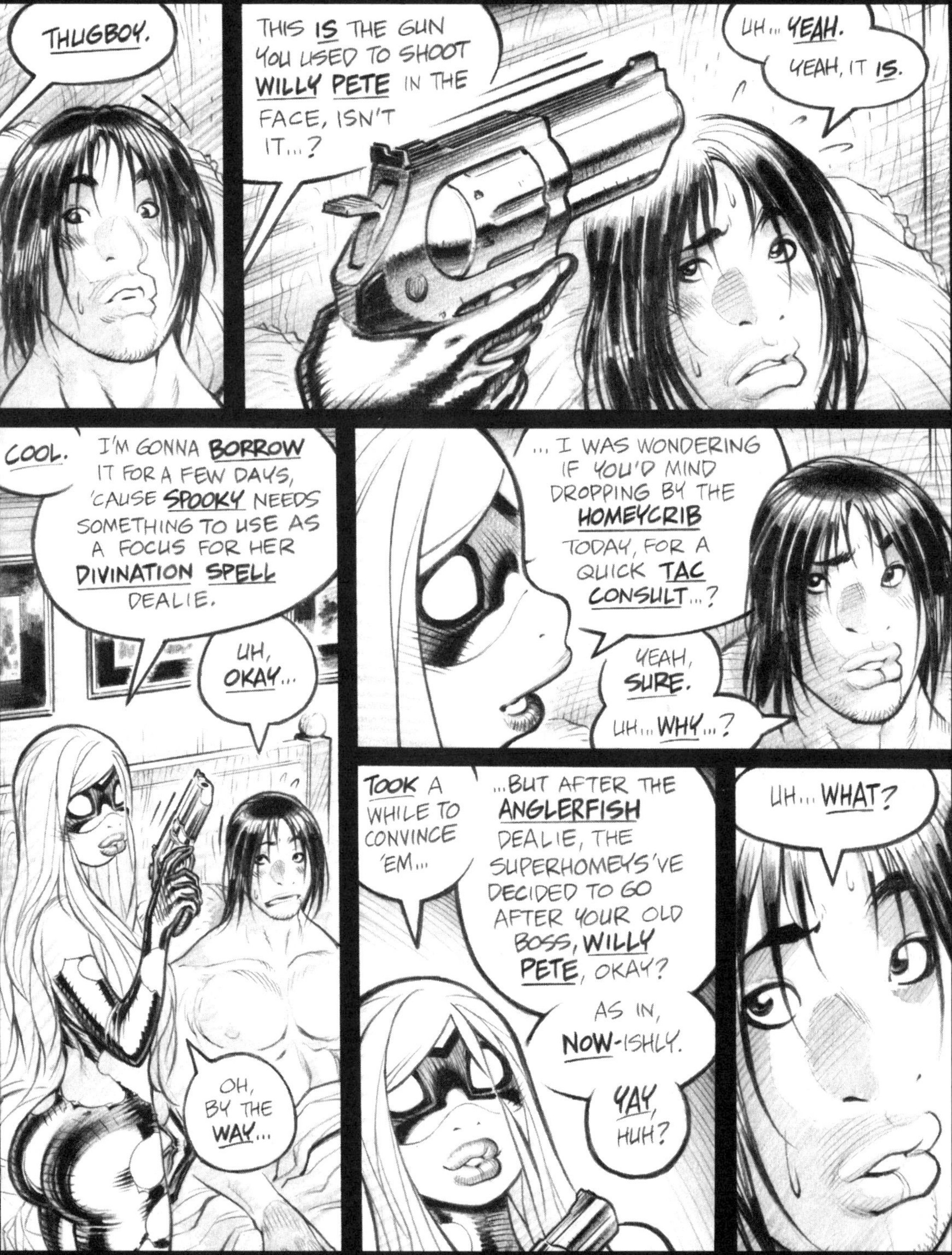
THUGBOY.
THIS IS THE GUN YOU USED TO SHOOT WILLY PETE IN THE FACE, ISN'T IT...?
UH... YEAH.
YEAH, IT IS.
COOL.
I'M GONNA BORROW IT FOR A FEW DAYS, 'CAUSE SPOOKY NEEDS SOMETHING TO USE AS A FOCUS FOR HER DIVINATION SPELL DEALIE.
UH, OKAY...
OH, BY THE WAY...
... I WAS WONDERING IF YOU'D MIND DROPPING BY THE HOMEYCRIB TODAY, FOR A QUICK TAC CONSULT...?
YEAH, SURE.
UH... WHY...?
TOOK A WHILE TO CONVINCE 'EM...
...BUT AFTER THE ANGLERFISH DEALIE, THE SUPERHOMEYS'VE DECIDED TO GO AFTER YOUR OLD BOSS, WILLY PETE, OKAY?
AS IN, NOW-ISHLY.
YAY, HUH?
UH... WHAT?

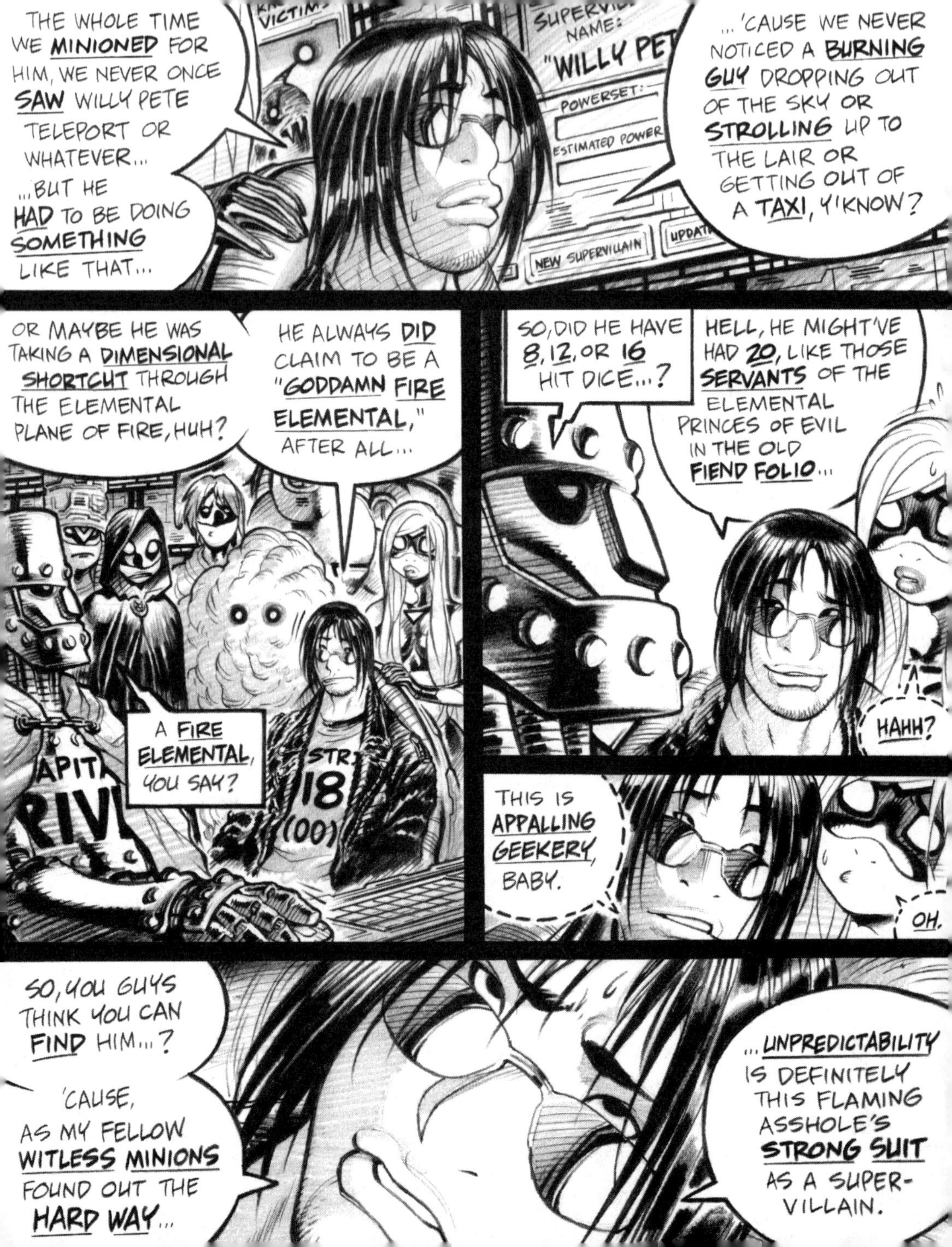
THE WHOLE TIME WE MINIONED FOR HIM, WE NEVER ONCE SAW WILLY PETE TELEPORT OR WHATEVER... ...BUT HE HAD TO BE DOING SOMETHING LIKE THAT...
NAME:
POWERSET:
ESTIMATED POWER
NEW SUPERVILLAIN
...'CAUSE WE NEVER NOTICED A BURNING GUY DROPPING OUT OF THE SKY OR STROLLING UP TO THE LAIR OR GETTING OUT OF A TAXI, Y'KNOW?
OR MAYBE HE WAS TAKING A DIMENSIONAL SHORTCUT THROUGH THE ELEMENTAL PLANE OF FIRE, HUH?
HE ALWAYS DID CLAIM TO BE A "GODDAMN FIRE ELEMENTAL," AFTER ALL...
A FIRE ELEMENTAL, YOU SAY?
18 (00)
SO, DID HE HAVE 8, 12, OR 16 HIT DICE...?
HELL, HE MIGHT'VE HAD 20, LIKE THOSE SERVANTS OF THE ELEMENTAL PRINCES OF EVIL IN THE OLD FIEND FOLIO...
HAHH?
THIS IS APPALLING GEEKERY, BABY.
OH.
SO, YOU GUYS THINK YOU CAN FIND HIM...? 'CAUSE, AS MY FELLOW WITLESS MINIONS FOUND OUT THE HARD WAY...
...UNPREDICTABILITY IS DEFINITELY THIS FLAMING ASSHOLE'S STRONG SUIT AS A SUPER-VILLAIN.

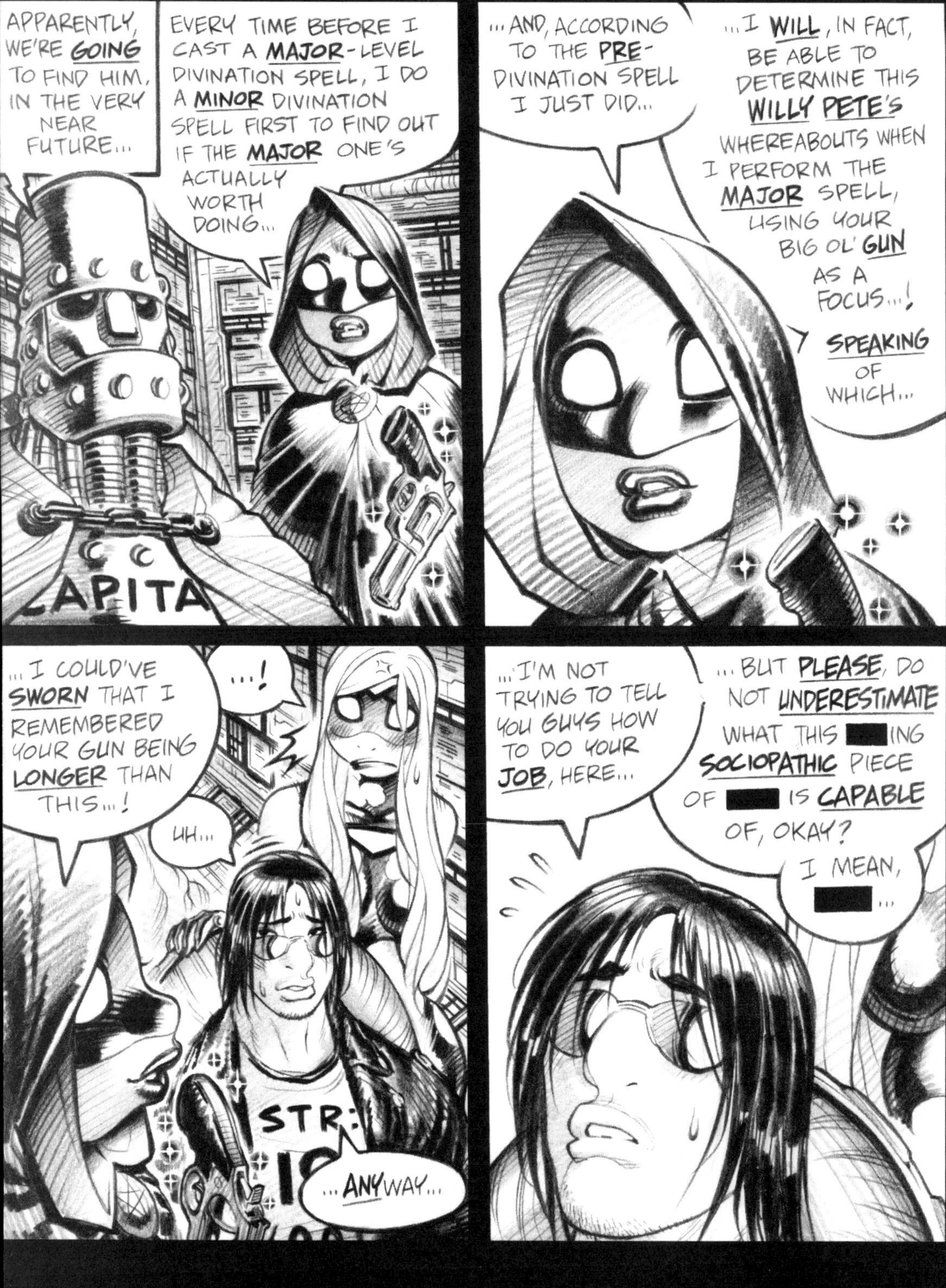
APPARENTLY, WE'RE GOING TO FIND HIM, IN THE VERY NEAR FUTURE...
EVERY TIME BEFORE I CAST A MAJOR-LEVEL DIVINATION SPELL, I DO A MINOR DIVINATION SPELL FIRST TO FIND OUT IF THE MAJOR ONE'S ACTUALLY WORTH DOING...
CAPITA
...AND, ACCORDING TO THE PRE-DIVINATION SPELL I JUST DID...
...I WILL, IN FACT, BE ABLE TO DETERMINE THIS WILLY PETE'S WHEREABOUTS WHEN I PERFORM THE MAJOR SPELL, USING YOUR BIG OL' GUN AS A FOCUS...!
SPEAKING OF WHICH...
...I COULD'VE SWORN THAT I REMEMBERED YOUR GUN BEING LONGER THAN THIS...!
...!
UH...
STR:
...ANYWAY...
...I'M NOT TRYING TO TELL YOU GUYS HOW TO DO YOUR JOB, HERE...
...BUT PLEASE, DO NOT UNDERESTIMATE WHAT THIS [redacted]ING SOCIOPATHIC PIECE OF [redacted] IS CAPABLE OF, OKAY?
I MEAN, [redacted]...

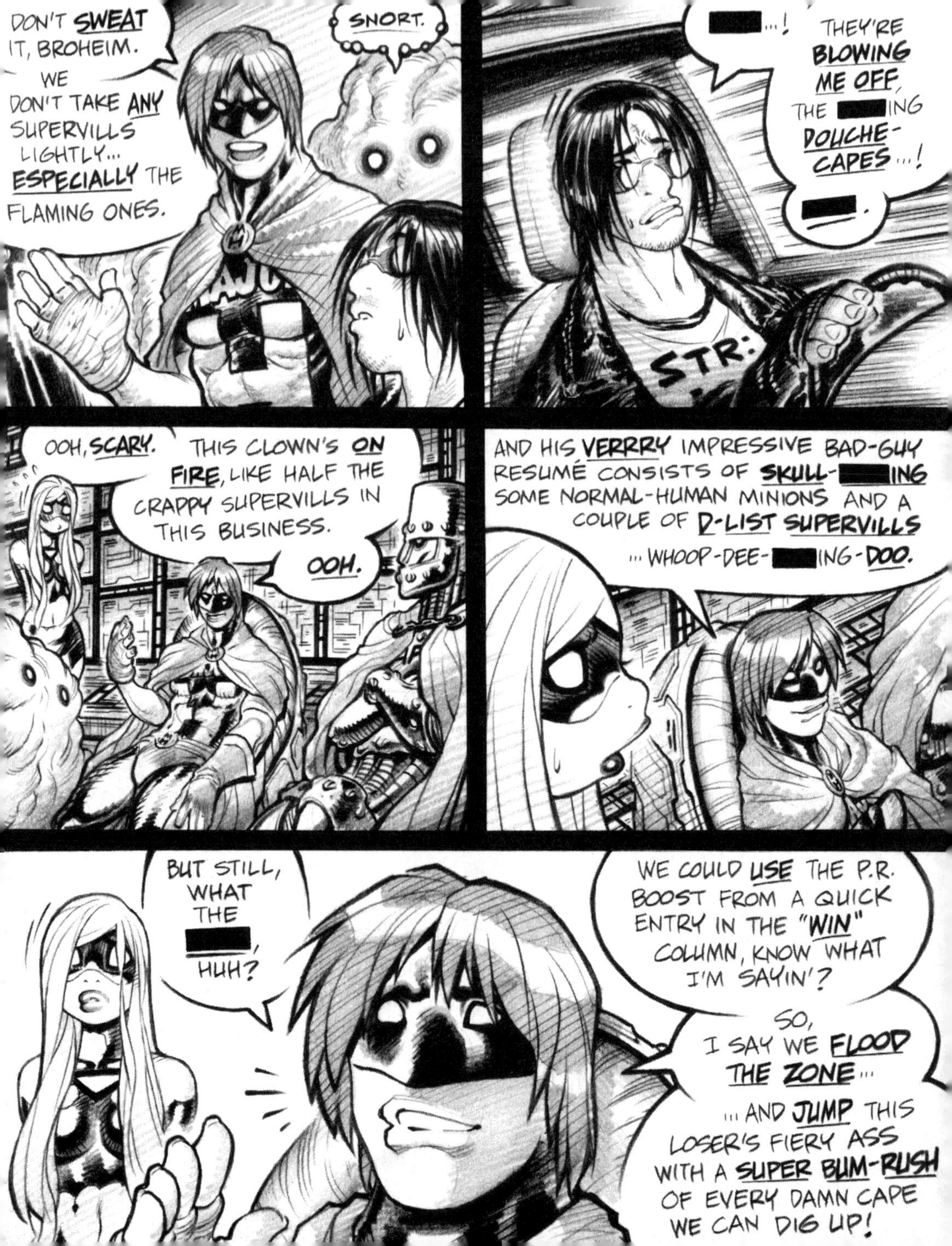
DON'T SWEAT IT, BROHEIM.
WE DON'T TAKE ANY SUPERVILLS LIGHTLY... ESPECIALLY THE FLAMING ONES.
SNORT.
[redacted]...!
THEY'RE BLOWING ME OFF, THE [redacted]ING DOUCHE-CAPES...! [redacted].
STR:
OOH, SCARY.
THIS CLOWN'S ON FIRE, LIKE HALF THE CRAPPY SUPERVILLS IN THIS BUSINESS.
OOH.
AND HIS VERRRY IMPRESSIVE BAD-GUY RESUMÉ CONSISTS OF SKULL-[redacted]ING SOME NORMAL-HUMAN MINIONS AND A COUPLE OF D-LIST SUPERVILLS ...WHOOP-DEE-[redacted]ING-DOO.
BUT STILL, WHAT THE [redacted], HUH?
WE COULD USE THE P.R. BOOST FROM A QUICK ENTRY IN THE "WIN" COLUMN, KNOW WHAT I'M SAYIN'?
SO, I SAY WE FLOOD THE ZONE...
...AND JUMP THIS LOSER'S FIERY ASS WITH A SUPER BUM-RUSH OF EVERY DAMN CAPE WE CAN DIG UP!

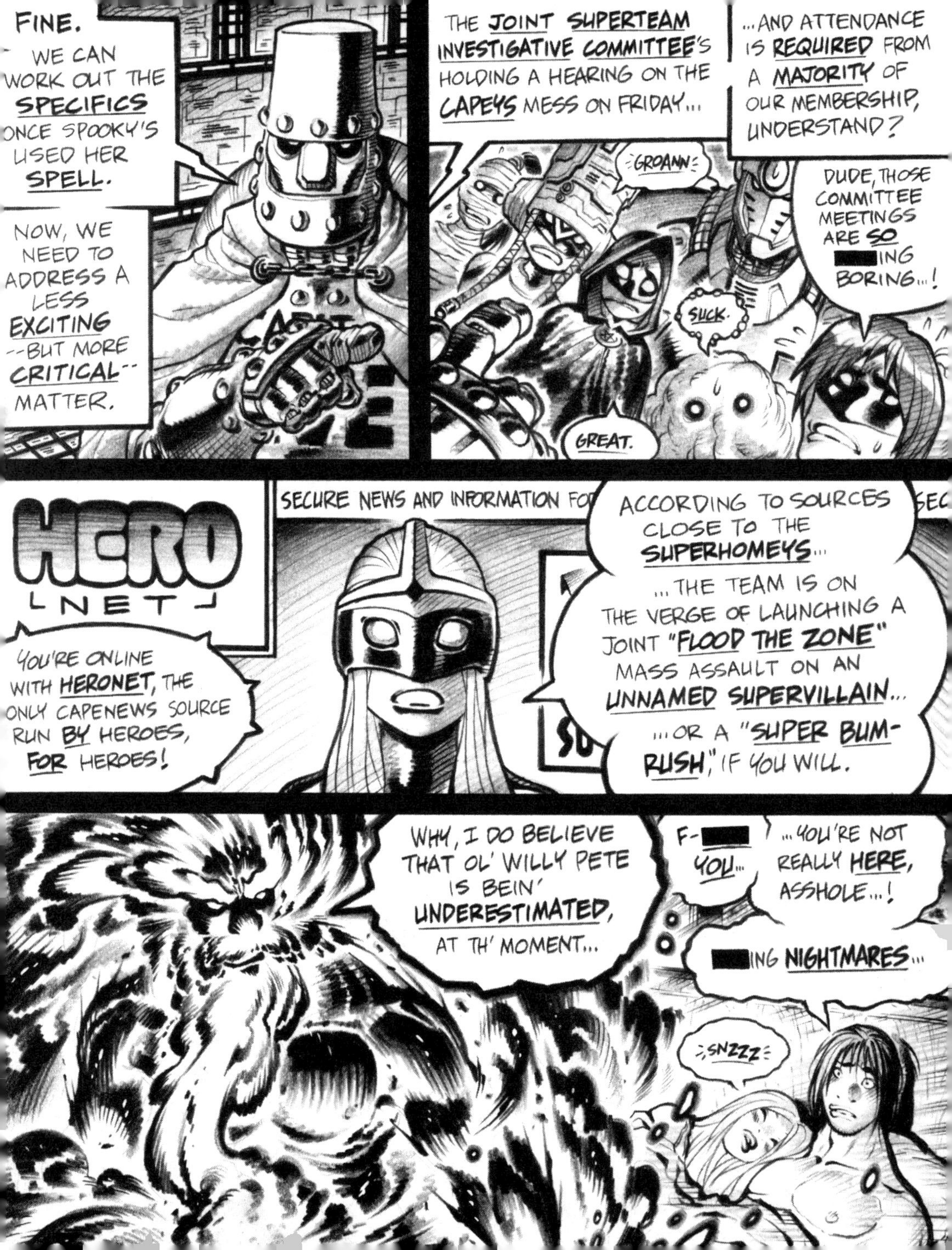
FINE.
WE CAN WORK OUT THE SPECIFICS ONCE SPOOKY'S USED HER SPELL.
NOW, WE NEED TO ADDRESS A LESS EXCITING --BUT MORE CRITICAL-- MATTER.
THE JOINT SUPERTEAM INVESTIGATIVE COMMITTEE'S HOLDING A HEARING ON THE CAPEYS MESS ON FRIDAY...
...AND ATTENDANCE IS REQUIRED FROM A MAJORITY OF OUR MEMBERSHIP, UNDERSTAND?
GROANN
DUDE, THOSE COMMITTEE MEETINGS ARE SO [redacted]ING BORING...!
SUCK.
GREAT.
HERO NET
SECURE NEWS AND INFORMATION FO
YOU'RE ONLINE WITH HERONET, THE ONLY CAPENEWS SOURCE RUN BY HEROES, FOR HEROES!
ACCORDING TO SOURCES CLOSE TO THE SUPERHOMEYS...
...THE TEAM IS ON THE VERGE OF LAUNCHING A JOINT "FLOOD THE ZONE" MASS ASSAULT ON AN UNNAMED SUPERVILLAIN...
...OR A "SUPER BUM-RUSH," IF YOU WILL.
WHY, I DO BELIEVE THAT OL' WILLY PETE IS BEIN' UNDERESTIMATED, AT TH' MOMENT...
F-[redacted] YOU...
...YOU'RE NOT REALLY HERE, ASSHOLE...!
[redacted]ING NIGHTMARES...
SNZZZ

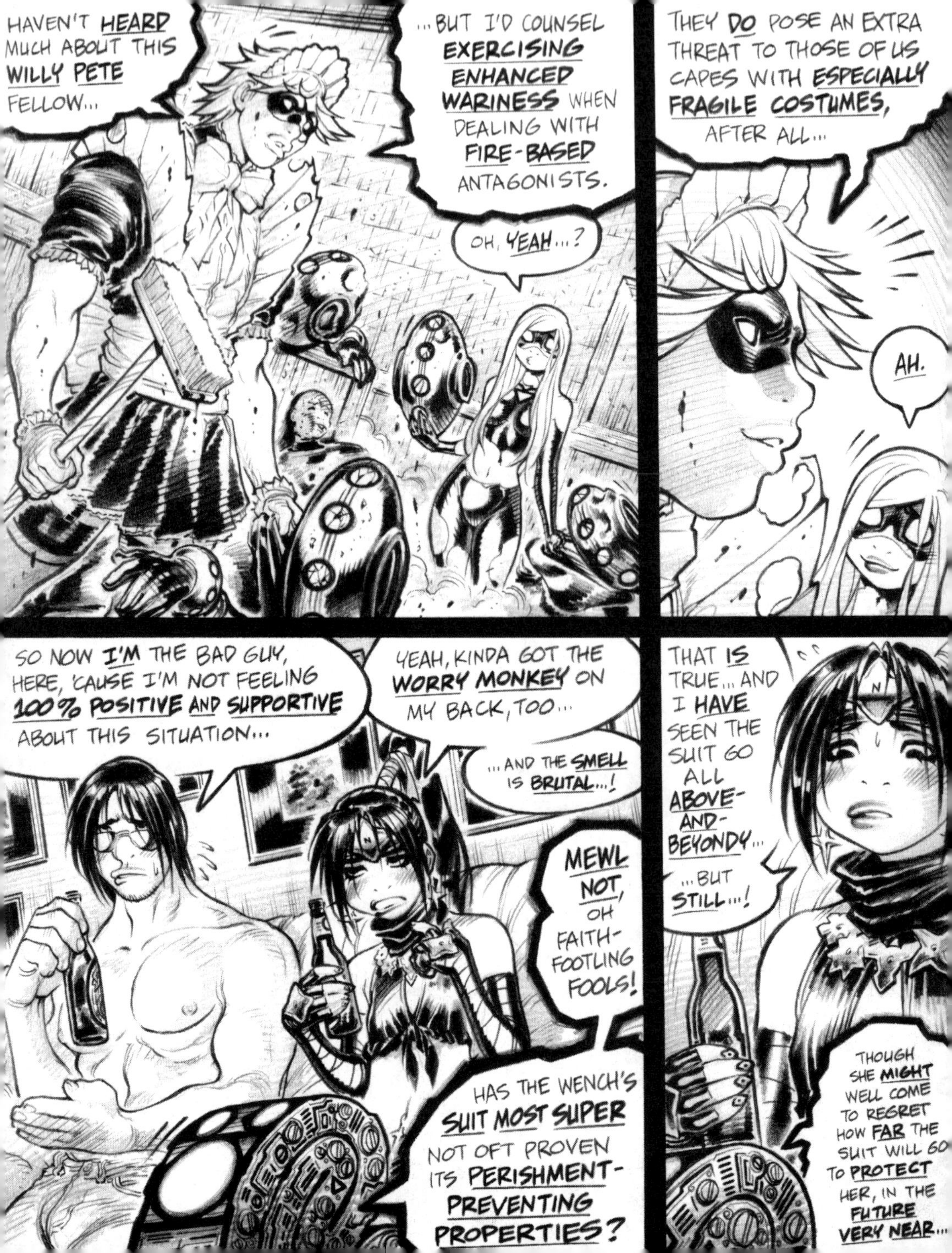
HAVEN'T HEARD MUCH ABOUT THIS WILLY PETE FELLOW...
...BUT I'D COUNSEL EXERCISING ENHANCED WARINESS WHEN DEALING WITH FIRE-BASED ANTAGONISTS.
OH, YEAH...?
THEY DO POSE AN EXTRA THREAT TO THOSE OF US CAPES WITH ESPECIALLY FRAGILE COSTUMES, AFTER ALL...
AH.
SO NOW I'M THE BAD GUY, HERE, 'CAUSE I'M NOT FEELING 100% POSITIVE AND SUPPORTIVE ABOUT THIS SITUATION...
YEAH, KINDA GOT THE WORRY MONKEY ON MY BACK, TOO...
...AND THE SMELL IS BRUTAL...!
MEWL NOT, OH FAITH-FOOTLING FOOLS!
HAS THE WENCH'S SUIT MOST SUPER NOT OFT PROVEN ITS PERISHMENT-PREVENTING PROPERTIES?
THAT IS TRUE... AND I HAVE SEEN THE SUIT GO ALL ABOVE-AND-BEYONDY...
...BUT STILL...!
THOUGH SHE MIGHT WELL COME TO REGRET HOW FAR THE SUIT WILL GO TO PROTECT HER, IN THE FUTURE VERY NEAR...

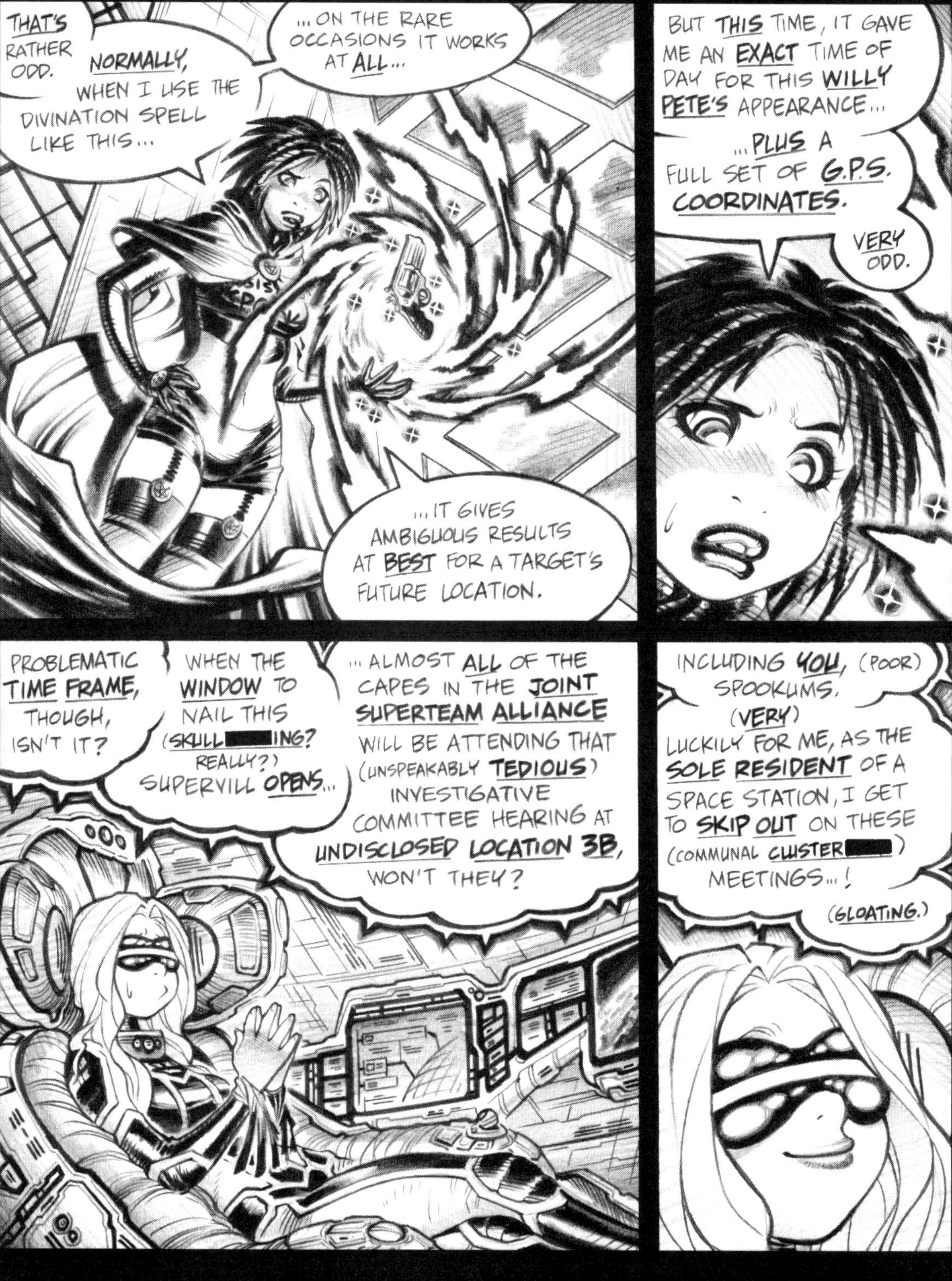
THAT'S RATHER ODD.
NORMALLY, WHEN I USE THE DIVINATION SPELL LIKE THIS...
...ON THE RARE OCCASIONS IT WORKS AT ALL...
...IT GIVES AMBIGUOUS RESULTS AT BEST FOR A TARGET'S FUTURE LOCATION.
BUT THIS TIME, IT GAVE ME AN EXACT TIME OF DAY FOR THIS WILLY PETE'S APPEARANCE...
...PLUS A FULL SET OF G.P.S. COORDINATES.
VERY ODD.
PROBLEMATIC TIME FRAME, THOUGH, ISN'T IT?
WHEN THE WINDOW TO NAIL THIS (SKULL[redacted]ING? REALLY?) SUPERVILL OPENS...
...ALMOST ALL OF THE CAPES IN THE JOINT SUPERTEAM ALLIANCE WILL BE ATTENDING THAT (UNSPEAKABLY TEDIOUS) INVESTIGATIVE COMMITTEE HEARING AT UNDISCLOSED LOCATION 3B, WON'T THEY?
INCLUDING YOU, (POOR) SPOOKUMS.
(VERY) LUCKILY FOR ME, AS THE SOLE RESIDENT OF A SPACE STATION, I GET TO SKIP OUT ON THESE (COMMUNAL CLUSTER[redacted]) MEETINGS...!
(GLOATING.)

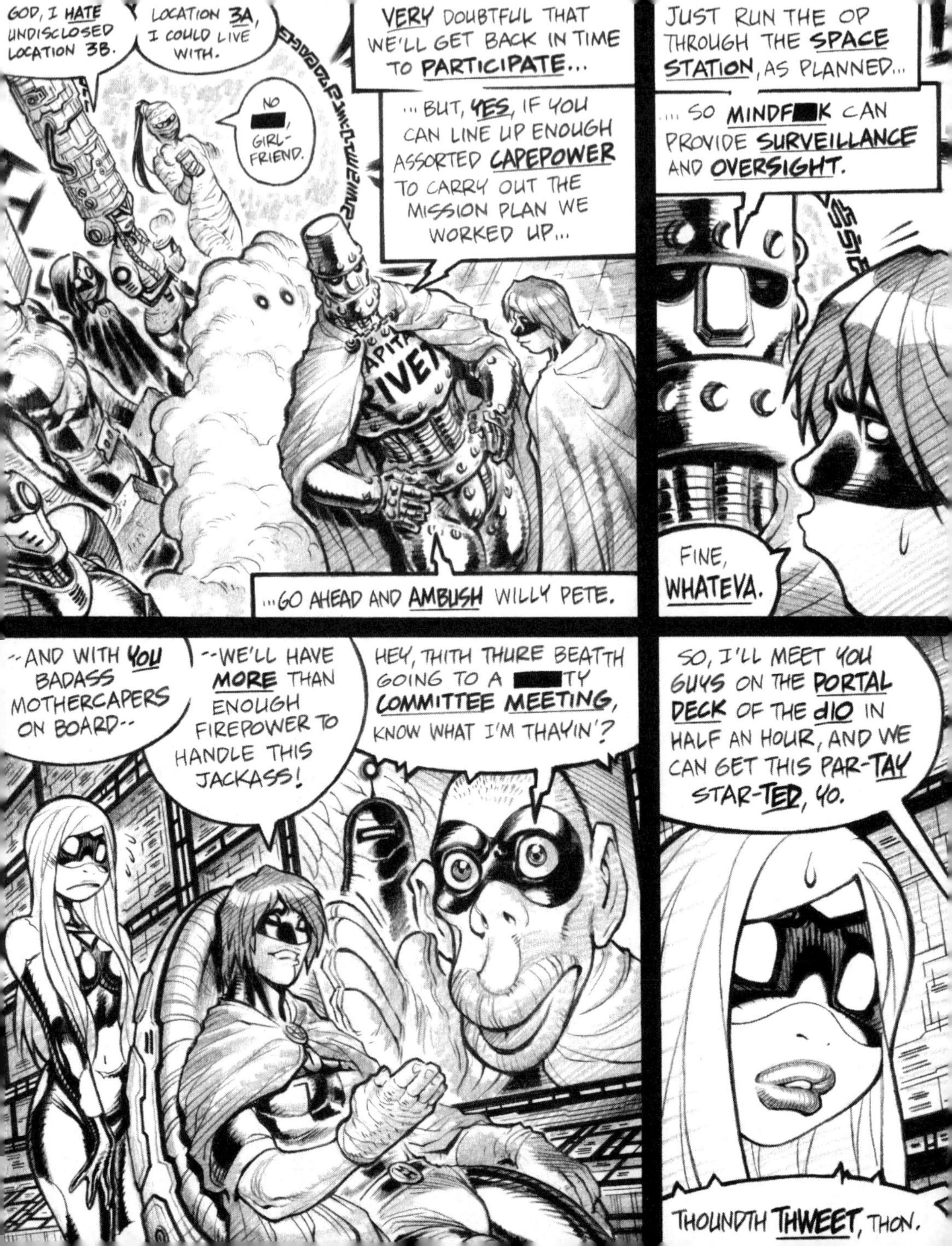
GOD, I HATE UNDISCLOSED LOCATION 3B.
LOCATION 3A, I COULD LIVE WITH.
NO [redacted], GIRL-FRIEND.
VERY DOUBTFUL THAT WE'LL GET BACK IN TIME TO PARTICIPATE...
...BUT, YES, IF YOU CAN LINE UP ENOUGH ASSORTED CAPEPOWER TO CARRY OUT THE MISSION PLAN WE WORKED UP...
...GO AHEAD AND AMBUSH WILLY PETE.
JUST RUN THE OP THROUGH THE SPACE STATION, AS PLANNED...
...SO MINDF[redacted]K CAN PROVIDE SURVEILLANCE AND OVERSIGHT.
FINE, WHATEVA.
--AND WITH YOU BADASS MOTHERCAPERS ON BOARD--
--WE'LL HAVE MORE THAN ENOUGH FIREPOWER TO HANDLE THIS JACKASS!
HEY, THITH THURE BEATTH GOING TO A [redacted]TY COMMITTEE MEETING, KNOW WHAT I'M THAYIN'?
SO, I'LL MEET YOU GUYS ON THE PORTAL DECK OF THE dIO IN HALF AN HOUR, AND WE CAN GET THIS PAR-TAY STAR-TED, YO.
THOUNDTH THWEET, THON.

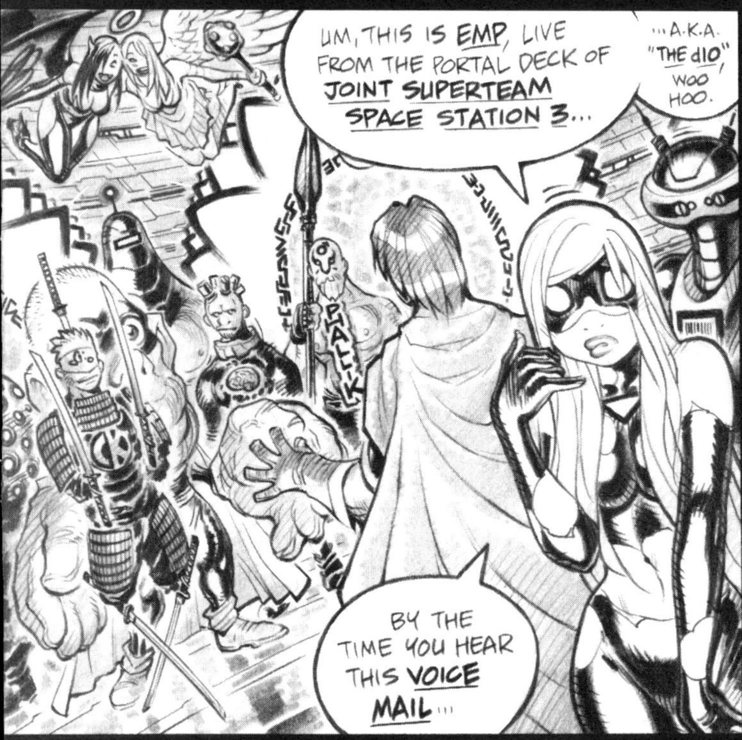
UM, THIS IS EMP, LIVE FROM THE PORTAL DECK OF JOINT SUPERTEAM SPACE STATION 3...
...A.K.A. "THE d10," WOO HOO.
PHALLIK
BY THE TIME YOU HEAR THIS VOICE MAIL...

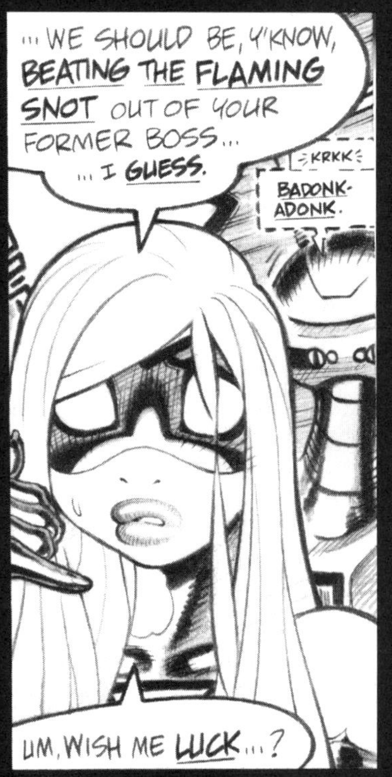
...WE SHOULD BE, Y'KNOW, BEATING THE FLAMING SNOT OUT OF YOUR FORMER BOSS... ...I GUESS.
KRKK
BADONK-ADONK.
UM, WISH ME LUCK...?

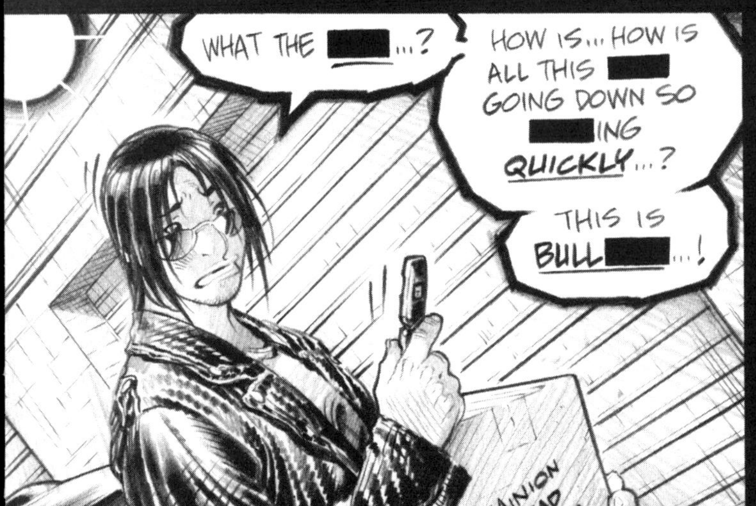
WHAT THE [redacted]...?
HOW IS... HOW IS ALL THIS [redacted] GOING DOWN SO [redacted]ING QUICKLY...?
THIS IS BULL[redacted]...!
MINION CRAP IS

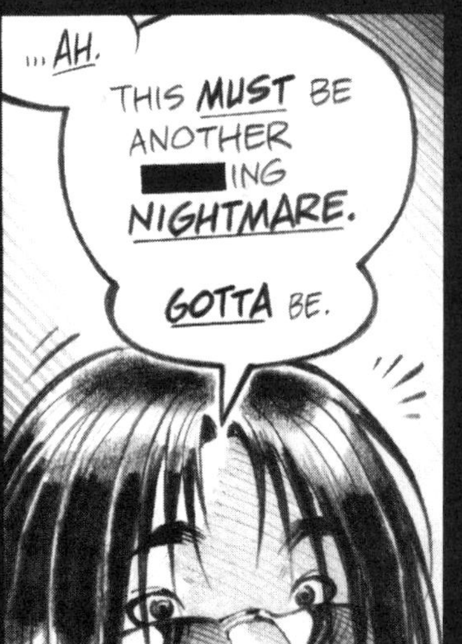
...AH.
THIS MUST BE ANOTHER [redacted]ING NIGHTMARE.
GOTTA BE.

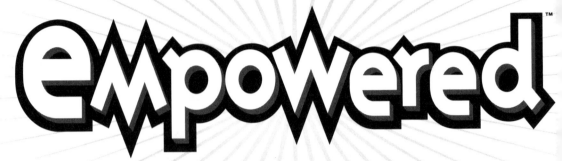

empowered™

Say That I Deserve This

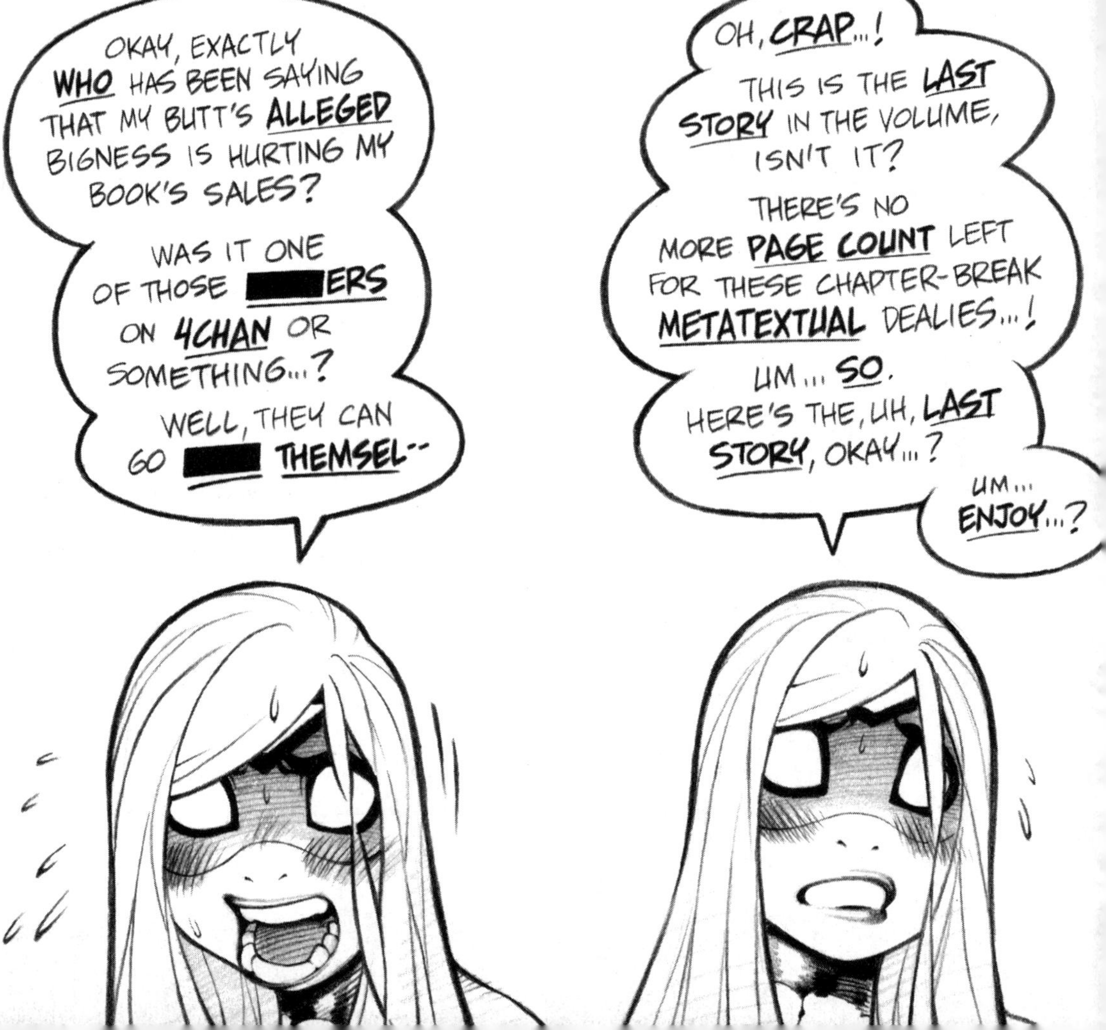
OKAY, EXACTLY WHO HAS BEEN SAYING THAT MY BUTT'S ALLEGED BIGNESS IS HURTING MY BOOK'S SALES?
WAS IT ONE OF THOSE [redacted]ERS ON 4CHAN OR SOMETHING...?
WELL, THEY CAN GO [redacted] THEMSEL--
OH, CRAP...!
THIS IS THE LAST STORY IN THE VOLUME, ISN'T IT?
THERE'S NO MORE PAGE COUNT LEFT FOR THESE CHAPTER-BREAK METATEXTUAL DEALIES...!
UM... SO. HERE'S THE, UH, LAST STORY, OKAY...?
UM... ENJOY...?

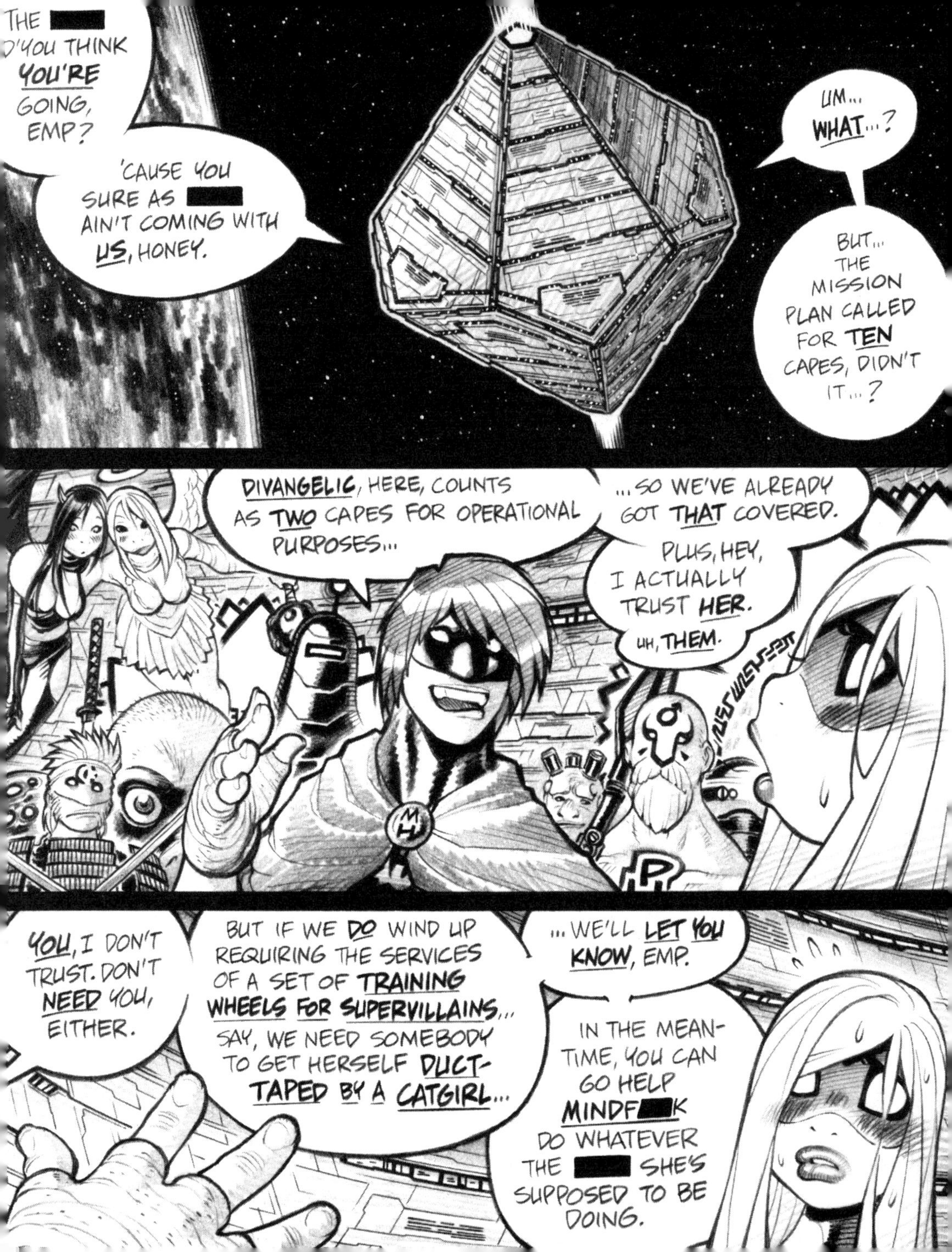
THE [redacted] D'YOU THINK YOU'RE GOING, EMP?
'CAUSE YOU SURE AS [redacted] AIN'T COMING WITH US, HONEY.
UM... WHAT...?
BUT... THE MISSION PLAN CALLED FOR TEN CAPES, DIDN'T IT...?
DIVANGELIC, HERE, COUNTS AS TWO CAPES FOR OPERATIONAL PURPOSES...
...SO WE'VE ALREADY GOT THAT COVERED.
PLUS, HEY, I ACTUALLY TRUST HER.
UH, THEM.
YOU, I DON'T TRUST. DON'T NEED YOU, EITHER.
BUT IF WE DO WIND UP REQUIRING THE SERVICES OF A SET OF TRAINING WHEELS FOR SUPERVILLAINS...
SAY, WE NEED SOMEBODY TO GET HERSELF DUCT-TAPED BY A CATGIRL...
...WE'LL LET YOU KNOW, EMP.
IN THE MEAN-TIME, YOU CAN GO HELP MINDF[redacted]K DO WHATEVER THE [redacted] SHE'S SUPPOSED TO BE DOING.

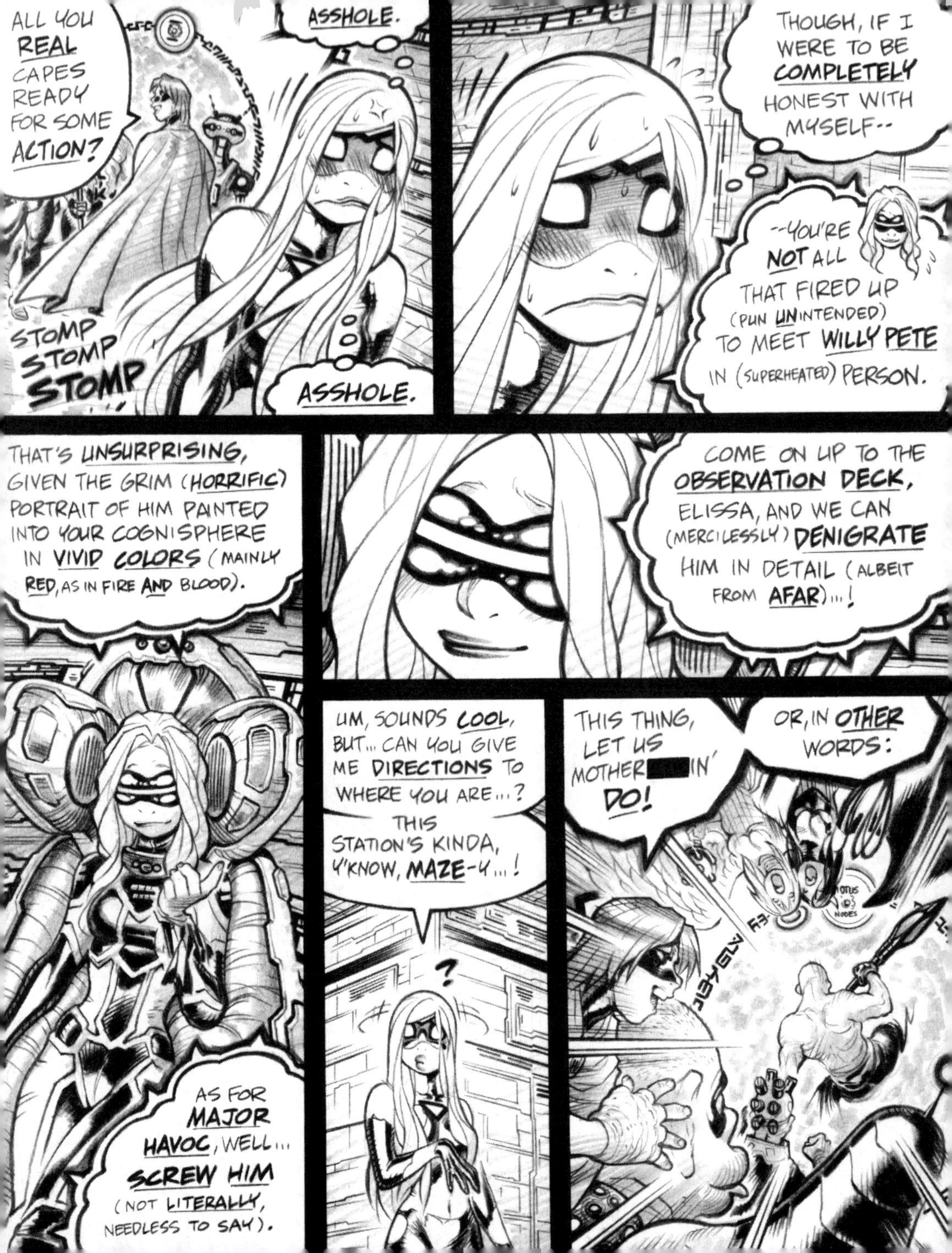

ALL YOU REAL CAPES READY FOR SOME ACTION?
ASSHOLE.
ASSHOLE.
STOMP STOMP STOMP
THOUGH, IF I WERE TO BE COMPLETELY HONEST WITH MYSELF--
--YOU'RE NOT ALL THAT FIRED UP (PUN UNINTENDED) TO MEET WILLY PETE IN (SUPERHEATED) PERSON.
THAT'S UNSURPRISING, GIVEN THE GRIM (HORRIFIC) PORTRAIT OF HIM PAINTED INTO YOUR COGNISPHERE IN VIVID COLORS (MAINLY RED, AS IN FIRE AND BLOOD).
AS FOR MAJOR HAVOC, WELL... SCREW HIM (NOT LITERALLY, NEEDLESS TO SAY).
COME ON UP TO THE OBSERVATION DECK, ELISSA, AND WE CAN (MERCILESSLY) DENIGRATE HIM IN DETAIL (ALBEIT FROM AFAR)...!
UM, SOUNDS COOL, BUT... CAN YOU GIVE ME DIRECTIONS TO WHERE YOU ARE...?
THIS STATION'S KINDA, Y'KNOW, MAZE-Y...!
?
THIS THING, LET US MOTHER[redacted]IN' DO!
OR, IN OTHER WORDS:
LOTUS NODES

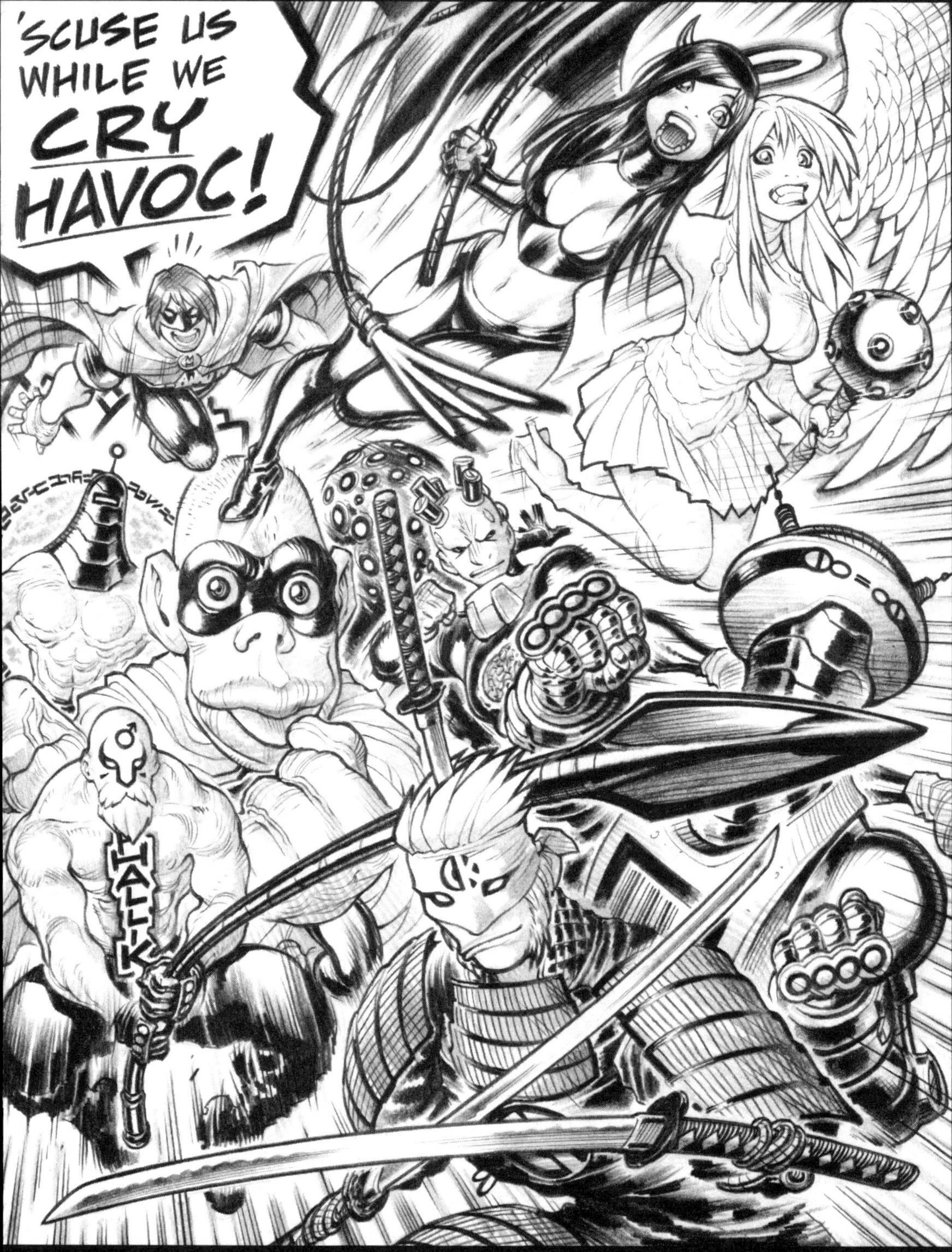
'SCUSE US WHILE WE CRY HAVOC!
HALLIK

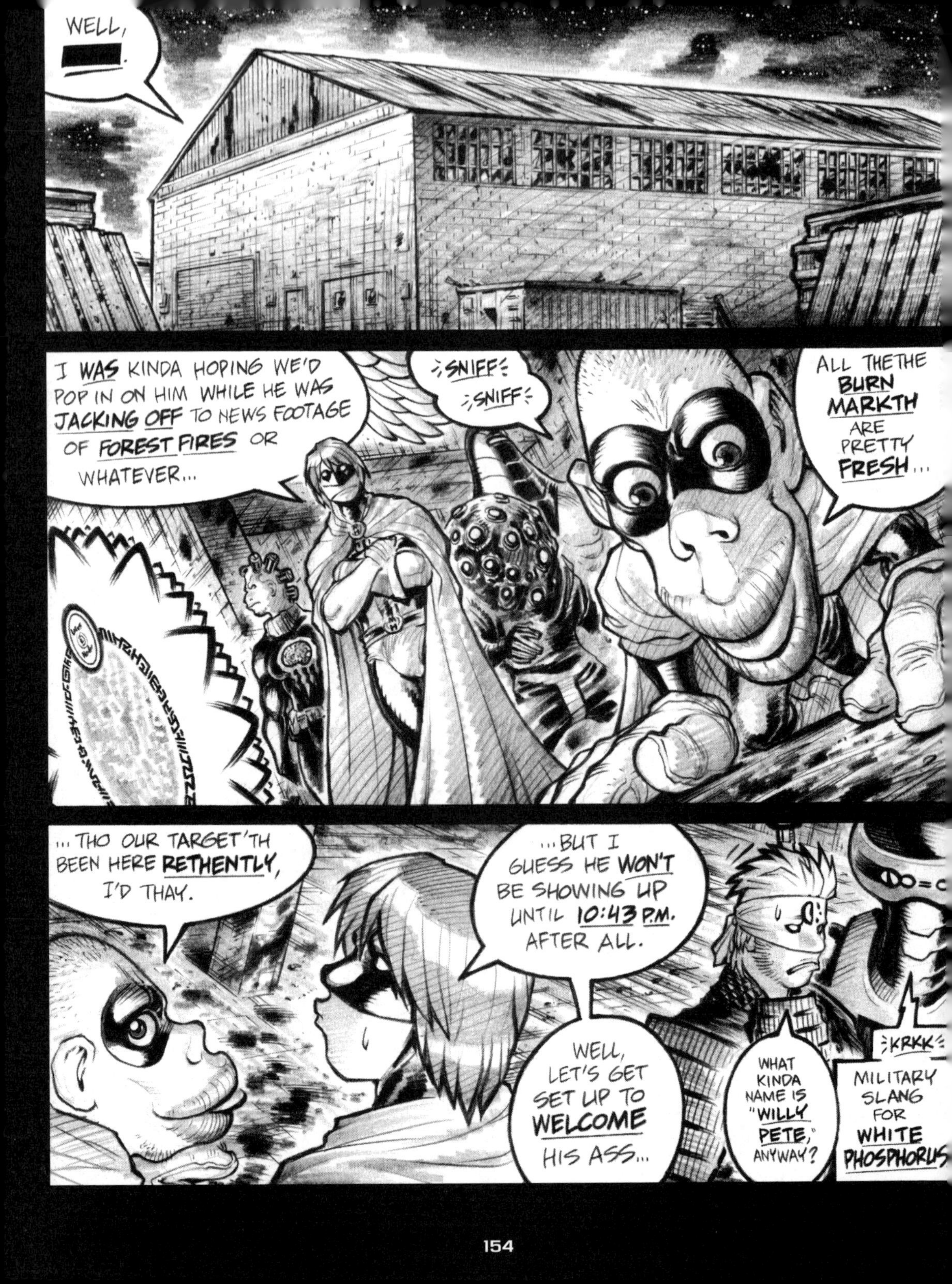
WELL, [redacted].
I WAS KINDA HOPING WE'D POP IN ON HIM WHILE HE WAS JACKING OFF TO NEWS FOOTAGE OF FOREST FIRES OR WHATEVER...
SNIFF
SNIFF
ALL THETHE BURN MARKTH ARE PRETTY FRESH...
...THO OUR TARGET'TH BEEN HERE RETHENTLY, I'D THAY.
...BUT I GUESS HE WON'T BE SHOWING UP UNTIL 10:43 P.M. AFTER ALL.
WELL, LET'S GET SET UP TO WELCOME HIS ASS...
WHAT KINDA NAME IS "WILLY PETE," ANYWAY?
KRKK
MILITARY SLANG FOR WHITE PHOSPHORUS

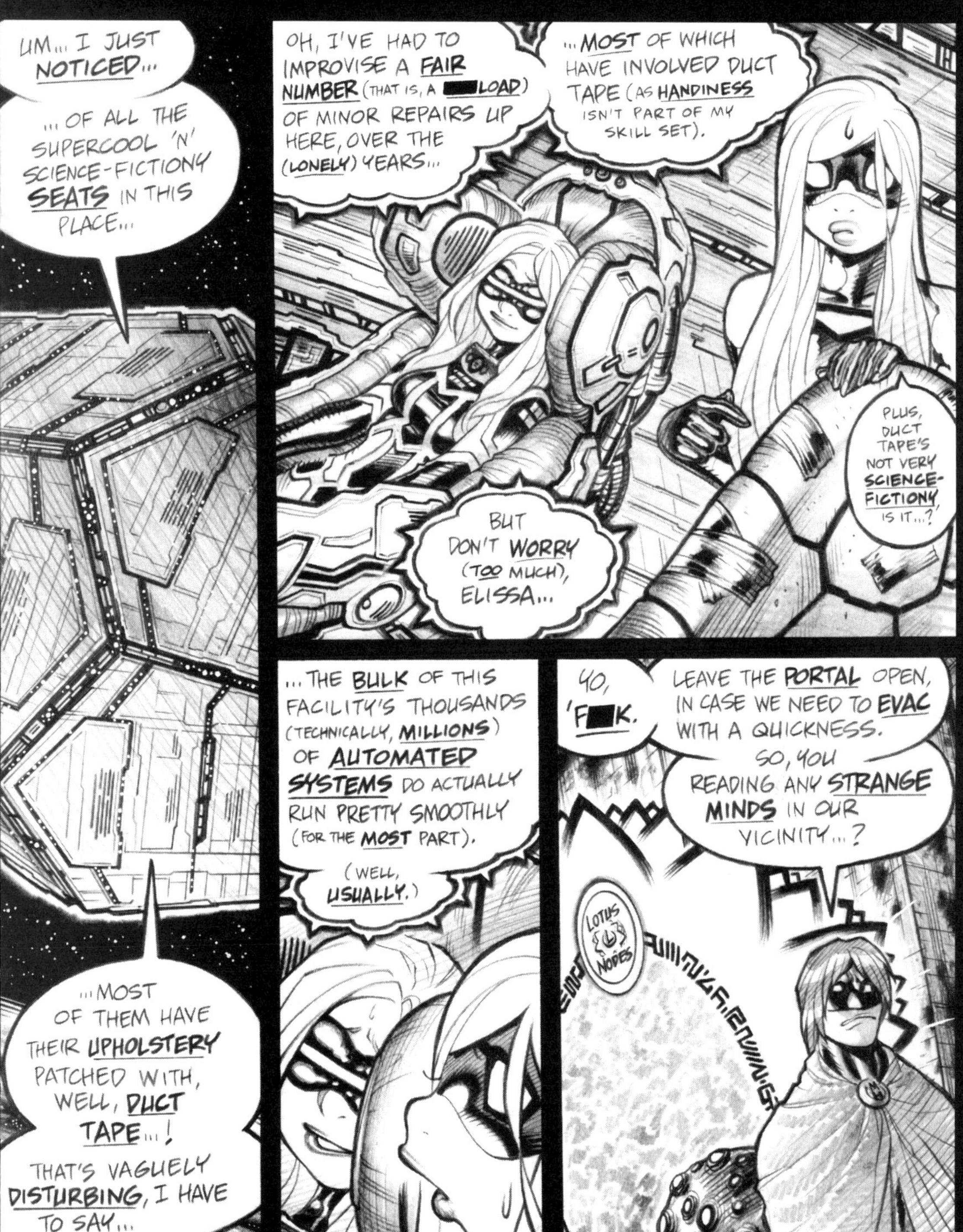

UM... I JUST NOTICED...
...OF ALL THE SUPERCOOL 'N' SCIENCE-FICTIONY SEATS IN THIS PLACE...
...MOST OF THEM HAVE THEIR UPHOLSTERY PATCHED WITH, WELL, DUCT TAPE...!
THAT'S VAGUELY DISTURBING, I HAVE TO SAY...
OH, I'VE HAD TO IMPROVISE A FAIR NUMBER (THAT IS, A [redacted]LOAD) OF MINOR REPAIRS UP HERE, OVER THE (LONELY) YEARS...
...MOST OF WHICH HAVE INVOLVED DUCT TAPE (AS HANDINESS ISN'T PART OF MY SKILL SET).
BUT DON'T WORRY (TOO MUCH), ELISSA...
PLUS, DUCT TAPE'S NOT VERY SCIENCE-FICTIONY, IS IT...?
...THE BULK OF THIS FACILITY'S THOUSANDS (TECHNICALLY, MILLIONS) OF AUTOMATED SYSTEMS DO ACTUALLY RUN PRETTY SMOOTHLY (FOR THE MOST PART).
(WELL, USUALLY.)
....
YO, 'F[redacted]K.
LEAVE THE PORTAL OPEN, IN CASE WE NEED TO EVAC WITH A QUICKNESS.
SO, YOU READING ANY STRANGE MINDS IN OUR VICINITY...?
LOTUS NODES

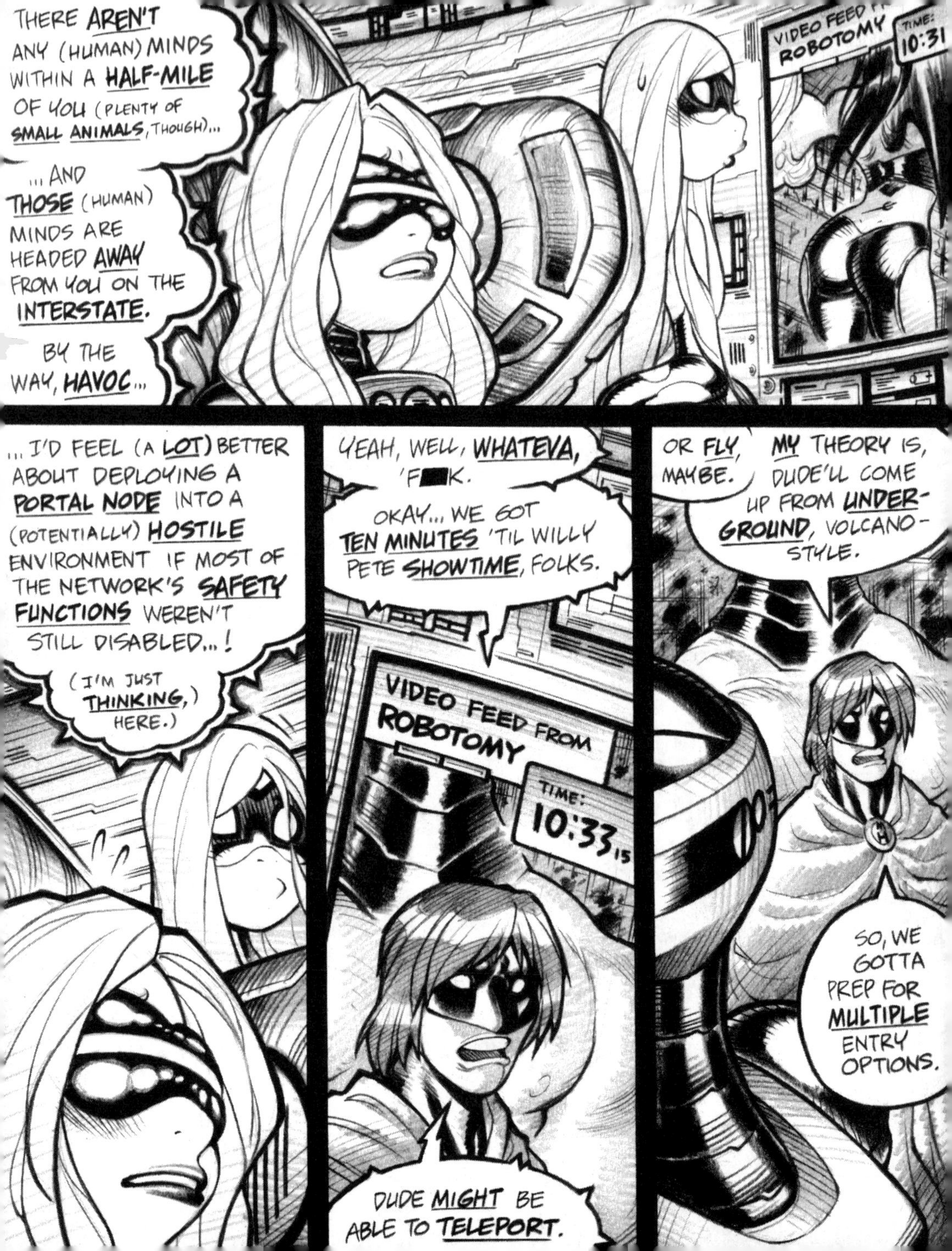
THERE AREN'T ANY (HUMAN) MINDS WITHIN A HALF-MILE OF YOU (PLENTY OF SMALL ANIMALS, THOUGH)...
...AND THOSE (HUMAN) MINDS ARE HEADED AWAY FROM YOU ON THE INTERSTATE.
BY THE WAY, HAVOC...
VIDEO FEED
ROBOTOMY
TIME: 10:31
...I'D FEEL (A LOT) BETTER ABOUT DEPLOYING A PORTAL NODE INTO A (POTENTIALLY) HOSTILE ENVIRONMENT IF MOST OF THE NETWORK'S SAFETY FUNCTIONS WEREN'T STILL DISABLED...!
(I'M JUST THINKING, HERE.)
YEAH, WELL, WHATEVA, 'F[redacted]K.
OKAY... WE GOT TEN MINUTES 'TIL WILLY PETE SHOWTIME, FOLKS.
VIDEO FEED FROM ROBOTOMY
TIME: 10:33 15
DUDE MIGHT BE ABLE TO TELEPORT.
OR FLY, MAYBE.
MY THEORY IS, DUDE'LL COME UP FROM UNDERGROUND, VOLCANO-STYLE.
SO, WE GOTTA PREP FOR MULTIPLE ENTRY OPTIONS.

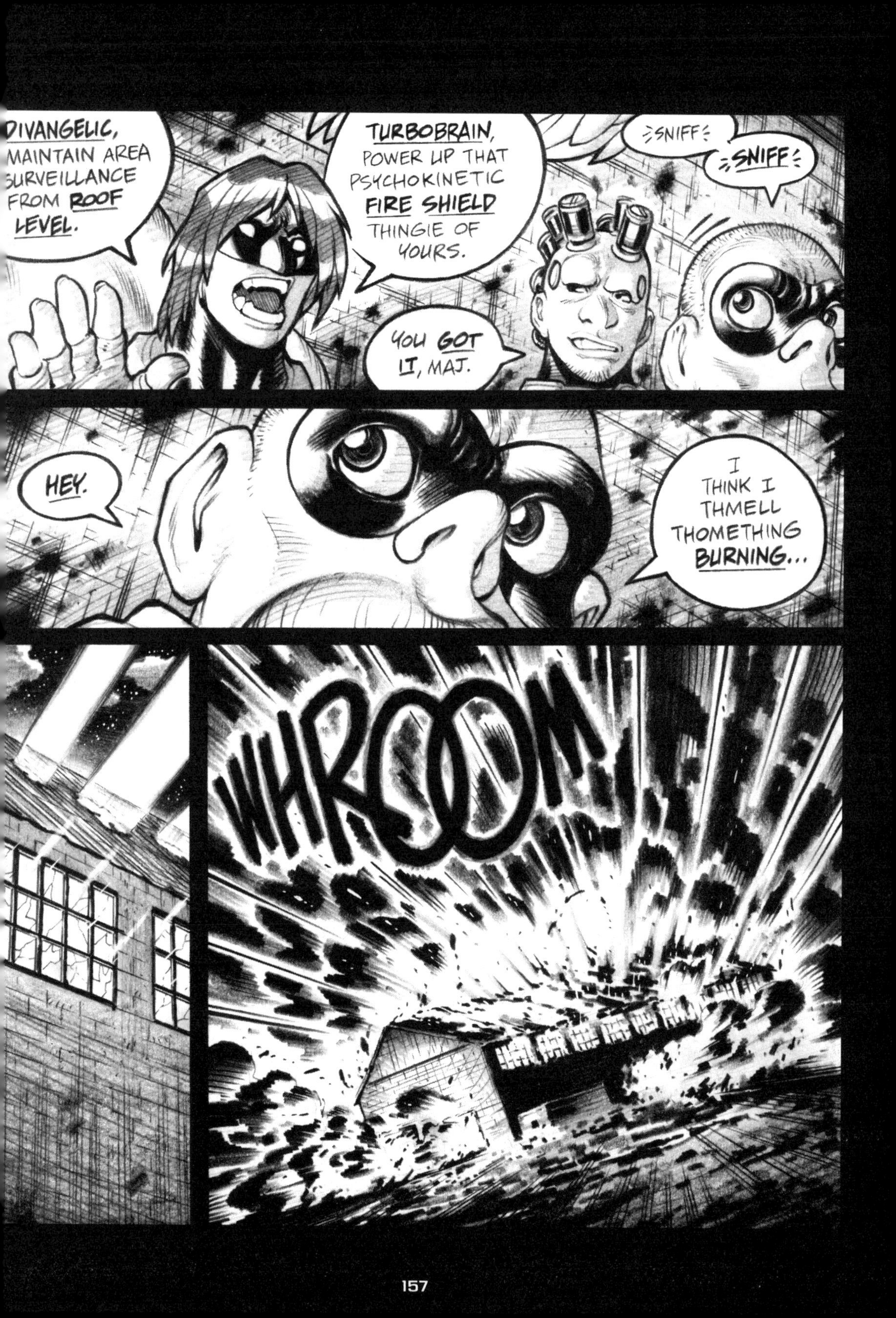
DIVANGELIC, MAINTAIN AREA SURVEILLANCE FROM ROOF LEVEL.
TURBOBRAIN, POWER UP THAT PSYCHOKINETIC FIRE SHIELD THINGIE OF YOURS.
SNIFF
SNIFF
YOU GOT IT, MAJ.
HEY.
I THINK I THMELL THOMETHING BURNING...
WHROOM

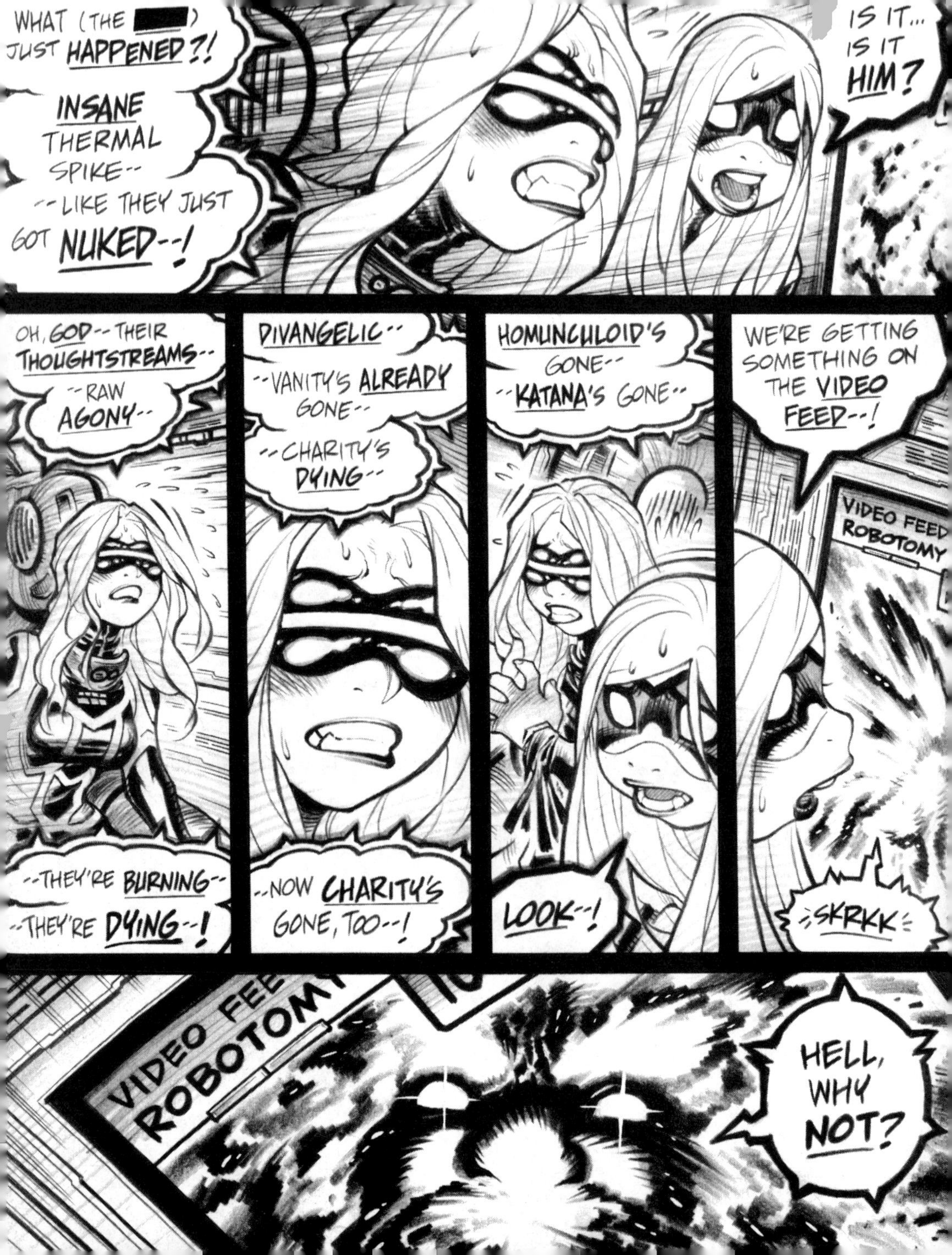
WHAT (THE [redacted]) JUST HAPPENED?!
INSANE THERMAL SPIKE--
--LIKE THEY JUST GOT NUKED--!
IS IT... IS IT HIM?
OH, GOD--THEIR THOUGHTSTREAMS--
--RAW AGONY--
--THEY'RE BURNING--
--THEY'RE DYING--!
DIVANGELIC--
--VANITY'S ALREADY GONE--
--CHARITY'S DYING--
--NOW CHARITY'S GONE, TOO--!
HOMUNCULOID'S GONE--
--KATANA'S GONE--
LOOK--!
WE'RE GETTING SOMETHING ON THE VIDEO FEED--!
VIDEO FEED
ROBOTOMY
SKRKK
VIDEO FEE
ROBOTOMY
HELL, WHY NOT?

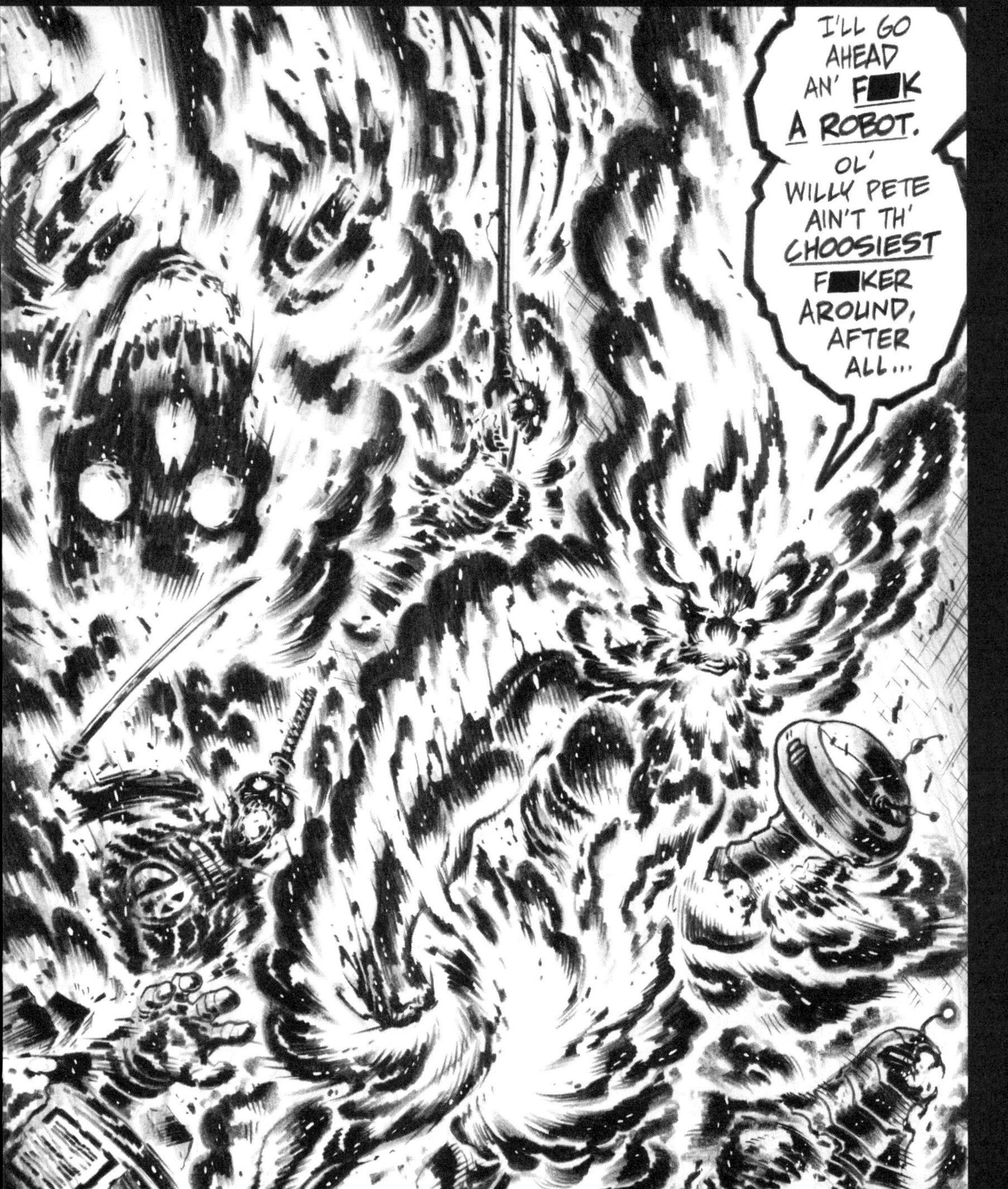
I'LL GO AHEAD AN' F[redacted]K A ROBOT. OL' WILLY PETE AIN'T TH' CHOOSIEST F[redacted]KER AROUND, AFTER ALL...

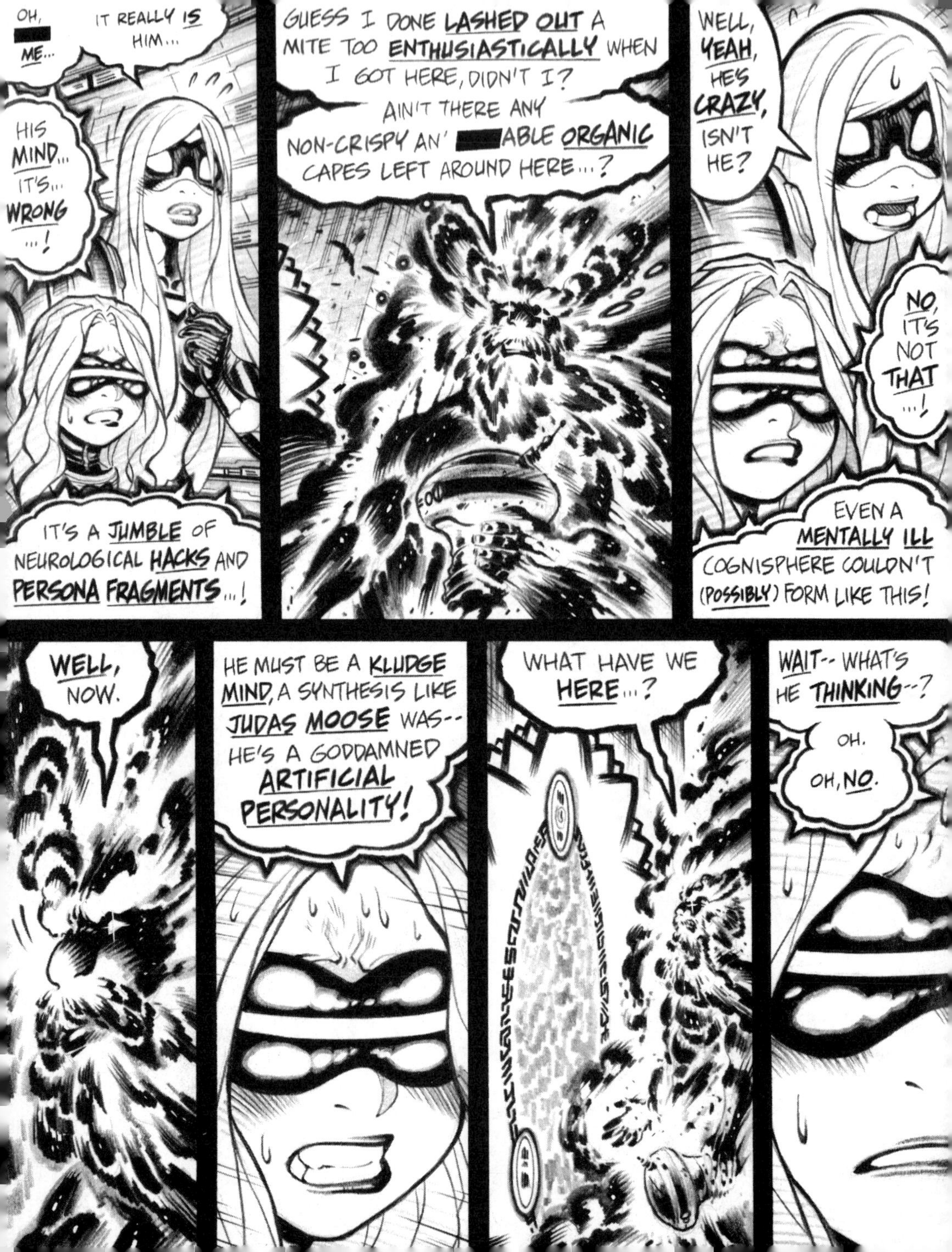
OH, [redacted] ME...
IT REALLY IS HIM...
HIS MIND... IT'S... WRONG...!
IT'S A JUMBLE OF NEUROLOGICAL HACKS AND PERSONA FRAGMENTS...!
GUESS I DONE LASHED OUT A MITE TOO ENTHUSIASTICALLY WHEN I GOT HERE, DIDN'T I?
AIN'T THERE ANY NON-CRISPY AN' [redacted]ABLE ORGANIC CAPES LEFT AROUND HERE...?
WELL, YEAH, HE'S CRAZY, ISN'T HE?
NO, IT'S NOT THAT...!
EVEN A MENTALLY ILL COGNISPHERE COULDN'T (POSSIBLY) FORM LIKE THIS!
WELL, NOW.
HE MUST BE A KLUDGE MIND, A SYNTHESIS LIKE JUDAS MOOSE WAS-- HE'S A GODDAMNED ARTIFICIAL PERSONALITY!
WHAT HAVE WE HERE...?
WAIT-- WHAT'S HE THINKING--?
OH.
OH, NO.

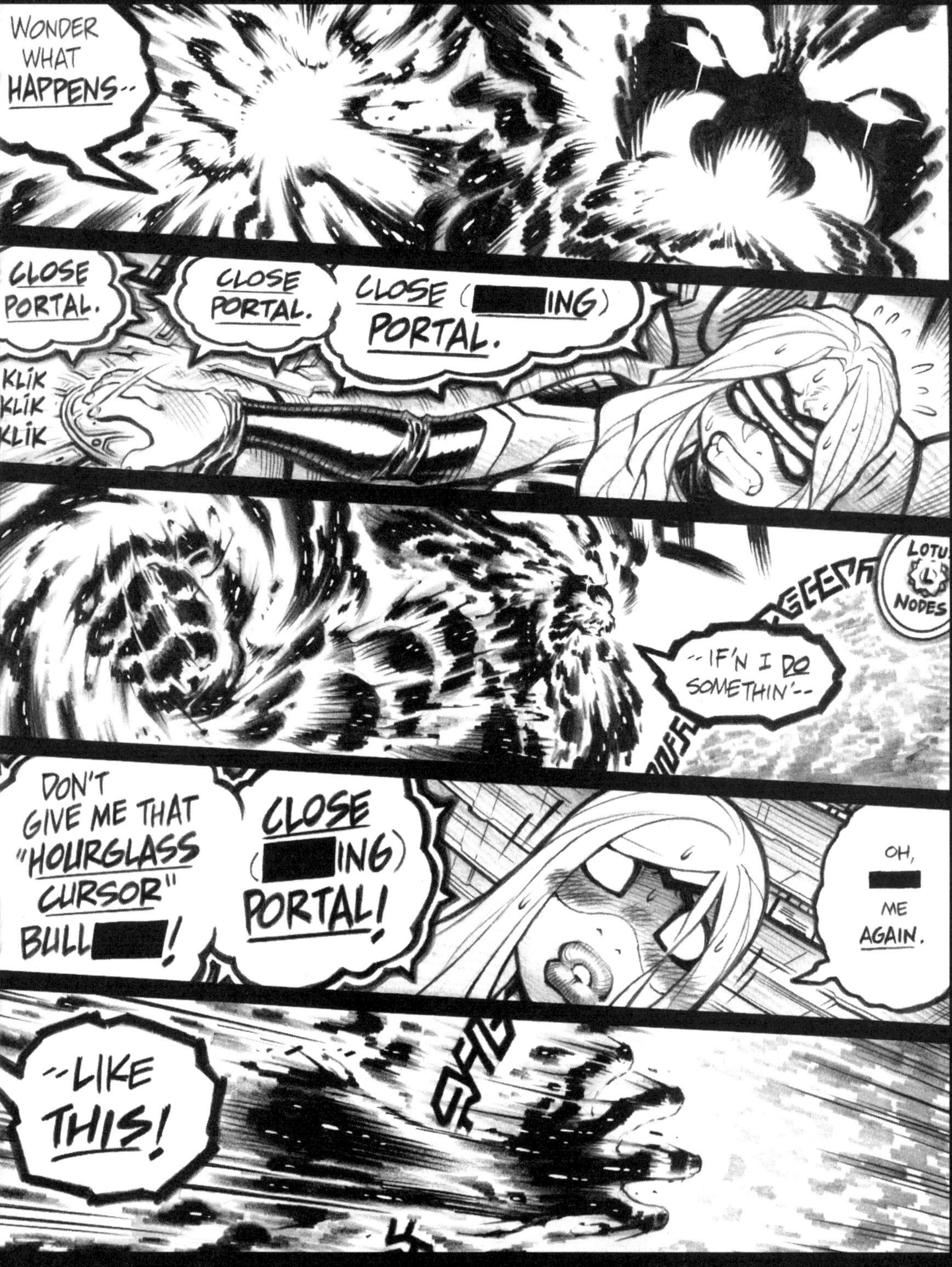

WONDER WHAT HAPPENS--
CLOSE PORTAL.
CLOSE PORTAL.
CLOSE ([redacted]ING) PORTAL.
KLIK KLIK KLIK KLIK
--IF'N I DO SOMETHIN'--
DON'T GIVE ME THAT "HOURGLASS CURSOR" BULL[redacted]!
CLOSE ([redacted]ING) PORTAL!
OH, [redacted] ME AGAIN.
--LIKE THIS!

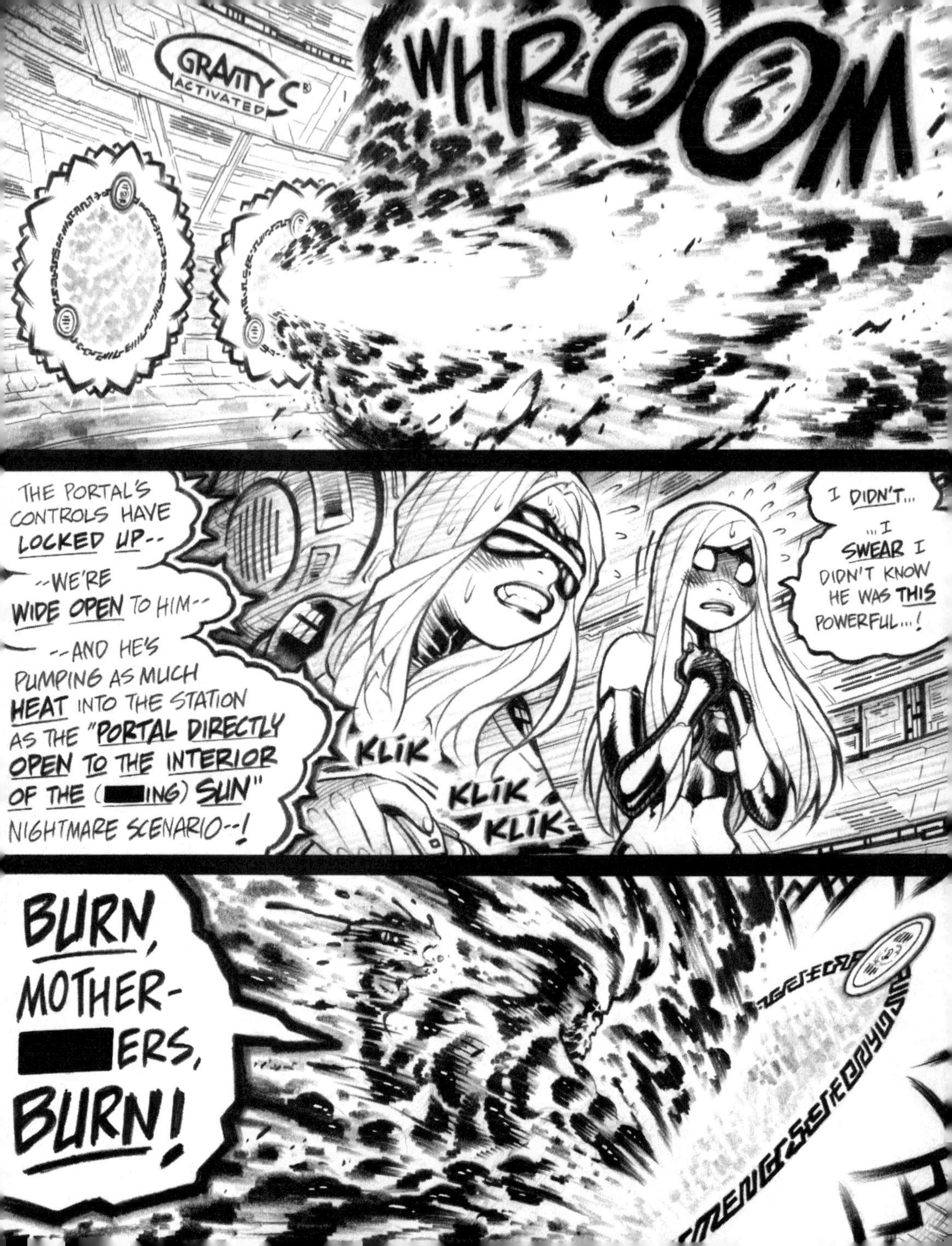
GRAVITY C® ACTIVATED
WHROOM
THE PORTAL'S CONTROLS HAVE LOCKED UP-- --WE'RE WIDE OPEN TO HIM-- --AND HE'S PUMPING AS MUCH HEAT INTO THE STATION AS THE "PORTAL DIRECTLY OPEN TO THE INTERIOR OF THE ([redacted]ING) SUN" NIGHTMARE SCENARIO--!
I DIDN'T... ...I SWEAR I DIDN'T KNOW HE WAS THIS POWERFUL...!
KLIK
KLIK
KLIK
BURN, MOTHER-[redacted]ERS, BURN!

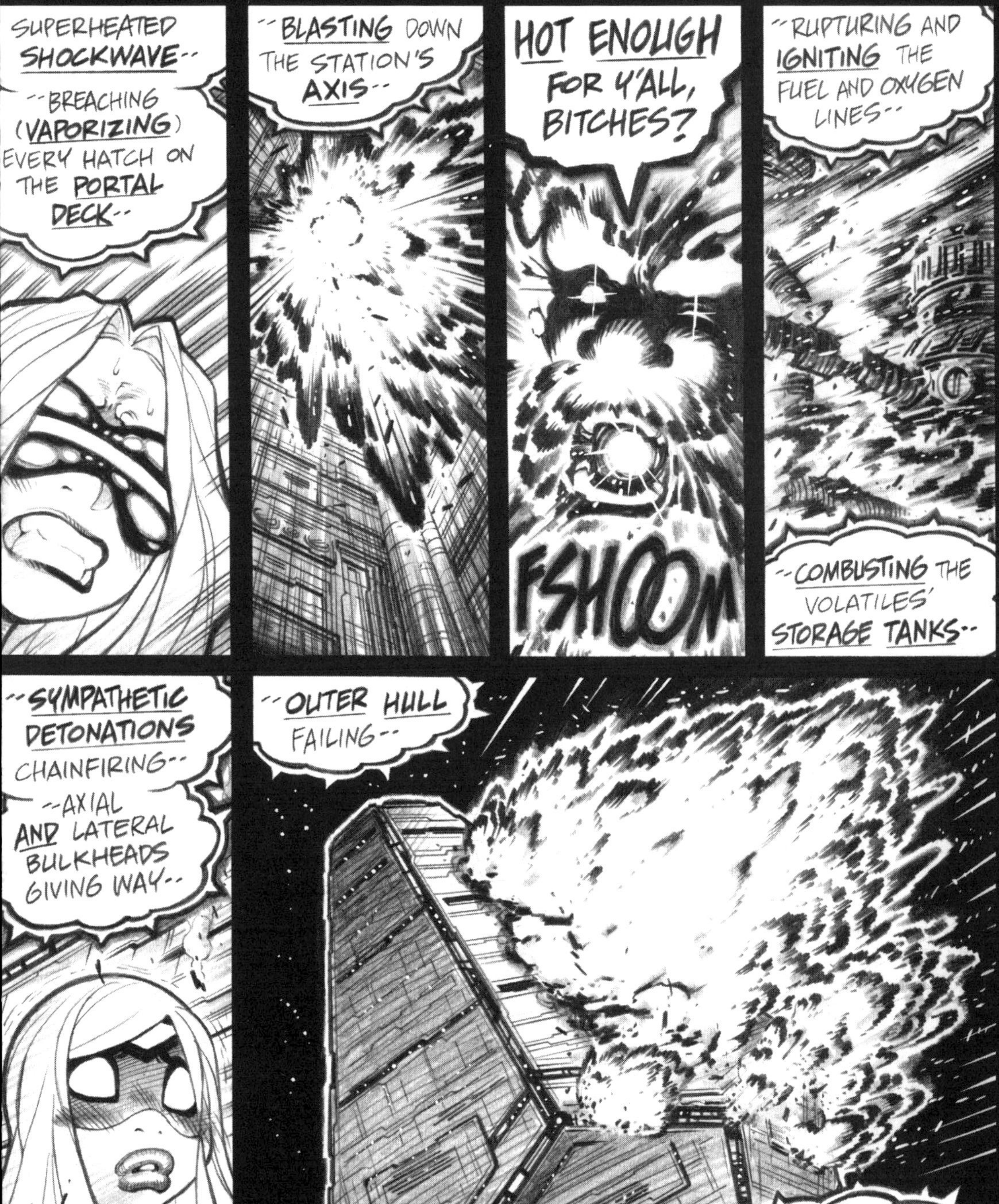
SUPERHEATED SHOCKWAVE--
--BREACHING (VAPORIZING) EVERY HATCH ON THE PORTAL DECK--
--BLASTING DOWN THE STATION'S AXIS--
HOT ENOUGH FOR Y'ALL, BITCHES?
FSHOOM
--RUPTURING AND IGNITING THE FUEL AND OXYGEN LINES--
--COMBUSTING THE VOLATILES' STORAGE TANKS--
--SYMPATHETIC DETONATIONS CHAINFIRING--
--AXIAL AND LATERAL BULKHEADS GIVING WAY--
RMBB
--OUTER HULL FAILING--
--EXPLOSIVE DECOMPRESSION--

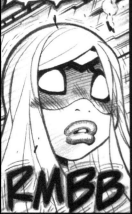

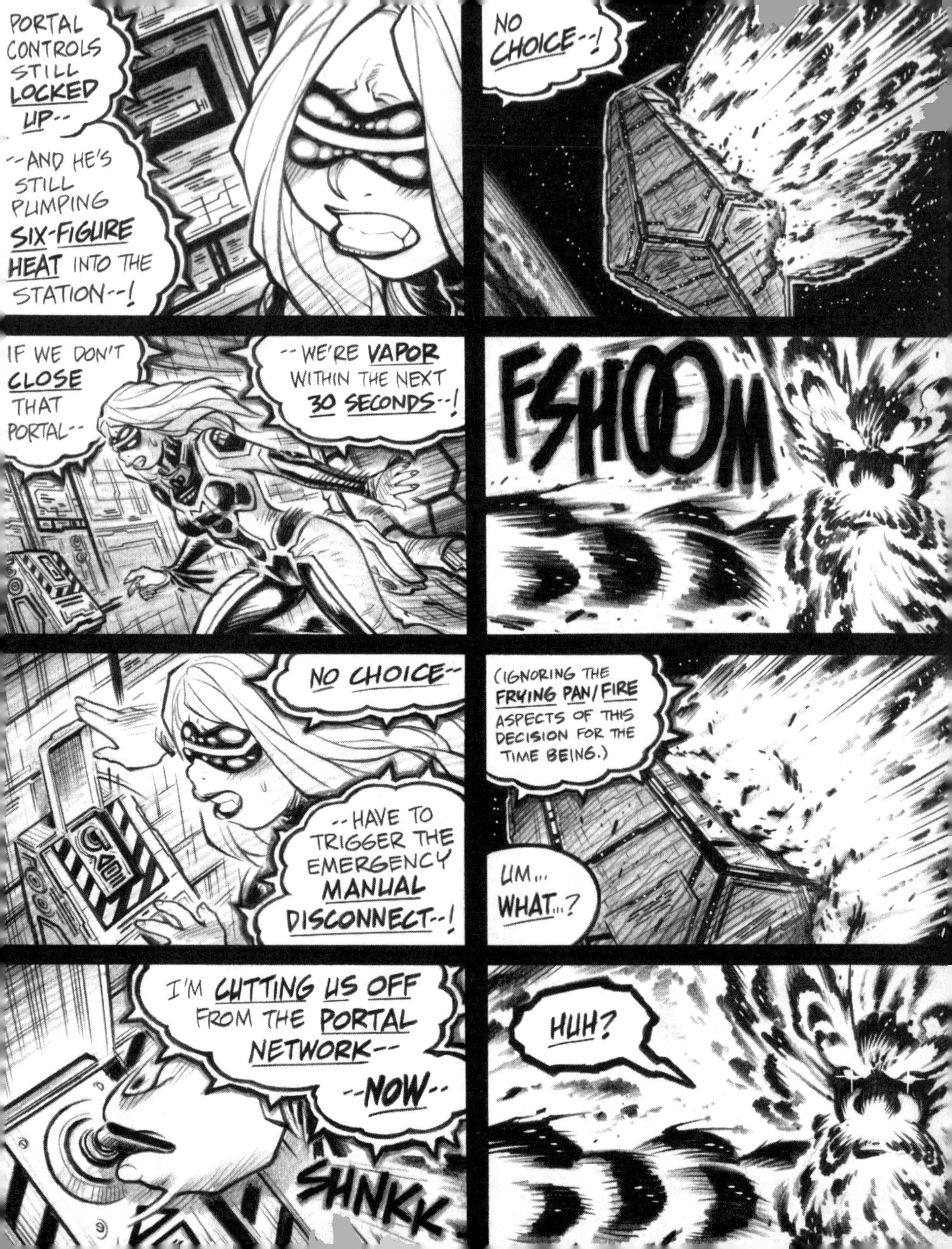
PORTAL CONTROLS STILL LOCKED UP--
--AND HE'S STILL PUMPING SIX-FIGURE HEAT INTO THE STATION--!
NO CHOICE--!
IF WE DON'T CLOSE THAT PORTAL--
--WE'RE VAPOR WITHIN THE NEXT 30 SECONDS--!
FSHOOOM
NO CHOICE--
--HAVE TO TRIGGER THE EMERGENCY MANUAL DISCONNECT--!
(IGNORING THE FRYING PAN/FIRE ASPECTS OF THIS DECISION FOR THE TIME BEING.)
UM... WHAT...?
I'M CUTTING US OFF FROM THE PORTAL NETWORK--
--NOW--
SHNKK
HUH?

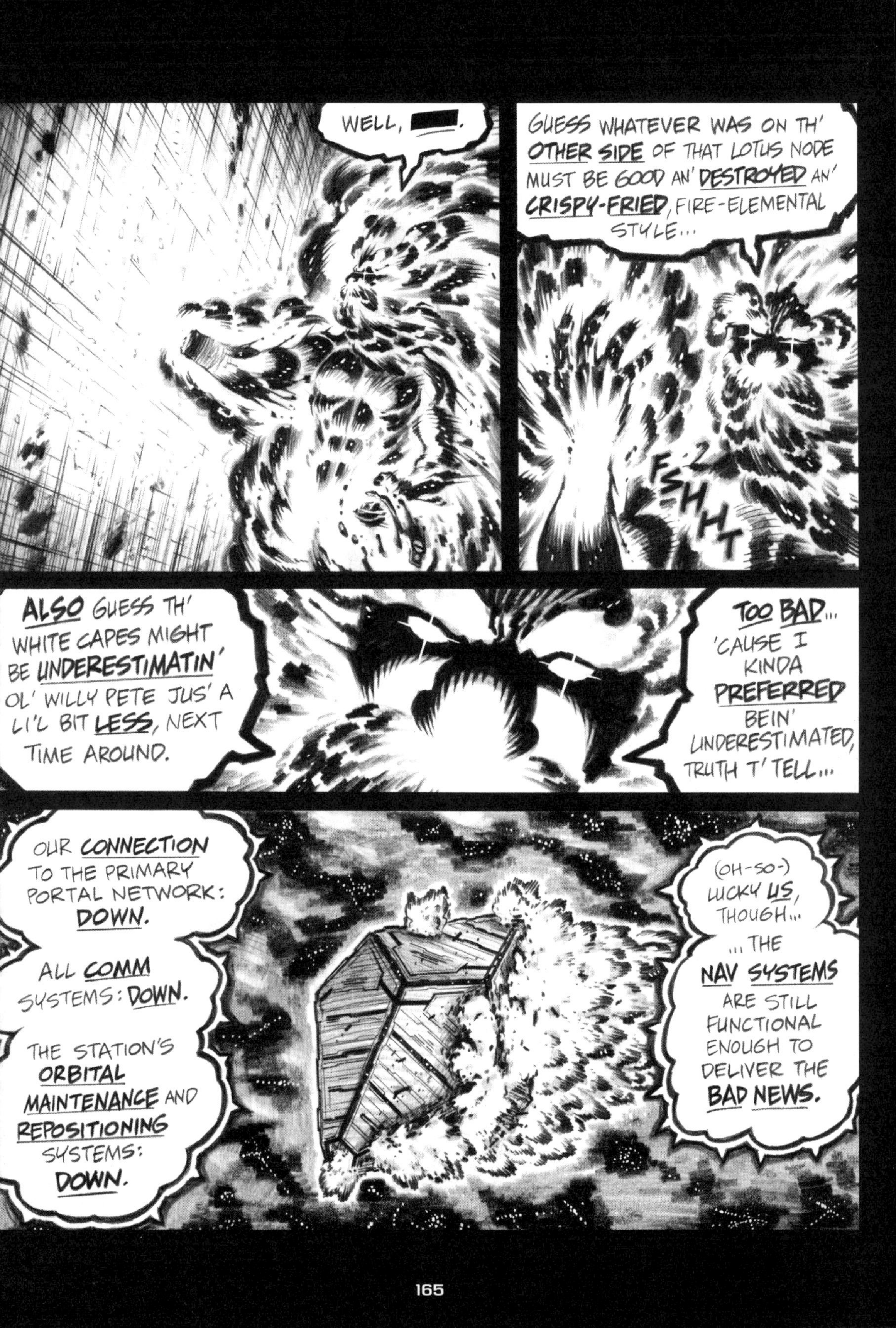
WELL, [redacted].
GUESS WHATEVER WAS ON TH' OTHER SIDE OF THAT LOTUS NODE MUST BE GOOD AN' DESTROYED AN' CRISPY-FRIED, FIRE-ELEMENTAL STYLE...
FSHHHT
ALSO GUESS TH' WHITE CAPES MIGHT BE UNDERESTIMATIN' OL' WILLY PETE JUS' A LI'L BIT LESS, NEXT TIME AROUND.
TOO BAD... 'CAUSE I KINDA PREFERRED BEIN' UNDERESTIMATED, TRUTH T' TELL...
OUR CONNECTION TO THE PRIMARY PORTAL NETWORK: DOWN.
ALL COMM SYSTEMS: DOWN.
THE STATION'S ORBITAL MAINTENANCE AND REPOSITIONING SYSTEMS: DOWN.
(OH-SO-) LUCKY US, THOUGH...
...THE NAV SYSTEMS ARE STILL FUNCTIONAL ENOUGH TO DELIVER THE BAD NEWS.

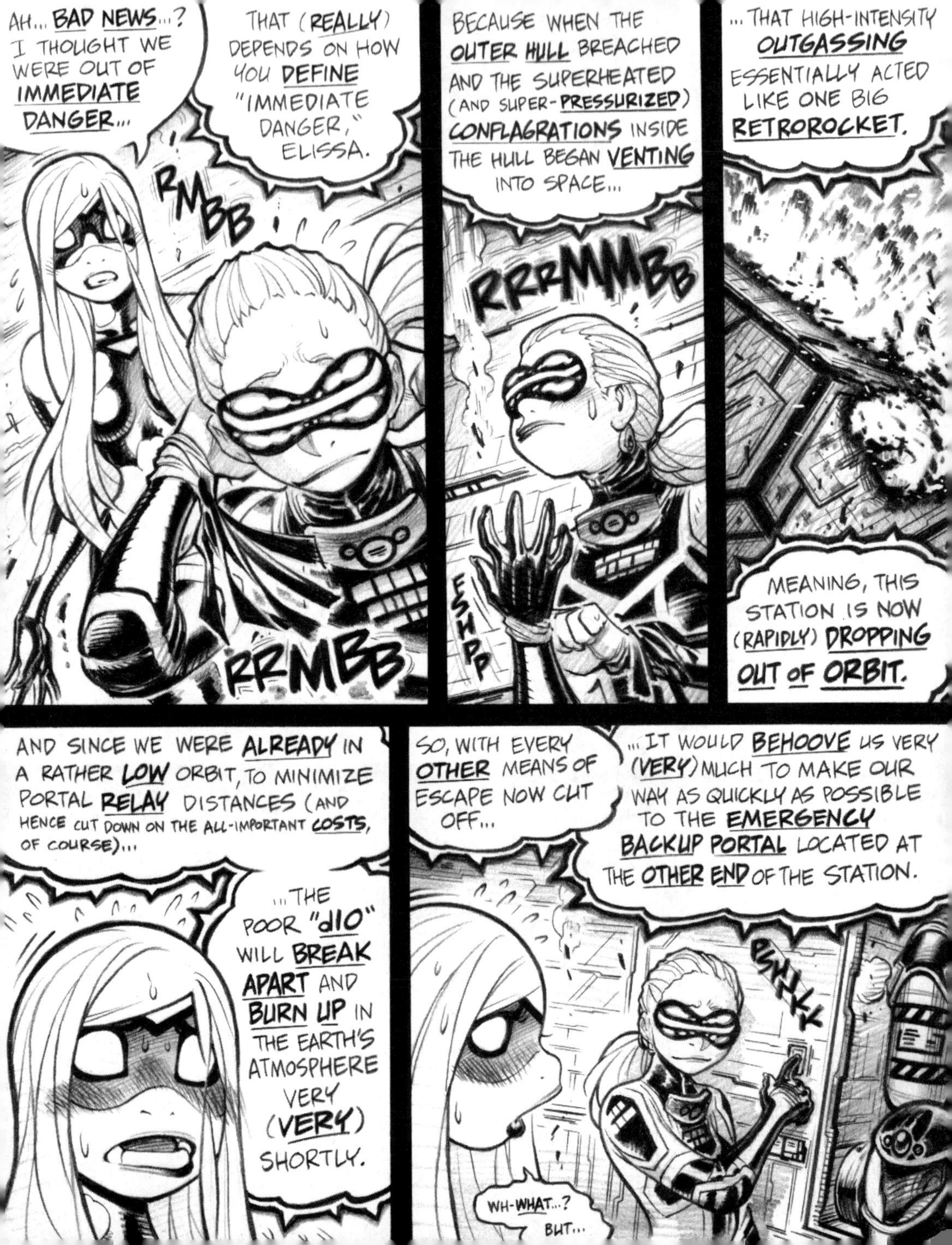
AH... BAD NEWS...? I THOUGHT WE WERE OUT OF IMMEDIATE DANGER...
THAT (REALLY) DEPENDS ON HOW YOU DEFINE "IMMEDIATE DANGER," ELISSA.
RMBB
RRMBB
BECAUSE WHEN THE OUTER HULL BREACHED AND THE SUPERHEATED (AND SUPER-PRESSURIZED) CONFLAGRATIONS INSIDE THE HULL BEGAN VENTING INTO SPACE...
RRRMMBB
FSHPP
...THAT HIGH-INTENSITY OUTGASSING ESSENTIALLY ACTED LIKE ONE BIG RETROROCKET.
MEANING, THIS STATION IS NOW (RAPIDLY) DROPPING OUT OF ORBIT.
AND SINCE WE WERE ALREADY IN A RATHER LOW ORBIT, TO MINIMIZE PORTAL RELAY DISTANCES (AND HENCE CUT DOWN ON THE ALL-IMPORTANT COSTS, OF COURSE)...
...THE POOR "dIO" WILL BREAK APART AND BURN UP IN THE EARTH'S ATMOSPHERE VERY (VERY) SHORTLY.
SO, WITH EVERY OTHER MEANS OF ESCAPE NOW CUT OFF...
...IT WOULD BEHOOVE US VERY (VERY) MUCH TO MAKE OUR WAY AS QUICKLY AS POSSIBLE TO THE EMERGENCY BACKUP PORTAL LOCATED AT THE OTHER END OF THE STATION.
PSHKK
WH-WHAT...? BUT...

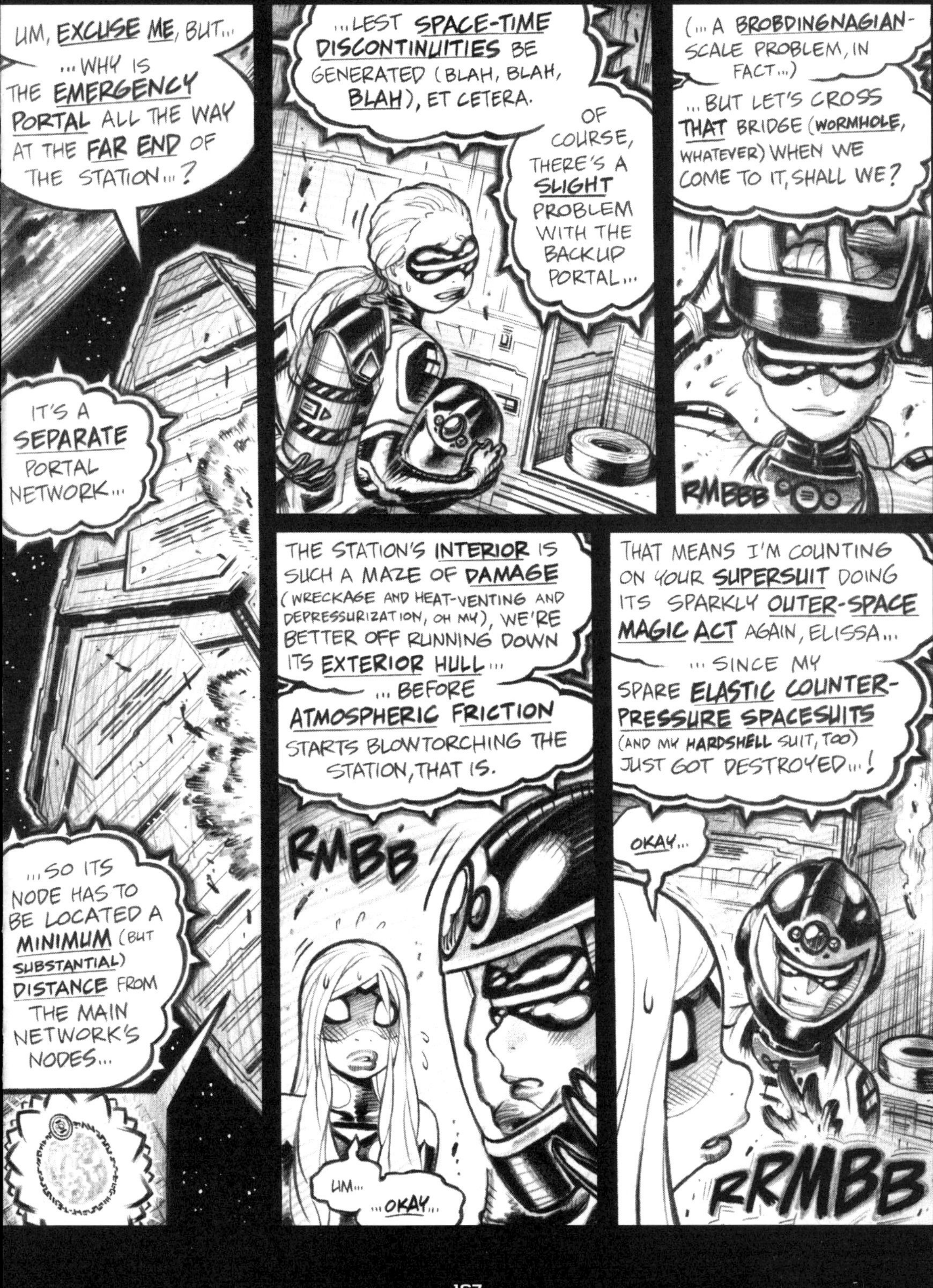

UM, EXCUSE ME, BUT... ...WHY IS THE EMERGENCY PORTAL ALL THE WAY AT THE FAR END OF THE STATION...?
IT'S A SEPARATE PORTAL NETWORK...
...SO ITS NODE HAS TO BE LOCATED A MINIMUM (BUT SUBSTANTIAL) DISTANCE FROM THE MAIN NETWORK'S NODES...
...LEST SPACE-TIME DISCONTINUITIES BE GENERATED (BLAH, BLAH, BLAH), ET CETERA.
OF COURSE, THERE'S A SLIGHT PROBLEM WITH THE BACKUP PORTAL...
(...A BROBDINGNAGIAN-SCALE PROBLEM, IN FACT...)
...BUT LET'S CROSS THAT BRIDGE (WORMHOLE, WHATEVER) WHEN WE COME TO IT, SHALL WE?
RMBBB
THE STATION'S INTERIOR IS SUCH A MAZE OF DAMAGE (WRECKAGE AND HEAT-VENTING AND DEPRESSURIZATION, OH MY), WE'RE BETTER OFF RUNNING DOWN ITS EXTERIOR HULL...
...BEFORE ATMOSPHERIC FRICTION STARTS BLOWTORCHING THE STATION, THAT IS.
RMBB
UM... ...OKAY...
THAT MEANS I'M COUNTING ON YOUR SUPERSUIT DOING ITS SPARKLY OUTER-SPACE MAGIC ACT AGAIN, ELISSA...
...SINCE MY SPARE ELASTIC COUNTER-PRESSURE SPACESUITS (AND MY HARDSHELL SUIT, TOO) JUST GOT DESTROYED...!
OKAY...
RRMBB

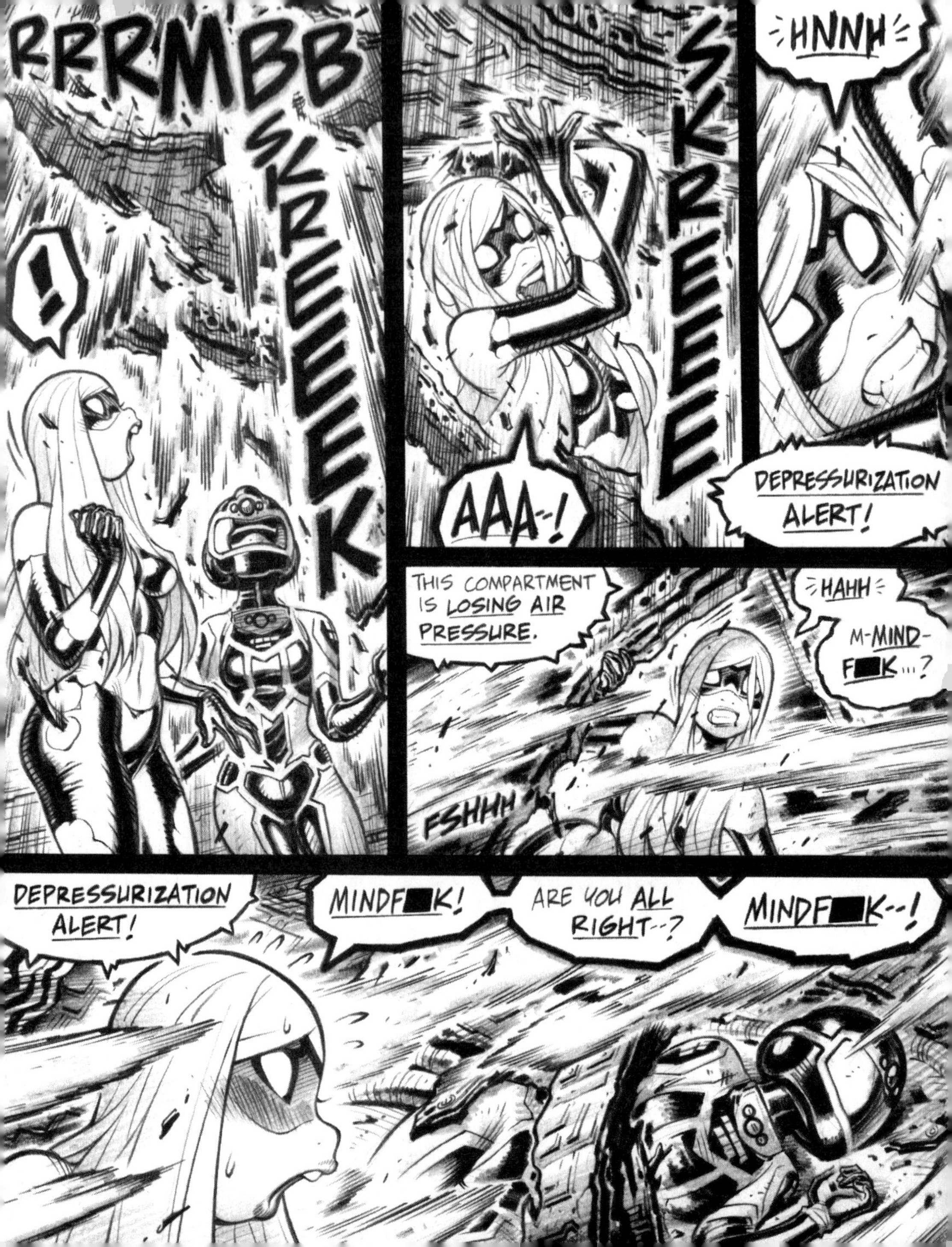
RRRMBB
!
SKREEEEK
SKREEE
AAA--!
HNNH
DEPRESSURIZATION ALERT!
THIS COMPARTMENT IS LOSING AIR PRESSURE.
HAHH
M-MIND-F[redacted]K...?
FSHHH
DEPRESSURIZATION ALERT!
MINDF[redacted]K!
ARE YOU ALL RIGHT--?
MINDF[redacted]K--!

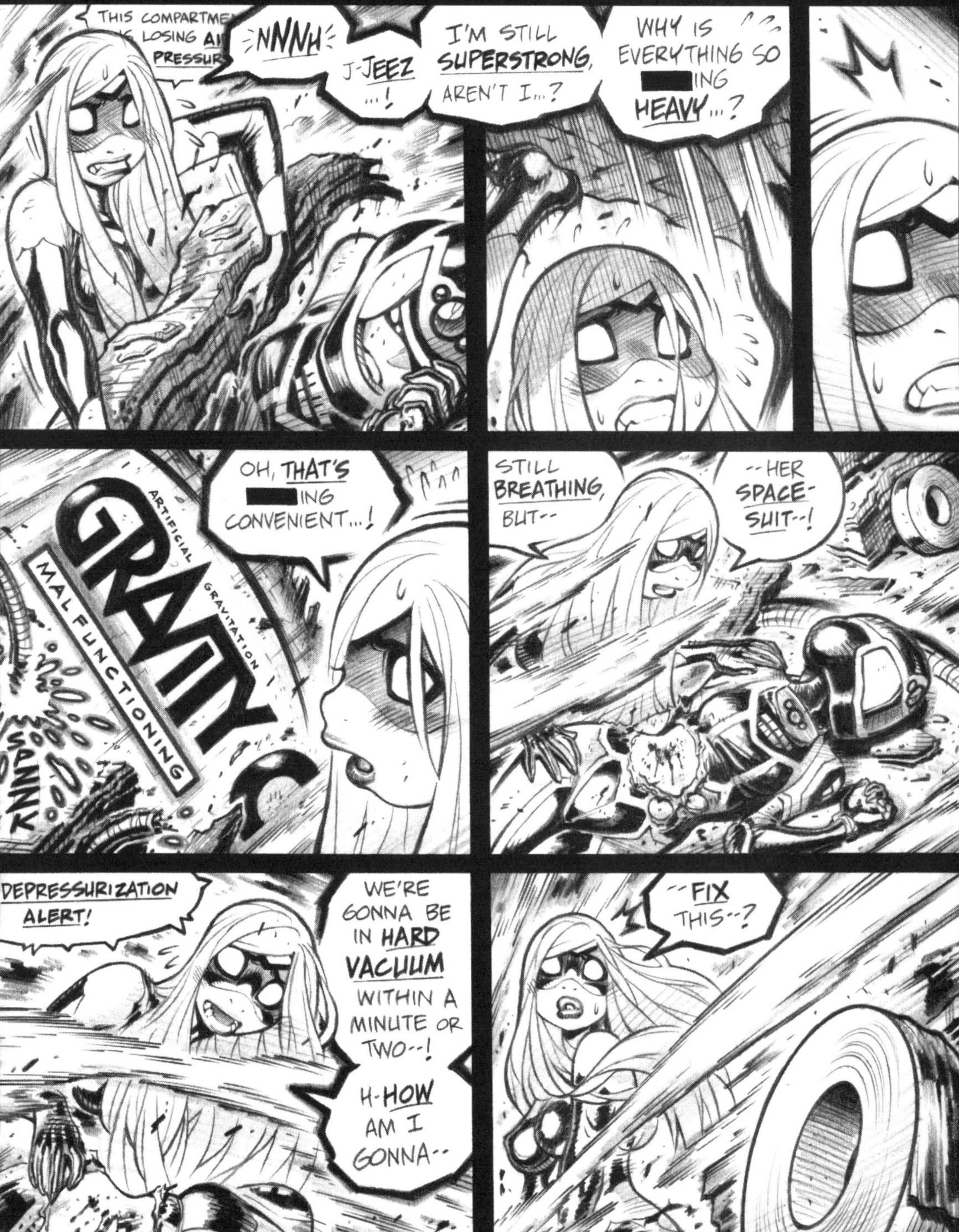

THIS COMPARTME LOSING AI PRESSUR
NNNH
J-JEEZ ...!
I'M STILL SUPERSTRONG, AREN'T I...?
WHY IS EVERYTHING SO [redacted]ING HEAVY...?
OH, THAT'S [redacted]ING CONVENIENT...!
ARTIFICIAL GRAVITATION
GRAVITY
MALFUNCTIONING
SPNNNK
STILL BREATHING, BUT--
--HER SPACE-SUIT--!
DEPRESSURIZATION ALERT!
WE'RE GONNA BE IN HARD VACUUM WITHIN A MINUTE OR TWO--!
H-HOW AM I GONNA--
--FIX THIS--?

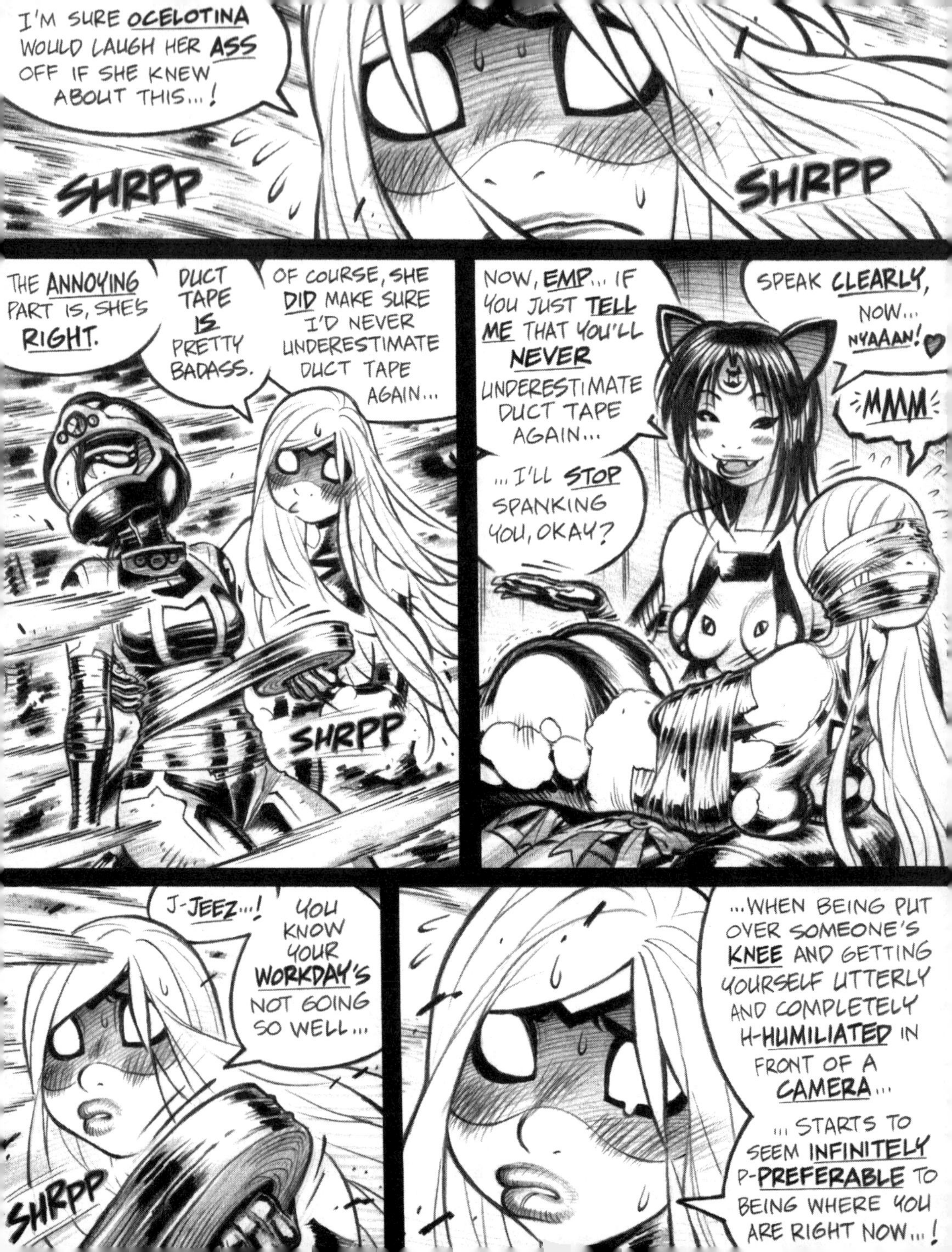

I'M SURE OCELOTINA WOULD LAUGH HER ASS OFF IF SHE KNEW ABOUT THIS...!
SHRPP
SHRPP
THE ANNOYING PART IS, SHE'S RIGHT.
DUCT TAPE IS PRETTY BADASS.
OF COURSE, SHE DID MAKE SURE I'D NEVER UNDERESTIMATE DUCT TAPE AGAIN...
SHRPP
NOW, EMP... IF YOU JUST TELL ME THAT YOU'LL NEVER UNDERESTIMATE DUCT TAPE AGAIN...
...I'LL STOP SPANKING YOU, OKAY?
SPEAK CLEARLY, NOW... NYAAAN!♥
MMM
J-JEEZ...!
YOU KNOW YOUR WORKDAY'S NOT GOING SO WELL...
SHRPP
...WHEN BEING PUT OVER SOMEONE'S KNEE AND GETTING YOURSELF UTTERLY AND COMPLETELY H-HUMILIATED IN FRONT OF A CAMERA...
...STARTS TO SEEM INFINITELY P-PREFERABLE TO BEING WHERE YOU ARE RIGHT NOW...!

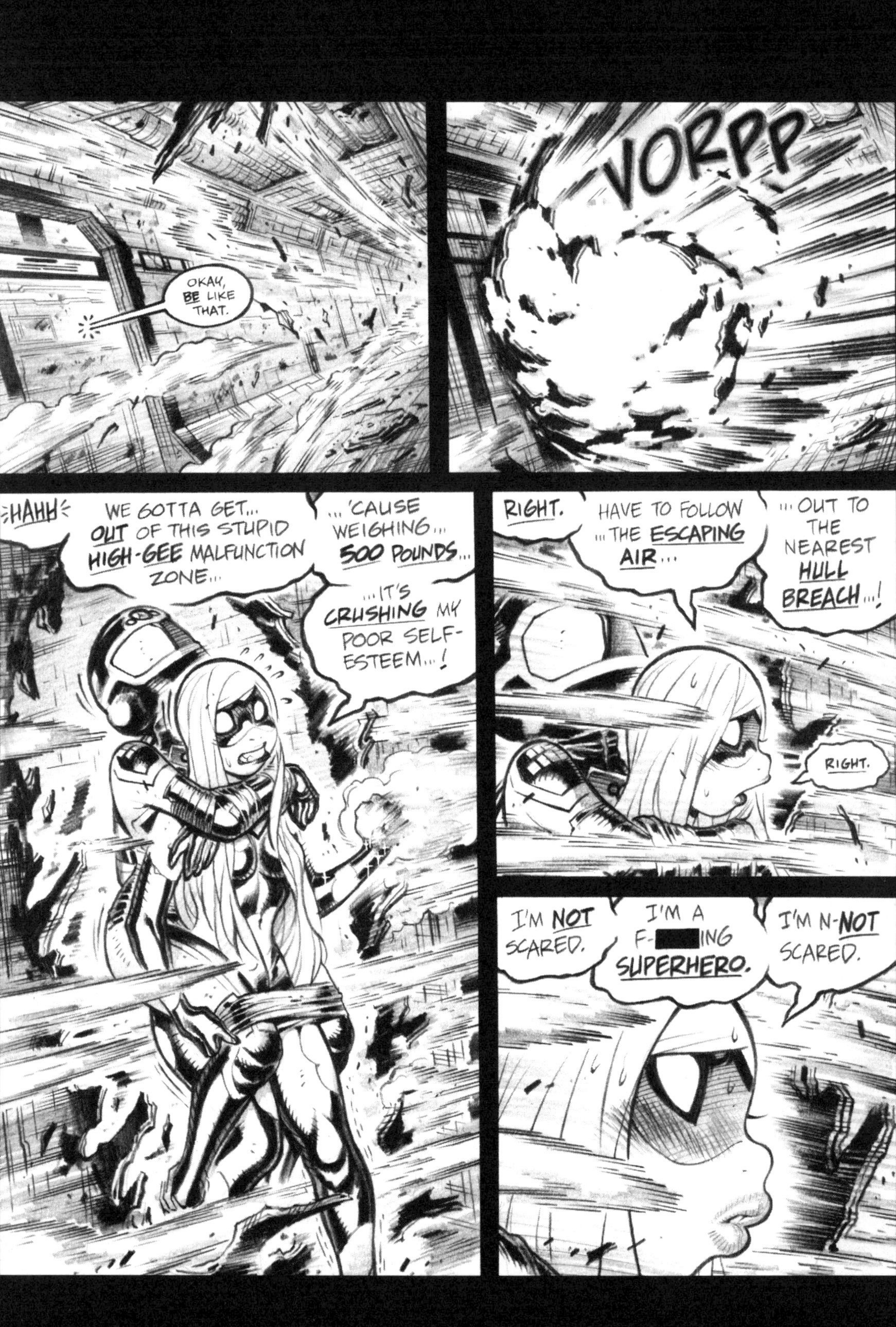
OKAY, BE LIKE THAT.
VORPP
HAHH
WE GOTTA GET... OUT OF THIS STUPID HIGH-GEE MALFUNCTION ZONE...
...'CAUSE WEIGHING... 500 POUNDS...
...IT'S CRUSHING MY POOR SELF-ESTEEM...!
RIGHT.
HAVE TO FOLLOW ...THE ESCAPING AIR...
...OUT TO THE NEAREST HULL BREACH...!
RIGHT.
I'M NOT SCARED.
I'M A F-[redacted]ING SUPERHERO.
I'M N-NOT SCARED.

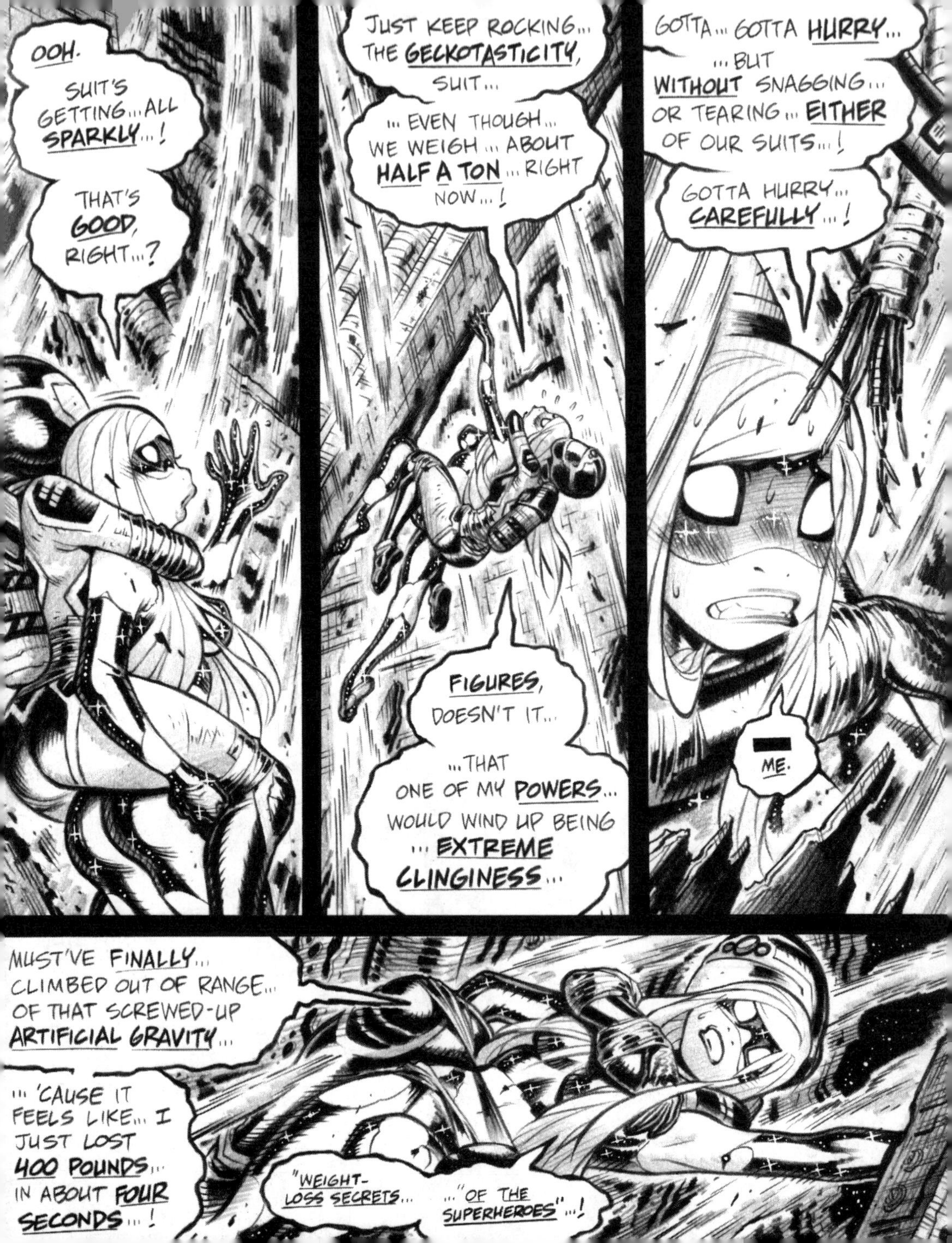

OOH.
SUIT'S GETTING... ALL SPARKLY... !
THAT'S GOOD, RIGHT...?
JUST KEEP ROCKING... THE GECKOTASTICITY, SUIT...
... EVEN THOUGH... WE WEIGH... ABOUT HALF A TON... RIGHT NOW... !
FIGURES, DOESN'T IT...
...THAT ONE OF MY POWERS... WOULD WIND UP BEING ... EXTREME CLINGINESS...
GOTTA... GOTTA HURRY... ...BUT WITHOUT SNAGGING... OR TEARING... EITHER OF OUR SUITS... !
GOTTA HURRY... CAREFULLY... !
[redacted] ME.
MUST'VE FINALLY... CLIMBED OUT OF RANGE... OF THAT SCREWED-UP ARTIFICIAL GRAVITY...
... 'CAUSE IT FEELS LIKE... I JUST LOST 400 POUNDS... IN ABOUT FOUR SECONDS... !
"WEIGHT-LOSS SECRETS...
..."OF THE SUPERHEROES"... !

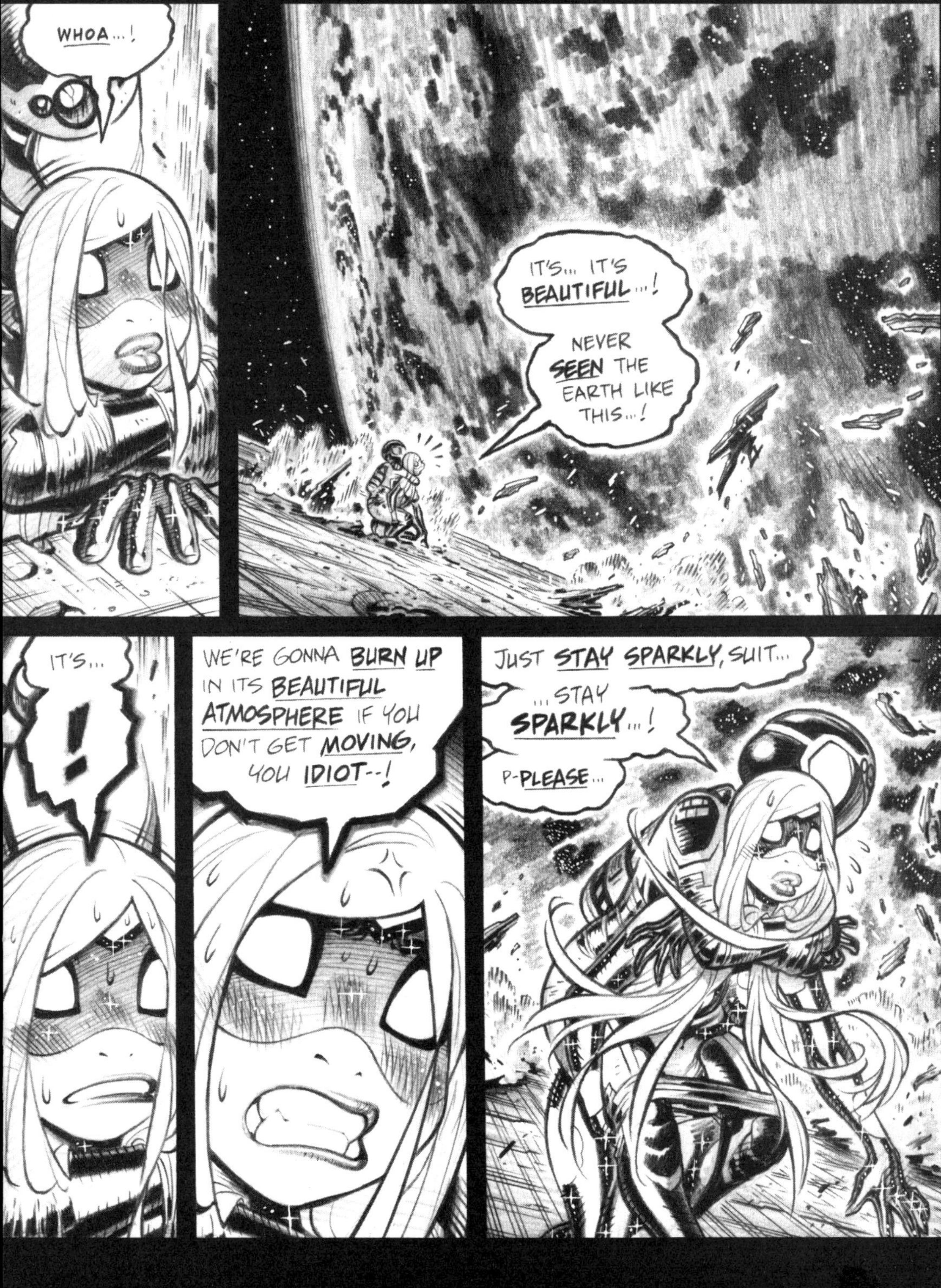
WHOA...!
IT'S... IT'S BEAUTIFUL...!
NEVER SEEN THE EARTH LIKE THIS...!
IT'S...
!
WE'RE GONNA BURN UP IN ITS BEAUTIFUL ATMOSPHERE IF YOU DON'T GET MOVING, YOU IDIOT--!
JUST STAY SPARKLY, SUIT...
...STAY SPARKLY...!
P-PLEASE...

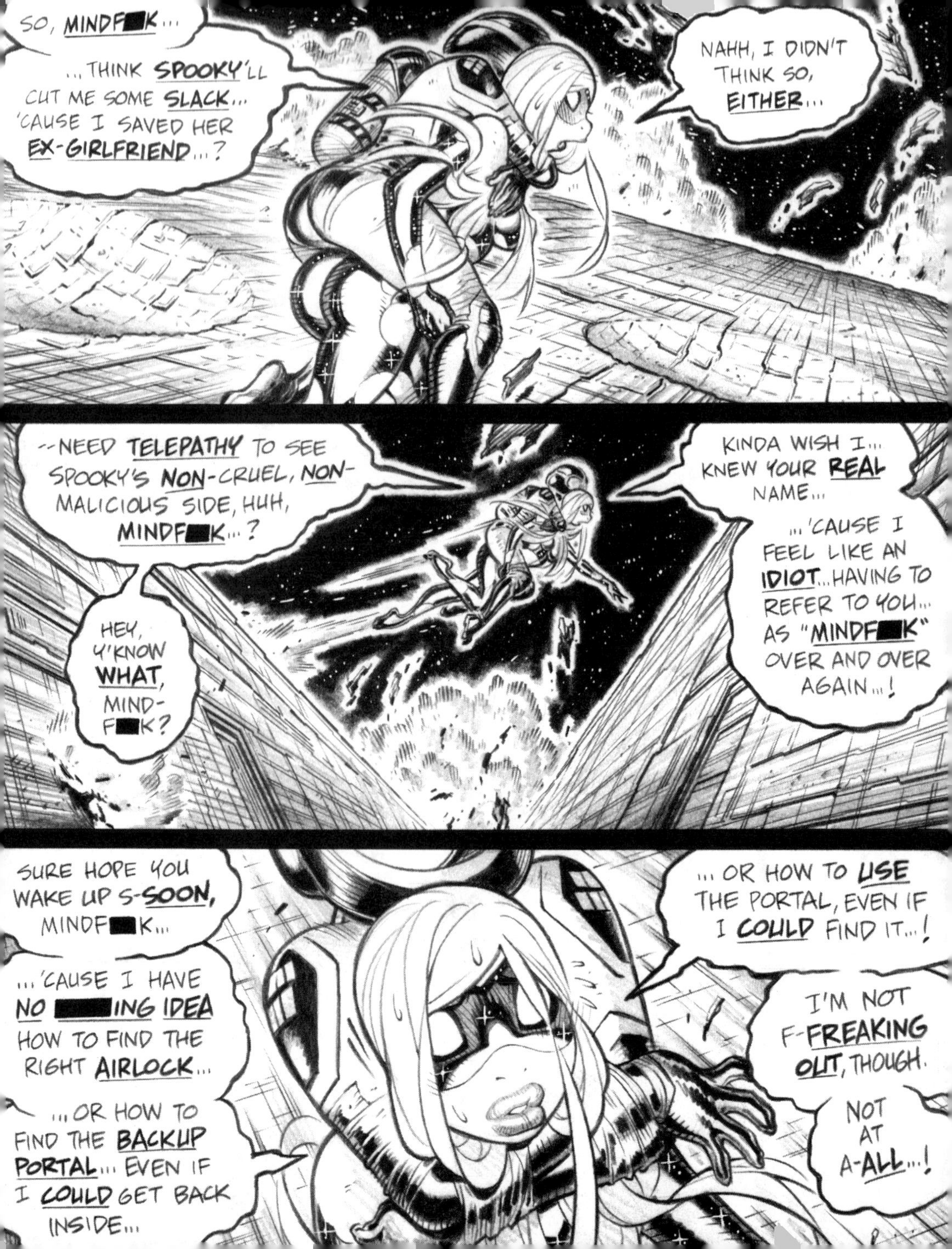
SO, MINDF[redacted]K...
...THINK SPOOKY'LL CUT ME SOME SLACK... 'CAUSE I SAVED HER EX-GIRLFRIEND...?
NAHH, I DIDN'T THINK SO, EITHER...
--NEED TELEPATHY TO SEE SPOOKY'S NON-CRUEL, NON-MALICIOUS SIDE, HUH, MINDF[redacted]K...?
HEY, Y'KNOW WHAT, MIND-F[redacted]K?
KINDA WISH I... KNEW YOUR REAL NAME...
...'CAUSE I FEEL LIKE AN IDIOT...HAVING TO REFER TO YOU... AS "MINDF[redacted]K" OVER AND OVER AGAIN...!
SURE HOPE YOU WAKE UP S-SOON, MINDF[redacted]K...
...'CAUSE I HAVE NO [redacted]ING IDEA HOW TO FIND THE RIGHT AIRLOCK...
...OR HOW TO FIND THE BACKUP PORTAL... EVEN IF I COULD GET BACK INSIDE...
...OR HOW TO USE THE PORTAL, EVEN IF I COULD FIND IT...!
I'M NOT F-FREAKING OUT, THOUGH.
NOT AT A-ALL...!

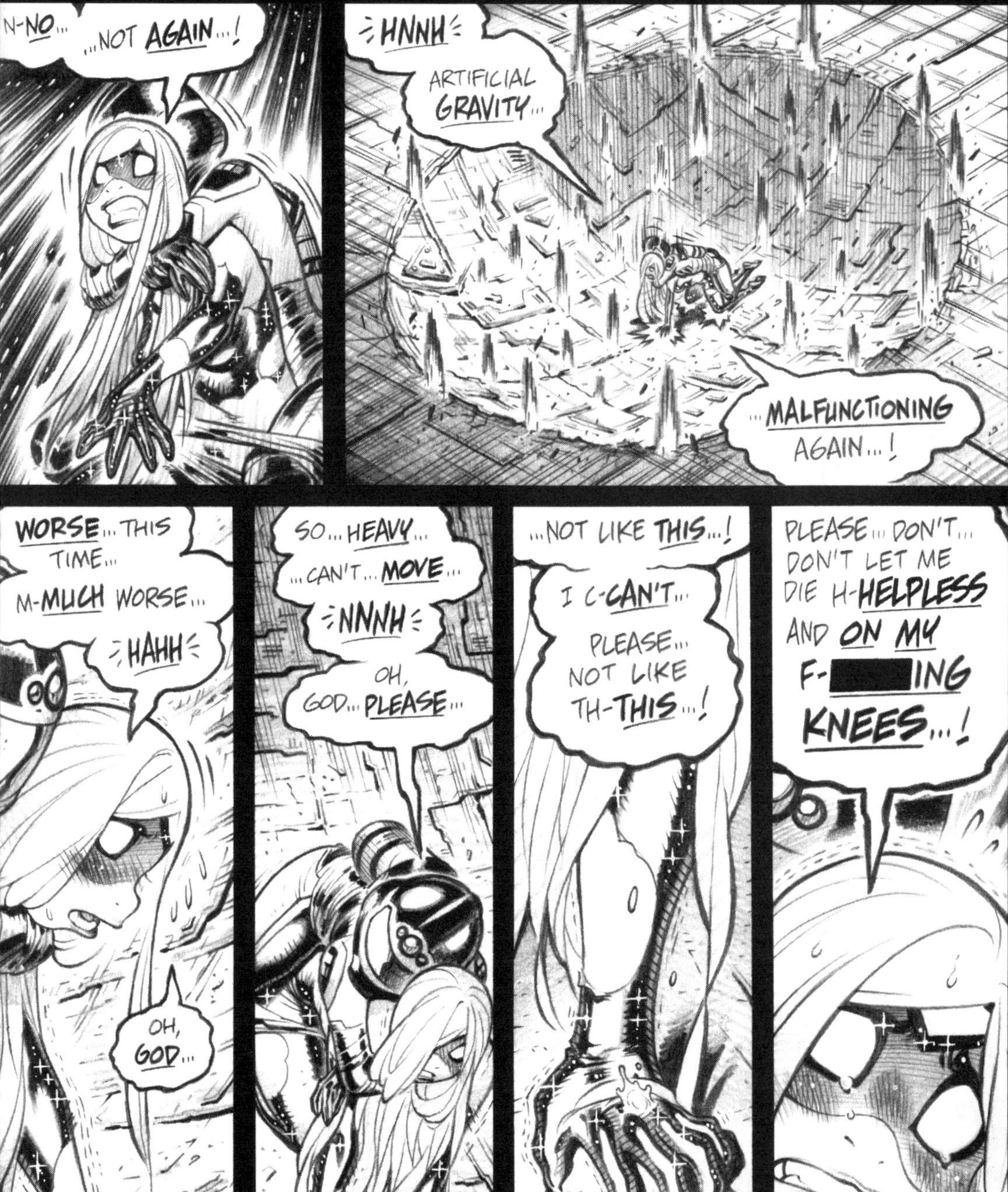
N-NO... ...NOT AGAIN...!
HNNH
ARTIFICIAL GRAVITY...
...MALFUNCTIONING AGAIN...!
WORSE... THIS TIME... M-MUCH WORSE...
HAHH
OH, GOD...
SO... HEAVY... ...CAN'T... MOVE...
NNNH
OH, GOD... PLEASE...
...NOT LIKE THIS...!
I C-CAN'T...
PLEASE... NOT LIKE TH-THIS...!
PLEASE... DON'T... DON'T LET ME DIE H-HELPLESS AND ON MY F-[redacted]ING KNEES...!

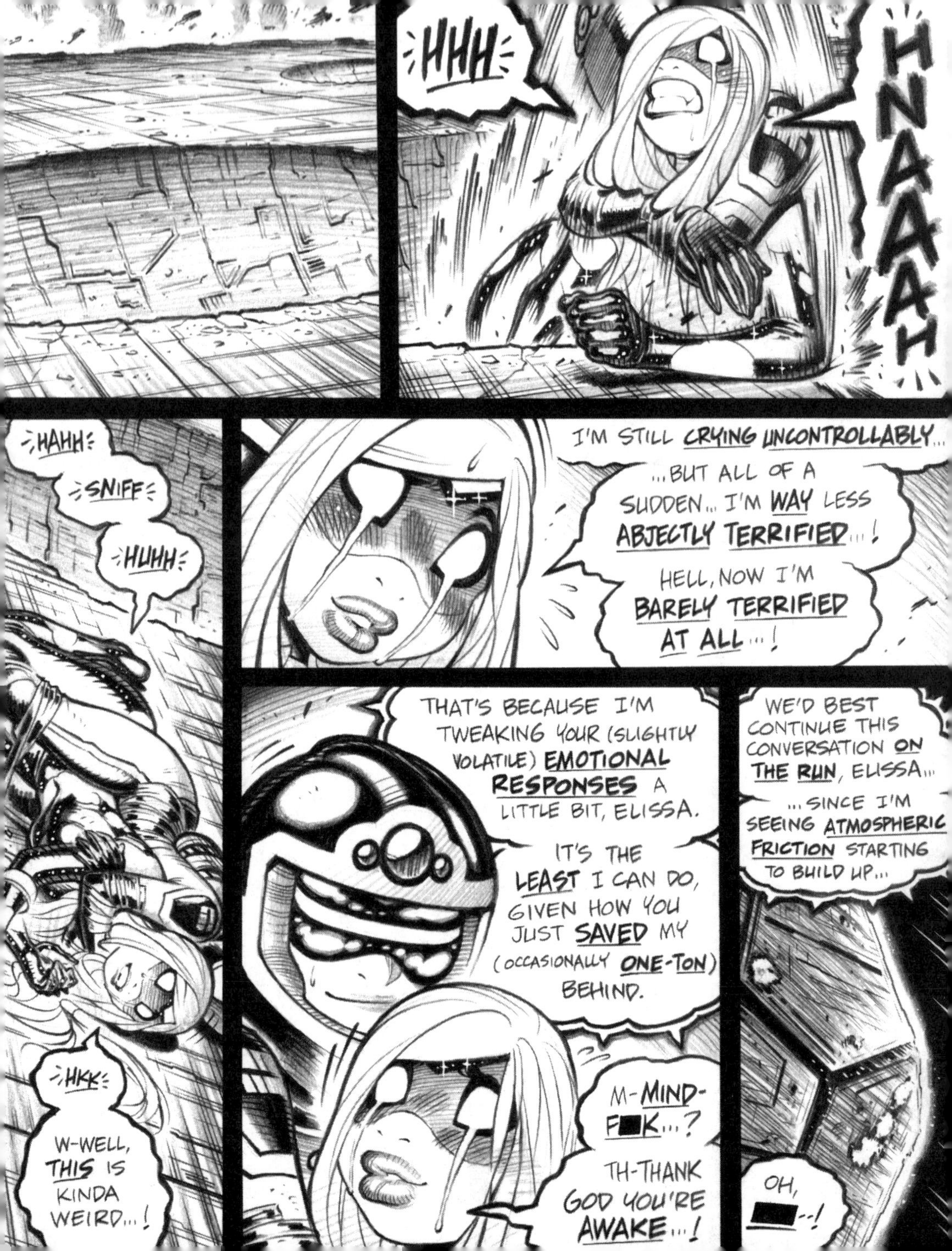
HHH
HNAAAH
HAHH
SNIFF
HUHH
HKK
W-WELL, THIS IS KINDA WEIRD...!
I'M STILL CRYING UNCONTROLLABLY...
...BUT ALL OF A SUDDEN... I'M WAY LESS ABJECTLY TERRIFIED...!
HELL, NOW I'M BARELY TERRIFIED AT ALL...!
THAT'S BECAUSE I'M TWEAKING YOUR (SLIGHTLY VOLATILE) EMOTIONAL RESPONSES A LITTLE BIT, ELISSA.
IT'S THE LEAST I CAN DO, GIVEN HOW YOU JUST SAVED MY (OCCASIONALLY ONE-TON) BEHIND.
M-MIND-F[redacted]K...?
TH-THANK GOD YOU'RE AWAKE...!
WE'D BEST CONTINUE THIS CONVERSATION ON THE RUN, ELISSA...
...SINCE I'M SEEING ATMOSPHERIC FRICTION STARTING TO BUILD UP...
OH, [redacted]--!

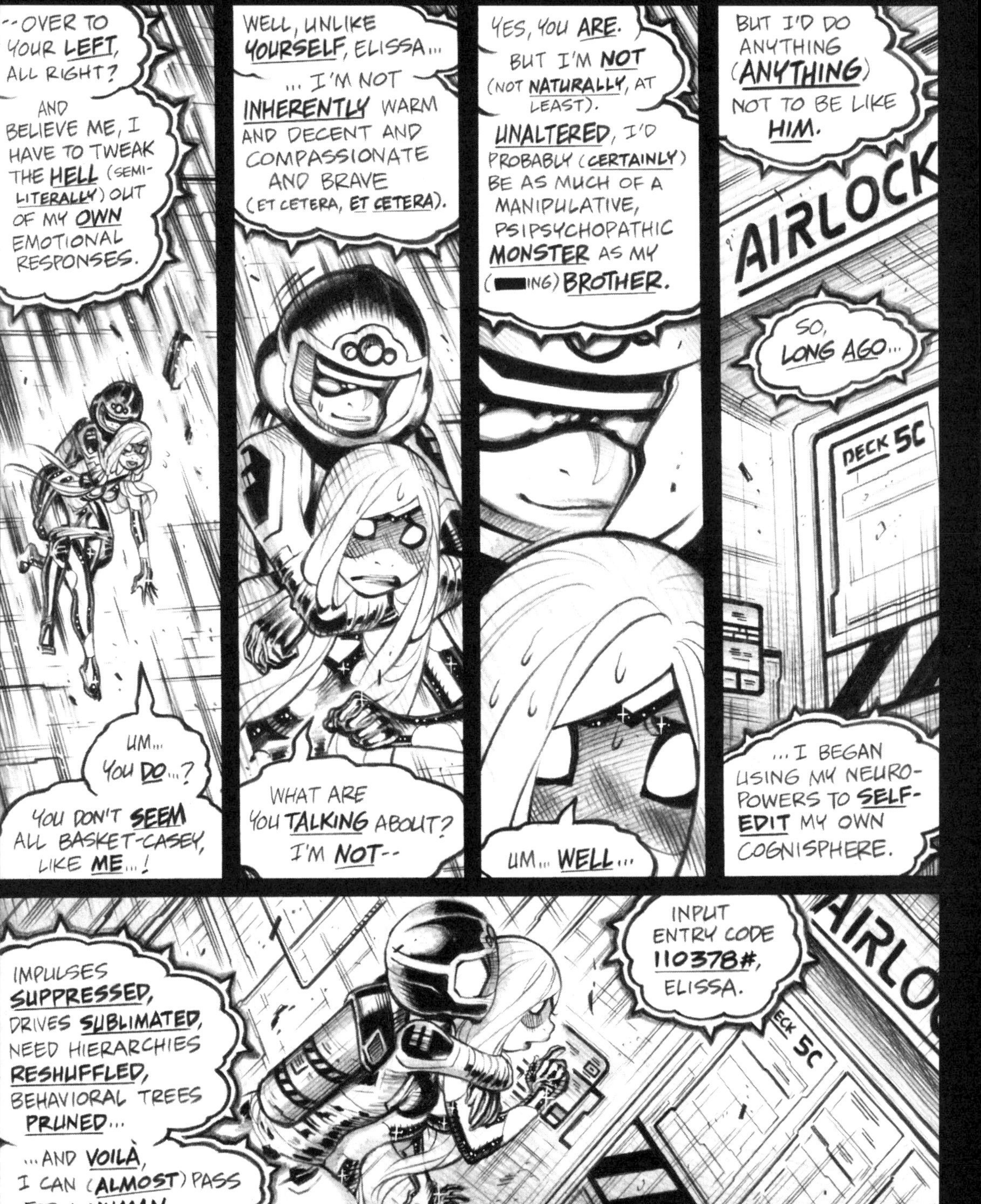
--OVER TO YOUR LEFT, ALL RIGHT?
AND BELIEVE ME, I HAVE TO TWEAK THE HELL (SEMI-LITERALLY) OUT OF MY OWN EMOTIONAL RESPONSES.
UM... YOU DO...?
YOU DON'T SEEM ALL BASKET-CASEY, LIKE ME...!
WELL, UNLIKE YOURSELF, ELISSA...
...I'M NOT INHERENTLY WARM AND DECENT AND COMPASSIONATE AND BRAVE (ET CETERA, ET CETERA).
WHAT ARE YOU TALKING ABOUT? I'M NOT--
YES, YOU ARE.
BUT I'M NOT (NOT NATURALLY, AT LEAST).
UNALTERED, I'D PROBABLY (CERTAINLY) BE AS MUCH OF A MANIPULATIVE, PSIPSYCHOPATHIC MONSTER AS MY ([redacted]ING) BROTHER.
UM... WELL...
BUT I'D DO ANYTHING (ANYTHING) NOT TO BE LIKE HIM.
AIRLOCK
SO, LONG AGO...
DECK 5C
...I BEGAN USING MY NEURO-POWERS TO SELF-EDIT MY OWN COGNISPHERE.
IMPULSES SUPPRESSED, DRIVES SUBLIMATED, NEED HIERARCHIES RESHUFFLED, BEHAVIORAL TREES PRUNED...
...AND VOILÀ, I CAN (ALMOST) PASS FOR A HUMAN.
INPUT ENTRY CODE 110378#, ELISSA.
AIRLO
ECK 5C

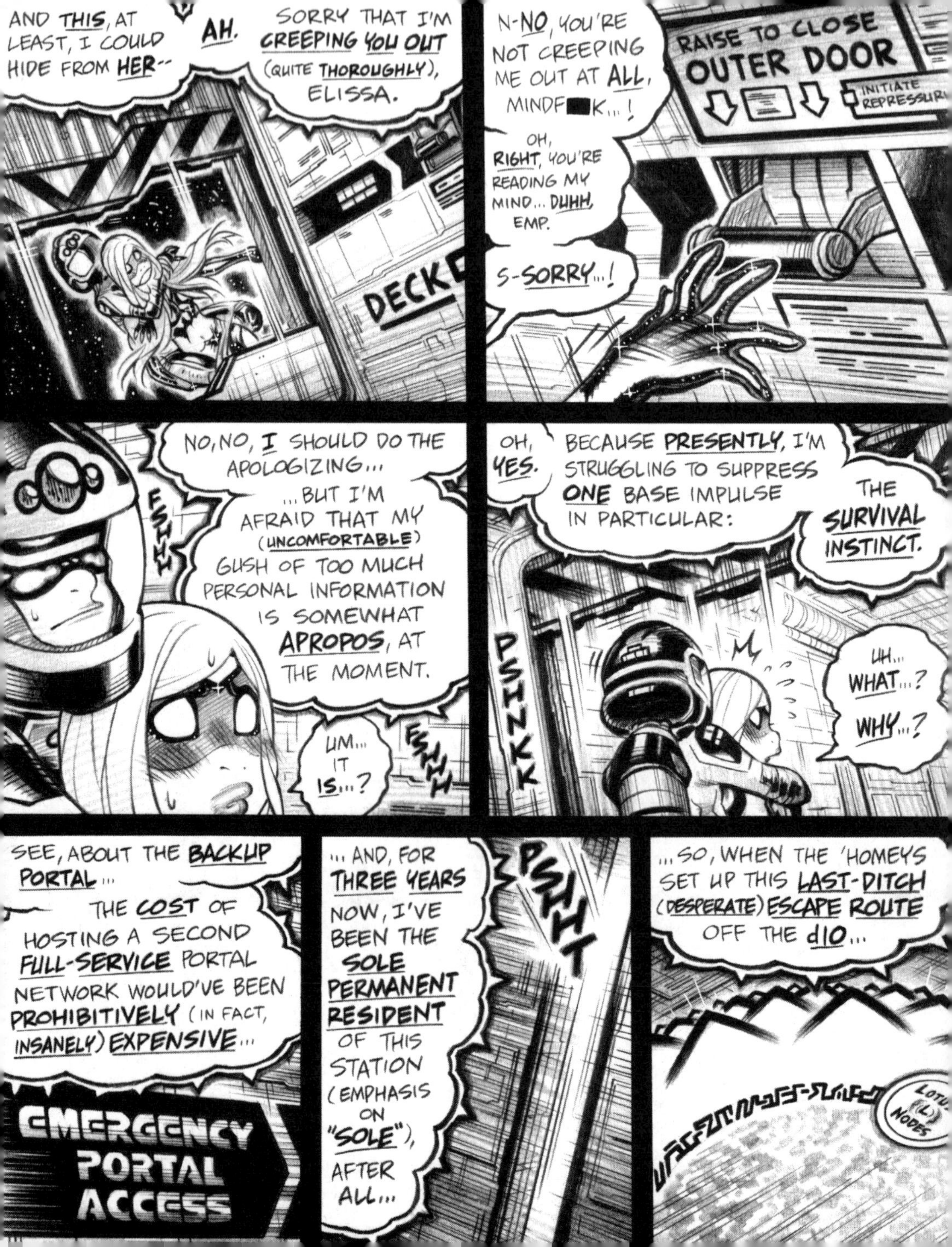
AND THIS, AT LEAST, I COULD HIDE FROM HER--
AH.
SORRY THAT I'M CREEPING YOU OUT (QUITE THOROUGHLY), ELISSA.
DECK
N-NO, YOU'RE NOT CREEPING ME OUT AT ALL, MINDF[redacted]K...!
OH, RIGHT, YOU'RE READING MY MIND... DUHH, EMP.
S-SORRY...!
RAISE TO CLOSE
OUTER DOOR
INITIATE REPRESSURI
NO, NO, I SHOULD DO THE APOLOGIZING...
...BUT I'M AFRAID THAT MY (UNCOMFORTABLE) GUSH OF TOO MUCH PERSONAL INFORMATION IS SOMEWHAT APROPOS, AT THE MOMENT.
FSHHH
UM... IT IS...?
FSHHH
OH, YES.
BECAUSE PRESENTLY, I'M STRUGGLING TO SUPPRESS ONE BASE IMPULSE IN PARTICULAR:
THE SURVIVAL INSTINCT.
PSHNKK
UH... WHAT...?
WHY...?
SEE, ABOUT THE BACKUP PORTAL...
THE COST OF HOSTING A SECOND FULL-SERVICE PORTAL NETWORK WOULD'VE BEEN PROHIBITIVELY (IN FACT, INSANELY) EXPENSIVE...
EMERGENCY PORTAL ACCESS
...AND, FOR THREE YEARS NOW, I'VE BEEN THE SOLE PERMANENT RESIDENT OF THIS STATION (EMPHASIS ON "SOLE"), AFTER ALL...
PSHHT
...SO, WHEN THE 'HOMEYS SET UP THIS LAST-DITCH (DESPERATE) ESCAPE ROUTE OFF THE d10...
LOTUS NODES

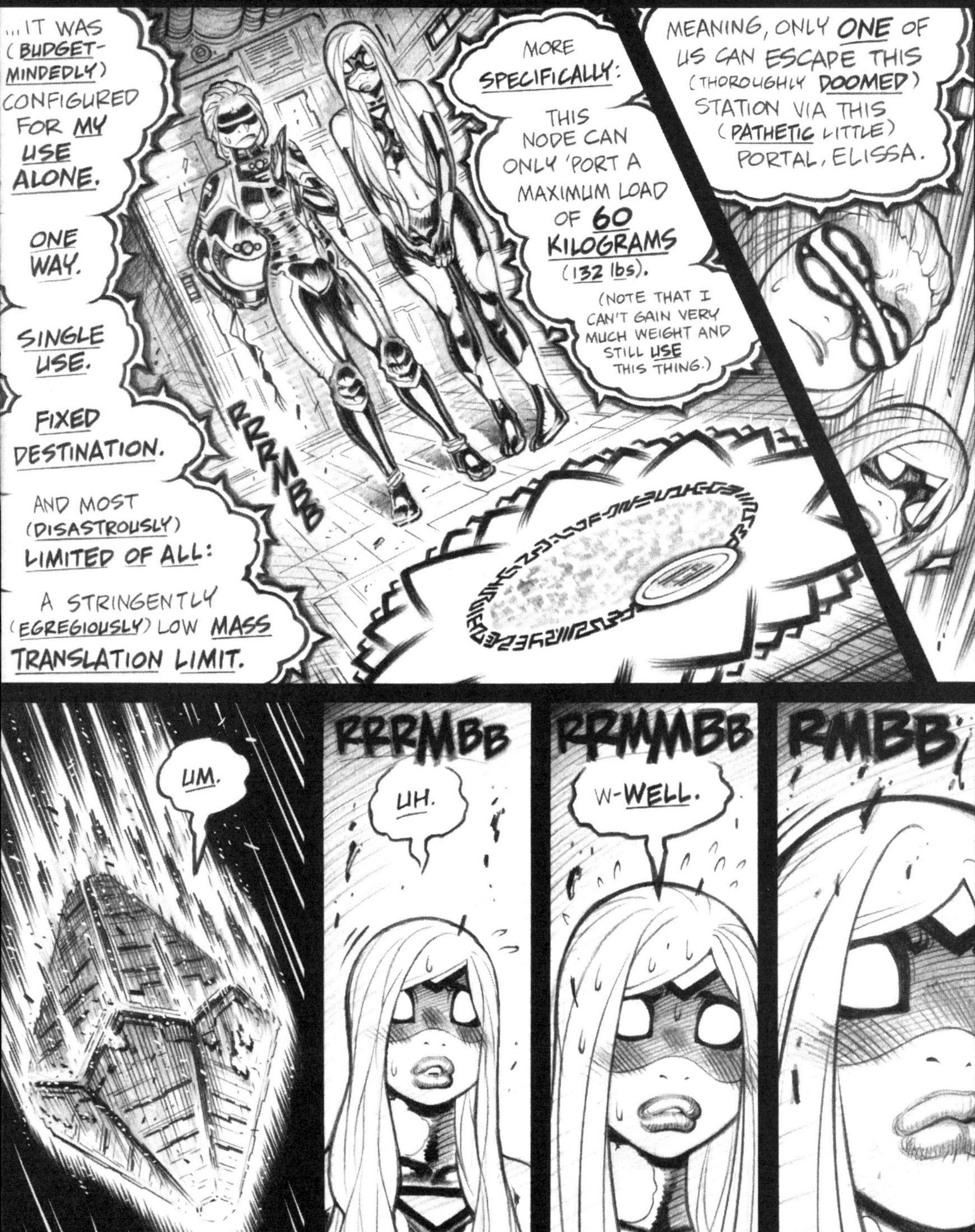

...IT WAS (BUDGET-MINDEDLY) CONFIGURED FOR MY USE ALONE.
ONE WAY.
SINGLE USE.
FIXED DESTINATION.
AND MOST (DISASTROUSLY) LIMITED OF ALL:
A STRINGENTLY (EGREGIOUSLY) LOW MASS TRANSLATION LIMIT.
RRRMBB
MORE SPECIFICALLY:
THIS NODE CAN ONLY 'PORT A MAXIMUM LOAD OF 60 KILOGRAMS (132 lbs).
(NOTE THAT I CAN'T GAIN VERY MUCH WEIGHT AND STILL USE THIS THING.)
MEANING, ONLY ONE OF US CAN ESCAPE THIS (THOROUGHLY DOOMED) STATION VIA THIS (PATHETIC LITTLE) PORTAL, ELISSA.
UM.
RRRMBB
UH.
RRMMBB
W-WELL.
RMBB

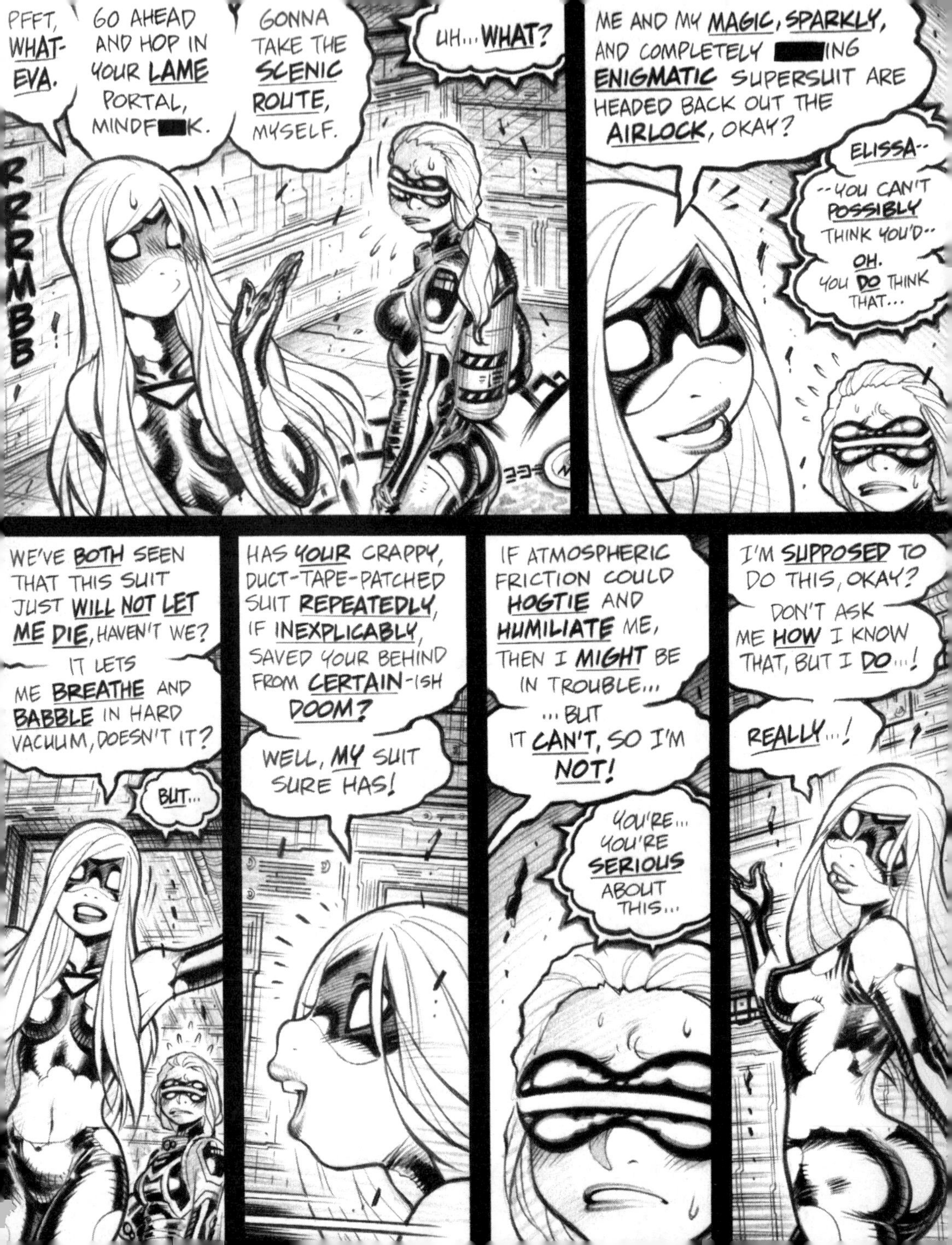
RRRRMBB
PFFT, WHAT-EVA.
GO AHEAD AND HOP IN YOUR LAME PORTAL, MINDF[redacted]K.
GONNA TAKE THE SCENIC ROUTE, MYSELF.
UH... WHAT?
ME AND MY MAGIC, SPARKLY, AND COMPLETELY [redacted]ING ENIGMATIC SUPERSUIT ARE HEADED BACK OUT THE AIRLOCK, OKAY?
ELISSA--
--YOU CAN'T POSSIBLY THINK YOU'D-- OH. YOU DO THINK THAT...
WE'VE BOTH SEEN THAT THIS SUIT JUST WILL NOT LET ME DIE, HAVEN'T WE?
IT LETS ME BREATHE AND BABBLE IN HARD VACUUM, DOESN'T IT?
BUT...
HAS YOUR CRAPPY, DUCT-TAPE-PATCHED SUIT REPEATEDLY, IF INEXPLICABLY, SAVED YOUR BEHIND FROM CERTAIN-ISH DOOM?
WELL, MY SUIT SURE HAS!
IF ATMOSPHERIC FRICTION COULD HOGTIE AND HUMILIATE ME, THEN I MIGHT BE IN TROUBLE...
...BUT IT CAN'T, SO I'M NOT!
YOU'RE... YOU'RE SERIOUS ABOUT THIS...
I'M SUPPOSED TO DO THIS, OKAY?
DON'T ASK ME HOW I KNOW THAT, BUT I DO...!
REALLY...!

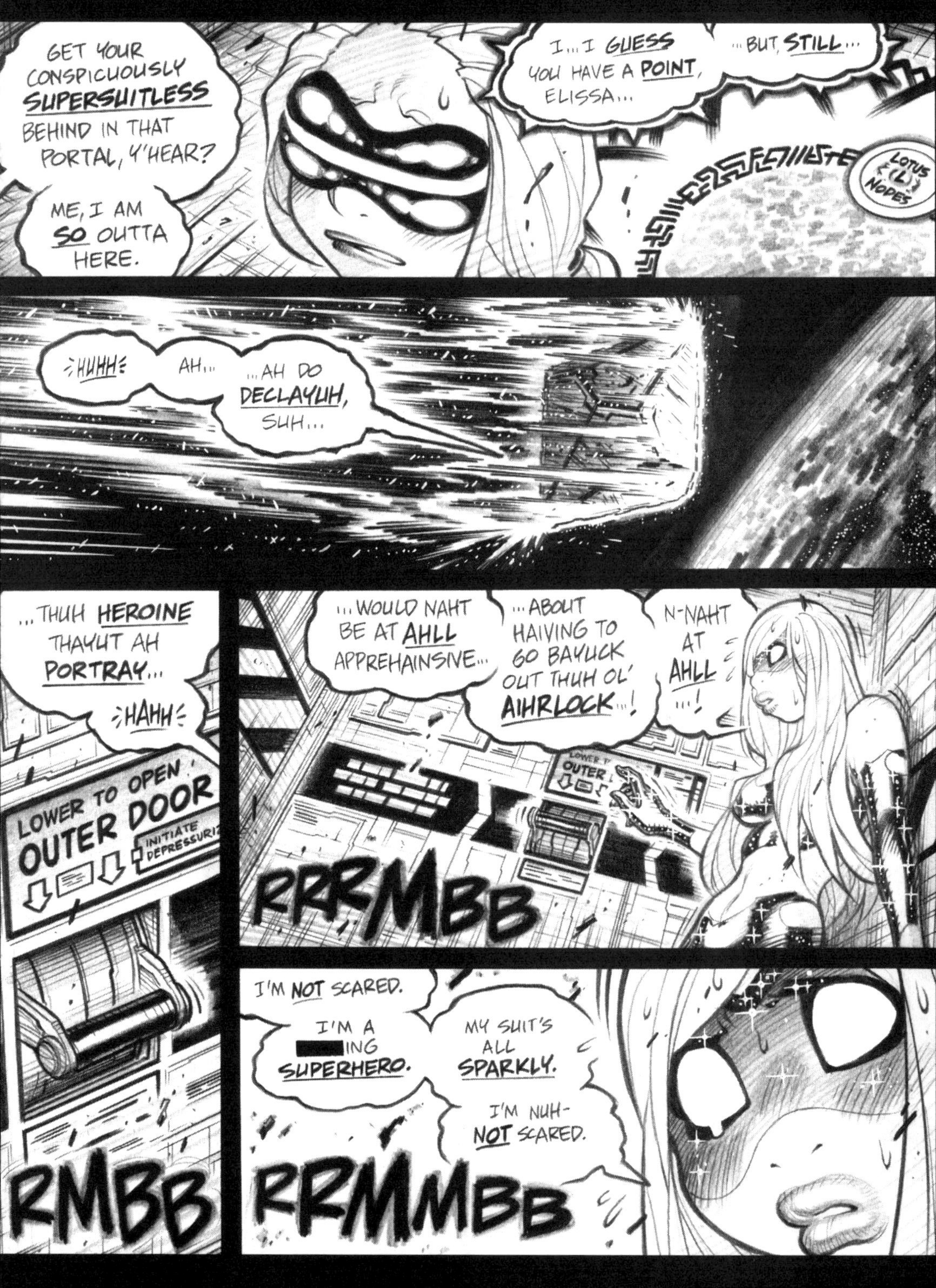
GET YOUR CONSPICUOUSLY SUPERSUITLESS BEHIND IN THAT PORTAL, Y'HEAR?
ME, I AM SO OUTTA HERE.
I... I GUESS YOU HAVE A POINT, ELISSA...
...BUT, STILL...
LOTUS NOPES
HUHH
AH...
...AH DO DECLAYUH, SUH...
...THUH HEROINE THAYUT AH PORTRAY...
HAHH
LOWER TO OPEN OUTER DOOR
INITIATE DEPRESSURIZ
RMBB
...WOULD NAHT BE AT AHLL APPREHAINSIVE...
...ABOUT HAIVING TO GO BAYUCK OUT THUH OL' AIHRLOCK...!
N-NAHT AT AHLL...!
RRRMBB
I'M NOT SCARED.
I'M A [redacted]ING SUPERHERO.
MY SUIT'S ALL SPARKLY.
I'M NUH-NOT SCARED.
RRMMBB

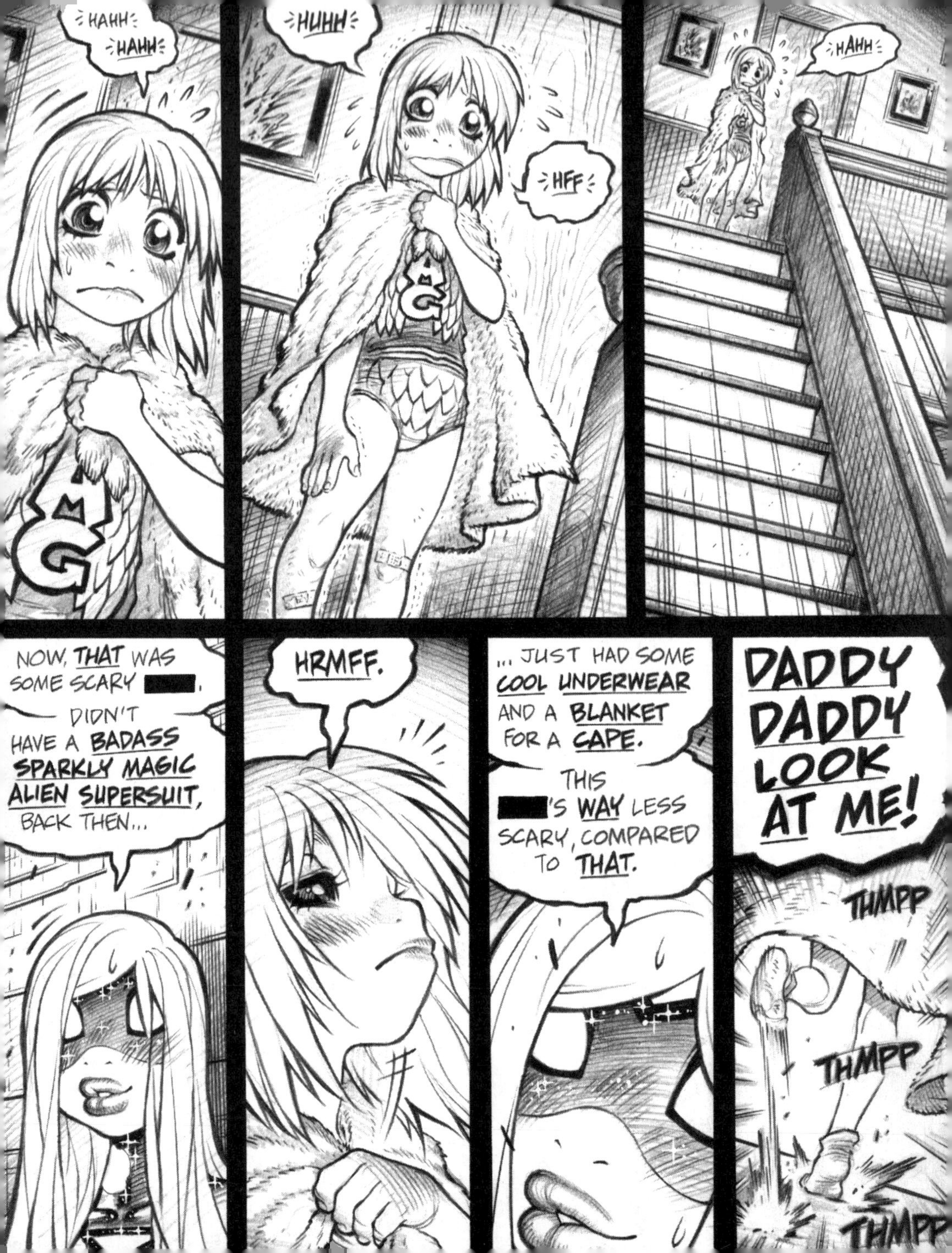
HAHH HAHH
HUHH
HFF
HAHH
NOW, THAT WAS SOME SCARY [redacted].
— DIDN'T HAVE A BADASS SPARKLY MAGIC ALIEN SUPERSUIT, BACK THEN...
HRMFF.
... JUST HAD SOME COOL UNDERWEAR AND A BLANKET FOR A CAPE.
THIS [redacted]'S WAY LESS SCARY, COMPARED TO THAT.
DADDY DADDY LOOK AT ME!
THMPP
THMPP
THMPP

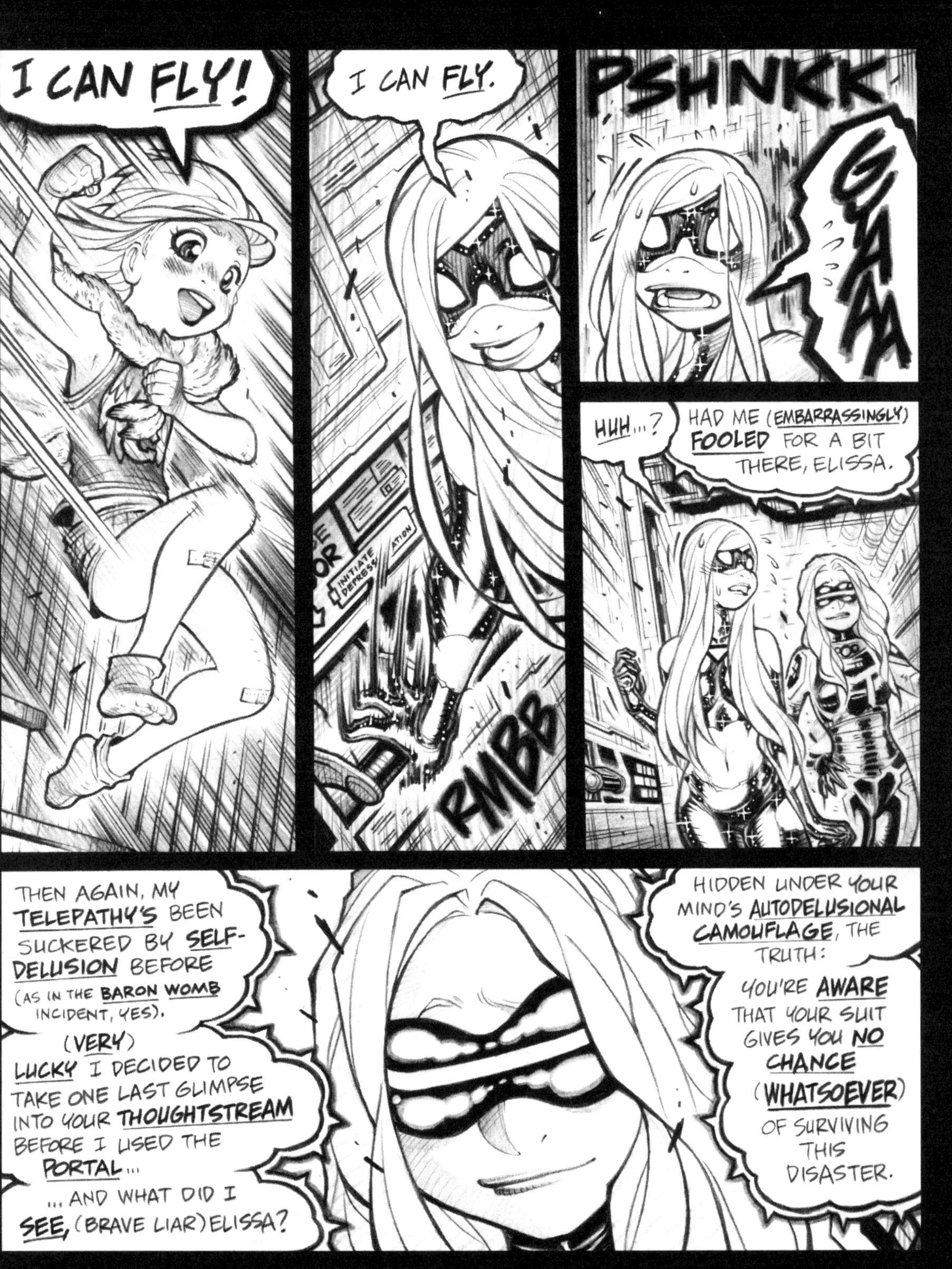
I CAN FLY!
I CAN FLY.
RMBB
PSHNKK
HUH...?
HAD ME (EMBARRASSINGLY) FOOLED FOR A BIT THERE, ELISSA.
THEN AGAIN, MY TELEPATHY'S BEEN SUCKERED BY SELF-DELUSION BEFORE (AS IN THE BARON WOMB INCIDENT, YES).
(VERY) LUCKY I DECIDED TO TAKE ONE LAST GLIMPSE INTO YOUR THOUGHTSTREAM BEFORE I USED THE PORTAL...
... AND WHAT DID I SEE, (BRAVE LIAR) ELISSA?
HIDDEN UNDER YOUR MIND'S AUTODELUSIONAL CAMOUFLAGE, THE TRUTH:
YOU'RE AWARE THAT YOUR SUIT GIVES YOU NO CHANCE (WHATSOEVER) OF SURVIVING THIS DISASTER.

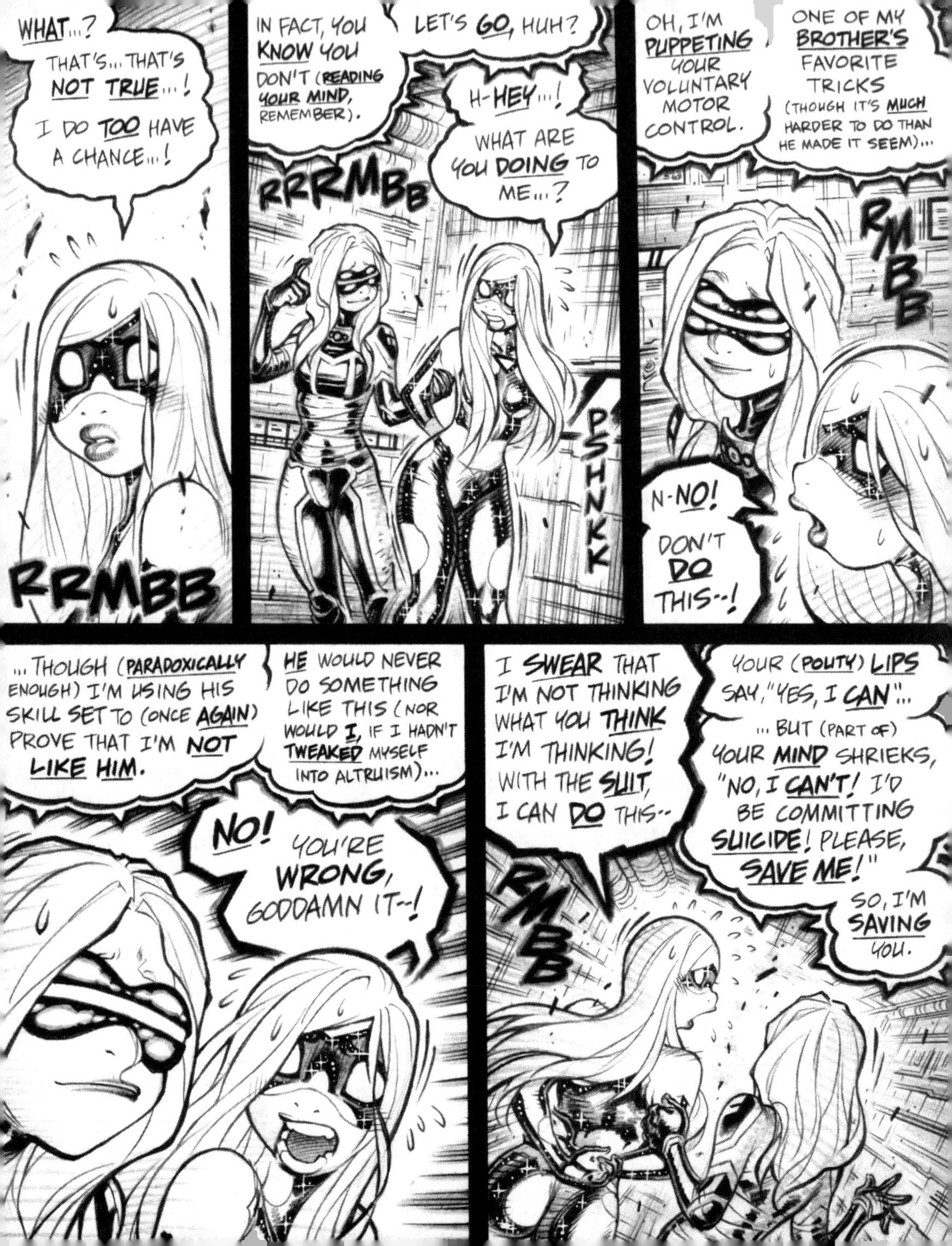
WHAT...? THAT'S... THAT'S NOT TRUE...! I DO TOO HAVE A CHANCE...!
RRMBB
IN FACT, YOU KNOW YOU DON'T (READING YOUR MIND, REMEMBER).
LET'S GO, HUH?
RRRMBB
H-HEY...! WHAT ARE YOU DOING TO ME...?
PSHNKK
OH, I'M PUPPETING YOUR VOLUNTARY MOTOR CONTROL.
ONE OF MY BROTHER'S FAVORITE TRICKS (THOUGH IT'S MUCH HARDER TO DO THAN HE MADE IT SEEM)...
RMBB
N-NO! DON'T DO THIS--!
...THOUGH (PARADOXICALLY ENOUGH) I'M USING HIS SKILL SET TO (ONCE AGAIN) PROVE THAT I'M NOT LIKE HIM.
HE WOULD NEVER DO SOMETHING LIKE THIS (NOR WOULD I, IF I HADN'T TWEAKED MYSELF INTO ALTRUISM)...
NO! YOU'RE WRONG, GODDAMN IT--!
I SWEAR THAT I'M NOT THINKING WHAT YOU THINK I'M THINKING! WITH THE SUIT, I CAN DO THIS--
RMBB
YOUR (POUTY) LIPS SAY, "YES, I CAN"...
...BUT (PART OF) YOUR MIND SHRIEKS, "NO, I CAN'T! I'D BE COMMITTING SUICIDE! PLEASE, SAVE ME!"
SO, I'M SAVING YOU.

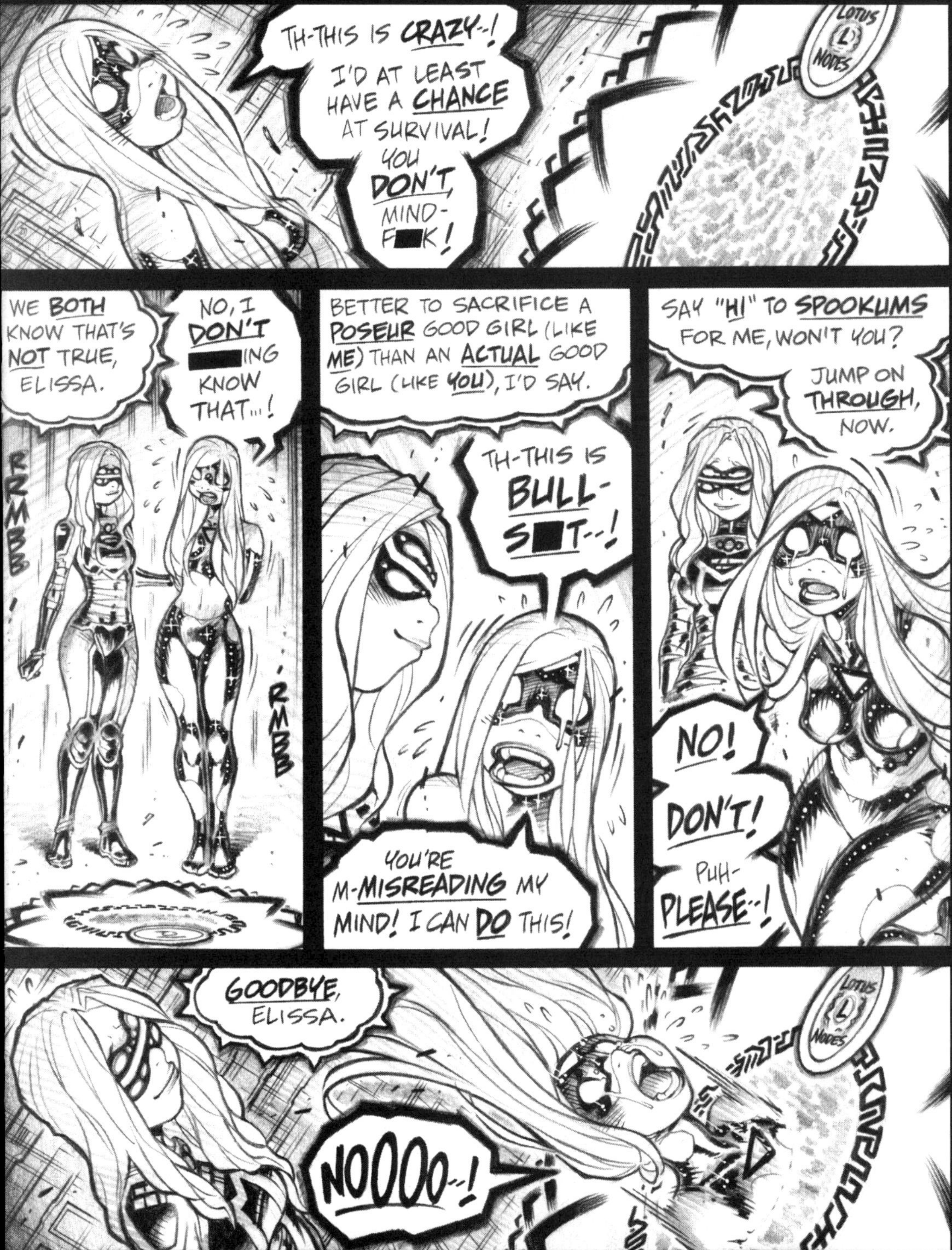
TH-THIS IS CRAZY--! I'D AT LEAST HAVE A CHANCE AT SURVIVAL! YOU DON'T, MIND-F[redacted]K!
LOTUS L NODES
WE BOTH KNOW THAT'S NOT TRUE, ELISSA.
NO, I DON'T [redacted]ING KNOW THAT...!
RRMBB
RMBB
BETTER TO SACRIFICE A POSEUR GOOD GIRL (LIKE ME) THAN AN ACTUAL GOOD GIRL (LIKE YOU), I'D SAY.
TH-THIS IS BULL-S[redacted]T--!
YOU'RE M-MISREADING MY MIND! I CAN DO THIS!
SAY "HI" TO SPOOKUMS FOR ME, WON'T YOU?
JUMP ON THROUGH, NOW.
NO!
DON'T!
PUH-PLEASE--!
GOODBYE, ELISSA.
NOOOO--!
LOTUS L NODES

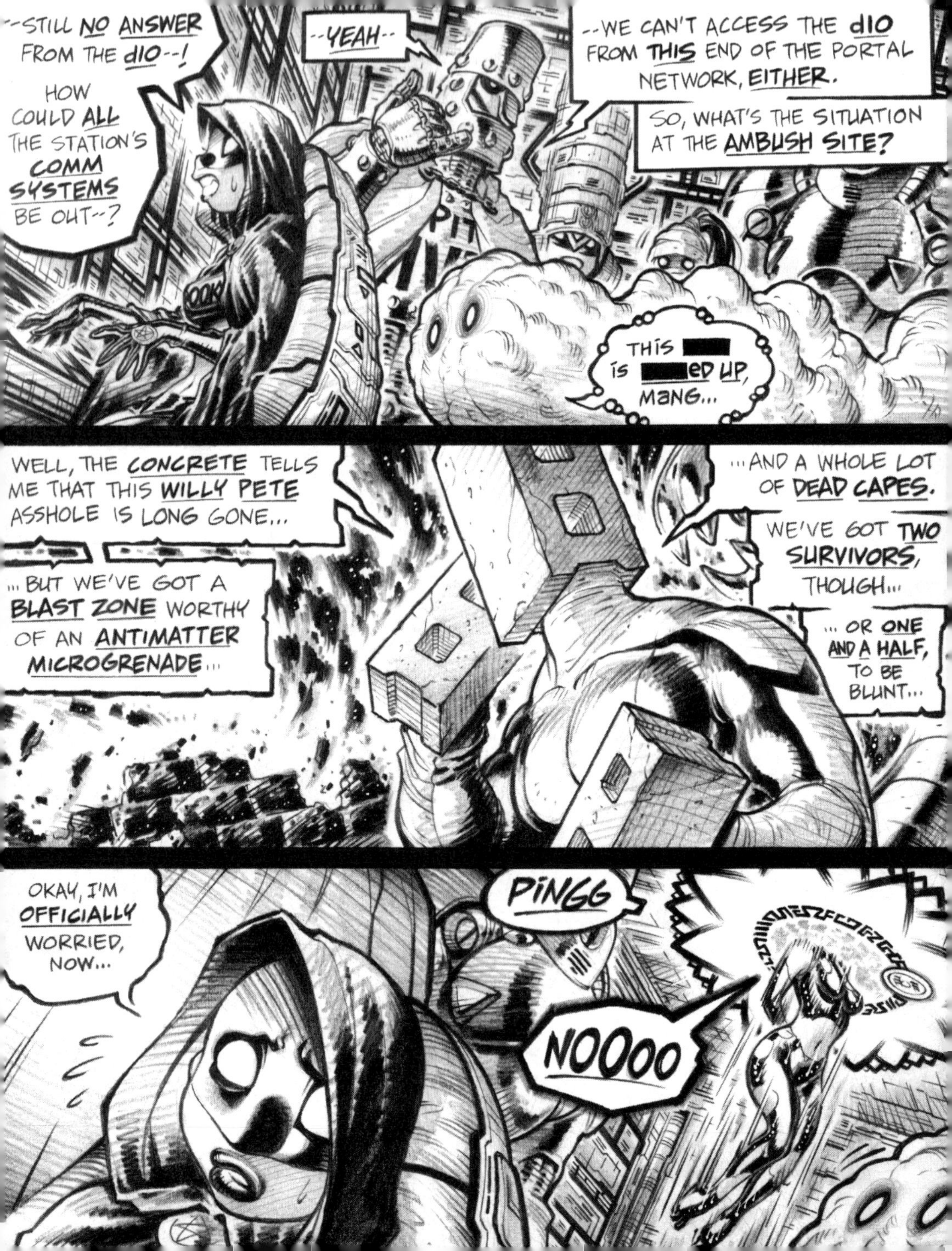
--STILL NO ANSWER FROM THE dIO--!
HOW COULD ALL THE STATION'S COMM SYSTEMS BE OUT--?
--YEAH--
--WE CAN'T ACCESS THE dIO FROM THIS END OF THE PORTAL NETWORK, EITHER.
SO, WHAT'S THE SITUATION AT THE AMBUSH SITE?
THIS [redacted] is [redacted]ED UP, MANG...
WELL, THE CONCRETE TELLS ME THAT THIS WILLY PETE ASSHOLE IS LONG GONE...
...BUT WE'VE GOT A BLAST ZONE WORTHY OF AN ANTIMATTER MICROGRENADE...
...AND A WHOLE LOT OF DEAD CAPES.
WE'VE GOT TWO SURVIVORS, THOUGH...
...OR ONE AND A HALF, TO BE BLUNT...
OKAY, I'M OFFICIALLY WORRIED, NOW...
PINGG
NOOOO

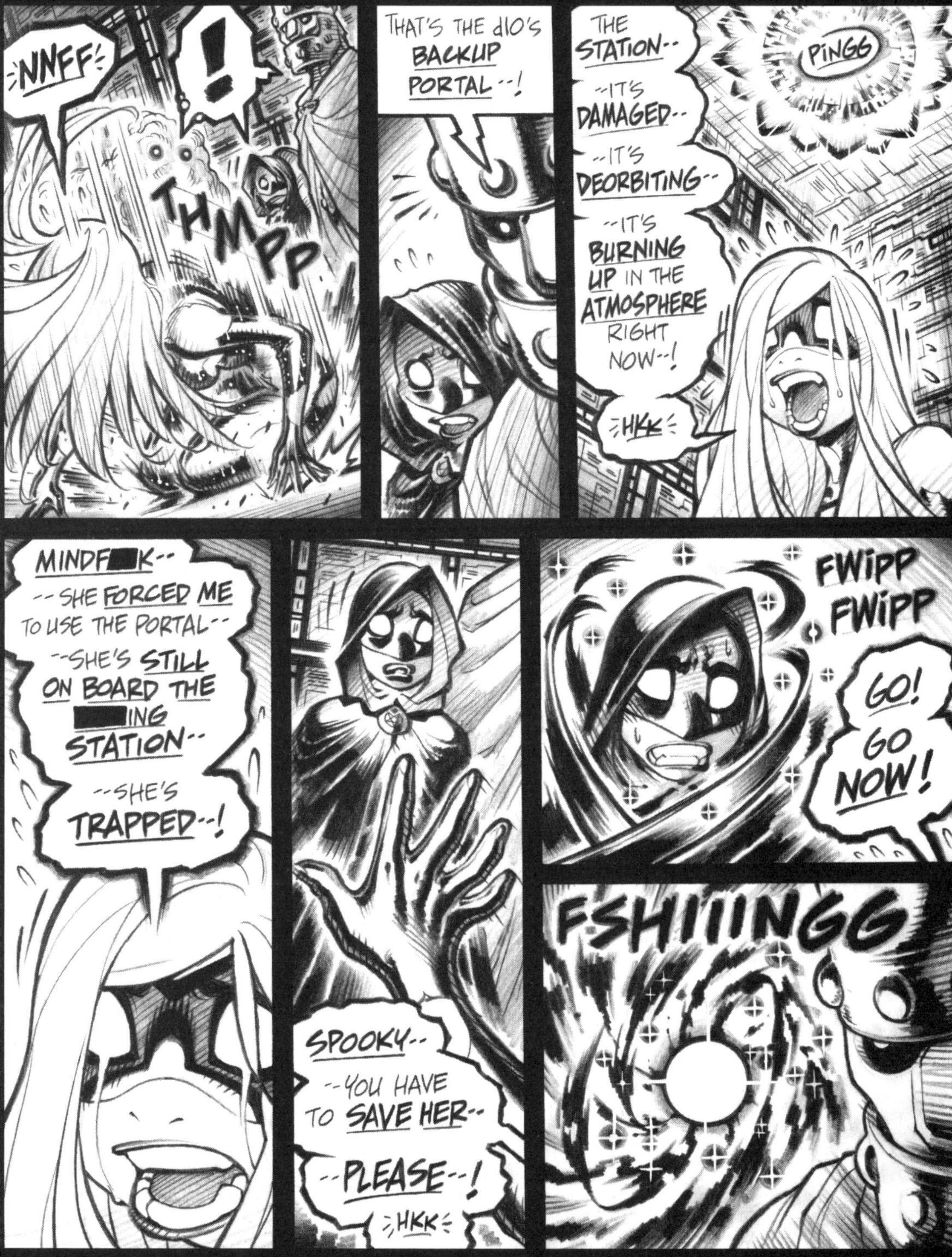
NNFF
!
THMPP
THAT'S THE dIO'S BACKUP PORTAL--!
THE STATION--
--IT'S DAMAGED--
--IT'S DEORBITING--
--IT'S BURNING UP IN THE ATMOSPHERE RIGHT NOW--!
PINGG
HKK
MINDF[redacted]K--
--SHE FORCED ME TO USE THE PORTAL--
--SHE'S STILL ON BOARD THE [redacted]ING STATION--
--SHE'S TRAPPED--!
SPOOKY--
--YOU HAVE TO SAVE HER--
--PLEASE--!
HKK
FWIPP FWIPP
GO! GO NOW!
FSHIIINGG

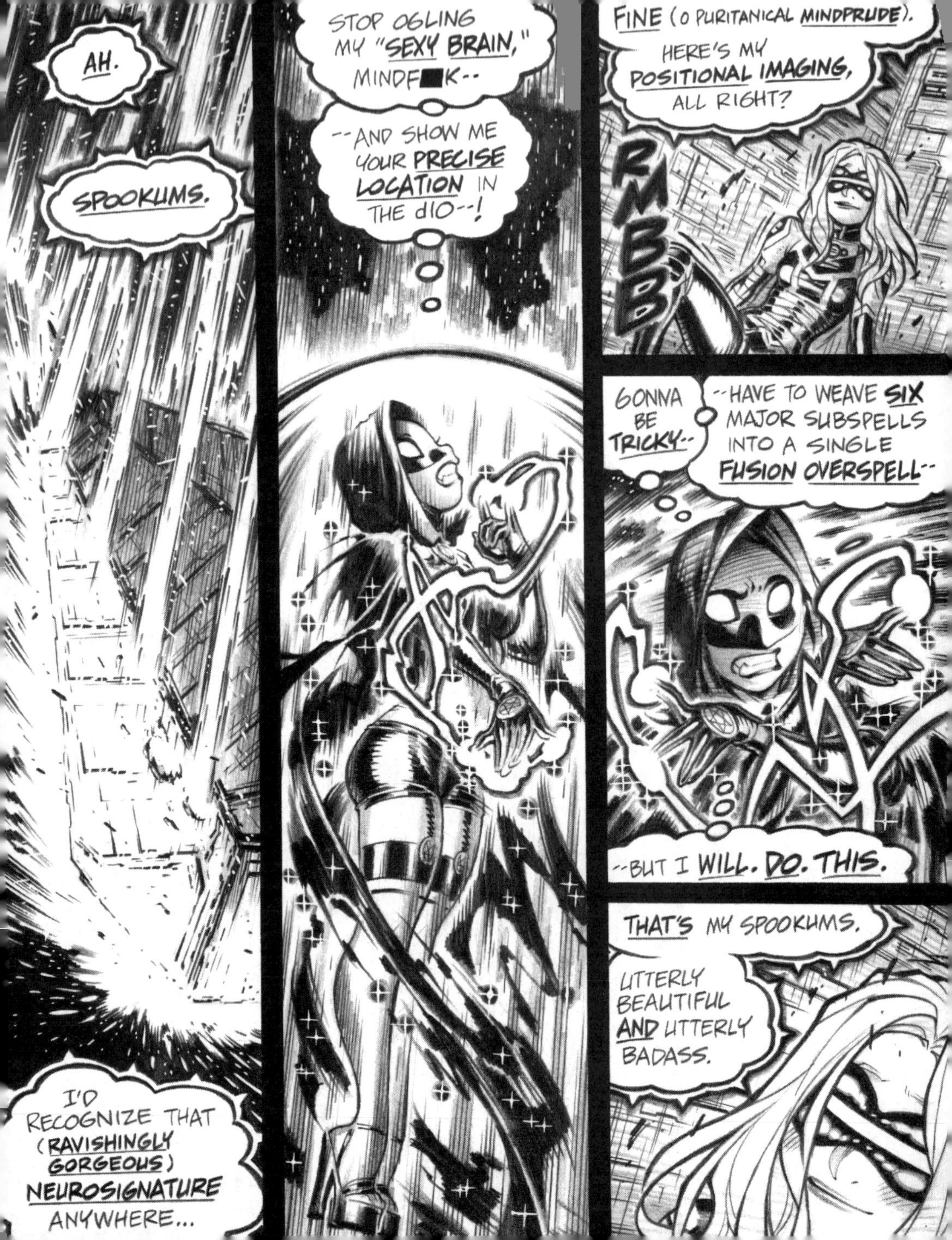
AH.
SPOOKUMS.
I'D RECOGNIZE THAT (RAVISHINGLY GORGEOUS) NEUROSIGNATURE ANYWHERE...
STOP OGLING MY "SEXY BRAIN," MINDF[redacted]K--
--AND SHOW ME YOUR PRECISE LOCATION IN THE dIO--!
FINE (O PURITANICAL MINDPRUDE).
HERE'S MY POSITIONAL IMAGING, ALL RIGHT?
RMBBB
GONNA BE TRICKY--
--HAVE TO WEAVE SIX MAJOR SUBSPELLS INTO A SINGLE FUSION OVERSPELL--
--BUT I WILL. DO. THIS.
THAT'S MY SPOOKUMS.
UTTERLY BEAUTIFUL AND UTTERLY BADASS.

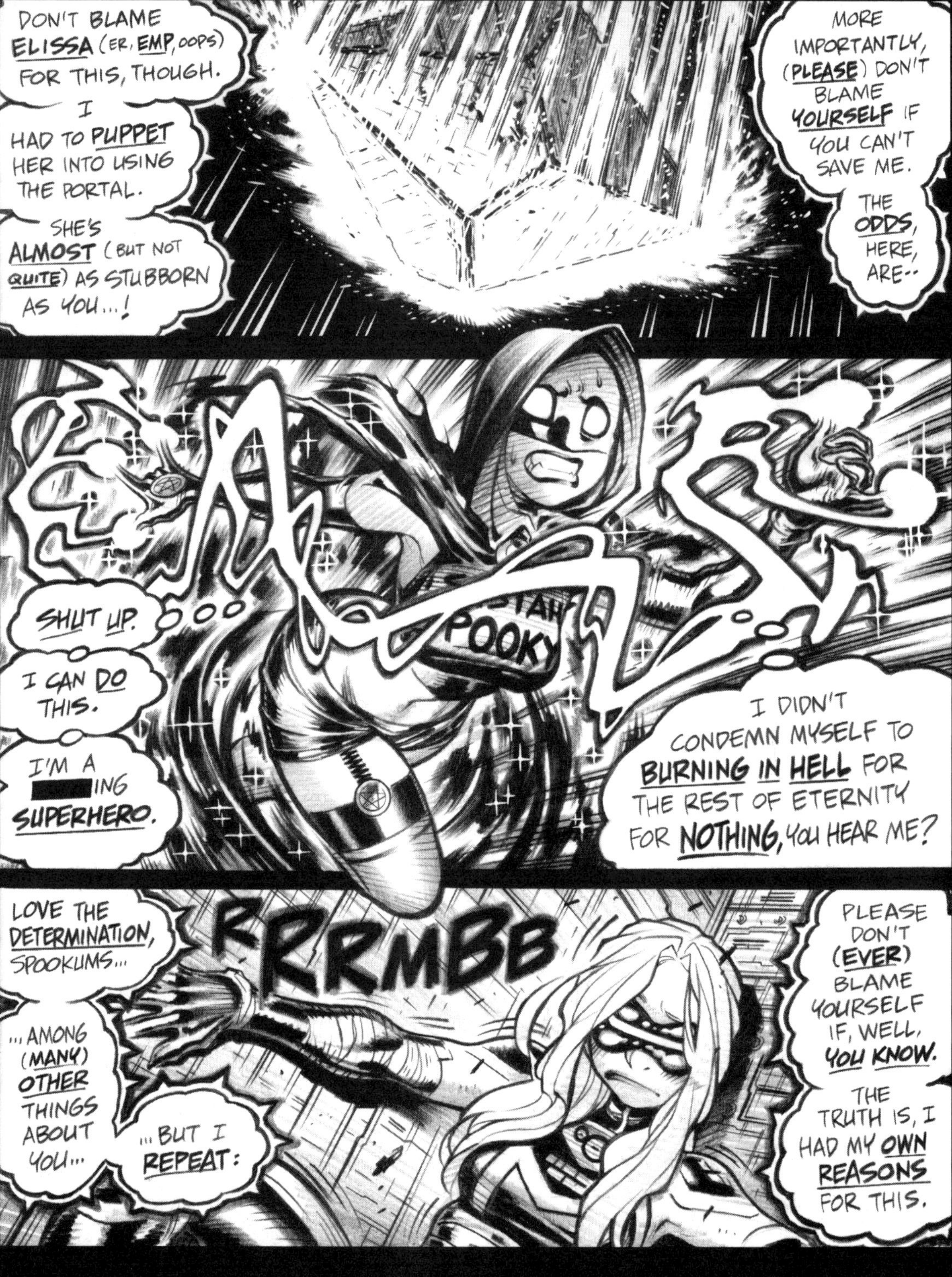
DON'T BLAME ELISSA (ER, EMP, OOPS) FOR THIS, THOUGH.
I HAD TO PUPPET HER INTO USING THE PORTAL.
SHE'S ALMOST (BUT NOT QUITE) AS STUBBORN AS YOU...!
MORE IMPORTANTLY, (PLEASE) DON'T BLAME YOURSELF IF YOU CAN'T SAVE ME.
THE ODDS, HERE, ARE--
SHUT UP.
I CAN DO THIS.
I'M A [redacted]ING SUPERHERO.
I DIDN'T CONDEMN MYSELF TO BURNING IN HELL FOR THE REST OF ETERNITY FOR NOTHING, YOU HEAR ME?
LOVE THE DETERMINATION, SPOOKUMS...
...AMONG (MANY) OTHER THINGS ABOUT YOU...
...BUT I REPEAT:
RRRMBB
PLEASE DON'T (EVER) BLAME YOURSELF IF, WELL, YOU KNOW.
THE TRUTH IS, I HAD MY OWN REASONS FOR THIS.

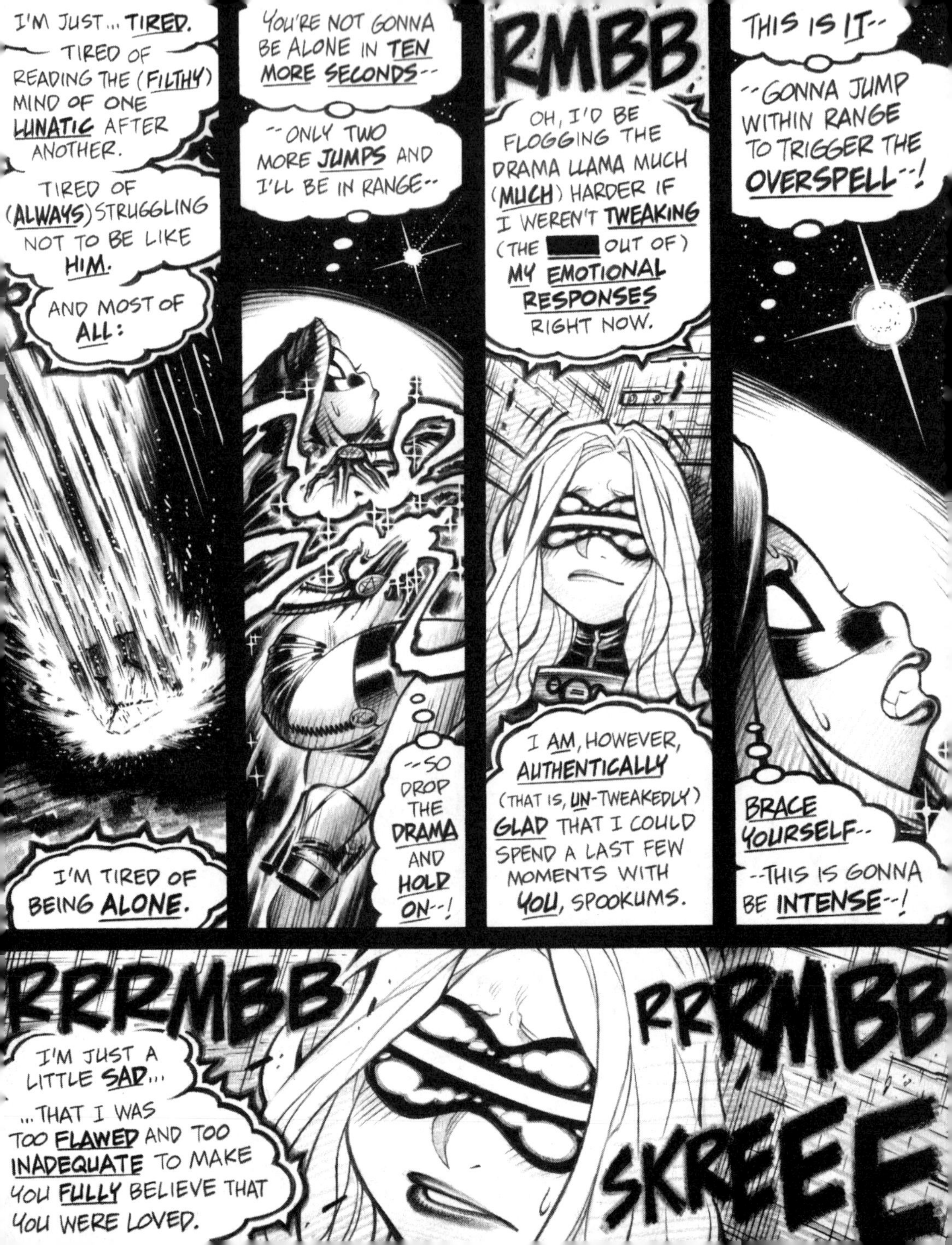
I'M JUST... TIRED.
TIRED OF READING THE (FILTHY) MIND OF ONE LUNATIC AFTER ANOTHER.
TIRED OF (ALWAYS) STRUGGLING NOT TO BE LIKE HIM.
AND MOST OF ALL:
I'M TIRED OF BEING ALONE.
YOU'RE NOT GONNA BE ALONE IN TEN MORE SECONDS--
--ONLY TWO MORE JUMPS AND I'LL BE IN RANGE--
--SO DROP THE DRAMA AND HOLD ON--!
RMBB
OH, I'D BE FLOGGING THE DRAMA LLAMA MUCH (MUCH) HARDER IF I WEREN'T TWEAKING (THE [redacted] OUT OF) MY EMOTIONAL RESPONSES RIGHT NOW.
I AM, HOWEVER, AUTHENTICALLY (THAT IS, UN-TWEAKEDLY) GLAD THAT I COULD SPEND A LAST FEW MOMENTS WITH YOU, SPOOKUMS.
THIS IS IT--
--GONNA JUMP WITHIN RANGE TO TRIGGER THE OVERSPELL--!
BRACE YOURSELF--
--THIS IS GONNA BE INTENSE--!
RRRMBB
I'M JUST A LITTLE SAD...
...THAT I WAS TOO FLAWED AND TOO INADEQUATE TO MAKE YOU FULLY BELIEVE THAT YOU WERE LOVED.
RRRMBB
SKREEEE

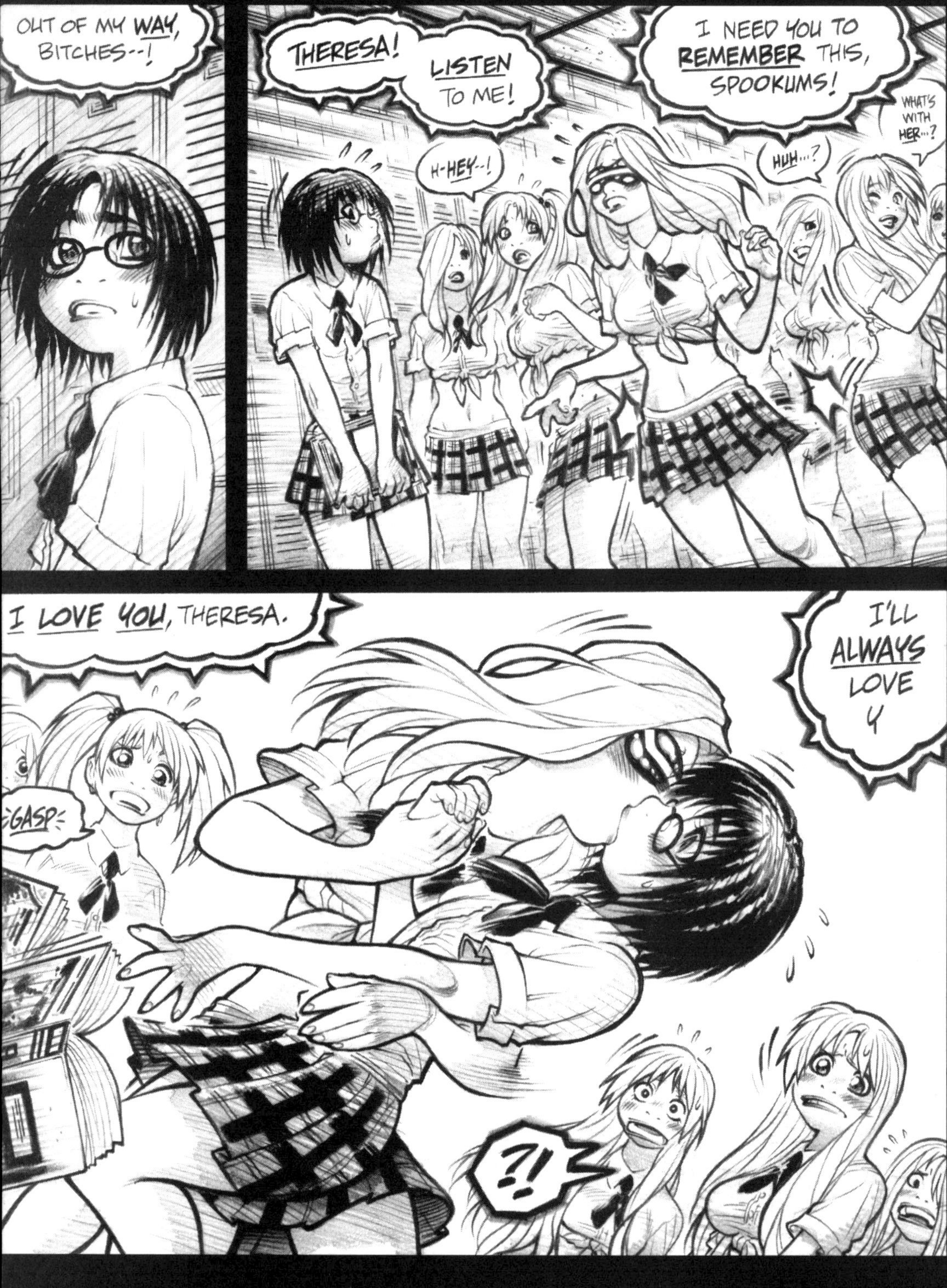

OUT OF MY WAY, BITCHES--!
THERESA!
LISTEN TO ME!
I NEED YOU TO REMEMBER THIS, SPOOKUMS!
H-HEY--!
HUH...?
WHAT'S WITH HER...?
I LOVE YOU, THERESA.
I'LL ALWAYS LOVE Y
GASP
?!

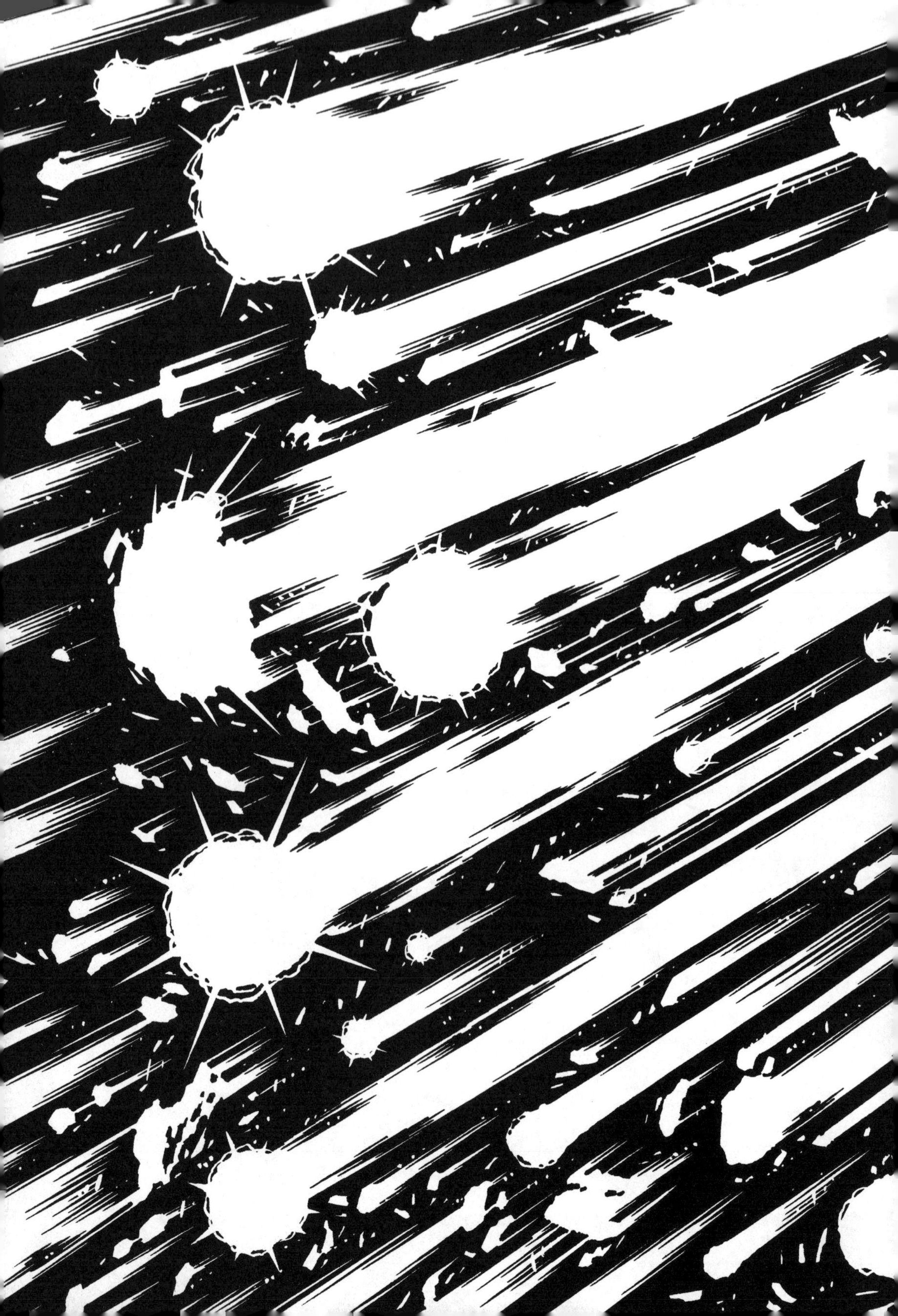

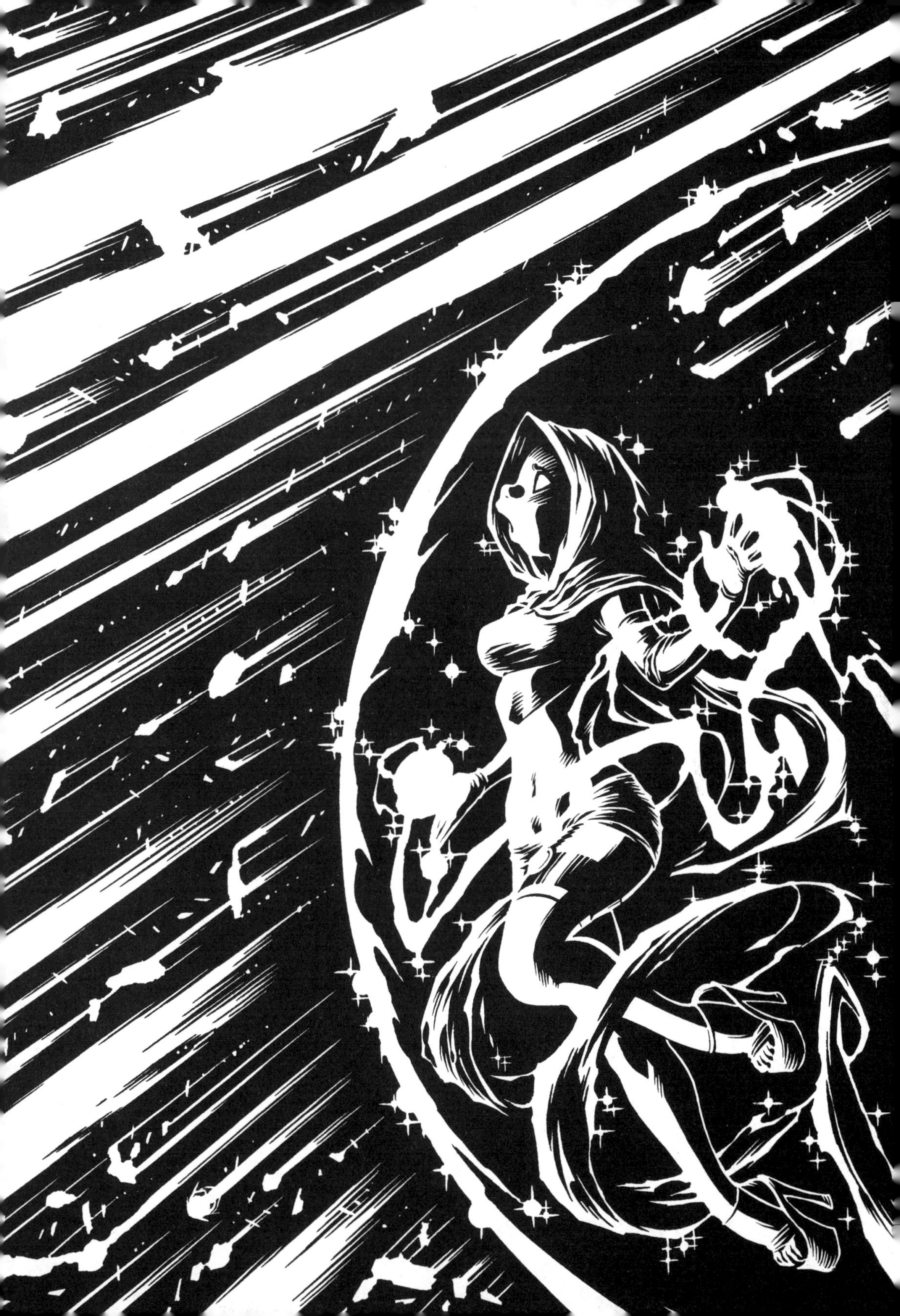

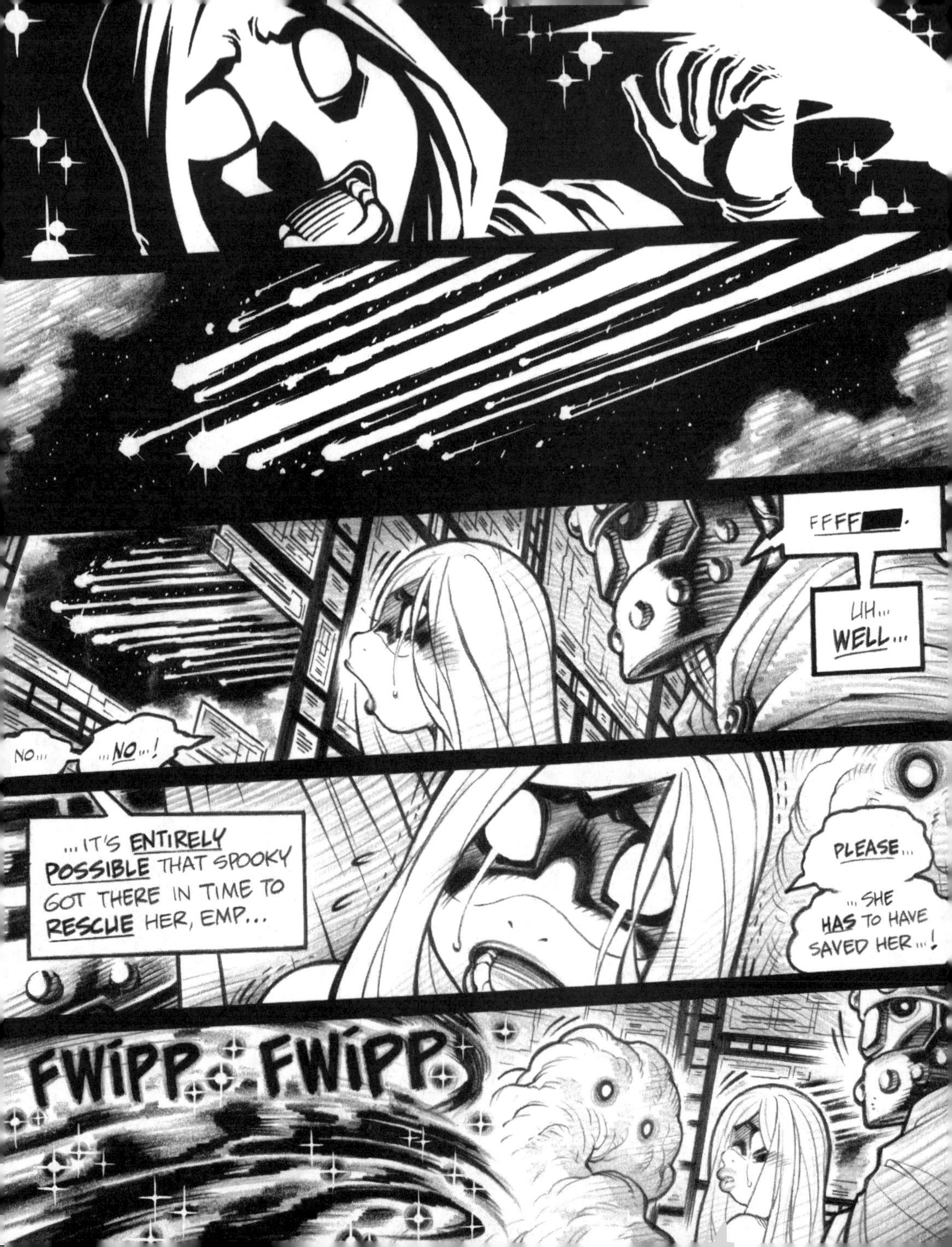

NO...
...NO...!
FFFF[redacted].
UH... WELL...
...IT'S ENTIRELY POSSIBLE THAT SPOOKY GOT THERE IN TIME TO RESCUE HER, EMP...
PLEASE...
...SHE HAS TO HAVE SAVED HER...!
FWIPP FWIPP

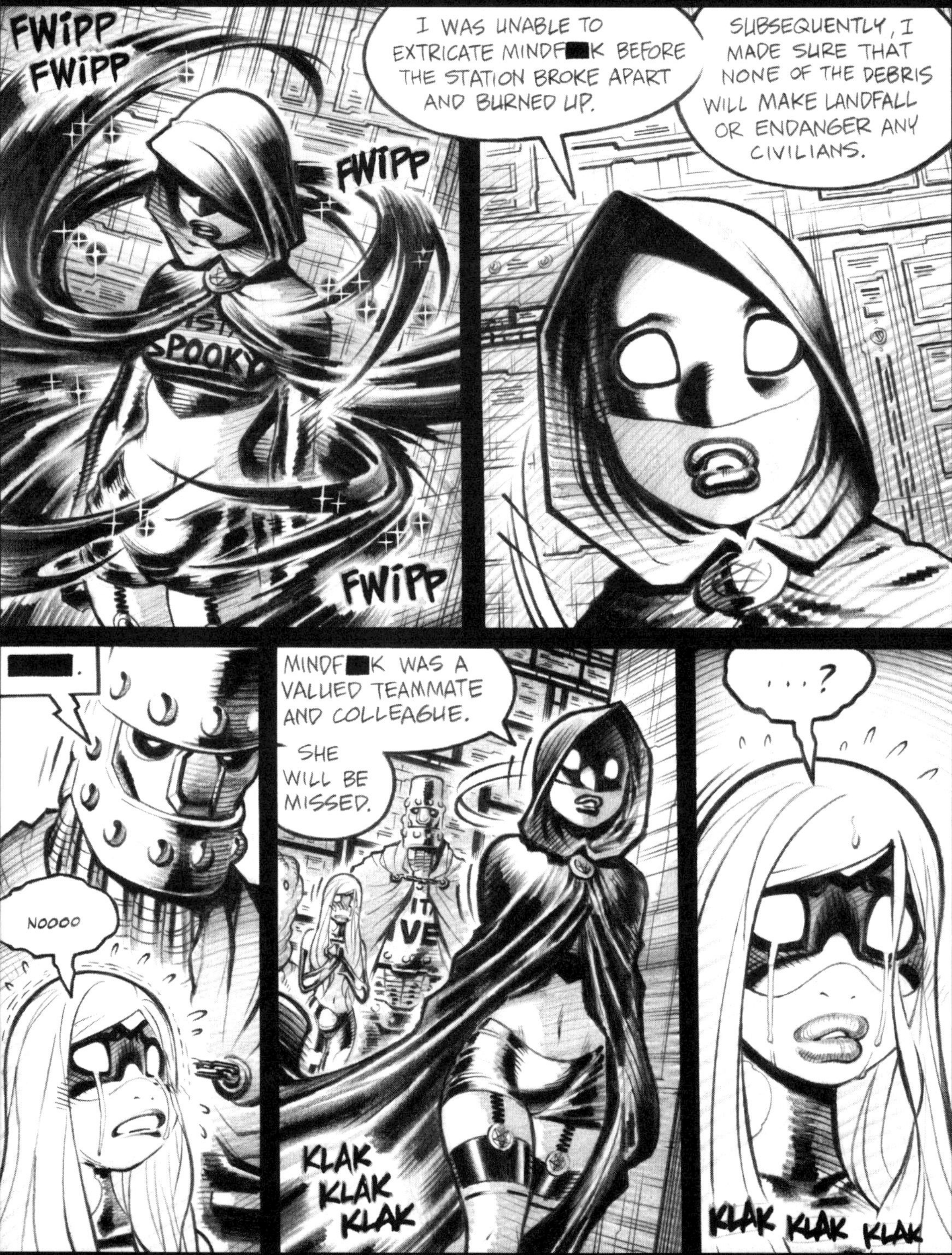
FWIPP
FWIPP
FWIPP
SPOOKY
FWIPP
I WAS UNABLE TO EXTRICATE MINDF[redacted]K BEFORE THE STATION BROKE APART AND BURNED UP.
SUBSEQUENTLY, I MADE SURE THAT NONE OF THE DEBRIS WILL MAKE LANDFALL OR ENDANGER ANY CIVILIANS.
[redacted].
NOOOO
MINDF[redacted]K WAS A VALUED TEAMMATE AND COLLEAGUE.
SHE WILL BE MISSED.
KLAK
KLAK
KLAK
...?
KLAK KLAK KLAK

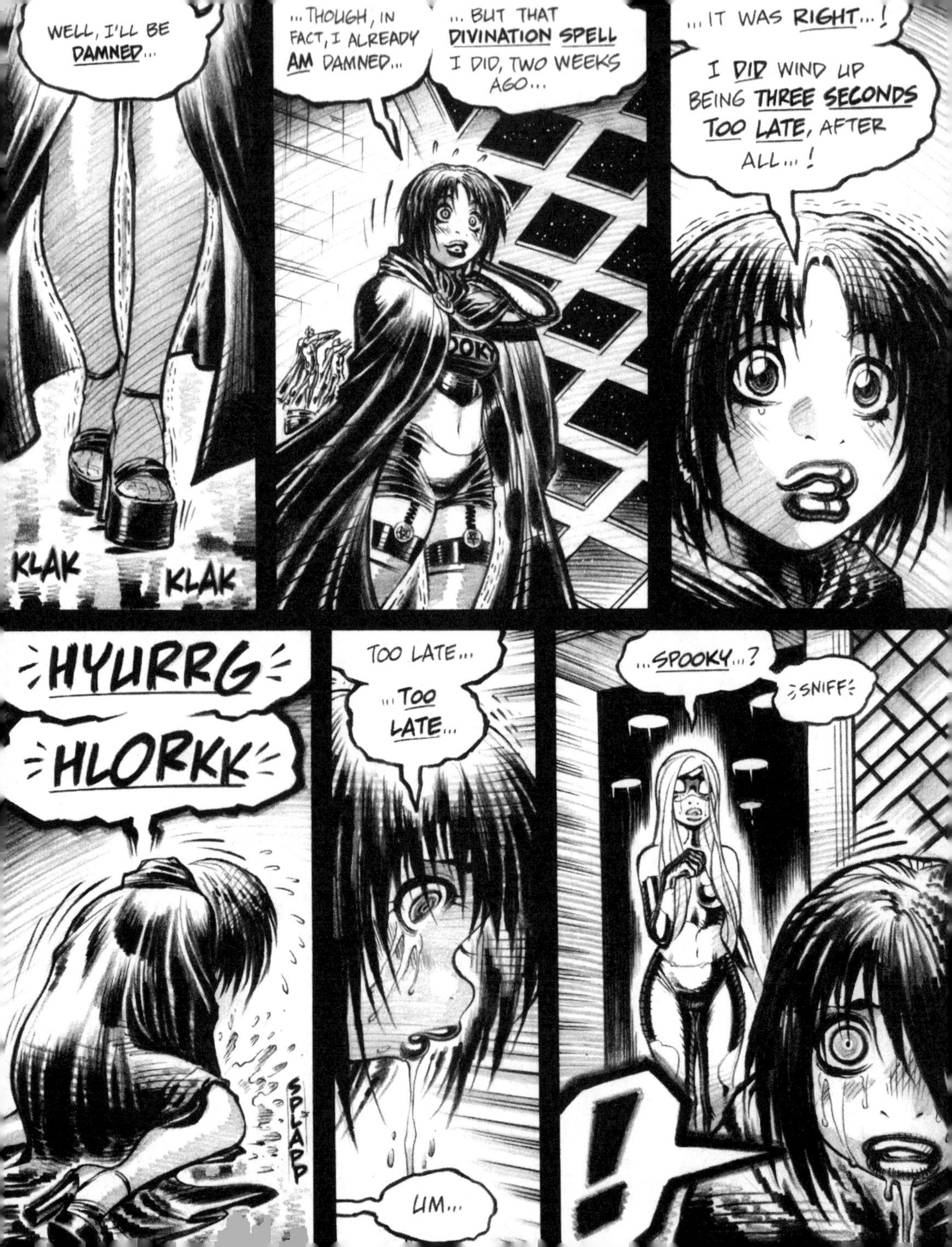
WELL, I'LL BE DAMNED...
KLAK
KLAK
...THOUGH, IN FACT, I ALREADY AM DAMNED...
...BUT THAT DIVINATION SPELL I DID, TWO WEEKS AGO...
...IT WAS RIGHT...!
I DID WIND UP BEING THREE SECONDS TOO LATE, AFTER ALL...!
HYURRG
HLORKK
SPLAPP
TOO LATE...
...TOO LATE...
UM...
...SPOOKY...?
SNIFF
!

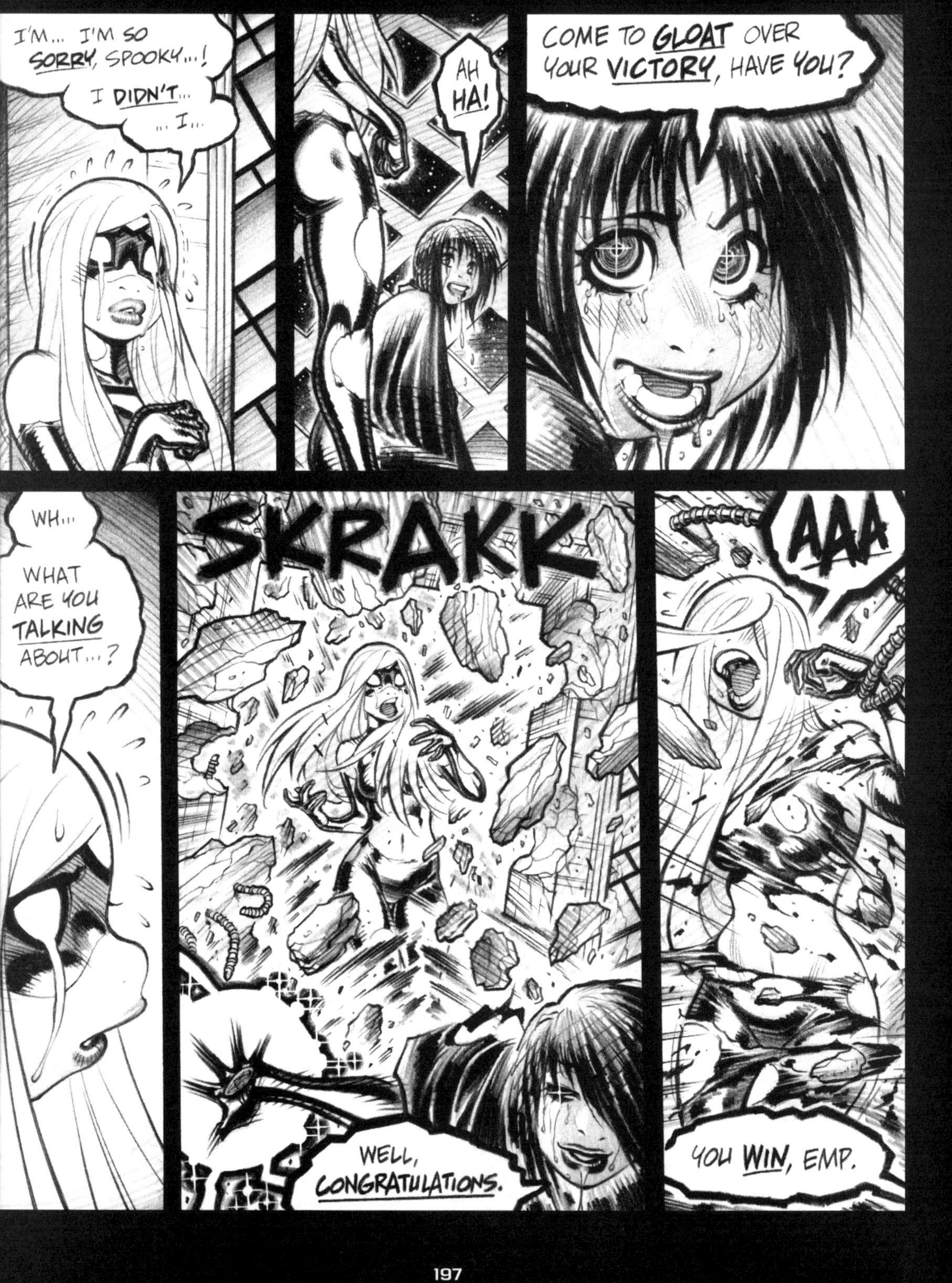
I'M... I'M SO SORRY, SPOOKY...!
I DIDN'T...
... I...
AH HA!
COME TO GLOAT OVER YOUR VICTORY, HAVE YOU?
WH...
WHAT ARE YOU TALKING ABOUT...?
SKRAKK
WELL, CONGRATULATIONS.
AAA
YOU WIN, EMP.

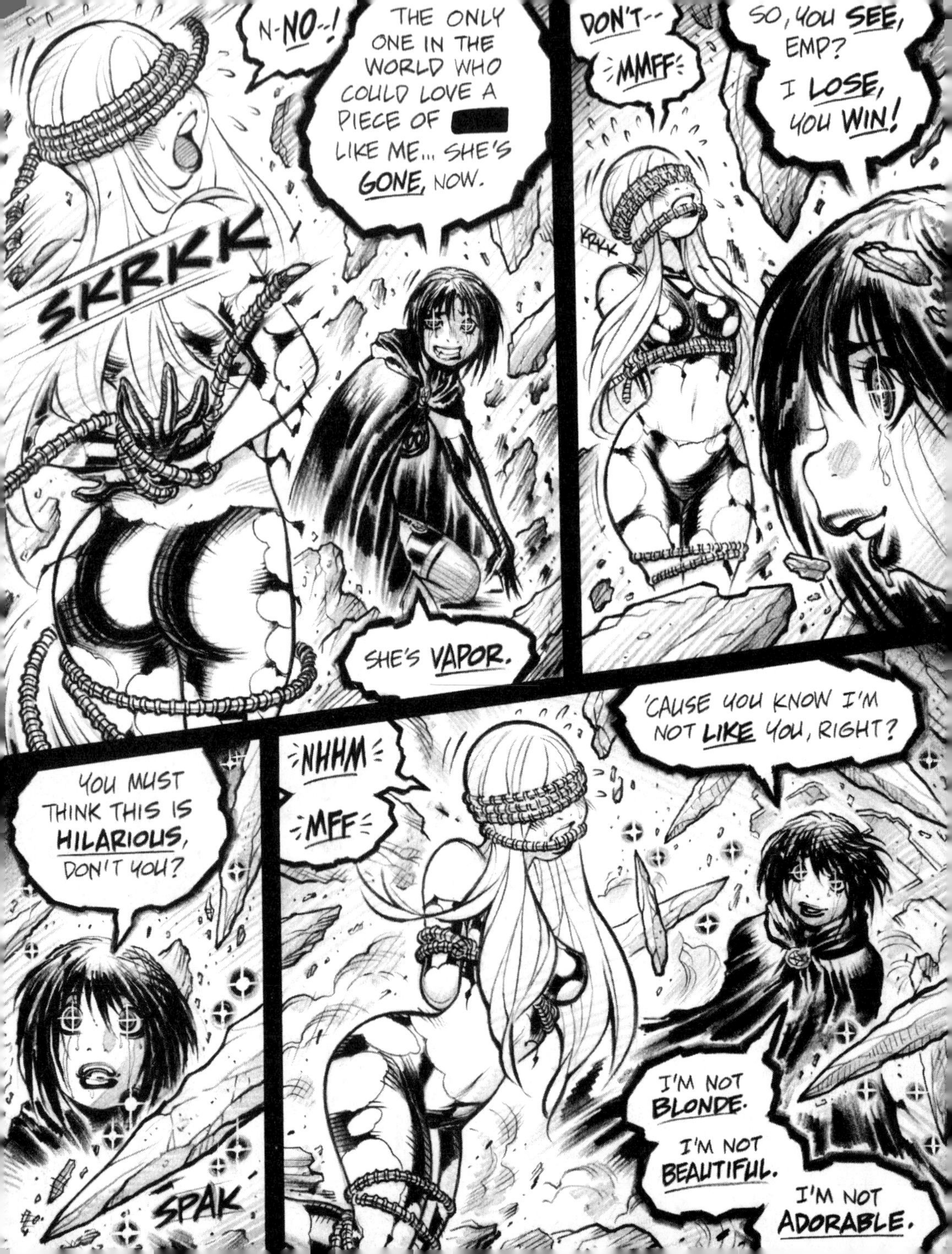
SKRKK
N-NO--!
THE ONLY ONE IN THE WORLD WHO COULD LOVE A PIECE OF [redacted] LIKE ME... SHE'S GONE, NOW.
SHE'S VAPOR.
DON'T--
MMFF
SO, YOU SEE, EMP?
I LOSE, YOU WIN!
KRKK
YOU MUST THINK THIS IS HILARIOUS, DON'T YOU?
SPAK
NHHM
MFF
'CAUSE YOU KNOW I'M NOT LIKE YOU, RIGHT?
I'M NOT BLONDE.
I'M NOT BEAUTIFUL.
I'M NOT ADORABLE.

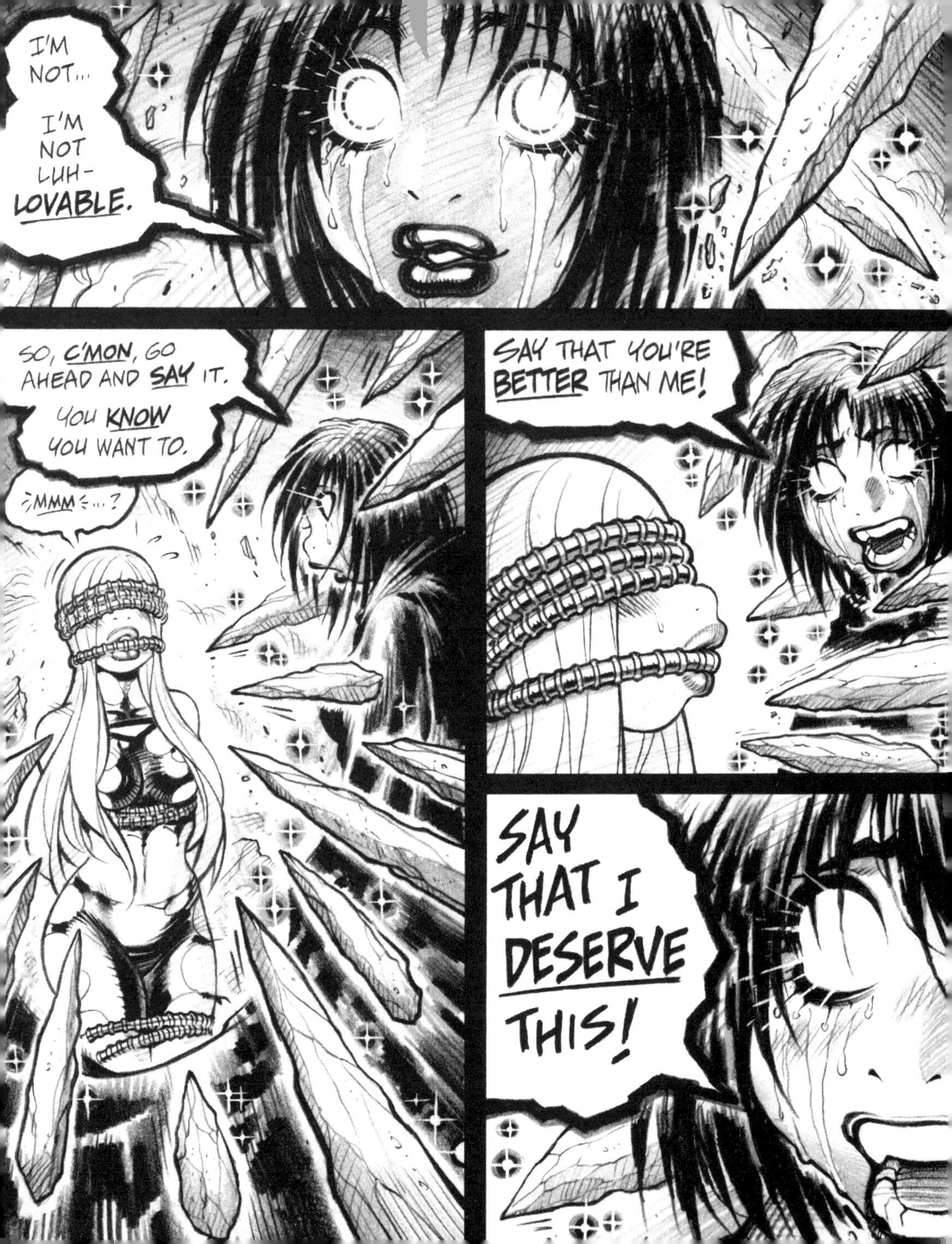
I'M NOT... I'M NOT LUH-LOVABLE.
SO, C'MON, GO AHEAD AND SAY IT. YOU KNOW YOU WANT TO.
MMM...?
SAY THAT YOU'RE BETTER THAN ME!
SAY THAT I DESERVE THIS!

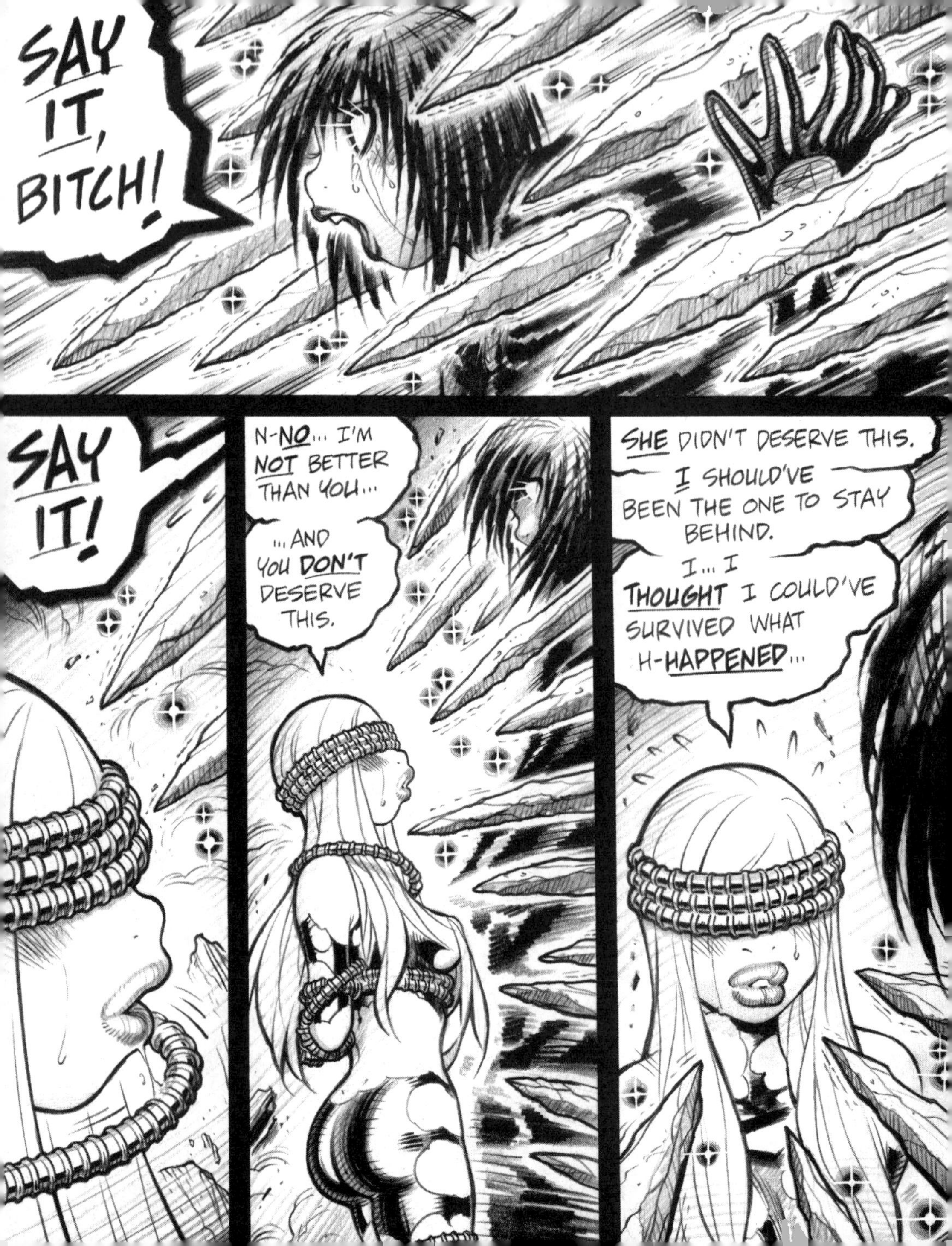
SAY IT, BITCH!
SAY IT!
N-NO... I'M NOT BETTER THAN YOU...
...AND YOU DON'T DESERVE THIS.
SHE DIDN'T DESERVE THIS.
I SHOULD'VE BEEN THE ONE TO STAY BEHIND.
I... I THOUGHT I COULD'VE SURVIVED WHAT H-HAPPENED...

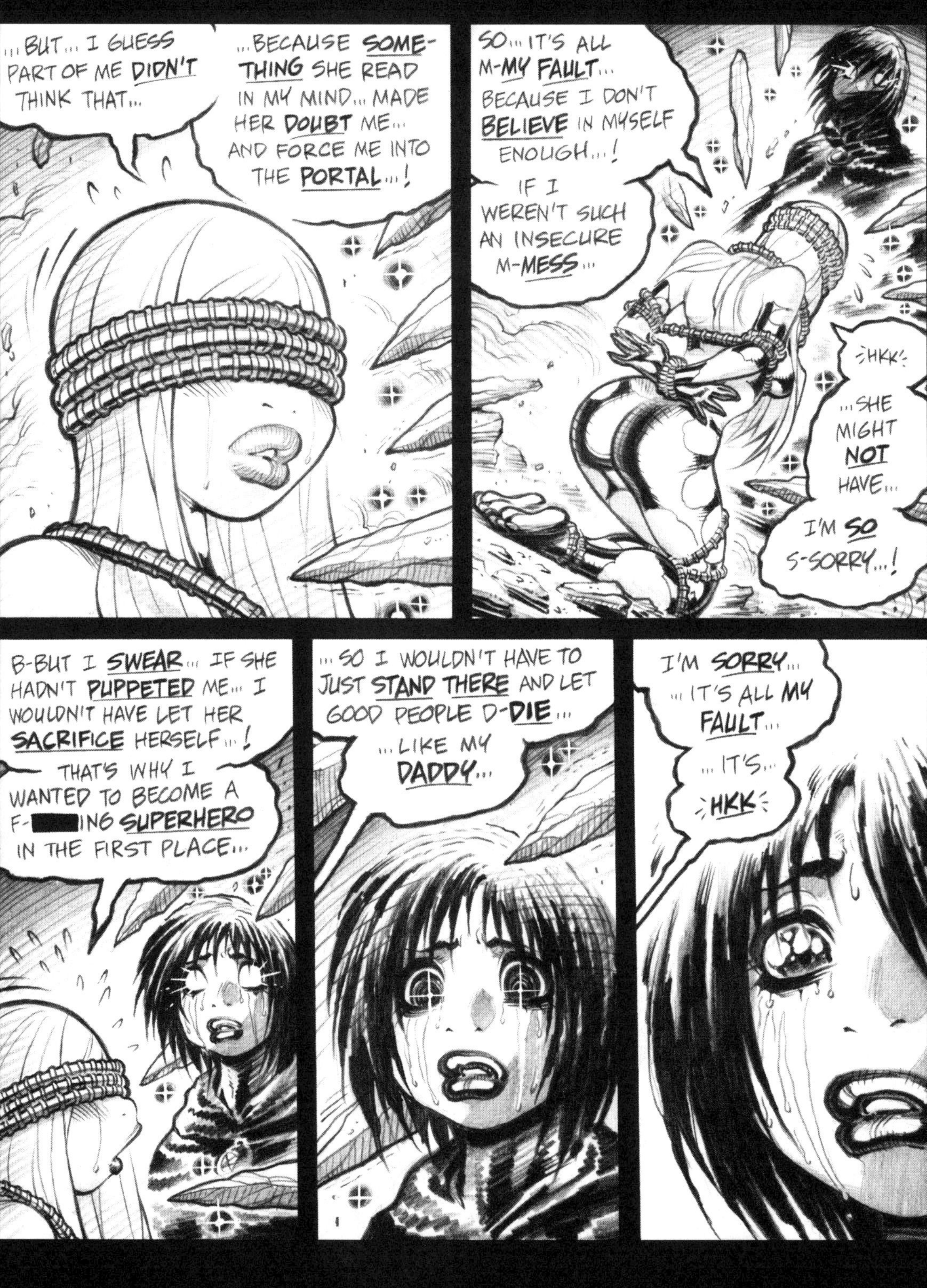
...BUT... I GUESS PART OF ME DIDN'T THINK THAT...
...BECAUSE SOME-THING SHE READ IN MY MIND... MADE HER DOUBT ME... AND FORCE ME INTO THE PORTAL...!
SO... IT'S ALL M-MY FAULT... BECAUSE I DON'T BELIEVE IN MYSELF ENOUGH...!
IF I WEREN'T SUCH AN INSECURE M-MESS...
HKK
...SHE MIGHT NOT HAVE...
I'M SO S-SORRY...!
B-BUT I SWEAR... IF SHE HADN'T PUPPETED ME... I WOULDN'T HAVE LET HER SACRIFICE HERSELF...!
THAT'S WHY I WANTED TO BECOME A F-[redacted]ING SUPERHERO IN THE FIRST PLACE...
...SO I WOULDN'T HAVE TO JUST STAND THERE AND LET GOOD PEOPLE D-DIE...
...LIKE MY DADDY...
I'M SORRY...
...IT'S ALL MY FAULT...
...IT'S...
HKK

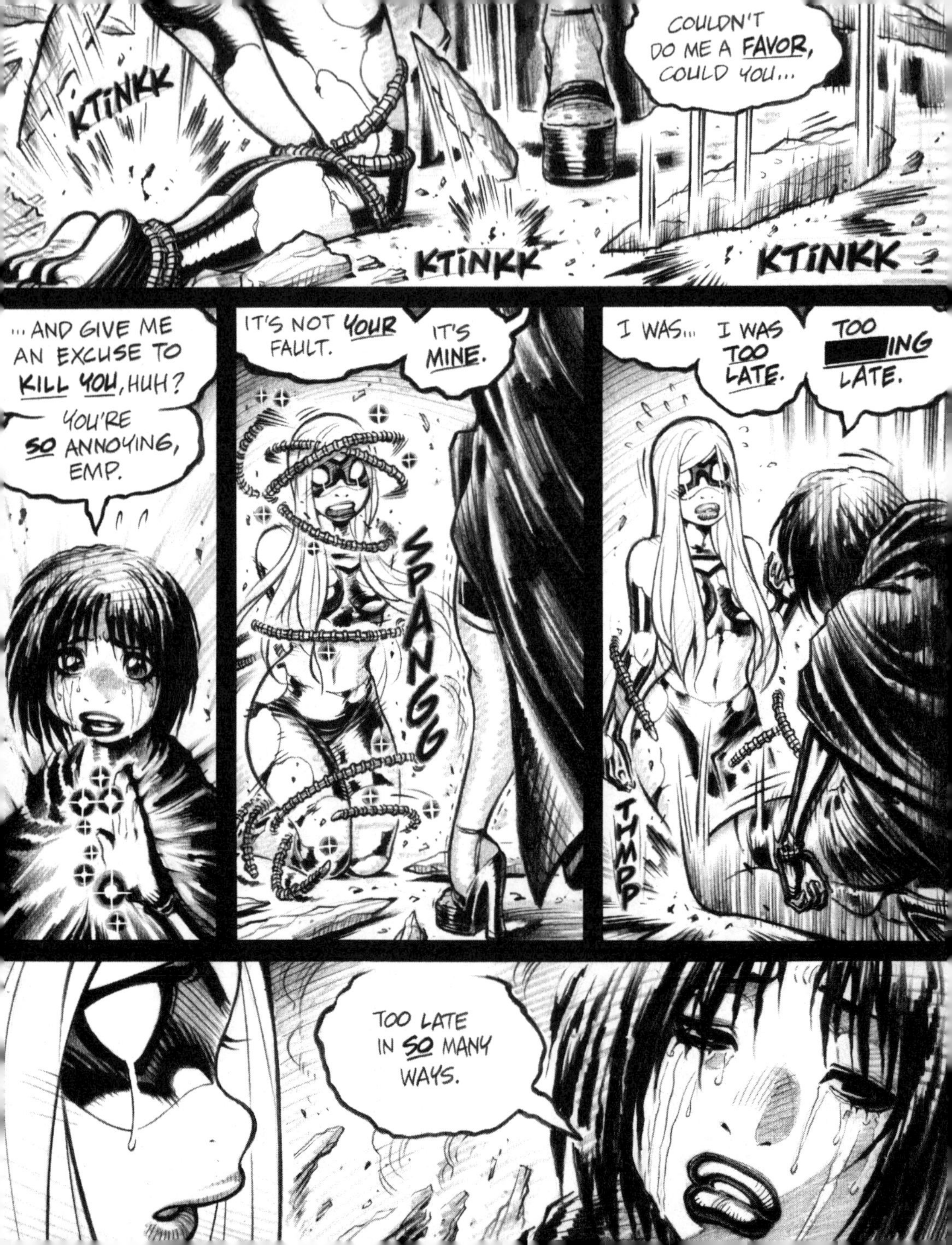
KTINKK
COULDN'T DO ME A FAVOR, COULD YOU...
KTINKK
KTINKK
...AND GIVE ME AN EXCUSE TO KILL YOU, HUH?
YOU'RE SO ANNOYING, EMP.
IT'S NOT YOUR FAULT.
IT'S MINE.
SPANGG
I WAS...
I WAS TOO LATE.
TOO [redacted]ING LATE.
THMPP
TOO LATE IN SO MANY WAYS.

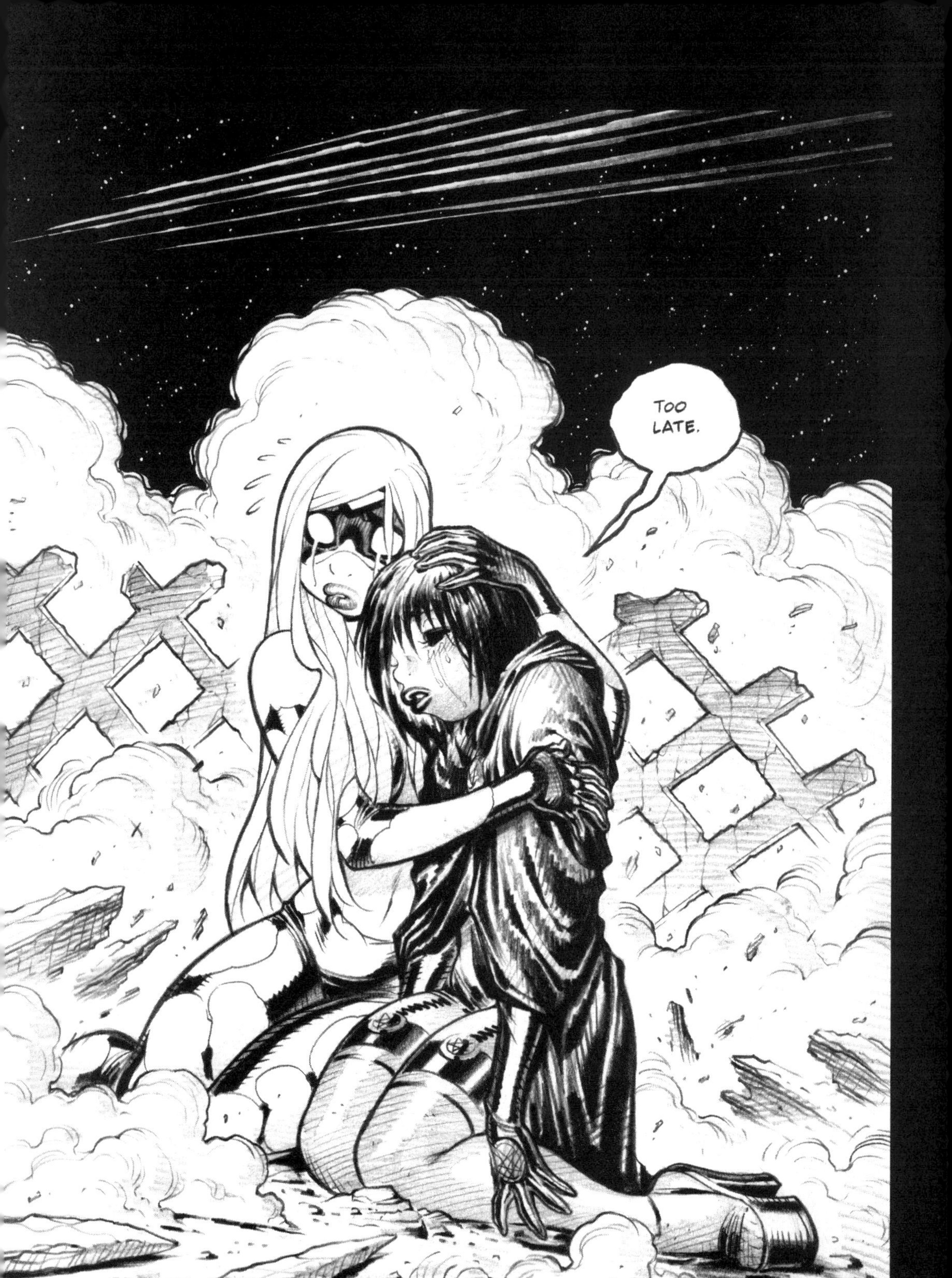
TOO LATE.

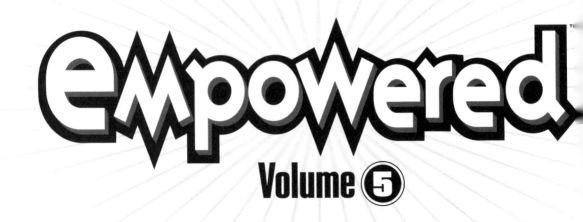

empowered™

Volume 5

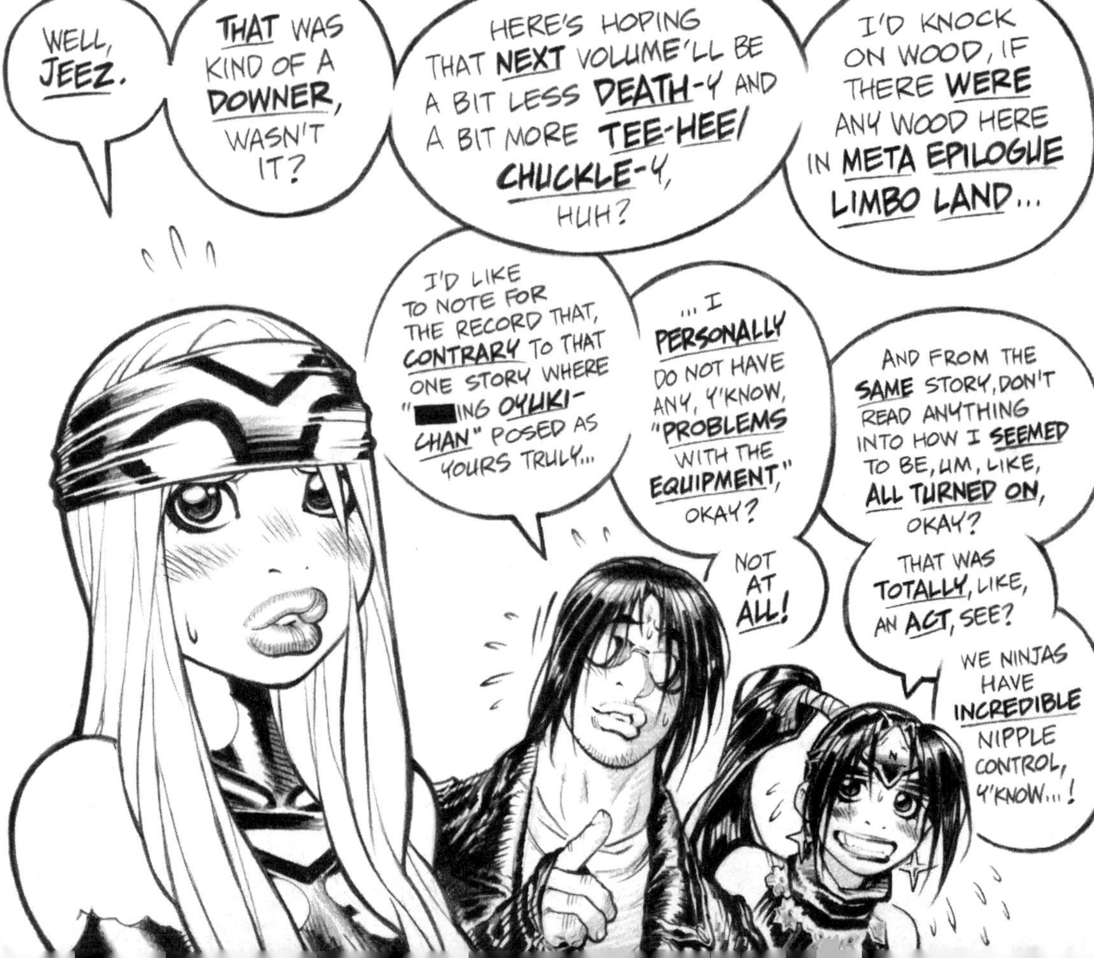

WELL, JEEZ.
THAT WAS KIND OF A DOWNER, WASN'T IT?
HERE'S HOPING THAT NEXT VOLUME'LL BE A BIT LESS DEATH-Y AND A BIT MORE TEE-HEE/CHUCKLE-Y, HUH?
I'D KNOCK ON WOOD, IF THERE WERE ANY WOOD HERE IN META EPILOGUE LIMBO LAND...
I'D LIKE TO NOTE FOR THE RECORD THAT, CONTRARY TO THAT ONE STORY WHERE "[redacted]ING OYUKI-CHAN" POSED AS YOURS TRULY...
...I PERSONALLY DO NOT HAVE ANY, Y'KNOW, "PROBLEMS WITH THE EQUIPMENT," OKAY?
NOT AT ALL!
AND FROM THE SAME STORY, DON'T READ ANYTHING INTO HOW I SEEMED TO BE, UM, LIKE, ALL TURNED ON, OKAY?
THAT WAS TOTALLY, LIKE, AN ACT, SEE?
WE NINJAS HAVE INCREDIBLE NIPPLE CONTROL, Y'KNOW...!

The End.

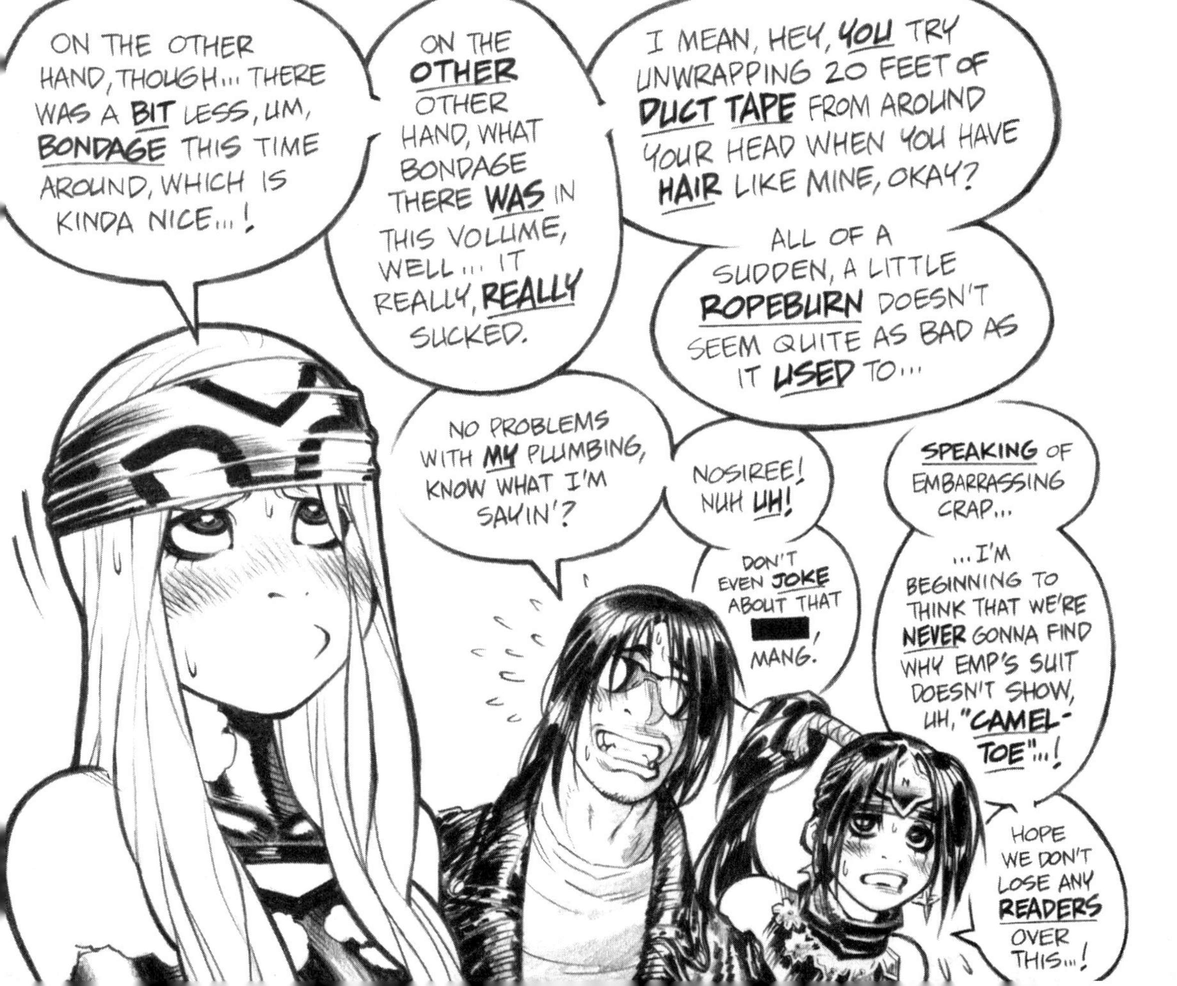
ON THE OTHER HAND, THOUGH... THERE WAS A BIT LESS, UM, BONDAGE THIS TIME AROUND, WHICH IS KINDA NICE...!
ON THE OTHER OTHER HAND, WHAT BONDAGE THERE WAS IN THIS VOLUME, WELL... IT REALLY, REALLY SUCKED.
I MEAN, HEY, YOU TRY UNWRAPPING 20 FEET OF DUCT TAPE FROM AROUND YOUR HEAD WHEN YOU HAVE HAIR LIKE MINE, OKAY?
ALL OF A SUDDEN, A LITTLE ROPEBURN DOESN'T SEEM QUITE AS BAD AS IT USED TO...
NO PROBLEMS WITH MY PLUMBING, KNOW WHAT I'M SAYIN'?
NOSIREE! NUH UH!
DON'T EVEN JOKE ABOUT THAT [redacted], MANG.
SPEAKING OF EMBARRASSING CRAP...
...I'M BEGINNING TO THINK THAT WE'RE NEVER GONNA FIND WHY EMP'S SUIT DOESN'T SHOW, UH, "CAMEL-TOE"...!
HOPE WE DON'T LOSE ANY READERS OVER THIS...!

Empowered™ EXTRAS

Here's the original title-page illo for this volume's story "When Titans Fornicate," back when said story was originally slated to run in *Empowered* Vol. 3. (Note that Vol. 3's back-cover illustration of cosplaying Emp and Thugboy was an unfortunate reference to "Titans," which wound up getting removed from the book due to space considerations.) This original version of the "Titans" title page featured a not-very-accurate caricature of the San Antonio Spurs' Manu Ginóbili; needless to say, likenesses are clearly not my strong suit as an artist. Belatedly, it occurred to me that San Antonio might no longer have a basketball franchise in the Empverse, due to the slight technicality of a good chunk of the city being blown to hell in Empverse continuity . . . Hence, my use of a Los Angeles Lakers player (as Ninjette's unlikely disguise) in the version that appears in this volume.

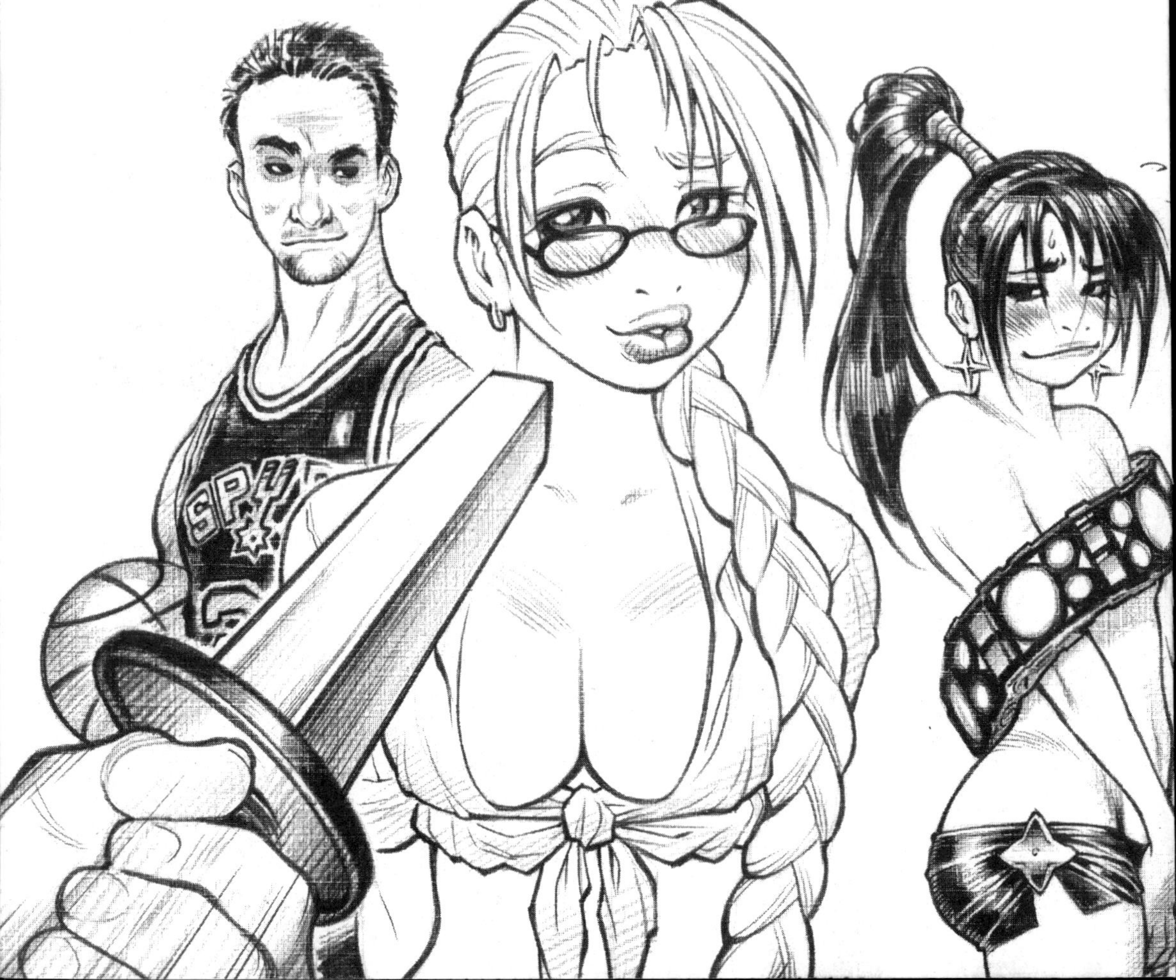

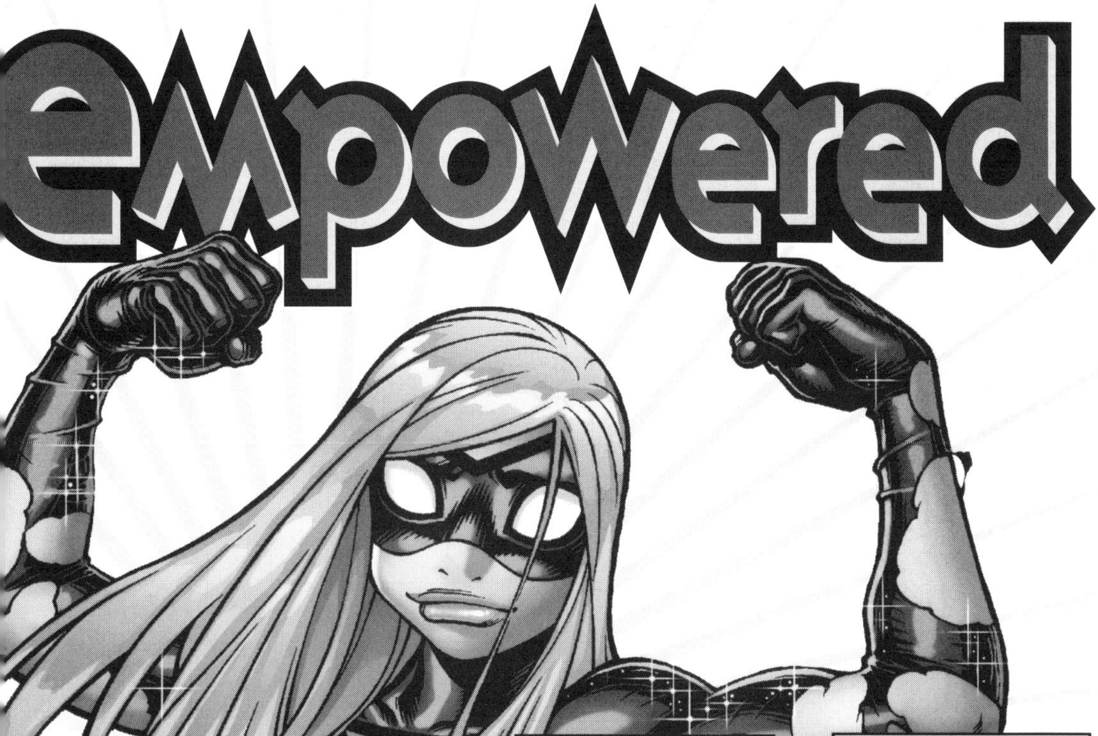
Empowered

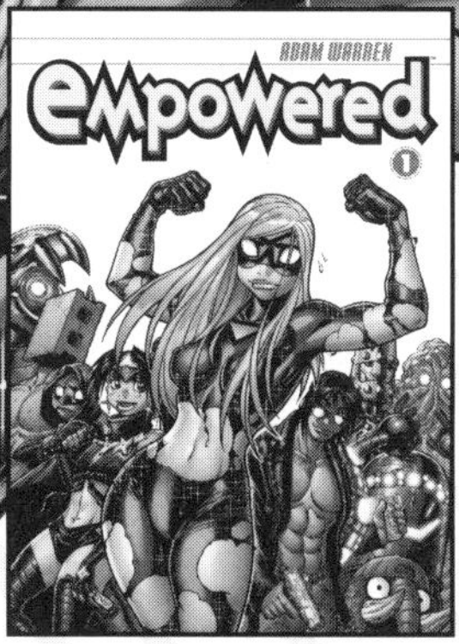
ADAM WARREN
Empowered
1

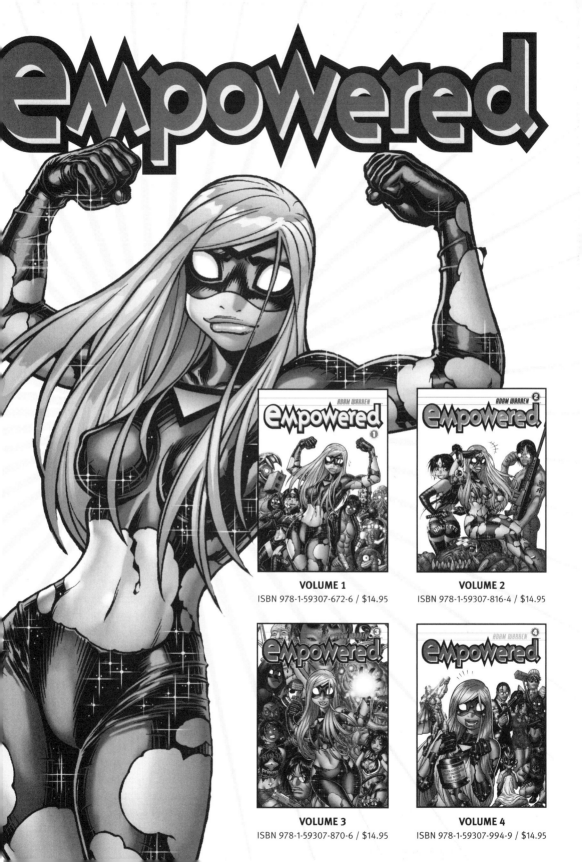

VOLUME 1

ISBN 978-1-59307-672-6 / $14.95

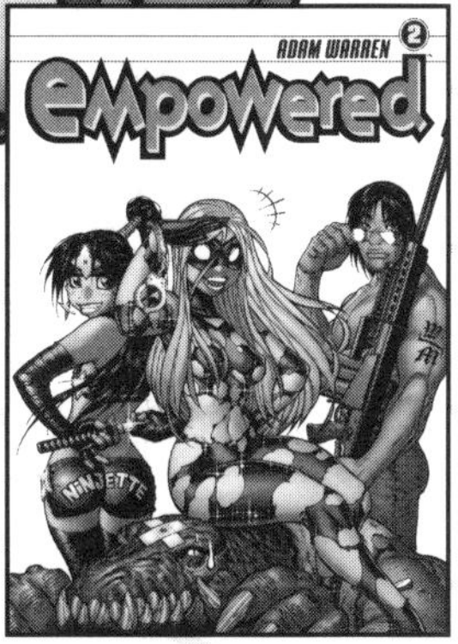
ADAM WARREN
2
Empowered

VOLUME 2

ISBN 978-1-59307-816-4 / $14.95

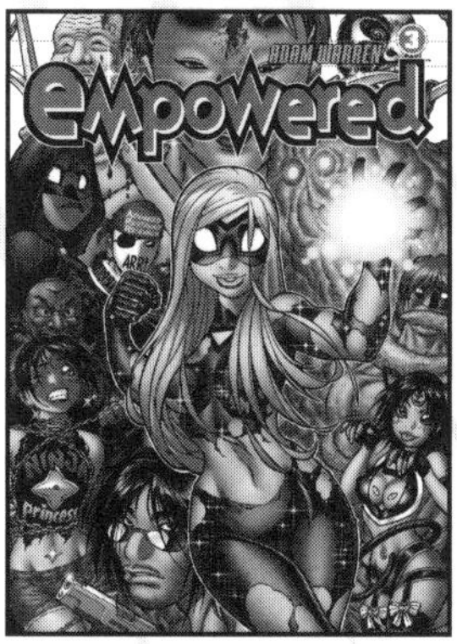
ADAM WARREN
3
Empowered

VOLUME 3

ISBN 978-1-59307-870-6 / $14.95

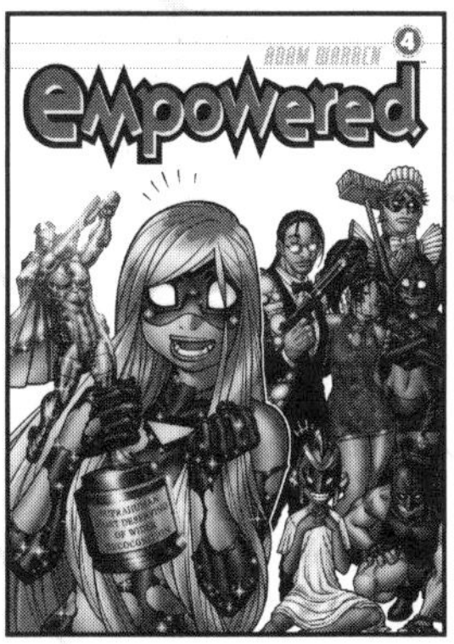
ADAM WARREN
4
Empowered

VOLUME 4

ISBN 978-1-59307-994-9 / $14.95

ADAM WARREN was one of the first writer/ artists in the American comics field to integrate the artistic and storytelling techniques of Japanese comics into his work. Yep, he was definitely a manga-influenced pioneer, even going so far as to ride around in a covered wagon and fire his six-shooters in the air while bellowing "Yee-Haw," pioneer-style. Okay, maybe he *didn't* actually go that far.

Off and on since 1988, he's written and drawn an idiosyncratic, English-language comics adaptation of the popular Japanese science-fiction characters known as *The Dirty Pair,* who first appeared in novels by award-winning author Haruka Takachi-ho and were popularized in a varying series of anime incarnations. The six *Dirty Pair* miniseries Adam worked on were known for their purty, purty artwork, future-shockalicious SF concepts, and obnoxiously satirical sense of humor . . . and at least one of which might be available as a trade-paperback collection from Dark Horse (hint, hint).

The rest of Adam's ripped and toned body of comics-related work ranges from forays into the teen-superhero, pop-culture saturation of Wild-Storm/DC's *Gen 13,* to a DC prestige-format, far-future iteration of the Teen Titans (*Titans: Scissors, Paper, Stone*), and even a take on old-school anime with a *Bubblegum Crisis* mini-series. More recently, he's created and written the mecha-superteam project *Livewires* for Marvel Comics, along with the miniseries *Iron Man: Hypervelocity.*

Beyond the comics field, he's dabbled in artistic miscellanea such as a dōjinshi "sketchbook" published in Japan and illustrations for magazines such as *Spin, GamePro, PSM, Wizard,* and *Stuff,* not to mention several (very) short-lived stabs into the fields of video games, CD-cover artwork, and TV animation. Currently, he's engaged in an epic, almost mythic feat of what might (very) loosely be described as "home repair"—indeed, the ordeal is remarkably akin to Hercules cleaning the Augean stables, but, alas, featuring a rather less impressive specimen of bearded manhood.

Adam lives a thrillingly reclusive lifestyle somewhere off in the deep woods, where hunting rifles boom, FedEx trucks get stuck in the mud, and grey squirrels the size of Labrador retrievers run up and down the sides of houses all ****ing day long, like the world's loudest and furriest ninja. His hobbies include: pegging himself in the eye with the snapped-off tip from a 3B pencil lead, dosing up with No-Doz®, dosing down with quality microbrews, reading an average of four to eight books per week, bailing over to the local Barnes & Noble to get an average of four to eight more books per week (whilst grinding his teeth at this particular store's repeated, maddening failure to stock *Empowered*), working out to *Dance Dance Revolution* for the maximum possible embarrassment value, bitching about the truly critical issues of the day (such as death, taxes, and whether or not KG will be available for the play-offs), and damaging what's left of his hearing with an iPod full of songs that are far, far too lame to admit listening to in public. His favorite colors are black and blue, which is almost certainly symbolic of something profoundly negative.

Find out more about Adam and his work on **DeviantART** and **MySpace**:
http://adamwarren.deviantart.com
http://www.myspace.com/adamwarrencomics